Protection and Implementation of International Human Rights in Domestic Law

Protection and Implementation of International Human Rights in Domestic Law

Atula Gaur

SERIALS PUBLICATIONS
NEW DELHI (INDIA)

First Published - 2010

ISBN: 978-81-8387-234-8

Published by

SERIALS PUBLICATIONS
4830/24, Prahlad Street, Ansari Road
Darya Ganj, New Delhi-110002 (India)
Phone: 23245225 Fax : 91-11-23272135
E-mail: serials@satyam.net.in

Dedicated to

The 'Have-Nots'
for Whom
Human Rights
Still Remain a 'Teasing Illusion'

CONTENTS

PREFACE

Each state has its own different history in relation to Human Rights. All nations incorporate in their respective constitution a significant place to Human Rights covering not only the traditional civil and political rights but also the new socio-economic rights. Similarly, each state has its own different approaches to Human Rights in relation to their enforceability. In India the great thinkers have expressed their concern to protect fundamental freedoms and 'human rights for all human being' since the vedic era and reflection on the dignity of man is found in the preaches of Lord Vishnu, Lord Shiva, Lord Krishna, Buddha, Mahabir and other saints. In British period, The Swaraj Bill, 1895; the Nehru Committee report, 1928; the karachi resolution, 1931 laid emphasis for the inclusion of fundamental human rights in a constitution to be framed by the Indians. In fact, Mahatama Gandhiji's Views to Human Rights predates the Universal Declaration of Human Rights. He proclaimed, "It has always been a mystery to me how men can feel themselves honoured by the humiliation of their fellow being." The Constitution of India adopted on November 26, 1949 contains express guarantee of the basic human rights as Fundamental Rights in Part III of the constitution and certain socio-economic rights, fundamental in the governance of the country, known as Directive Principles of State Policy have been incorporated in part IV of the constitution. The fundamental rights have been made as justiciable rights and constitutional remedy is available in case of their violation or encroachment by executive or legislative action. Although the constitution makes directive principles as non-justiciable but the Supreme Court of India has used the directive principles to enlarge the scope and content of the fundamental rights.

The expression 'Human Rights' includes every aspect of human dignity. To achieve this object the definition stated in domestic law must be in conformity to the Universal Declaration of Human Rights as well as to the International Covenants. In India, the Protection of Human Rights Act, 1993, defines 'Human Rights' as rights relating to life, liberty, equality and dignity of the individual guaranteed by the Constitution or embodied in the International covenants and enforceable by courts of India. Thus the statutory definition of human rights is wide enough to cover the Fundamental Rights in the constitution as well as Civil, Political, Economic, Social and cultural Rights in the two major covenants.

Article 51 of the Indian constitution provides for promotion of International peace and security and ordains the state to foster respect for international law and treaty obligations. Under Article 253 the Parliament has been empowered to make any law for the whole or any part of the territory of India for implementing treaty agreement or convention with any country or countries or any decision made at any international conference, association or other body. The Protection of Human Rights Act, 1993 is an enactment made by the parliament, inter alia, in exercise of the powers conferred under Article 253.

The first International workshop on 'national institutions for the promotion and profection of human rights was held in Paris, in 1991. It was an important event for the establishment of the normative frame work of national institutions. The 'Paris Principles' emphasized that a national institution should have the function to submit recommendations, proposals and reports on any matter relating to human rights; to promote confirmity of national laws and practices with international human rights standards and to co-operate with the United Nationas, regional institutions and national institutions of other countries. Later on the United Nations and the Vienna conference in 1993 endorsed many of the Paris Principles. Amnesty international has also laid down directives for the establishment of such national institution. Therefore, the Indian Parliament enacted the Protection of Human Rights Act 1993, under which a National Human Rights commission has been set up.

As far as implementation of international human rights is concerned it can be implemented by casting a duty over the states by adopting an inter-state complaint mechanism and by establishing a mechanism by which individuals would have an easy access to international commission or regional commissions, courts or tribunals. When the UN charter was adopted, the member states of the United Nations promised to promote and encourage respect for human rights and basic freedoms for all despite their race, religion, language or sex. At regional level European convention on Human Rights and the American Convention on Human Rights have laid down ample provision on implementation of Human Rights. The enforcement and effective implementation of human rights on international level is not left to the United Nations and its organs only. Most of the countries have established National Human Rights Commission with a view to ensure that laws relating to protection of human rights are forcefuly implemented.

In India, the framers of the Constitution incorporated the human rights as fundamental rights in our Constitution. The Indian Parliament has enacted 'The protection of Human Rights Act', in 1993. The Act provides for the Constitution of a National Human Rights Commission, State Human Rights Commissions, and Human Rights Court for better protection of Human Rights and for the purpose of providing speedy trial of offences arising out of violation of human rights.

'All human rights for all' and the world is one family are concepts which have depended on the expanded meaning of Human Rights assuring full dignity to every member of the human race in the global village. Globalization of human rights by making it universally accepted, removing the global inequities is the clarion call of the prevailing human rights movement. With the globalisation of human rights, it becomes significant for the judicial system around the world, to inquire the possibility of and the necessity for application in their domestic jurisdiction, of International Human Rights Law. Sujata Manohar J. has posed key questions regarding it-can Judges apply international human rights treaty law and non-treaty instruments or their principles, in the adjudication of domestic litigation? If so, to what extent and in what manner which is jurisprudentially acceptable? The Apex Court of India, in this regard has taken the view that international human rights law can be applied in domestic jurisdiction, if there is no national law which is inconsistent with it. Thus international human rights norms can be used for widening the scope of fundamental rights and for covering the field not covered by existing domestic legislation. This has enabled the court to lay down guidelines for preventing sexual harassment of women at the work-place.

The United Nations Secreatary General Kofi Annan, on Human Rights day 10th December, 2006, observed, "Basic Human Rights-the right to a decent standard of living to food and essential health care, to opportunities for education or decent work or to freedom from discrimination-are precisely what the world's poorest need most. Yet, by virtue of their enfeebled status, they are the ones least able to achieve or defend such 'universal' rights. As a result, human rights are jeopardized wherever and whenever a man, woman or child subsists in extreme poverty. If we are to be serious about human rights, we must demonstrate that we are serious about deprivation. As suggested by this year's International Human Rights day observance, we must answer the call to fight poverty as a matter of obligation, not charity....Viewing poverty through a human rights lens heightens our moral imperative to act. But it brings other benefits as well. Since human rights norms emphasize individual empowerement, a rights-based approach can help, empower and enable the poor. Today, development, security and human rights go hand in hand; no one of them can advance very far without the other two. Indeed, any one who speaks forcefully for human rights but does nothing about human security and human development or vice versa-undermines both his credibility and his causes. So let us speak with one voice on all three issues, and let us work to ensure that freedom from want, freedom from fear and freedom to live in dignity carry real meaning for those most in need." speaking at a function organized by National Human Rights commission, H.E. Shri B.S. Shekhawat vice-President of India pointed out, "that what is needed is to make the poor strong enough so that no one exploits them. The rights of the poor are to be protected and this can only happen when we are able to make them aware of their rights, what we need is the grassroot level awareness of the human rights so that a country like India with a vast population is able to distribute the fruits of development judiciously. Dignity is the spine of Human Rights and the very foundation on which human rights rest. Human Rights have a direct relationship with human development and therefore, universality of human rights demands eradication of global inequities and to achieve this end the importance of 'Right to development' cannot ever be over-emphasized." On this occassion, the Acting chair-person of National Human Rights commission Dr. Justice Shiv Raj V. Patil highlighted that "persistence of poverty in many parts of the world points out not only to an inequitable distribution of economic, social and political opportunities but also to violation of Human Rights. Violation of Human Rights is thus both a cause and consequence of poverty and poverty is not only a development goal but also a central challenge for human rights. There is a need for determination and dedicated efforts to prevent violation of human rights. Building a world of respect for human dignity and social justice is a job a responsibility for every one. There is imperative need to build and encourage Human Rights culture at all levels in all segments of society and mere words will not suffice and what we need are deeds and this will require sustained individual and collective efforts." Accordingly, in this work the author has tried to study, elucidate and explore the issues relating to 'Protection and implementation of International Human Rights in Domestic law.

I take this opportunity to express my deep sense of gratitude to my reverred teacher Prof. V. Tayal, Principal N.M. Law P.G. College, Hanumangarh (Former, Vice-chancellor,

University of Bikaner) who was kind enough to help and guide me at every stage of the work. I am thankful to the publisher 'Serials Publications' for printing and publishing the work in an elegant manner.

Last but not the least, I am grateful to my husband Dr. Anil Kumar, whose constant unfailing help and care made it possible for me to complete this work and I record my deep and warm affections to my dear daughters Miss Priyanka (Scientist), Miss Charu and lovely son Abhishek, who permitted me to complete this task.

Atula Gaur

1

Introduction

Throughout history, every society has sought to define the concept of human dignity, in the sense of seeking to ascertain the qualities and inherent value, if any, of each person and his relationship to society. These questions have been answered in various ways, whether on the basis of the social obligations and duties owed by individuals, in terms of social hierarchy based on birth or sex, through submission to the will of royal or divine forces or on the basis of the over-riding importance attached to the maintenance of social harmony. Invariably, the ethical, religious or political bases by which each society has premised its answers to these questions have been reflected to a large extent, in the values and systems by which that society has in turn been governed.[1]

It is in this context that the concept of human rights a concept which tends to emphasize the worth of the individual and to recognize his or her rights as against their society arises. As generally used today, the term human rights covers the series of often disparate rights and freedoms asserted by many to be universally accepted and essential prerequisites for people's enjoyment of a life based on the centrality of human dignity. Proponents of human rights regard them as being inherent, inalienable and universal, inherent in the sense that they are the birth rights of all human beings and people enjoy them simply by virtue of their human existence and as such, they do-not have to be granted to them by any superior or sovereign authority; inalienable in the sense that people cannot agree to give them up or have them taken away from them; and universal in the sense that they do not just apply to individuals as citizens or groups but to all persons regardless of their group identities.[2]

The concept of human rights is as old as the human race. These rights have their roots in antiquity. The roots for the protection of the human rights may be traced as far as back as in the Babilonian laws, Assyrian laws and in the Dharam of the vedic period in India. Writings of plato and other Greek and Roman philosophers also depict for the prtoection of human rights though they had a religious foundation. The city state of Greece have equal freedom of speech, equality before law, right to vote, right to be elected to public office, right to trade and right of access to justice to their citizens. Similar rights were secured to the Roman by the Jus civil of Roman Law.[3]

In this background it is desirable to analyse the meaning, nature, evolution, kinds, sources of International human rights law, globalization and human rights perpsective as well as the Constitution and Human Rihgts Culture.

'MEANING' OF HUMAN RIGHTS

Human Rights may be defined, as those minimal rights which every individual must have against the state or other public authority by virtue of his being a 'member of the human family', irrespective of any other consideration. Bennett says,[4] "Human Rights include those areas of individual or group freedom that are immune from governmental interference or that, because of their basic contribution to human dignity or welfare, are subject to governmental guarantee, protections or promotion."

Human beings are rational beings. They by virtue of their being human possess certain basic and inalienable rights which are commonly known as human rights. Since these rights belong to them because of their very existence, they become operative with their birth. Human rights, beings the birth rights, are, therefore, inherent in all the individuals irrespective of their caste, creed, religion, sex and nationality.

These rights are essential for all the individuals as they are consonant with their freedom and dignity and are conducive to physical, moral, social and spiritual welfare. They are also necessary as they provide suitable conditions for the material and moral uplift of the people. Because of their immense significance to human beings, human rights are also sometimes referred to as fundamental rights, basic rights, inherent rights, natural rights and birth rights. Human rights is a generic term and it embraces civil rights, civil liberties and social, economic and cultural rights. However, it can be said that the rights that all people have by virtue of being human are human rights. These are the rights which no one can be deprived without a grave affront to justice.[5]

The Human rights resemble to natural rights because they have not been created by any legislative enactment. A civilized society or nation is bound to recognise these inalienable rights. The legal obligation to protect them includes the legal obligation to respect them. Members of the United Nations have committed themselves to promote respect for and observance of human rights and fundamental freedoms.[6]

International concern with Human rights is not a modern idea but in fact, heir to all the great historic movements for man's freedom to the enduring elements in the tradition of natural law and natural rights and in the most of the world's great religious and philosophies and the findings of contemporary science about interrelations of simple respect for human dignity and other individual and community values.[7]

Prof Louis Henkin explained 'Human Rights' as .... claims which every individual has or should have, upon the society in which he or she lives.[8]

Human dignity is the essence of human rights. All those rights which are essential for the protection and maintenance of dignity of individuals and create conditions in which every human being can develop his personality to the fullest extent may be termed as human rights.[9] However, dignity can not be defined exactly, but it accords with justice and good society.[10] In 1993 a world conference on Human Rights was held it was stated in its declarations that all human rights derive from the dignity and worth in herent in the human person and that the human person is at the centre of human rights and fundamental freedoms.

Gavison is of the view that human rights are rights that belong to every person and do not depend on the specifics of the individual or the relationship between the right-holder and the right grantor. Moreover, human rights exist irrespective of the question whether they are granted or recognized by the legal and social system within which we live. They are devices to evaluate these existing arrangements : ideally, these arrangements should not violate human rights. In other words, human rights are moral, pre-legal rights. They are not granted by people nor can they be taken away by them. They can only be respected or violated by them.[11]

Thus, Human Rights are those rights which belong to an individual as a result of being human as a means to maintain the human dignity and honour. These are the rights which all men every where at all times ought to have, something of which no one may be deprived without a grave affront to justice.[12]

Human Rights come in the category of those rights which are available to all individual beings and are necessary for the development of the personality of an individual.

When Human Rights are treated as immunities they impose a corresponding duty on the others that some thing should not be done. This aspect lays down that human beings due to their humanity, ought to be protected against unjust treatment. The idea of protecting the human rights is a concept of civilized society only. In other words one cannot think of their protection and implementation in a state of anarchy. Human rights can be said to be exemptions from the operation of arbitrary powers of the state.

The appalling atrocities of the Nazis against the Jews and against other races during the second world war led to a strong movement for the international protection of the fundamental human rights and the charter embodies numerous reference to them.[13] As a matter of fact, with the horrors perpetrated by Nazi and Fascist leaders still in their minds, the makers of the charter were determined that the rights of the individual be made an international concern.[14] Human Rights are mentioned for the first time.. in any international treaty (not counting the treaties for the protection of minorities concluded after the First world war, which related to the rights of special groups but not to human rights in general) because the drafters of the charter were.... looking behind the facts of war to its causes, that is to say to the existence of dictatorship which makes wars possible.[15]

The provisions concerning human rights run throughout the U.N. Charter "like a golden thread."[16] Much of the credit for this goes to the determined lobbying by non Governmental organisations at the san Fransisco conference. The delegates of some of the states at the san Francisco conference were in favour of the adoption of even stronger provisions concerning human rights. An attempt which proved abortive, was also made to incorporate in the U.N. Charter an International Bill of Human Rights.[17]

Human Rights refers to the concept of human being as having universal rights or status, regardless of legal jurisdiction or other localizing factors such as ethnicity, nationality and sex. As is evident in the United Nations Universal Declaration of Human Rights, human rights at least in the post-war period are conceptualized as based on inherent human dignity, retaining their universal and inalienable character.[18]

The colour of the skin may be white or black, the level of the mental make up may be high or low, the way of life of a people may be modern or primitive to the core, the essential reality of all belonging to species of human race cannot be dismissed by any stretch of imagination.[19] According to A.J.M. Milne, "There can be no human Community without rights. Having rights is part of what is to be member of any community. A community necessarily consists of members who have rights and obligations. Unless there are members, there cannot be community. There have to be rights if there is to be any social life. Thus rights enable an individual with at least some of the elements of a place an identity and a role in the social milieu. 'Human Rights', in the words of R.J. Vincent, are the rights that every one has.... by virtue of their very humanity. They are grounded in our appeal to human nature. Following the same argument, David Sebby says, "Human Rights pertain to all persons and are possessed by everybody in the world because they are human being, they are not earned, bought or inherited, nor are they created by any contractual undertaking." A.A. Said opines that, "Human Rights are concerned with the dignity of the individual the level of self esteem that secures personal identity and promotes human community." Plano and olton states that human rights are those rights which are considered to be absolutely essential for the survival, existence and personality development of a human being. Davidson presents a very precise definition by saying, "The concept of human rights is closely connected with the protection of individuals from the exercise of state, government or authority in certain areas of their lives, it is also directed towards the creation of societal conditions by the state in which individuals are to develop their fullest potential".[20]

Sec. 2(d) of the protection of Human Rights Act, 1993 says 'Human Rights' means the rights relating to life, liberty, equality and dignity of the individual guaranteed by the constitution or embodied in the International Covenants and enforced by courts in India.

A close scrutiny of the above definitions shows that they are universal in nature, belong to all human beings at all times and at all places. They do not depend on status of a person or gender or race. They neither differ with history nor with the geography. It is the duty of the state to recognise, protect and implement them.

NATURE OF HUMAN RIGHTS

Human Rights are a sub-class of rights. Human Rights are rights that belong to every person and do not depend on the specifics of the individual or the relationship between the right-holder and the right grantor. More over, human rights exist irrespective of the questions whether they are granted or recognized by the legal and social system within which we live. They are devices to evaluate these existing arrangements : ideally, these arrangements should not violate human rights. In other words, human rights are moral pre-legal rights. They are not granted by people nor can they be taken away by them. They can only be respected or violated by them. Human rights are often complexes of the types of benefits listed by Hohfeld (claims, rights, liberties, immunities and powers). What ever their type, their special function is to justify the imposition of duties on others. These duties in turn, make meaningful the sense in which the right holder has entitlement. Demanding that a right be protected or that a duty corresponding to it be performed, is thus not a matter of charity or even of justice. The right holder is entitled to the performance of the corresponding duty.[21]

According to Gavison rights are strong entitlements. This is a distinct or extra characteristics of a right. Even if one does not accept Dworkin's position that rights act as trumps, precluding their violation for reasons of prudence or utility or Nozick's conception of rights as side-constraints, rights do provide more than regular reasons for action. For instance, they confer the right to do wrong, i.e. they protect the right-holder against interference, even if the particular instance of exercising of the right cannot be justified by an all things considered judgment. All rights-natural, moral, constitutional and legal-enjoy this peremptory nature. Only human or natural rights have the additional feature that they exist irrespective of any social or institutional endorsement, based only on moral justification and the humanity of the right holder. This distinct combination is the source of both the great appeal of the notion and of its weakness. It also explains the unease often felt when courts play out the institutional implications of this Combination, giving priority to claims of human rights, as such, over practical judgments made by legislature or communities. The pre-political nature of human rights suggests that they do not require social endorsement for their recognition. Ideally, all societies should voluntarily abide by these constraints. However, wise societies know that there are forces which systematically seek to undermine the rights of others. They therefore construct institutional mechanisms to protect the rights of inhabitants even against legislatures and executives. These mechanisms often include granting constitutional status to some rights, enforceable by independent (Constitutional) courts. Presumably, their nature as pre-legal rights influenced the decision to accord them constitutional status but in turn their effectiveness within the system depends on that status.[22]

Human Rights justify the imposition of duties and thus have moral import. But their enforcement needs a political will and force. If such rights are not controversial i.e. acceptable to the society, then these rights are enforceable. A 'thin' reading of human rights suggests that, within particular societies, human rights discourse should focus on persuading the political branches of the need to promote the relevant concerns by defining them as rights within the system. This approach is superior to for both moral and institutional reasons, to trying to 'force' them to legislate and implement these policies through international and external pressures, invoking the duty of these countries to protect and promote human rights.

'Thin' readings are the ones truly shared by all, or at least rights that can seriously claim Universality. Basic rights to human dignity and freedom are obvious candidates. Torturing killing or persecution of political dissidents or of members of a certain race or religion, are unjustified violations of human rights. The courts of a political system should declare such activities illegal and make the perpetrators accountable. But case should be taken when we move into arrangements, which may be presented as unjustified violations of human rights only under thicker readings of such rights. Human rights are unique in that they justify the imposition of duties, even if social and political powers reject such duties. For effective protection and implementation of right moral force with real acceptance is required.[23]

EVOLUTION OF THE CONCEPT OF HUMAN RIGHTS

Different movements and establishment of United Nations organisation makes it clear that the concern for human rights became popular especially in 20th century, though it had its roots in one or the other form since time immemorial. It is not static but a part of continuing dialectic process through which progress in the field might be and manifestly has been made.[24] Most of the students of human rights trace the historical origin of the concept back to ancient Greece and Rome where it was closely linked with the pre-modern natural law doctrine of Greek stoicism. This school of the thought which was initially founded by zeno of citium, held the view that a "universal working force pervades all creation and that human conduct, therefore, should be judged according to and brought into harmony with the law of nature.[25]

The philosophy of human rights appears to have its existence in the domain of natural law. According to the philosophy of natural law jurists, the natural law denotes natural justice, an instrument which can harmonise the whole mankind and bestow happiness essential for good living of a society. To the Greek philosophers, the sophists, Socrates, plato and Aristotle natural law is both a way of living as well as thinking. Their philosophy has been that natural law enables a man to realise good life that is living according to virtue. Aristotle argues that the philosophy of human rights derives its strength from the principles of natural law. Sophists also focussed on ethical and moral values to prepare the young men of Athens to be efficient citizens. Grotian has a strong conviction that natural law is binding one overrules all other laws. They believe that natural law predicate men to recognise divine will in human affairs. Man availing himself of natural law automatically participates in the wisdom of God. Grotian observes that by the inclusion of natural law in a legal system, it becomes the link between the minds of the men and the mind of God. Christ himself said, "Thou shalt love thy neighbour as thyself. All things, therefore, what so ever you would that man should do to you do you also to them.[26]

Similarly St. Thomas Aquinas (1225-1274), the first eminent theologist, in his famous work Summa Theologica considered law as a means to end and therefore stresses that man ought to follow the divine law as embodied in Ten Commandments which is repository of divine revealed wisdom contained in the scriptures. He believes that precepts of natural law teach us to live honourably; to injure no one; and to give every man his due.[27]

The natural law contents in Hugo Grotius, Thomas Hobbs, John Locke, Rousseau and Immanuel Kant strongly propagate the existence of human rights securing of life, property and happiness and subjects by the social institutions. Thus the principle of natural law hammers out a charter of human rights to be protected as the basis of survival of the human being. The crux of the natural law philosophy is that it makes the life, liberty and property the cardinal rights of man, which greatly dominates and influence the further course of the development of human right philosophy the world over.[28]

The appeal to equate natural rights with human rights is also ordained in vedas. The Philosophy envisaged in Rig veda commands that all human beings are equal and that conduct is just which is based on the principles of equality. Vedic ethics idealised an equality of treatment. Ahtharv veda ordains that all human beings are equal and that conduct is moral which is based on the principles of equality. Thus human rights are the modern name for what had been traditionally known as natural rights in Greece, Rome, India and elsewhere.

Notwithstanding all the polemics of natural law jurists, the condition of man in world over remained greatly unchanged. He was still in the shackle though he had known of the 'natural rights of man' through the philosophy of natural law. The situation changed with the dawn of Renaissance the intellectual revival which inundated Europe with a new ideas of all the spheres of human life. It opened a new vista in the era of human life. The result was that even the king in England was forced to sign Magna carta (the great charter of human rights) said to be the first mile stone on the road to the liberties of the people of England in 1215 A.D. It is imperative to add here that the philosophy of human rights was added and strengthened specifically after the introduction of Magna carta. The Magna carta was followed by the petition of Rights, 1627 and the Bill of Rights, 1639. The Bill of Rights may be said to be the third charter of human rights which assumed the natural law rights to the people. Events in England profoundly affected. France and other countries of the continent with the result that France Declaration of the Rights of Man came into existence in 1789 with the prime objective to resist oppression on man. Declaration not only set out a number of human rights...... but clothed them in political philosophy with the words "the main of all political association is the protection of natural and imprescriptible rights of man...... liberty property, security and resistance to oppression.[29]

The charter of New Plymonth of 1620 contained the principles of human rights in the United states of America. The Declaration of Independence in the United states of America declared that all men are born equal; that they are endowed by the creator with certain inalienable rights; that among these are life, liberty and the pursuit of happiness; that whenever any form of Government becomes destructive of these ends, it is the right of the people to revolt against it and to install a new government based upon such principles and organising its powers in such forms as to them shall seem most likely to effect their safety and happiness........ but when a long train of abuses and usurpations, pursuing invariable the same object, evinces a design to reduce then under absolute despotism, it is their right, it is their duty to throw off such government and to provide new guards for their future security.

The concept of human rights as natural rights was not free from controversies because of its abstract nature and the connection with religious dogmas. Political as well as philosophical liberals rejected this concept or idea and the principle of natural rights was attacked by the contemporary liberals. In England, Edmund Burke and David Hume questioned the foundation of this principle. Jeremy Bentham emphasised that "Right is the child of law, from real law come real right; but from imaginary laws, from law of nature' come imaginary rights...... Natural rights is simple nonsense; natural and imprescriptibly rights, rhetorical non sense, nonsense upon stilts'. David Hume took the view that natural laws and natural rights are not real but these are metaphysical phenomenon. Thus the idea of natural rights was attacked during 18th century and was broadened during the coming two centuries. Jurists like sir Henry Maine, J.S. Mill and Karl Von Savigny asserted that rights are the product of cultural and environmental variables and so are very unique to particular society.

In 19th century with the rising of spirit of Nationalism in Europe, the Marxian school of law came into being which argued that the rights belong to the Community or the whole society and not only to individuals. This school of new thought emphasised on social rights by narrowing down the parameters of natural rights, still the idea natural rights remained alive. Various reforms like abolition of slavery fixing of working hours for labourers in the factories, and origin of trade unions in 19th century witnesses that still the concept of natural rights was alive. The atrocities in Germany by passing and enforcing laws authorising the extermination of Jews and other minorities, permitting search and seizure by police, ordering imprisonment or execution of death sentence without fair trial emerged a new idea that law and morality, are to be kept alive, despite the adoption of any theory – utilitarianism or Marxism. With the emergence of this idea the dignity of the individual became the centre point. As a result some institutions were developed to protect the people's rights in a systematic manner, one of these institutions was League of Nations.

In 1929, the Institute of International law resolved a declaration known as 'Declaration of International Right of Man'. Article 1 of the Declaration said, "It is the duty of every state to recognise the equal right of every individual to life, liberty and property, and to accord to all within its territory the full and entire protection of these rights without distinction as to nationality, sex, race or language or religion."

Though Human rights were not expricitly-mentioned in the Covenant of the League of Nations the organization was alive to the task of seeking to protect the rights of people in two particular spheres, namely, the minorities and persons inhabiting the colonies of the defeated powers. Another important feild from the human rights perspective in which the League was active was on the protection of worker's rights and indeed the goal of fair and humane conditions of labour for man and children.[30]

The Dumbarton Oaks Conference of 1944 among the four Big powers led to the first tentative draft of a new world organisation. In 1945, in yalta conferance, the Great power of the world proclaimed a declaration of liberated Europe where principles of Atlantic charter and Declaration of United Nations were affirmed.

After world war-II in 1945 the United Nations Organization was formed and the charter of declaration of human rights was signed by its member nations. The United Nations charter reflects its deep attachement and concern to human rights. The object of the charter is to save the humanity from the scourge of war and the complete development of human personality his liberties and scope for the same. The 20th century brought a new and changing political context for human rights and transformed the philosophical and ideological debates about it, the second half of the century has seen a universal acceptance of human rights in principle and general agreement on its content.[31]

In the preamble of United Nations charter, the people of United Nation expressed their faith in fundamental human rights and in the dignity and worth of human persons, in the equal rights of men and women. Article I of the charter declares the aim of United Nations in the following words, "to achieve international co-operation is solving International problems of an economic, social and cultural or humanitarian charter and in promoting and enlarging respect of human rights and for fundamental freedoms for all without discriminations as to race, sex, language or religion. Article 13 of the charter lays down that General Assembly shall initiate studies and make recommendation for the purpose of assisting for relisation of human rights. Article 55 Cass an obligation on the UN to promote universal respect for and observance of human rights and fundamental freedoms for all without distinction as to race, sex, language or religion.

The historic Universal Declaration of Human Rights (UDHR) was adopted and proclaimed by the United Nations General Assembly on December 10, 1948 is said to be a first step in formulation on an International Bill of Human rights. UDHR is universally regarded as a common standard of achievements for all people and all nations to strive by teaching and education to promote respect for those rights and freedom. In the preamble of the declaration it is stated, that it is essential if man is not to be compelled to have recourse, as a last resort, to rebellion against tyranny and oppression, that human rights should be protected by the rule of law.

The Universal Declaration of Human Rights Contains 30 Articles. Article 1 of declaration proclaims, "all human beings are born free and equal in dignity and rights". Article 3 laysdown, "Every one has right to life, liberty and security of person". Article 5 says, "No one shall be subjected to torture or to cruel, in human or degrading treatment or punishment.

An urgent need was felt to safeguard the political and civil rights of individual and to provide them economic and social security. For this purpose two International covenants, viz. International covenant on civil and Political Rights (ICCPR) and International covenant on Economic, social and cultural Rights (ICESCR) 1966 were prepared. The ICESCR came into force on January 3, 1976 and by the end of 1998 it was ratified by 138 countries while ICCPR came into force on March 23, 1978 and till the end of 1998 it was ratified by 140 nations.

In India the desire for civil rights struck deep roots in the 19th century. It was implicit in the formation of the Indian National Congress Resolution passed at successive sessions of the congress stresses the importance of the rights to personal liberty and other human rights. Consequently when the Constitution was drafted, constitutional guarantee for the protection of the human rights were incorporated in Part III of the Constitution.[32] It was also provided that any law or executive order which infringed the rights contained in Part III of the Constitution would be void.[33]

In 1979, India adopted the International covenant on Civil and Political Rights, 1966. It is to be noted here that the Indian

Constitution was drafted even before the Universal Declaration of Human Rights, 1950, but is was adopted at a time when the deliberation for the Universal Declaration were in the air, so that the framers of the Indian Constitution were influenced by the concept of human rights, and already guaranteed most of the human rights which later came to be embodied in the International Covenant in 1966. Even prior to the framing of the Constitution for free India, Mahatama Gandhi had announced before the Second Round Table Conference that his aim was to establish a political society in India in which there would be no distinction between high class and low class people, that women should enjoy the same rights as men, and dignity and justice, social, economic and political would be ensued to the teeming millions of India. This was one of the objects which inspired Pandit Jawahar Lal Nehru in drafting the historic objective Resolution in the Constituent Assembly, and which was adopted on January 22, 1947. Clause (5) of the Resolution stated:

"WHEREIN shall be guaranteed and secured to all the people of India Justice, social economic and political, equality of status, of opportunity, and before the law; freedom of thought, expression, belief, faith, worship, vocation, association and action subject to law and public morality....." It is thus evident that during the period between 1946 and 1949, India had formulated the concept of human rights.[34]

KINDS OF HUMAN RIGHTS

Human rights can be classified into the following categories:

Natural Rights

Natural rights are those rights which are considered to be inherent and integral to human nature. The crux of the natural law philosophers is that it makes the life, liberty and property the cardinal rights of man which influence the future course of the development of human right philosophy. The doctrine of natural law lays down a charter of human rights to be protected as the foundation for comfortable living of human beings. Some of the reconized rights were-All Citizens have a right to concur, either personally or through their representatives, in its formation. No man should be accused, arrested or held in confinement, except in cases determined by the law, and according to the forms which it has prescribed.

Fundamental Rights

Some rights have been treated as basic rights which came to be known as fundamental rights. The doctrine of fundamental rights tried to overthrow absolutism. In the beginning these rights were not in the form of substantive rights, they were merely remedies against wrong doers. In Europe during the 18th century it was recognized that a man possessed, a right to enjoyment of all those conditions which were necessary for attaining the purpose of life. The state had no power to deprive a person of these conditions. These rights thus became fundamental. They are treated as sacrosanct, immutable and inviolable and find place in most of the modern Constitutions. The Supremacy of fundamental rights implies that a negative duty on the state has been imposed to refrain from infringing or violating those rights. The first fundamental right that was declared was right and freedom to choose one's rulers. This substituted the King's right to rule with the support of divine authority. The logical concomitant to this right 'to choose ruler' was the fundamental freedom to treat the rulers responsible for their act or conduct. Due to this fundamental right accountability of the rulers to man was established.

As a logical consequence, there came into existence the fundamental rights to freedom of thought and expression coupled with the right to bear arms. At that time a feeling prevailed was that the right to resist the undemocratic rulers would be useless if the citizen have no right to bear arms.

Legal Rights

The legal rights are those rights which are not fundamental rights. In other words the rights other than the fundamental or basic rights protected and enforced under law of the land are known as legal rights. These rights are also uniform and available to all persons irrespective of their Caste, Creed, Colour, race or sex.

Civil and Political Rights

The rights essential for civilized life granted by a civil society state or Government may be called as civil and political rights.

In 16th and 17th centuries we find middle class of bourgeois flanked by artists, physicians, lawyers, teachers and men of letters. This category of persons was educated energetic, competent and highly intelligent. These people raised their voice against feudal class. This was the era of dawn of industralisation. If industralisation was to flourish, the feudal class had to go and if necessary, the feudal order too. This led to the emergence of new ideas. The philosophers of natural law asserted that the positive law as subordinate to natural law. It was proclaimed that law is an expression of the will of the community. The Industrial Revolution Consumed the entire feudal order and installed on the throne of the state new Goddess of Equality, Liberty and Fraternity. Thus it dawned the era of fundamental rights, particularly, the political rights like freedom to choose one's ruler. Along with the political rights, other rights known as civil right were also recognized.

Article 1 of the Universal Declaration of Human Rights says that all Human beings are born free and equal in dignity and rights. They are endowed with reason and conscience and should act towards one another in a spirit of brotherhood. Thus this Article 1 provides the inherent freedom and equality in dignity and rights of all human beings. The declaration include the under mentioned civil and political rights:

1. Right to life, liberty and security of persons.[35]
2. Prohibition of slavery and slavery trade.[36]
3. Prohibition of torture, cruel, inhuman or degrading treatment or punishment.[37]
4. Right to be recognized as a person before law.[38]
5. Equality before the law and equal protection of law against any discrimination in violation of the Declaration.[39]

6. Right to effective remedy by the competent national tribunals.[40]
7. Prohibition of arbitrary arrest, detention or exile.[41]
8. Right to a full equality to a fair and public hearing by an independent and impartial tribunal.[42]
9. Right to be presumed innocent until proved guilty according to law in public trial.[43]
10. Freedom from ex-post facto laws.[44]
11. Freedom from arbitrary interference with privacy, family, home, correspondence or attack on honour or reputation and right to protection by law against such interference.[45]
12. Right to freedom or movement and residence within the borders of State.[46]
13. Right to leave any country, including his own, and to return to his country.[47]
14. Right to seek and enjoy in other countries asylum from prosecution in respect of political crimes.[48]
15. Right to nationality.[49]
16. Freedom from arbitrary deprival of nationality and right to change nationality.[50]
17. Right to marry and to found a family and equal rights as to marriage, during marriage and at its dissolution.[51]
18. Right to own property and freedom from arbitrary deprival of property.[52]
19. Right to freedom of thought, conscience and religion.[53]
20. Right to freedom of opinion and expression.[54]
21. Right to freedom of peaceful assembly and association.[55]
22. Right to take part in the government of his country.[56] and
23. Right to equal access to public service in his country.[57]

Part III of the constitution of India include the following political and civil rights, termed as fundamental rights:

(I) Right to equality[58]

(II) Right to six freedoms[59]

- (i) freedom of speech and expression,
- (ii) freedom to assemble peaceably and without arms,
- (iii) freedom to form association or unions,
- (iv) freedom to move freely throughout the territory of India,
- (v) freedom to reside and settle in any part of the territory of India, and
- (vi) freedom to practice any profession or to carry on any occupation, trade or business.

(III) Right to life and personal liberty[60]

(IV) Right to freedom of religion[61]

(V) Cultural and educational rights[62]

(VI) Right to property[63]

(VII) Right against exploitation, and[64]

(VIII) Right to constitutional remedies.[65]

Above enumerated rights make it clear that Article 3 to 16 of the UDHR deals with civil rights, that is individual freedoms that belong to each individual member of a society. The idea behind the protection of these rights is to guarantee an individual a certain sphere to protect him against interference from public authorities. Article 19 and 20 protect the general political rights, viz., the right to freedom of opinion and expression and the right to freedom of peaceful assembly and association. Article 21 guarantees specific political right, the right to vote in free elections and the right to equal access to public service in one's country. These political rights differ from civil rights in that they protect the participation of an individual in the function of an organized society. The nature of political and civil rights differ from each other but they are so much inter-related, this is the cause which led to the framing of one covenant covering both civil and political rights i.e. International covenant on civil and political rights.

Economic, Social and Cultural Rights

The economic depression of thirties struck a blow at the lofty philosophy of individualism. The social reality came in the light. It was apparent that beneath the lofty idealism of laiseez faire lay hidden the ugly aspect of capitalism. In this regard Julius stone took the view:

"The fallacy of supposing that a work man, living from hand to mouth on daily labour, resents legislative protection for his wage level and conditions of labour in the way as a great commercial or industrial corporation resents restrictions on its free bargaining is now well recognized."[66]

The two products of industrial revolution were 'fundamental rights' and working class. With the advancement of capitalism, it was realized that the fundamental rights remained fundamental rights of capitalist class only and they had no meaning for the working class. The economic depression revealed that though the doctrine of laisez faire triumphed its ultimate result was a divided society, which was divided between the privileged and underprivileged. In this regard President Roosvelt observed:

"One third of our population, the overwhelming of which is in industry and agriculture is ill-nourished, illclad and ill housed."[67]

In the words of professor Wills, "the number of unemployed under capitalistic system had been on a constant increase. Around ten millions of people are now out of the employment which means that there are about thirty or forty millions in the United states without source of revenue. The result of permanent unemployment is indescribable. The physical denials and suffering which accompany it are bad but they do not compose with the mental agony and spiritual disintegration which follow it. Neither capitalist order could endure, nor general economic progress be protected so long as this problem of unemployment remained unsolved.[68]

This state of affairs led to rethinking. It was felt that if fundamental rights were to have any meaning to the millions, it was necessary that their contents must change. If rights were considered to be the condition for the fulfilment of life, then the working class too should have these rights. As a result some more fundamental rights were recognised, they were named as 'social and economic rights'. They can be defined as rights claimed by an individual, in order to eradicate social inequality, economic imbalance and to limit the disadvantage caused due to various reasons.

Economic, social and cultural rights are concerned to the guarantee of minimum necessities of the life to human beings. These rights are positive in nature so the state is bound to take positive action for their fulfilment. The state is not bound to meet these rights all at once. It depends upon the economic resources of the state. The Constitution of Soviet Union adopted these rights without reservation. A trend to include these rights in the Constitution started after the first world war. The Constitution of USSR and the Rublican Constitution of Waimer guaranteed these rights as fundamental rights. In the modern Constitutions of many countries these rights, in some form or the other, are included, though there is no concensus about the details of their contents. They include the right to work, right to employment, right to leisure, rights to public assistance in case of unemployment, old age or sickness, right to collective bargaining, right to education, right to health care, right to special care during childhood and during motherhood.

The economic, social and political right included in the UDHR are as under:

1. Right to social security and the right to realization of the economic, social and cultural rights indispensable for his dignity and the free development of his personality.[69]
2. Right to work, free choice of employment, just and favorable conditions of work and protection against unemployment.[70]
3. Right to equal pay for equal work.[71]
4. Right to just and favourable remuneration.[72]
5. Right to form and to join trade Unions.[73]
6. Right to rest and leisure.[74]

7. Right of living adequate for the health and well-being of himself and his family.[75]
8. Right to all children to enjoy same social protection.[76]
9. Right to education.[77]
10. Right of parents to choose the kind of education for their children.[78]
11. Right to participate in cultural life of the community.[79] and
12. Right to protection of moral and material interests resulting from any scientific, literary or artistic production of which he is the author.[80]

Part IV of the Constitution of India incorporates economic, social and cultural rights termed as 'Directive principles of State Policy,' which are as under:

(a) Right to adequate means of livelihood.[81]
(b) Right against economic exploitation—'that the ownership and control of the material resources of the community are so distributed as best to subserve the common good.[82]
(c) Right to equal pay for equal work for both men and women.[83]
(d) Right to equal justice and free legal aid.[84]
(e) Right to work.[85]
(f) Right to education.[86]

    Right to public assistance in case of unemployment, old age, sickness and disablement.[87]
(g) Right to just and humane conditions of work and for maternity relief.[88]
(h) Living wage for workers, conditions of work ensuring a decent standard of life and full enjoyment of leisure and social and cultural opportunities.[89]

    Some provisions relating to Directive principles of state policy do not confer rights but imposes obligations on the state in the followings manner:

(a) To secure the participation of workers in management of industries.[90]

(b) Free and compulsory education for children.[91]

(c) Promotion of educational and economic interests of schedule castes, scheduled Tribes and other weaker sections.[92]

(d) To raise the level of nutrition and the standard of living of its people and the improvement of public health.[93]

SOURCES OF LAW RELATING TO INTERNATIONAL HUMAN RIGHTS

The law relating to International Human Rights is growing extensively since the formation of the United Nations. The main feature of this developing law is that it prescribes a set of rules for all members of the human family i.e. for all the people of all the states. The following are the main sources of International human rights law:

International Treaties

International treaties are the most important source of International human rights law. Now a days, a number of multilateral treaties are in force and which are binding on the state parties. United Nations charter is the best example of such type of treaty. It is legally binding on all the nations of the world and it prescribes general obligations to honour and promote human rights.

The general assembly of the United Nations adopted Universal Declaration of Human Rights on December 10, 1948 with the hope that ultimately nations will include these human rights in their constitutions.

Besides it there are regional treaties like European convention on Human Rights, American Convention on Human Rights and African Charter on Human and People's Rights which are binding on the contracting states.

International Customs

It is treated as the oldest and the original source of International law as well as of municipal law. In the field of International human rights law also it was regarded as one of the prominent source for a long time. Certain international human rights have gained the status of customary International law because must of the states have adopted them in their practice. Restatement (third) of the Foreign Relation law of the United Nations makes a provision to the effect that customary International law protects at least certain basic human rights sec. 702 of the Restatement says, "A state violates International law if as a matter of state policy it practices, encourages or condones (a) genocide, (b) slavery or slave trade, (c) the murder or causing the disappearance of individuals, (d) torture or other cruel inhuman or degrading treatment or punishment, (e) prolonged arbitrary detention, (f) systematic racial discrimination, or (g) a consistent pattern of gross violations of internationally recognized human rights". The above enumerated list of human rights is not complete in itself but there seems to be widespread agreement among the nations that a number of rights are at present embodied with in the customary international law and as a result they are the source of international human rights law. It would be of immense value if a study is conducted to make a list of those human rights which have acquired the status of international customary law.

International Instruments

A number of international instruments relating to human rights adopted time to time also constitute the source of International human rights law. The prominent among these is the Universal Declaration of Human Rights of 1948 which contains a long list of civil and political rights; economic, social and cultural rights. The general assembly proclaimed the UDHR as a common standard of achievement for all people and all nations, to the end that every individual and every organ of society, keeping this declaration constantly in mind, shall strive by teaching and education to promote respect for these freedoms and by progressive measures, national and international, to secure their universal and effective recognition and observance, both among the people of member states themselves and among the people of territories under their jurisdiction.

The International Covenant on Economic, social and cultural right and the International Covenant on civil and political rights are other instruments which have established broadly recognised standards relating to human rights issues. Tehran Conference (1968) and the Vienna Conference (1993) adopted declarations with can also be treated as the source of international human rights laws.

International Judicial Decisions

Decision of the various International judicial bodies are helpful in determining the rules relating to human rights issues. In the modern time International court of Justice in the main International judicial tribunal. It may be noted have that the decision of International Court of Justice does not create a binding general rule of International law. According to Article 38(1)(d) of the statute International Court of Justice, subject to the provisions of Article 59 judicial decisions are "subsidiary means for the determination of rules of law".

Besides the International Court there are regional Courts, such as European Court of Human Rights, Inter-American Court of Human rights, municipal court on human right, the decisions of all these Court on human rights matters have contributed to the development of International human rights law "State Judicial decisions are treaty as weighty precedents. In this regard Marshall C.J. of Supreme Court of America observed, "The decision of the court of every country show how the law of the nations in the given case is understood in that country will be considered in adopting the rule which is to prevail in that Case."[94]

In addition to the decisions of court, the decisions of the Arbitral Tribunals are treated as weighty precedents and can be regarded as source of International human rights law.

Official Documentation

The United Nations and its specialized agencies have produced official documentation relating to human rights issues which is also a subsidiary source of human rights law. Human Rights

Law Journal, European Law Review and Human Rights Review are such documentation of immense value.

GLOBALIZATION AND HUMAN RIGHTS PERSPECTIVE

The term globalisation is a post-soviet phenomenon. It changed the very intellectual comprehension of world politics and economy, apart from the global power equations. It is a Western model of market economy.[95] Globalization is primarily a removal of national barriers to trade and investment. It is associated with contemporary phenomenon of privatisation, de-regulation, the expanded provision of incentives for entrepreneurial behaviour, structural adjustment programmes and related pressures on developing countries to open-up their markets for international financial institutions and developed countries.[96]

Globalization both as a description and as a prescription has proved several contradictory responses.[97] Globalization demands deregulation and regulation at the same time.[98] Globalization has removed borders regarding trade but not regarding several other important issues such as access to food or medicine, labour movement, employment and immigration.[99] Globalization which is a matter of celebration and resistance at the same time both in the west and in the rest, is either inevitable or irreversible or is an example of western imperialism in an era of neo-liberalism and therefore, whether reversible is a moot point.[100] Whether Globalization poses a threat to human rights or gives impetus to their realization is a disputed question. According to Hertz, globalization is resulting in alienation of people by bringing them together, there is no consensus whether the brining of people closer and thus striving for global homogeneity- uniformity - conformornity is a good development, or is at the heavy cost of destroying indigenous of local beliefs and culture.[101] Similarly, whether globalization increases or decreases poverty as well as economic disparity is a hotly debated and contested issue; what is, however, hardly contested is the fact that globalization has serious implications positive or negative for the relaization of human rights every where, but more so in developing countries.[102]

Dunning defines 'globalization' as connectivity of individuals and institutions across the globe.[103] Gidden say it as 'local happenings are shaped by events occurring many miles away.[104] 'An intense interchange of people, ideas, capital and technology across international space' is globalization.[105] Thus it has been defined in various ways the central idea behind it is that globalization is about movement across the natural and/or (mostly) man-made border barriers in a speedy, efficient way and with minimum restrictions. This movement is ensured through the 4-Ds, deregulation, denationalization, disinvestment and digitalization.

Globalization has not only affected the nature, and elements (contents) of human rights but also the implementtion mechanism. In this regard a number of questions arises:

(i) Whether globalization is anti-human rights or it is pro-human rights; or

(ii) is it a neutral Concept?

In fact, globalization as a concept is neither pro nor anti-human rights; Conceptually globalization could offer opportunities both for the promotion and abridgment of human rights, at the national level as wells as internationally.[106] Dunning takes the view that globalization is a morally neutral concept. In itself it is neither good, nor bad but it may be motivated for good or bad reasons and used to bring about more or less good or bad results.[107] What is, however, critical is the 'way' in which this conception is operationlized, that is, the process of globalization. The direction of the way will depend on many factors, including the composition of actors behind it and their objectives. The apparent actors are states and states-led international institutions such as the United Nations, World Bank, International Monetary Fund and the World Trade Organization.[108] For determining the relationship between globalization and human rights, the following factors needs a close examination:

State's Position and Role Changed

Hertz took the view that the state has been stepping back and the market has been taking over; Globalization has attacked the traditional concept of State Sovereignty; the project of globalization.... lies in "rolling back the state"[109] one should not, however, assume lightly that states or their sovereignty are withering away totally. There is not a loss of sovereignty but only a reconstitution or transformation of it.[110] States, in principles still possess the power of regulation or intervention, but the exception is that states will exercise their power only when it suits the interests of global capital, even if doing so harms the interests of local communities. Moreover, state, even with a democratic set up, might not be able take an activist position towards fulfilling their human rights obligations under pressure from international bodies. In this state of things, it is doubtful whether states could still be trusted for solely guarding, to the best of their ability, the human rights of their populace.

Influence of Multinational Corporations

Increase in the number of multinational Corporations has influenced the human rights jurisprudence—one can easily say that our present as well as fulture is in the hands of large corporations. Despite the fact that Multi-national Corporations of today dwarf many modern states in terms of their economic might, their activities by and large are still not subject to concrete, legally binding human rights obligations flowing from either Constitutional law or international law. Not only this but these corporations are also able to influence policy and law making in key areas such as public health, child labour, workers' rights, consumer protection, foreign investment, environment protection, women's rights at work place and indigenous peoples' rights. Although it can be argued that the arrival of multinationals in local markets benefits consumers and or that they could also have some positive impact on human rights, this has not been the case always. Corporation undoubtedly produce wealth but they also produce risks both to humans and to the eco system.[111]

It is said that there is nothing new about the involvement of corporations or companies in human rights violation, the Indian experience shows that as early as in 17th century the British East India Company had been a great violator of human rights, that was a time when the concept of human rights in its present scenario was not prevalent.

Technology

The most important feature of globalization is exchange of 'technology' because it has helped in the circulation of ideas, goods and people at global level. It has the potential to shape the nature of human rights and could have impact on their realization. The Internet not only enabled the transmission of information to consumers swiftly and in a cost-effective manner but also enabled Non-Governmental organisations to foster alliances all over the world to fight against what of globalization is perceived against human rights. The internet has also raised issues related to right to privacy or child pornography. Similarly, digitalization and biotechnology could have serious implications for the realization of various human rights.[112]

Though technology could be used to promote human rights, there are reasons to believe, given the economic considerations involved in its production, transfer and dissemination, that the final balance-sheet might paint a gloomy picture as far as the human rights in concerned.[113] The Human Development report narrates, "Policies are urgently needed to turn the advances in the new technologies into advanced for all or human kind, and to prevent rules of globalization from blocking poor people and poor countries out of the knowledge economy.[114]

Foreign Investment

The foreign investment is certainly an important factor which has helped in development. But according to eminent economists it is challenge for developing countries to create an atmosphere conducive to foreign direct investment and to ensure that it does not hamper the local developmental needs or the realization of human rights. Surya Deva raises two issues one whose development and at what cost.[115] States may in fact, be ready to barter even their power of regulation in favour of short terms economic gains.[116] Many developing countries often compete for their share of foreign direct investment, this leads to a 'race to the bottom' regarding human rights, including environmental and labour standards.[117]

Treaties Among States

The international as well as regional treaties also govern the relationship between globalization and human rights. Globalization requires cooperation between the states. Due to this cooperation the line between municipal and international governance issues is getting blurred and more issues are being regulated or governed by international or regional treaties. Upendra Baxi says that there are two effects of this regulation issue : First, it limits the leeway and discretion, which is a vital attribute, available to states to react to their respective special human rights needs. For example, a member state of world Trade organization could no longer act, even if demanded by its constitution, to tackle an epidemic or health emergency in disregard to the TRIPs Agreement and the Doha declaration, Second, the process promotes centralization by going further away from the people. Third, it is undemocratic in operation because, oftenly, the obligations imposed by the treaty are undertaken by the executive limb of the government which results in depriving of the people or their representations to discuss the issues before taking the decision.[118]

Consumerism and free Market Economy

Free market economy is one of the result of globalization or considered as supplement to it. Such a market can promote the human rights in several ways. But it can also violate the human rights. It cannot be said with certainty whether free market economy will flourish the human rights. In fact, state regulation or intervention is necessary so that such a market may promote the human rights.

Multi-national companies or Corporations have two motives, namely to earn more and more profit and second, to capture more market. In this process consumerism is increasingly used as a device for 'market creation, the interests of the consumers are the obvious casualties.[119] Consumer choices are molded even at the cost of their health and safety, for example the use of Mega stars or women in sexually explicit advertisements. As 'chick-choca chips culture', which has started taking its roots even in villages, dictates life priorities, the culture of consumerism poses a serious challenge to the realization of human rights of all. In these circumstances, one can only wonder if we need to have a second look at those aspects of globalization which promote a culture of consumerism, something incompatible with sustainable development.[120]

Role Played by Academics, Media and Non-Government Organisations

Rajagopal says that academicians, public spirited social workers, lawyers, Non-government organisations and media have assumed an important role in global governance. They affect not only the policy but law making decisions also at the state and international level.[121] Our past experience shows that the media and NGOs have raised the issues relating to human rights at appropriate forums and thus played a positive role in the promotion of human rights. But media playing in the hands of certain big corporate houses and dependence of Non-government organisations on donations is a considerable matter or a matter of high concern.

Certainly the globalization has influenced the human rights. This new concept has also reduced the reliance on role played by the state in implementation of human rights. In due course of time and in coming days the non-state entities, non-government organisations, public spirited people, academics, organized consumers, social workers, trade unions and media would seek to ensure effective implementation of human rights obligations.

The above discussion makes it clear, first, though globalization as a concept is not inherently anti or pro-human rights, the same can not be said about globalization as a process. In view of the nature and motive of the actors involver, the process of globalization is widely seen more as a foe than a friend of the human rights of all. Second, as globalization offers opportunities both for promotion and abridgment of human rights, at the national level as well as internationally, at a given point of time the position of globalization vis-a-vis human rights will ultimately depend on how effectively human rights activists are able to utilize those opportunities qua other competing actors. Third, it is highly unlikely that any one interest constituency will have a long lasting monopoly over the process of globalization so as to derive more benefits. Though, to date it is primarily driven by something else than the human rights of all, especially of the poor oppressed illiterate masses, this may change in future.[122]

In India the adoption of New Economic Policy in the early 1990 had been a debatable issue regarding its suitability and impact. It is widely accepted that liberalization was the need of the hour, it seems that the state did not ensure that the enforcement of human rights, especially of the down trodden class remained an important variable at the time of law making or policy decision taking. Mc Corquodale and Fairbrother points out that the government did not control adequately the direction of Foreign investment, and probably made bad policy decisions in terms of investment prioritization.[123] This resulted in a situation where people in villages have access to Pepsi or coca cola but not safe drinking water, adequate food, health case, electricity, roads or school.[124]

Second, the amended laws relating to foreign investment, factories, industrial dispute, contract labour, monopolistic practices and trade union had adversely affected the human rights of labourer class. Third, the executives's decision to override the authority of Legislature to undertake international obligations on important issues is a matter of high concern, as it is against the canons of parliamentary democracy. Fourth, the Government did not pursued extradition of Warran Anderson, the ex-CEO of Union Carbide Corporation by this a Wrong message was transmitted to foreign companies regarding their human rights obligations. Fifth, when there was a hue and cry regarding presence of toxic pesticides in soft drinks like Pepsi, the Central Government took a decision to ban the supply of such drinks in parliament premises but did not ban the same for ordinary consumers thus left them at the mercy of multi-national corporations.

A very important component of economic constitutionality is the Constitutional settlement of the basic economic and social rights of citizens. These basic rights should be based on guarantee of social security, the improvement of equality of opportunity and the principle of social justice. Among these rights, the following have particular importance: The rights to work the right of free selection of profession and work place, the right to social security to leisure the right to strike and further more the right to establish organizations for representing interests. Confronted with new developments at the international level and the desire that India should not be left behind in economic development, the new laws and policies are framed in this direction to integrate Indian economy and market with the global economy, but nothing has been done to ensure that the individuals, particularly marginalized sections of society, do not suffer from the on slaught of these developments and their human rights are ensured. Thus, the fundamental challenge before the government is that while it should march with the world economic order, it should not lag behind on the human resource development, by providing a conducive socio-legal and economic conditions. For this reason, the constitutional mechanism on the regulation must be provided to ward off the ill effects of globalisation and to reap its benefits. It may be relevant to note that India's economy is primarily agricultural and majority of its population lives in villages........ A large segment of the society is illiterate and lives below the poverty line. Hence, it is required that the economic policy of the government should be more focused with definite aims, otherwise the development will never be wholesome and the market forces will spell a havoc for the Indian State. It is feared that under pressure of globalization, the poor and downtrodden will further be marginalized. It is also feared that the small scale and cottage industry will lose-out the competition. Whereas, it shall be duty to protect the interests of these entrepreneurs, it is also the duty of the state to provide adequate socio-legal framework in which the welfare of the deprived sections should be central to legal reforms.... India has declared it self as a 'socialist' republic in the preamble of its Constitution. Even if it is swayed by the winds of globalization, it must act to fulfil that mandate by giving a proper place to the rights of the individual, which are enshrined in the Constitution and for which it is internationally obliged to comply under various human rights treaties to which it is a party.[125]

This does not suggest that the Government has been totally oblivious to the impact of globalization on its Constitutional obligation of realizing human rights of all and of the impoverished especially, for example, it launched a social security scheme for the unorganized sector; amended the Constitution to provide for free and compulsory education;[126] released a charter on corporate responsibility for environmental protection, made environmental clearance mandatory for new big urban projects; and recently proposed an Employment guarantee scheme to provide at least 100 days of employment to every house hold in rural India.[127]

Indian Constitution and Human Rights Culture

The Constitution of United States of America incorporated human rights in its constitution in 1789. After world war II, almost all the countries of the world have embodied the basic human rights in their text. On December 10, 1948 the general assembly of United Nations adopted the Universal Declaration of Human Rights and in pursuance of it two covenants- International covenant on civil and political rights and International covenant on Economic, social and cultural rights, 1966 were prepared.

The history of the inclusion of fundament rights in the constitution of India is a long one. For the first time, the Indian National Congress prepared a proposed draft of the Indian constitution (constitution of India Bill, 1895) incorporating certain fundamental rights to all citizens irrespective of their religion, race and caste. Article 16 of this Bill laid down a variety of rights including free speech, imprisonment only by competent authority and of free state Education. The next development was Mrs. Beasent's commonwealth of India Bill, 1925 which included individual liberty, freedom of conscience, free expression of opinion, free assembly, equality before law and no disqualification or disability on the ground of sex. the other provisions contained in the bill were : all persons in the commonwealth of India were to have the right to free elementary education and all persons were to have equal rights to the use of roads, courts of justice and other places of business or resort dedicated to the public.

The fortythird Annual session of the congress at Madras in 1927 passed resolution that the working committee should be empowered to set up a committee to draft a Swaraj Constitution for India on the basis of a declaration of right. The committee was set up under the chairmanship of Motilal Nehru, the report of the committee spoke, "It is obvious that our first care should be to have our fundamental Rights guaranteed in a manner which will not permit their withdrawl under any circumstances....[128] In 1931, the congress session held at Karachi adopted resolution on Fundamental rights and Economic and social change which was both a declaration of rights and a humanitarian socialist manifesto. The Karachi resolution, as it came to be called, meant that the social revolution would have a vital share in shaping India's future constitution, and the provisions did in fact become the spiritual, and in some cases the direct, antecedents of the Directive Principles.[129] The Karachi resolution stated that, 'in order to end the exploitation of masses, political freedom must include the real economic freedom of the serving millions. According to the resolution state was obliged to safeguard the interests of industrial workers, ensuring that suitable legislation should secure them a living wage, healthy conditions, limited hours of labour, and protection from the economic consequences of old age, sickness and unemployment.

The next effort in this direction was the Sapru Report of 1945. The report laid down a constitutional scheme for India and the part of the report dealing with fundamental rights laid emphasis mainly on the minority problem. The Report said, 'that what the constitution clemands and expects is perfect equality between one section of the community and another in the matter of political and civic rights, equality of liberty and security in the enjoyment of the freedom of religion, worship and the pursuit of the ordinary application of life.[130]

The idea of framing of the Indian constitution through a sovereign constituent Assembly owes its origin to the philosophy of popular sovereignty, current in the west during the 18th century. The demand of a constituent Assembly for India for determining her political destiny may be traced back to the assertion of Mahatma Gandhi as early as in 1922. He said, "Swaraj will not be a free gift of the British Parliament. It will be a declaration of India's full self expression expressed.... through the freely chosen representative."[131] The Indian National Congress passed resolution in December, 1936 which read, "The Congress stand for a genuine democratic state in India ...... such state can only come into existence through a constituent Assembly.[132]

The Constituent Assembly of India was Convened as per the provisions of the Cabinet Mission Statement of 16th May, 1946. The objective resolution moved by Pandit Jawahar Lal Nehru on December 13, 1946 was in the nature of a pledge, a statement of policy and an introduction to the philosophy of the Constitution.[133] The relevant clause (5) of the resolution lays down. "WHEREIN shall be guaranteed and secured to all the people of India Justice, social economic and political, equality of status, of opportunity, and before the law, freedom of thought, expression, belief, faith worship, vocation, association and action, subject to law and public morality." The first task after the resolution was to constitute an Advisory

Committee. The Advisory Committee appointed five sub-committees one of them was fundamental rights sub-committee. The Sub-committee drafted the rights during ten meetings held in March and April 1947 and submitted its report to the Advisory Committee which presented an interim report on the rights to the Constituent Assembly on 29th Apl., 1947. The Assembly after a due debate finalized the rights by the mid of December, 1948.

For the incorporation of human rights in the Constitution, Granville Austin analysing the position says, that the decade of the 1940's generally was marked by a resurgence of interest in human rights. The denial of liberties under German and Russian totalitarianism and elsewhere resulted in the Atlantic charter, the United Nations Charter and the activities of the United Nations Human Rights Commission. Assembly members were sensitive to these currents which supported their own faith in the validity of written rights. By 1947, it was a commonly accepted belief that the state bore a major responsibility for the welfare of its citizens. Nehru, the Indian socialists, and the very winds of social and political thought had brought to India the ideas of Marx, T.H. Green, Laski, the webbs and many others The expression of such ideas had begun before the end of the nineteenth century with the views of Swami Vivekanand and continued with those of R.C. Dutt and M.Visvesvaraya, among other.[134]

The sublime and substantive provisions concerning human rights emphasised in the Universal Declaration of Human Rights, 1948, Finds good and extensive incorporation and expression in Part III and IV of Indian Constitution dealing with the Fundamental Rights and Directive Principles of State Policy. The Chapter on Fundamental Rights in called Magna Carta of India. It is the ground work of the state. Part III and IV of Indian Constitution cover almost the entire field of the Universal Declaration of Human Rights. Human Rights Jurisprudence in India has a constitutional status and sweep so that this Manga Carta may well toll the knell of human bondage beyond civilised limits.

The human rights enshrined in Part III of Indian Constitution has been made non-derogable under article 13(2) and their enforcement has been guaranteed under Article 32 of the Constitution as one of the basic rights. These rights are essential for good life as essential as light, air, food and clothing are for human existence. The rights enumerated in Part III of the Indian Constitution include namely:

(i) Right to equality, guaranteed under Articles 14 and 16.

(ii) Freedom of speech, assembly and association etc., guaranteed in Article 19.

(iii) Right to life and personal liberty enshrined in Article 21 and 22.

(iv) Right against exploitation enshrined in Articles 23 and 24.

(v) Right to religion, cultural and educational etc., enshrined in Articles 25, 28, 29 and 30.

The Constitution of India is a document rich in human rights jurisprudence.[135] The Preamble concisely sets out quintessence of human rights, which represents the aspirations of the people who have established the Constitution. Democracy, secularism, liberty and equality as they appear in the Preamble of the Constitution, are considered as the basic features of the Indian Constitution which cannot be taken away or amended, to deprive them of their significance, even by a constitutional amendment.[136]

The Constitution of India is one of the most elaborated Charter of human rights, yet framed by any state.[137] Many of the human rights and freedoms in the Universal Declaration of Human Rights, 1948, and in the International Covenant on Civil and Political Rights, 1966 are guaranteed in Part III of the Constitution as Fundamental Rights. In fact, Part III of the Constitution may be characterised as the Magna Carta of India. It embodies and sanctifies certain fundamental, individual justifiable rights which are primarily mend to protect and promote the basic human rights of the people and protect the individual against state action by imposing negative obligations.

Our National Charter endeavors to aim at the establishment of free and egalitarian social order based on the rule of law. The directive principles aim at the betterment of the individual as an integrated component of the society. Elimination of inequality of income, opportunities and status and securing a just social order is the philosophical foundation of Part IV, embodying the concept of welfare state.[138] The specific economic rights include the right to adequate means of livelihood distribution of ownership and control of material resources for the common good, equal pay for equal work for men and women, the protection against abuse of health and strength of childhood and youth. The protection of child and youth against exploitation is a fundamental right. The state is enjoined "within the limits of its economic capacity[139] and development" to provide for securing the right to work, to education and public assistance in case of unemployment, old age, sickness, disablement and "other cases of observing want" and to secure just and humane conditions of work, and maternity relief.[140] A significant advantage is Article 43 which promises living wage, condition of work, ensuring a decent standard of life, full enjoyment of leisure and social and cultural opportunities. Primary education has been made out not only free but compulsory until the completion of 14 years of age.[141] Equal opportunities for securing justice by legal aid, is another landmark in the quest of social justice. The trial of poor accused in a criminal case is vitiated if the state does not offer at its expense the service of a lawyer.[142]

In addition to Fundamental rights and Directive principles of state policy, the constitutional has several provisions on human rights providing for negative rights as well as for positive obligations. For example, the equal right of all to participate in the political process on the basis of adult franchise is provided in Articles 325 and 326 and the fairness of electoral process is ensured in Articles 324 to 329. Part XVI, comprising Articles 330 to 342 makes special provisions for the representation of SCs, STs and the Anglo-Indians in the national parliament and state legislatures by reserving certain number of seats for them. It also make provision for special educational grants and representation in certain state services for the Anglo-Indians and also for the SCs and STs.[143] Other provisions in that part provide for elaborate machinery for the protection of the SCs, STs and other Backward classes, including the appointment of commissions from time to time for the STs and other backward classes and a permanent national commission for all of them.[144] Special safeguards and machinery are also provided for the linguistic minorities in part XVII of the constitution.[145] For the better administration of the predominantly tribal areas special provisions are made in Articles 244 and 244A and in schedules V and VI of the constitution. Provision is also made for the appointment of a tribal welfare minister in some of the states.[146] On the same line some amendments of the constitution have introduced special provisions for the SCs, STs, women and other weaker sections of the society. For example, part IVA comprising Article 51A introduced in 1976, imposes certain fundamental duties on the citizens which, among others, ensure dignity of women, common brother hood among people and protection of environment. Parts IX and IXA, introduced in 1992, make special provisions for the representation, including in the chief executive position of the SCs, STs and woman in the village panchayat and the municipalities respectively.

From the above description of the provisions of the Constitution it is clear that almost coinciding with the Universal Declaration of Human Rights and much before the ICCPR and the ICESCR, the Constitution of India had expressed all that is covered in those documents and more. The most notable aspect of the constitution is the recognition of state's obligation to ensure human rights to everyone and not only to those who can make full use of them.[147]

Besides the Constitutional provision, the National Human Rights Commission and State Human Rights Commissions constituted under the Protection of Human Rights Act, 1993 keep a vigil on violation of human rights. This Act was enacted for better protection of human rights. The functions of the Commission include inquiring into violation of human rights, to study treaties and other International instruments on human rights and to make for their effective implementation, to undertake and promote, restrict in the field of human rights, to spread human rights literacy among various sections of the society and promote awareness of safeguards available for the protection of these rights and recommend measures for effective implementation of the safeguards provided by or under the Constitution or any law. There is no doubt that National Human Rights Commission and State Human Rights commissions have been playing a significant role in, protecting the human rights. The very idea to bring the Human Rights commission into existence is to give practical shape to the entire gamut of human rights philosophy by executing the intention of the legislatures manifested in different social legislations in consonance with the philosophy enshrined in our national character.[148]

NOTES

1. Human Rights Manual, Department of Foreign Affairs and Trade, (1993) p. 10.
2. Human Rights Manual, Department of Foreign Affairs and Trade, (1993) p. 10.
3. LAWS Promulgated in the reigns of Urukagina of Lagash, (3260 B.C.), Sargon of Akkad (2300 B.C.) and Hammurabi of Babylon, (1750 B.C.) Cited by P.N. Bhagawati J. in inaugural address in the "seminar on Human Rights" organised by International Law Association, Allahabad Centre, (1980), p. 9.
4. D. D. Basu (2003), *Human Rights in Constitutional Law*, p. 8.
5. Dr. H. O. Aggrawal (2005) , '*International Law and Human Rights*', p. 695.
6. J. E. S. Fawcett (1968), *The Law of Nations*, p. 15.
7. M. S. Mc Dougal and Bebr (1964), "Human Rights in the United Nations, *A.J.I.L.* Vol. 56, P. 604.
8. 'Rights Here and there', 81 Columbia Law Review 1582 (1981).
9. Bhagwati J. (1978), in *Maneka Gandhi v. Union of India,* A.I.R. SC 597, at p. 619
10. David P. Forsythe, 'The Internationalisation of Human Rights, p. 1.

11. The Globalization of Human Rights, editea by Jean Marc Colcaud, Michael W. Doyle & Anne Mari Gardner (2004) p. 25.
12. Maurice Cranston, What are Human Rights, p. 36.
13. J. L. Brierly (1963), *'The Law of Nations'* Sixthed, p. 292.
14. Stephen S. Goodspeed (1967), 'The Nature and Functions of International Organisation, 2nd ed., p. 516.
15. A. H. Robertson (1961) , The Law of International Institution in Europe, pp. 52-53.
16. Humphrey (1967), 'The U.N. Charter and the UN Declaration of Human Rights' in Laurd (ed.) The International Protection of Human Rights.
17. Dr. S. K. Kapoor, *International Law and Human Rights*, 14th ed. p. 765.
18. Wikipedia-The Free Encyclopaedia *'Human Rights'*, p. 1.
19. J. C. Johari (1996) , Human Rights and New World Order: Towards Perfection of the Democracticway of Life, p. 2.
20. Arun Ray (2004) , 'National Human Rights Commission of India', p. 46.
21. 'The Globalization of Human Rights' edited by Jean Marc Colcaud, Michal W. Doyle & Anne Mari Gardner (2004) p. 25-26.
22. Gavison (2004), 'Relation Between Rights' in Globalization of Human Rights (ed.) by Marc, Gardner, at p. 26-27.
23. The Globalisation of Human Rights edited by Jean Marc etc. at p. 29.
24. Scott Davidson (1993), "Human Rights", p. 45.
25. Richard pierre claude and H. weston Burns (ed.) Human Rights in the world community: Issues and Actions (1989).
26. Mehta & Jaswal 'Human Rights: concept and ideology' p. 122.
27. Altor Chand (1985) , Politics of Human Rights and Civil Liberties-A Global Survey, 45, p. 74.
28. *Ibid*, p. 75.
29. F.N. 26, p. 123.
30. Human Rights Manual Department of Foreign Affairs and Trade, Australian Govt. Publication Service, 1993, p. 11.
31. L. Henkin (1979), "The Right of Man Today", p. 18-19.

32. H.R. Khanna, J. (1998), "Human Rights—Dimension and Challenges", AIR , *Journal Section*, Page 49.
33. See Article 13(2) of the Constitution of India.
34. D. D. Basu (2003), "*Human Rights in Constitutional Law*"', 2nd ed., at pp. 16-17.
35. Article 3.
36. Article 4.
37. Article 5.
38. Article 6.
39. Article 7.
40. Article 8.
41. Article 9.
42. Article 10.
43. Article 11, para 1.
44. Article 11, para 2.
49. Article 15, para 1.
50. Article 15, para 2.
51. Article 16, para 1.
52. Article 17.
53. Article 18.
54. Article 19.
55. Article 20.
56. Article 21, para 1.
57. Article 21, para 2.
58. Article 14-16.
59. Article 19.
45. Article 12.
46. Article 13, para 1.
47. Article 13, para 2.
48. Article 14.
60. Articles 20-22.
61. Articles 25-28.

62. Articles 29 & 30.
63. Article 31 (44th Amendment Act, 1978 has deleted this right and re-enacted it in Article 300A, as constitutional right).
64. Article 23 & 24.
65. Article 32.
66. The Province and Function of Law, Ist Ed. P. 265.
67. Public Papers and address of Franklin D. Roosvelt, 223.
68. Constitutional Law (1936), 792.
69. Article 22.
70. Article 23, para 1.
71. Article 23, para 2.
72. Article 23, para 3.
73. Article 23, para 4.
74. Article 24.
75. Article 25, para 1.
76. Article 25, para 2.
77. Article 26, para 1.
78. Article 26, para 3.
79. Article 27, para 1.
80. Article 27, para 2.
81. Article 39(a) of the Constitution of India.
82. Article 39(b) of the Constitution of India.
83. Article 39(d) of the Constitution of India.
84. Article 39(A) of the Constitution of India.
85. Article 41 of the Constitution of India.
86. Article 41 of the Constitution of India.
87. Article 41 of the Constitution of India.
88. Article 42 of the Constitution of India.
89. Article 43 speaks as under "The state shall endeowour to secure.... to all workers..... a living wage, condition of work ensuring a decent standard of life and full enjoyment of leisure and social and cultural opportunities and in particular, the state shall endeavour promote cottage industries on an individual or co-operative basis in rural areas."

90. Article 43A of the Indian Constitution.
91. Article 45 of the Indian Constitution.
92. Article 46 of the Indian Constitution.
93. Article 47 of the Indian Constitution.
94. Thirty Hogheseads of Sugar, Bentzon v. Boyle, (1815) 9 Cranch (9).
95. Asghar Ali Engineer (1997), "Globalization, Democracy and Threat to Diversity," Mainstre am 10, Nov. 1.
96. Stenier and Alston (ed.), (1993), International Human Rights in Context, (1996), Citing Sigrun Skogly "Structural Adjustment and Development: Human Rights—An agenda for change, 15 HRS G. 751.
97. Upendra Baxi (2002), "The Future of Human Rights", p. 133.
98. Joseph E. Stiglitz (2002), "Globalization and its discontents".
99. U.N. General Assembly, 'Preliminary Report of the Secretary General on Globalisation and its Impact on the Full Enijoyment of the Human Right', (August 31, 2000) Para 37.
100. Noam Chomsky (1999), 'Profit Over People Neoliberalism and Global order.
101. Hertz (2001), "The Silent Takeover, Global Capitalism and the Death of Democracy, 1-5.
102. Antony Anghie (2000), "Time Present and Time Past; Globaliazation, International Financial Institutions and the Third World. New York University *Journal of International Law and Policy*, 32, 243.
103. John H. Dunning (2003), "The Moral Imperative of Global Capitalism", p. 12.
104. Gidden (1990), "The Consequences of Modernity, Polity Canabridge 64.
105. Richard Peet (2003), "World Bank and WTO, p. 1.
106. Surya Deva (2007), "Globalization and its Impact on the Relization of Human Rights-Indian Perspective on a global Canvas' in Human Rights, Justice and Constitution Empowerment by Raj Kumar, p. 240-241.
107. John H. Dunning (2003), "Making Globalization good-The Moral Challenges of Global Capitalism.

108. John Braithwaite and Peter Drahos (2000), "Global Business Regulation, p. 511-12.

109. Upendra Baxi (2002), "The Future of Human Rights", p. 133.

110. Saskia Sassen, Losing Control? Sovereignity in an age of Globalization, (1996).

111. Surya Deva (2003), Human Rights Violations by Multinational Corporation and International Law, *Jounral of International Law,* 19, 1.

112. Upendra Baxi (2003), "The Future of Human Rights.

113. Raj Kumar (2007), "Human Rights, Justice and Constitutional Environment, p. 246.

114. Human Development report (1999) p. 72.

115. Surya Deva (2004), "The Sangam of Foreign Investment, Multinational Corporations and Human Rights: An Indian Perspective for a Developing Asia, Singapore *Journal of Legal Studies.*

116. Steven R. Rother (2001), 'Corporation and Human Rights: A Theory of Legal Responsibility Yale *Law Journal,* 443.

117. K. Chockalingam (2007), Human Rights, Justice and Constitutional Empowerement, p. 245.

118. Upendra Baxi (2002), "The Future of Human Rights" 135.

119. Robert Mc Corquodale and Richard Fairbrother (1999), "Globalization and Human Rights", *Human Rights Quarterly,* 21 735.

120. Surya Deva (2007), 'Globalization and its Impact on the Realization of Human Rights' in Human Rights, Justice and Constitutional Empowerement (ed) by Raj Kumar, 247.

121. Rajagopal (2003), 'International Law and Social Movements Challenge of Theorising Resistance' *Columbia Journal of Transnational Law* 41, 397.

122. Raj Kumar & K. Chockalingam (2007), "Human Rights, Justice and Constitutional Empowerement, 250-251.

123. "Globalization and Human Rights", *Human Rights Quarterly,* 21 (1999) 750.

124. Is India Shining? Frontline (Feb. 28-March 12, 2004).

125. Prof. S. K. Verma (2000), "Globalisation, marketistation and Cosntitutional Mandate", 42 JILI, 401-402.

126. Article 21A, inserted by Constitution (86th Amendment) Act 2002 Says, "The State shall provide free and compulsory Education to all children of the age of six to furteen years in such manner as the state may, by law, determine. By the same amendment 51-A(k) inserted in part IV-A (Fundamental duties) lays down," who is a parent or guardian to provide opportunities for education to his child or, as the case may be, ward between the age of six and fourteen years.

127. Surya Deva (2007), "Globalization and its Impact on the Realization of Human Rights" in Human Right, Justice and Constitutional Empowerement, p. 252-253.

128. Report of a Committee to Determine Principles of the Constitution for India, the Nehru Report, pp. 89-90.

129. Granville Austin (1966), "The Indian Constitution: Cornerstone of a Nation", p. 56.

130. Constitutional Proposals of the Sapru Committee Report p. 260.

131. C.A.D., I. P. 5

132. C.A.D., I., P. 6

133. C.A.D., I., PP. 58-60

134. Granville Austin (1966), "The Indian Constitution: Cornerstone of a Nation", pp. 59-60.

135. See, G.H. Gutjals (1986), "Human Rights the Indian Law", 26.1 and 2 *Indian Journal of International Law*, 55, Jan.-June.

136. For detail see constitution of India, Article 13(2) and 368.

137. See, Subhash C. Kashyap, Human Rights and Parliament, 33 (Metropolitan, New Delhi 1977).

138. Article 38 reads as under: (1) The state shall strive to promote the welfare of the people by securing and protecting as effectively as it may, a social order in which Justice, social, economic and political shall inform all the institutions of the national life. (2) The state shall in particular, strive to minimize the inequalities in income, and endeavour to eliminate inequalities in status facilities and opportunities, not only amongst individuals but also amongst groups of people residing in different areas engaged in different vocations.

139. Ind. Const. Art. 47.

140. Ind. Const. Art. 42.

141. Constitution of India Art. 45.

142. Constitution of India Art. 39-A.

143. Articles 335-337.

144. Articles 338-340 Constitution (89th Amendment) Act, 2003 inserted a new Article 338A which provides for establishment of National commission for the scheduled Tribes.

145. Articles 350-351.

146. Article 164, See also constitution (94th Amendment) Act, 2006.

147. M.P. Singh (2007), "Constitualization and Human Rights in India" in Human Rights, Justice and Constitutional Empowerement (e.d.) by C. Raj Kumar and K. Chockalingam, p. 32.

148. See, P.L. Mehta and Neena Verma (1999), Human Rights under the Indian Constitution 4, Deep & Deep Publication Pvt. Ltd. New Delhi.

2

INTERNATIONAL AND REGIONAL IMPLEMENTATION OF HUMAN RIGHTS

GENERAL

Some authors[1] argue that the idea of human rights is the contemporary concept, especially the post world war II phenomenon. This is misapprehended or misconceived approach. It is possible to say that the public movement for respect of human rights has started after the 13th century. But the conception of human rights is as old as the history of human being. To ensure this resort craft be made to the teachings of Holy Bible and Holy Quran. The foundation of human rights is essentially theological and is rooted in the obligation owed by human beings to God. Therefore considering human rights as peculiar to the modern world is misunderstanding which arises from the fact that when democratic movements started in the European countries during the 18th Century.[2]

It is incontrovertible that human rights has got international concern after the World War II. During the Second World War it was proved that one dangerous aspect of Hitler's rule was its lack of concern for peoples lives and liberties[3]. After looking the devastating effect of the war the promotion and protection of human rights was considered as an integral and essential element for the preservation of World peace and co-operation. The atrocities of Second World war led to a determination to do some thing to prevent war, to build an international organization that could remove international crises and provide a forum for discussion and mediation. This gave birth to the United Nations Organization in the year 1945 which has played a significant role in the development of the present international human right norms and in the establishment of international human right implementation machineries. In the forthcoming sections attempt has been made to see these norms and implementation mechanisms established therein.

Universalization of Human Rights and Doctrine of Incorporation in Domestic Jurisprudence

According Henkin, the modern human rights movement has sought to achieve, "the universalisation of human rights, the transformation of the idea of constitutional rights in a few countries to a universal conception and a staple of international politics and law." The effect of this transformation when the global standards are incorporated in domestic law needs to be considered. Claire Archbold has raised some questions in this regard, which are as under:

(i) Do the standards survive intact or as they are adopted and integrated into national law, do they become less universal?

(ii) Does national incorporation mean that standards are flexible enough not to be monolithic or so flexible as to become something other than universal?

How International norms can become part of domestic law, Archbold pointed out that human rights—the moral and/or legal claims arising from the inherent dignity of human beings were part and parcel of a Lockian view of constitutionalism, and their potential political effects were perhaps most notably demonstrated in revolutionary France and America at the end of the eighteenth century. At that time, rights were seen as liberties of the individual which had to be ringfenced against invasion by the state. They were negatively phrased and absolute. In the twentieth century, this liberal idea of rights has developed and evolved as circumstances have changed, and commentators now refer to a roughly chronological development of three generations of rights. First generation rights are those civil and political liberties recognizable to the eighteenth century constitutional drafters. Second generation rights are social and economic rights, such as the rights to basic nutrition, shelter, education, and health care. Third generation rights are a mixed bag. consisting of more recently developed individual rights, such as the right to a healthful environment, as well as minority and group rights. Although human rights are often described as indivisible, indicating that the effective guarantee of any right requires the respect for all of them. the diverse nature, and occasionally competing demands of each generation of rights, can seem to give rise to tensions.

The question of how rights are to be made effective within nation states requires that they be incorporated into national law and practices. Human rights consciousness and énforcement "trickle down" from international to national levels in several ways. At the broadest level, the language of human rights is used when the community of nations attempts to put pressure on nations which have little regard for the rights of their citizens. Within nation state, the language of rights is used by non-governmental organizations and human rights monitors, as well as by politicians, as a motor for social or political change. In more concrete terms, national governments sign human rights treaties, and several United Nations treaties requrie them to make periodic reports on the extents towhich the rights in question are secured for their citizens. Other treaties, such as the European Convention on Human Rights, have their own judicial institutions, and can be effective in indicating areas in which human rights protection could be better. But a human rights culture will only really be created in a particular society if huamn rights are incorporated into its national law. This may be by "ordinary" legislation, or, in the common law world in particular, by judicial application of internationally recognized human rights norms in national courts. But the most effective way to secure human rights for national citizens is by enacting them as entrenched legislation, which has a special status and cannot be easily changed, such as a Bill of Rights or constitution.

In the Vienna Declaration of 1993, the United Nations stated that civil and political, social and economic, group and individual rights are unified and indivisible. However, when it comes to incorporation and implementation of human rights at nation state level, this statement is less selfevident. Human rights norms are not incorporated into national law without some element of selection and modification resulting from national political and social circumstances. This process may be most evident in the debate surrounding enactment of an entrenched national Bill of Rights. Canada and South Africa, both provide examples of this process. Both are states which have chosen to entrench particular human rights norms in their law as part of a process of constitutional transition. However, selection and modification do not mean that human rights norms are entirely mutable when enacted at a national level. The selections made in both jurisdictions have indicated the points of tension in those societies. Further, engagement with international human rights discourse can in its turn modify national political and constitutional discourses in terms of international human rights thinking.

The road to incorporation of Internatiaonal human rights in domestic law may be indicated by taking example of Canada and Australia. Canada has a burkean constitutional heritage, arising from its origins within the British Empire. The dominion of Canada was founded by The British North America Act of 1867, and has a highly decentralized federal system of government. After the Balfour Declaration of 1926, by which the British government expressed its intention that Comonwealth countries should become autonomous and self-governing, the Canadian provincial governments met, and it became clear that Canada would not be able to agree a means of amending a national constitution. The Statute of Westiminster granted Canada self-governing autonomy in other regards, but provided that the Canadan Constitution would continue to be amended in London. Formulas for constitutional amendment were negotiated amongst the provicial premiers at Charlorttetown in 1964, at Victoria in 1971, and in the negotiations which rumbled or throughout the 1970s, but were unacceptable to some of the provinces, particularly to Quebec, which became increasing nationalist and separatist as its so-called Quiet Revolution grathered force from 1965. The explicit human rights discourse included in the debate, most notably by Pierre Trudeau after 1965. The focus of attention in Canada was on those human rights which were at the site of the constitutional problems-groups rights; in particular the linguistic and cultural rights of the people of Quebec, and their right to seelf-determination. One aspect was Trudeau's attempt to raise support for the idea of individual human rights held equally by all Canadians as a "fundamental Canadain value" was a way of trying to shift the debate away from this impasse, reflecting the idea that "universal" rights are uncontentious. The other aspect was that individual rights have become associated with one side of the constitutional disagreement in Canada, but even in this context without necessarily losing their substantive conceptual power. The ongoing history of how human rights have been "personalized" to the Canadian discourse illustrates both how national experience acts to modify expressions of universal human rights and how human rights discourse soaks into the fabric of national constitutional debate, facilitating the constitutional conversation.

Individual human rights made their first significant appearance in national debate in the 1958 elections, when a Canadian Bill of Rights was an electoral platform of the Prime Minister John Diefenbaker. When enacted in 1960, it was a first step towards a constitutional declaration of rights. Macklem-suggest that the Bill of Rights had a number of shaping influences; notably the Universal Declaration of Human Rights, the liberal interpretations of the US Supreme Court in the 1950s, fear of expanding government, a sense that the Cold War was, at its heart, a struggle for individual rights, and finally, unease at certain denials of civil liberties which had taken place in

Canada during World War II and in the post-War period. Despite good intentions, however, the Bill of Rights was limited document, particuarly because it was narrowly interpreted by the courts. The United Kingdom Canada Act 1982 granted Canada full independence from Britain, and added the Charter of Rights and Freedoms to the Existing Constitution (contained in the British North America Act and subsequent enactments of the UK Parliament), as well as recognizing the "existing" rights of Canada's aboriginal people. However, it did not create a completely new Constitution. The next important development was the Meech Lake Accord of 1987. At this point, while indiviudal enjoyment of equal rights was the value which won support of most English-speaking Canadians, for French-speakers, the prime constitutional value was still maintaining and developing their distnict indentity. Candians had tasted a more democratic form of constitution-building, and meech Lake, a return to the closed-door relite accommodations of the past, was bitterly attacked by the interest groups which had been successful in the 1982 process. Nor did Meech satisfy interests in Quebec, and perhaps the strongest opposition to Meech was among the aboriginal peoples of Maintoba and the population of Newfoundand, which, like other maritime and western provinces, felt outnumbered and unrepresented in the agreement. The Federal Government's proposals for constitutional reform in Shaping Canada's Future Together (1991) would have added a "Canada clause," containing a statement of national identity, to the Constitution, amended the Charter to recognize Quebec as a distinct society, guaranteed property rights and amended the notwithstanding clause so that a 60 per cent majority would be necessary to pass non-compatible legislation. These proposals were the subject of a series of conferencess which culminated in the Beaudoin-Dobbie Report and became the basis of the Charlottetown Accord. The characteristics of accord were:

1. Parliamentary democracy and Canadian federalism;
2. Right of Aboriginal people;
3. Quebec's distinct society;

4. Linguistic dulity;
5. Racial and ethnic equality;
6. Respect for individual and collective human rights and freedoms of all people;
7. Equality of women and men;
8. The equality of provinces, while recognizing their diverse characteristics.

The Human rights focus which resulted in the Canadian Charter and which was so deeply ingrained in later negotiations did not provide a "quick fix" to the tensions causing constitutional disagreement in Canadian society. Furthermore, the range of rights included in the Charter may be seen to be largely limited to first generation (civic and political) and linguistic/cultural rights. Although international human rights norms may be seen as a unified and indivisible whole, indidivuals societies prioritize those rights which are most relevant to the points of tension in their culture and circumstances.

However, the achievements of the Charter were twofold. First, the Charter consultations were the first to include a broad base of non-parliamentary Canadians and were the occasion for many more voices to enter the constitutional dialogue, expressing and understanding their claims in human rights terms. Second, despite the unfinished nature of Canadain Constitution making, the courts have used the Charter to develop a strongly rights and equality-based jurisprudence which is seen in many cases by other jurisdictions as a model of the way in which human rights may be ingrafted to national jurisprudence. Both the process and the substances of the Charter, therefore have contributed to the support it has gained from, and the affection with which it is seen by, the majority of Canadians. The process of interacting with human rights norms itself can modify the political life of the society and begin to remake it in line with those norms.[3a]

In Australia the dualist theory of relationship betwen international and national law has been followed. The well established principle of the Common law is that a treaty not terminating a state of war has no legal effect upon the rights and duties of Australian citizens and is not incorporated into Australian law on it ratification by Australia. In this respect Australian law differs from that of the United States where treaties are self executing and create rights and liabilities without the need of legislation by congress. As Barwich C.J. and Gibbs. J. observed in *Bradley v. The Commonwealth*[4], the approval by the Commonwealth Parliament of the charter of the United Nations in the charter of the United Nations Act, 1945 did not incorporate the provisions of the charter into Australian law. To achieve this result the provisions have to be enacted as part of our domestic law, whether by commonwealth or State statute. Section 51, the external affairs power arms the Commonwealth Parliament to legislate so as to incorporate into our law the provisions of international conventions.[5]

In *Minister for Immigration and Ethnic Affairs v. Wu Shan Liang,*[6] the High Court was required to return to the meaning and operation of the Refugees Convention, being the Convention Relating to the Status of Refugees which was completed at Geneva on 28 July 1951, as amended by the Protocol relating to the Status of Refugees which was completed at New York on 31 January 1967. The Refugees Convention, so amended, is incorporated into Australian domestic law by the provisions of the Migration Act 1958.[7] In *Chan v. Minister for Immigration and Ethnic Affairs,*[8] the High Court had considered how the test for determining a `refugee' was to be applied. Wu's case was concerned with how the chance of persecution was to be ascertained from the multiple facts presented to the administrative decision-maker and the courts—given the inherent difficulty of predicting the future—should the putative refugee be returned to the State of origin or nationality.[9]

Again in *Applicant A v. Minister for Immigration and Ethnic Affairs,*[10] the High Court considered the definition of `refugee' and specifically that part of the Refugees Convention definition which refers to `membership of a particular social group'. The applicants were Chinese nationals. They had sought asylum in Australia on the basis that they were parents of a child born in China and, if returned to China, would face forcible sterilisation under that State's one child policy. The Minister did not dispute that forcible sterilisation would amount to persecution: the well-founded fear of which by members of a particular social group would give rise to `refugee' status. However, he contended that any such persecution would not be owing to' the appellants' membership of any particular social group. On that question the High Court divided. The majority (Dawson, McHugh and Gummow JJ) held that the appellants were not members of a 'particular social group'. Accordingly, they were not refugees. Chief Justice Brennan and Michael Kirby, J. dissented. The Chief Justice pointed out that protection of fundamental rights and freedoms was an object of the Refugees Convention, reflected in the definition of 'refugee' adopted in domestic law in terms of the Convention.[11] All of the opinions in the High Court reviewed the international jurisprudence that has developed around the ambiguous language of the Refugees Convention.

In *De L v. Director General, NSW Department of Community Services,*[12] the High Court was required to construe the Convention on the Civil Aspects of International Child Abduction 1980 (Child Abduction Convention). Subsequently, the High Court returned to the language of that Convention in order to construe Regulation 7 of the Family Law (Child Abduction Convention) Regulations made in exercise of the power conferred by the Family Law Act 1975. Once again, the High Court was concerned to reflect, in the meaning given to national law, the language and purpose of an international treaty to which Australia is a party that had been incorporated into Australian domestic law.[13]

Another case concerned to international human rights norms was *Croome v. Tasmania.*[14] The case involved the constitutional validity of the Human Rights (Sexual Conduct) Act 1994. That Act was the vehicle for incorporating into Australia's domestic law the requirement of sexual privacy held by the United Nations Human Rights Committee to be inherent in the International Covenant on Civil and Political

Rights to which Australia is a party. A preliminary point was taken in the case. It concerned the standing of the applicants. When that point was determined against the State of Tasmania, the constitutional question seemed ready for hearing. However, the Criminal Code (Amendment) Act 1997 (Tas) was then enacted, obviating the necessity to consider the constitutional validity of the Federal statute. The law criminalising adult, consensual homosexual conduct was repealed. The case of Mr Croome illustrates quite vividly the way in which international human rights law can sometimes stimulate, or require, change in Australia's domestic laws.[15]

Two other decisions relating to Australia's International obligations were, the first. *Project Blue Inc v. Australian Broadcasting Authority*[16] it was concerned to the Australia New Zealand closer Economic Relations-Trade Agreement and the Trade in services protocol to the trade agreement said to be referred to and incorporated in Australian law, by the Broadcasting services Act, 1992. Under Section 160(d) of the Act, the Australian Broadcasting Authority is required to perform its function in a manner consistent with Australia's obligations under any convention to which Australia is a party. Several Federal statutes and Regulations have provisions similar to that of Broadcasting services Act.[17] Qantas Airways Ltd. case[18] involved alleged discrimination against a Qantas air pilot on the ground of his age, contrary to obligations accepted by Australia and laid down by the International Labour organisation. Although, the High court, by a majority rejected the complaint. But the court examined not only the Australian legislation invoked by captain christie but also the ILO conventions that legislation was designed to implement.

Linden v. Commonwealth of Australia [No 2][19] involved an application by the Commonwealth to strike out a statement of claim. That document sought declarations reflecting questions submitted at the same time to the International Court of Justice. Those questions sought an Advisory Opinion concerning the illegality of the threat or use of nuclear weapons.[20] The proceeding was, in a sense, a continuation of earlier attempted challenges by Mr. Linden, to the Joint Defence Space Research facility near Alice Springs (commonly known as 'Pine Gap').[21] The process was struck out. A similar fate befell a statement of claim filed by the plaintiff in *Thorpe v. Commonwealth of Australia [No 3]*.[22] Mr. Thorpe, an Aboriginal Australian, had sought a declaration that the Commonwealth was obliged by fiduciary duty to `move in the United Nations General Assembly for an Advisory Opinion from ... the International Court of Justice as to the separate rights and legal status of the original peoples of this land'.[23] The Commonwealth argued that any such declaration would involve a wholly impermissible invasion of the constitutional prerogatives of the executive government.[24] The court upheld the Commonwealth's submission, concluding:

"The Court has no knowledge of the many considerations which would have to be taken into account in deciding whether Australia should seek such a resolution from the General Assembly. It has no means of knowing how any such application would affect Australia's international relations generally or its relations with particular countries or its other activities within the United Nations and its agencies. These are all matters which the Australian Constitution reserves to the executive government of the Commonwealth. They defy judicial application. They turn on a multitude of considerations unknown to this Court. They are matters upon which the Australian government speaks to the international community with a single voice. That voice is the voice of the executive government chosen from the Parliament elected by the people of Australia. It is not the voice of this Court."[25]

Mr. Thorpe's case is an illustration of developments which have been seen in other jurisdictions, notably the US,[26] wherein parties, discontented with what they see as the unsatisfactory conduct of domestic and foreign policy, resort to the courts in the hope of securing orders directed to the Executive. It will be obvious from the reasons in Thorpe that the single bench consider that great care must be taken by courts against intruding impermissibly into the conduct of the external affairs of the nation.

INTERNATIONAL IMPLEMENTATION MECHANISM

U.N. Charter and Human Rights

Discussions regarding international implementation of human rights relates to the United Nation and its Principal organs as well as special agencies. United Nations Organization was created primary as a mechanism to maintain world peace and security. The UN Charter gives due attention to the importance of international cooperation in dealing with economic and social problems and to the need for safeguarding basic human rights. As stated under article 1 of the Charter, the basic aim of UN is to "develop friendly relations among nations based on respect for the principle of equal rights and self-determination of people and to take other appropriate measures to strengthen universal peace" and "to achieve international co-operation in solving international problems of an economic, social, cultural, or humanitarian character, and in promoting and encouraging respect for human rights and for fundamental freedoms for all without distinction as to race, sex, language or religion".

The UN Charter focuses on the correlation between peace and observance of Fundamental human rights. This was emphasized by president Truman in his closing address to the San Francisco Conference:

> The charter is dedicated to the achievement and observance of human rights and Fundamental Freedoms. Unless we can attain these objectives for all men and women everywhere "without regard to race, language, or religion-we cannot have permanent peace and security."[27]

The charter contains a number of provisions for the promotion of human rights and fundamental freedoms in the Preamble and in Article 1, 13(1)(b), 55, 56, 62(2), 68 and 76(c) which are as follows:

(1) The Preamble of the Charter in its first substantive paragraph lays down that.... 'we the peoples of the United Nations determined to reaffirm faith in

fundamental human rights, in the dignity and worth of the human person, in the equal rights of men and women and of nation large and small.'

(2) Para 3 of Article 1 of the Charter provides that the achievement of international co-operation in promoting and encouraging respect for human rights and for fundamental freedoms for all without distinction as the race, sex, language or religion shall be one of the purposes of the United Nations. The above provision shows that the desirability of promoting and encouraging respect for human rights and fundamental freedoms' without distinction as to race, sex, language or religion was generally recognised. There was a general agreement that all human beings are entitled to some basic rights. It marked the birth of the international and universal recognition of human rights. However, despite the difference as to what rights and freedoms are, the achievement of the maximum freedom and dignity of the human beings was the primary aim of the United Nations.

(3) The General Assembly and the Economic and Social Council were given the task for the realisation of the promotion of human rights and fundamental freedoms. By the terms of Article 13, the General Assembly was empowered to initiate studies and make recommendations for the purpose of assisting in the realisation of human rights and fundamental freedoms for all without distinction as to race, sex, language or religion.

Most of the items relating to human rights are considered by the Assembly's Third Committee (Social, Humanitraian and Cultural Committee), but other may be referred to other Committees such as the Sixth Committee (Legal) or the First Committee (Political and Security) or the Special Political Committee. The Assembly has also established subsidiary organs for dealing with issues relating to specific human rights such as Special Committee on Decolonization, the Special Committee on Apartheid and the Special Committee to Investigate Israeli Practices in the Occupied Territories.

(4) Article 55 provides that the United Nations shall promote: (a) higher standards of living, full employment and conditions of economic and social progress and development; (b) solutions of international economic, social, health and related problems, and international cultural and educational cooperation; and (c) universal respect for, and observance of, human rights and fundamental freedoms for all without distinction as to race, sex, language or religion. It is to be noted that Article 55 is not self-explanatory. Wordings of the Article suggest that human rights are limited to those subjects which are mentioned in paragraph (c), and the subjects in paragraphs (a) and (b) are not rights at all but only policies that should be promoted.

(5) Article 56 provides that the members of the United Nations pledged themselves to take joint and separate action in co-operation with the Organisation for the achievement of the purposes set forth in Article 55.

(6) Article 62 of the Charter authorizes the Economic and Social Council to 'make recommendations for the purpose of promoting respect for, and observance of, human rights and fundamental freedoms for all'.

(7) Article 68 directes the Council to set up commissions in economic and social fields and for the promotion of human rights, and such other commissions as may be required for the performance of its functions. The commission on Human Rights and the Commission on the State of Women are the subsidiary bodies of the Economic and Social Council.

(8) Para(c) of Article 76 stipulates that one of the basic objectives of the trusteeship system is to encourage respect for human rights and for fundamental freedoms for all without distinction as to race, sex,

language or religion, and to encourage recognition of the interdependenace of the peoples of the World.

In addition to the above provisions, the Charter has referred repeatedly the concept of 'fundamental human rights', 'the dignity and worth of the human person', 'equal rights', 'justice', 'social progress' and fundamental freedoms. The Charter devoted three Chapters to the self-determination of people.

The above provisions of the Charter make it clear that the State's treatment of its own citizens has become a matter of international concern. Although there was no universal agreement as to the precise extent of the 'human rights and fundamental freedoms' guaranteed to all by the Charter, there is at present no dissent from the view that they have become one of the basic principles of international law.

The Charter by incorporating the provisions relating to promotion of human rights and fundamental freedoms opened a new dimension towards the progressive development of International Law. Individuals became a focus of international concern by acquiring their own rights. All member States were required to promote observance of fundamental human rights without distinction as to race, sex, language or religion. The Charter universalized and internationalized the concept of human rights which hitherto was adopted in some countries since last 200 years. It was universalized in the sense that there was a general acceptance of rights by national governments and was internationalized because the treatment of citizens in one country became the business of other countries as well. It was the first international document which recognised the respect for human rights and fundamental freedoms as a principle of International Law. Their recognition and their further realisation was deemed necessary as they were regarded as one of the methods of achieving greater unity between the States and also because they are indispensable for the maintenance of international peace and security. It is clear from thewordings of Article 55 of the Charter which lays down that the United Nations shall promote universal respect for, and observance of human rights and fundamental freedoms for all without distinction as to race, sex, language or religion with a view to the creation of conditions of stability and well-being which are necessary for peaceful and friendly relations among nations. The observance of human rights therefore contains an essential element of peace, justice and well-being necessary to ensure the development of friendly relations and cooperation among themselves as among all States. President Truman at the closing address to the San Francisco Conference as to relationship of the promotion of human rights and the maintenance of international peace and security had stated-that:

> The Charter is dedicated to the achievement and observance of human rights and fundamental freedoms. Unless we can attain these objectives for all men and women everywhere without regard to race, language or. religion one cannot have permanent peace and security in the world.

It is to be noted that the Charter is a global constitution without a bill of rights. It neither defined the human rights nor they were enumerated therein. There is no provision in the Charter laying down expressio verbis that there is a legal obligation resting upon nations to observe human rights and fundamental freedoms.[28] Courts in various States which have been called on to consider the legal effect of the Charter provisions relating to human rights have differed in their conclusions. Some have affirmed the binding nature and direct enforceability of the Charter provisions,[29] while others have denied it,[30] others while considering them as binding have declined to enforce them on the ground that they had not been formally incorporated as part of the law of the land,[31] and others still, while denying to them, the character of rules binding directly in the internal law of the State have them, directly or indirectly, as relevant in the sense that they form part of the public policy of a State as a signatory of the Charter.[32] The guarantee for the protection of human rights and fundamental freedoms was also not provided in the Charter. Although it was proposed by the Latin American States during the drafting of the Charter at San Francisco Conference that it should contain an 'International Bill of Rights', a specific list of rights could not be prepared due to lack of sufficient time, and therefore, promotion as well as protection of human rights was explicitly rejected. Provisions relating to human rights in the Charter are therefore general and vague. However, since the adoption of the Charter, international human rights law has been developing in an unprecedented way, and presently, it has become a substantive part of international law as a whole.

Promotion and Protection of Human Rights by the United Nations

Promotion and encouragement of respect for and observance of human rights and fundamental freedoms is one of the purposes of the United Nations. The Charter of United Nations mentions the term promotion of human rights seven times, but makes no reference to "protection" of "human rights". A question arises how this purpose is achieved by the United Nations? It is to be noted that the role and scope of U.N. action in promoting and protecting human rights have tremendously increased in the last fifty seven years. The term promotion of human rights may mean setting of international standard of human rights, education and dissemination. The prime responsibility for the promotion of human rights under the U.N. Charter rests in the General Assembly, in the Economic and Social Council and its subsidiary body—the Commission on Human Rights. The General Assembly by adopting treaties has set standards and socializes into those standards. Holding conferences and seminars to spread the World about human rights values found in these international documents are also included in the promotion of human rights.

The term protection of human rights which may mean implementation and enforcement action does not find place in the U.N. Charter. Among the United Nations agencies only the Security Council and the International Court of Justice can engage in enforcement action; only they have a competence to pass a binding resolution or issue a binding judgment. The Security Council can threaten or vote sanctions in relation to its own previous actions or that of the Court. Enforcement is thus the authoritative application of human rights. All other actions beyond promotion but short of enforcement may be considered as implementation efforts[33] Implementation thus includes passing non-binding resolutions about specific problems or States. When a U.N. agency approves a resolution calling on a specific State to take specific human rights action, it is considered to generate political pressure on the target and thus an effort at protection, not just promotion. United Nations in the past has been able to promote and protect human, rights by a number of ways which are as follows:

Human Rights Consciousness

The first and the most important role which the United Nations has played is that it has made the people and the States conscious about the human rights and fundamental freedoms. It has set a pace in establishing minimum standards of acceptable behaviour by States. The proclamation of the Universal Declaration of Human Rights containing the universal code of human rights may be regarded as the first step towards the promotion and protection of human rights.

Codification of the Law of Human Rights

The United Nations has codified the different rights and freedoms by making treaties for all sections of the people such as women, child, migrant workers, refugees and stateless persons. In addition to the above, the prohibition on the commission of inhuman acts such as genocide, apartheid, racial discrimination and torture have been brought Within the international rule of law.

Monitoring of Human Rights

Treaty bodies, Special Rapporteurs and Working Groups[34] of the Commission on Human .Rights have procedure and mechanism to monitor compliance with conventions .and investigate allegations of human rights' abuses. A number of expert committees have been established under particular treaties. They are not subsidiary organs of the United Nations, but are autonomous. The Committees are termed U.N. Treaty Organs. Their resolutions on specific cases carry a moral weight that few Governments are willing to defy. In the past, U.N.

Human Rights monitors have been sent to many countries including El Slavador and Cambodia. Human Rights monitors have also worked as part of peace keeping operations in Haiti, Rwanda, Guatemala and the formerYugoslavia.

Procedure for Individual's Complaints

A number of human rights treaties permit individuals to make petition before the appropriate international bodies. For instance, the Optional Protocol to the International Covenant on Civil and Political Rights, the International Convention on the Elimination of All Forms of Racial Discrimination, Convention Against Torture and the International Convention on the Protection of the Rights of All Migrant Workers and their families have permitted individuals to make petitions against their States that have accepted relevant international legal procedures. Also, under procedures .established by the Commission on Human Rights, and its Sub-Commission on the Promotion and Protection of Human Rights (earlicr known as Sub-Commission on Prevention of Discrimination and Protection of Minorities) and their Working Groups, hear numerous complaints annually submitted by individuals as well as by non-governmental organisations (NGO).

The Commission on Human Rights is authorized to discuss human rights situations anywhere in the World and examine information from individuals, NGOs and other sources.

The Economic and Social Council in 1970 adopted Resolution 1503 entitled 'Procedure for Dealing with Communications Relating to Violations of Human Rights and Fundamental Freedoms commonly known as '1503 Resolution' wherein individuals and non-governmental organisations (NGO) were allowed to make a communication to the Commission concerning "situations which appear to reveal a consistent pattern of gross and reliably attested violations of human rights.[35] A communication i.e., a complaint is sent to the Office of the UN High Commissioner for Human Rights in Geneva. The Commission has focused the 1503 procedure mainly on civil and political rights using rapporteurs and Working Groups in specific countries and specific problems, it is to be noted that the individual petitions help to provide some check on governmental violations of human rights as they provide a source; of information to international organisations.

Compilation of Informations on the Violations of Human Rights

The original mandate of the Commission on Human Rights to examine situations where massive violations of rights appear to be taking place has been complemented by a new function, i.e., compiling informations on the incidence of certain kinds of violations, or violation in a specific country. This task is performed by Special Rapporteurs/ Representative or Working Groups. They gather facts, keep contacts with local groups and government authorities, conduct on-site visits when Governments permit, and make recommendations. on how human rights institutions might be strengthened.

Examination of Human Rights Situations

The Commission on Human Rights may ask the Secretary-General to intervene or send an expert to examine a human rights situation in any State with a view to prevent flagrant violations. Such tasks may be performed by the Secretary-General himself in the exercise of his good offices and may establish the U.N/s legitimate concern and curb abuses. The Secretary-General or his special representative and the High Commissioner for Human Rights, confidentially raise human rights concerns with member States, including items such as the release of prisoners, commutation of death sentences and other issues.

Coordination of Human Rights Activities

The post of High Commissioner for Human Rights was created in 1993. with the intention of strengthening ihe coordination and impact of UN Human Rights activities. He is charged with promoting and protecting the effective enjoyment by all of all human rights and maintains a permanent dialogue with the member States.

By Providing Advisory Services

The Center for Human Rights provides advisory services to Government seeking to improve their human rights performance. Assistance may be given to draft a constitution, to improve electoral laws, establish or upgrade human rights institutions, prepare new criminal codes, or overhaul the judiciary.

The above points go to prove that the United Nations has been performing a variety of functions successfully to promote and protect human rights and it has promoted global culture of human rights through education and awareness. Human rights which was regarded as a matter of domestic jurisdiction of the States, has acquired the international character, vis-a-vis, international human rights. It is appropriate to call international human rights because firstly, human rights is increasingly a well established issue area of international politics secondly, States are increasingly obligated to respect human rights norms, and thirdly, individuals have increasingly obtained legal personality, in the form of partial subjectivity, with regard to human rights matters. However, it has to be conceded that the impact of the U.N. activities on interational human rights issues has been indirect and it has long term effect. All of its promotion effort and most of its protection attempts entail considerable time to have an impact The result is that human rights continue to be widely violated around the globe fundamental rights of individual's life, liberty and physical security, right to health, housing and work as well as cultural rights continue to be threatened by forces of repression, ethnic hatred and exploitation. Torture, cruel and inhuman punishment for seemingly minor -crimes to spousal and child abuse have led to the description of societies and ethnic, religious and other conflicts. In the face of these challenges, the United Nations has to be more active. It has to intervene in cases of massive human rights violations. It has to work with the cooperation of the member States to strengthen the commitments of promoting and protecting human rights.[36]

UNIVERSAL DECLARATION OF HUMAN RIGHTS[36a]

After the coming into force of the UN charter the preparatory commission of the United Nations recomended[37] that the Economic and Social Council should establish a commission on Human Rights and the later is to formulate "an International Bill of Rights" and to prepare studies and recommendations in the field of human rights. The General Assembly by Resolution Number 7(1), 12th of February 1946 approved this recommendation and the ECOSOC established a Commission on Human Rights and directed it to submit to the council the proposals, recommendations and reports regarding an "International Bill of Rights"[38].

The Economic and Social Council was of the view that "the purpose of the United Nations with regard to the promotion and observance of human rights, as defined in the charter of the United Nations, can only be fulfilled if provisions are made for the implementation of human rights and of an International Bill of Rights[39]. The commission on Human Rights took the duty of drafting the International Bill of Rights. Although there was controversy as to the nature of the instruments, the General Assembly completed the first step towards International Bill when it adopted and proclaimed unanimously on 10th December 1948 the Universal Declaration of Human Rights[40]. The controversy was that some favoured for binding convention, some merely for declaration of bill of rights. One distinctive feature of the declaration is that it is neither addressed to nations nor to member states of the United Nations but to every individual, and is not a legal declaration in the sense that it is not a legal instrument having a binding force on its ratifiers.[41] The declaration "is the mine from which other conventions as well as national constitutions protecting these rights have been and are being quarried.[42]

The Universal Declaration of Human Rights was adopted and proclaimed by the General Assembly as a common standard of achievement for all peoples and all nations, to the end that every individual and every organ of society, keeping this Declaration constantly in mind, shall strive by teaching and education to promote respect for these rights and freedoms and by progressive measures, national and international, to secure their universal and effective recognition and observance, both among, the peoples of Member States themselves and among the peoples of territories under their jurisdiction.

Forty-eight States voted in favour of the Declaration, none against, with eight abstentions. In a statement following the voting, the President of the General Assembly pointed out that adoption of the Declaration was "a remarkable achievement, a step forward in the great evolutionary process. It was the first occasion on which the organized community of nations had made a Declaration of human rights and fundamental freedoms. The instrument was backed by the authority of the body of opinion of the United Nations as a whole, and millions of people -men, women and children all over the world-would turn to it for help, guidance and inspiration.

The Declaration consists of a preamble and 30 articles, setting forth the human rights and fundamental freedoms to which all men and women, everywhere in the world, are entitled, without any discrimination.

Article 1, which lays down the philosophy on which the Declaration is based, reads:

> All human beings are born free and equal in dignity and rights. They are endowed with reason and conscience and should act towards one another in a spirit of brotherhood.

The article thus defines the basic assumptions of the Declaration: that the right to liberty and equality is man's birthright and cannot be alienated: and that, because man is a rational and moral being, he is different from other creatures on earth and therefore entitled to certain rights and freedoms which other creatures do not enjoy.

Article 2, which sets out the basic principle of equality and non discrimination as regards the enjoyment of human rights and fundamental freedoms, forbids "distinction of any kind, such as race, colour, sex, language, religion, political or other opinion, national or social origin, property, birth or other status".

Article 3, the first cornerstone of the Declaration, proclaims the right to life, liberty and security of person-a right essential to the enjoyment of all other rights. This article introduces articles 4 to 21, in which other civil and political rights are set out, including: freedom from slavery and servitude; freedom from torture and cruel, inhuman or degrading treatment or punishment; the right to recognition everywhere as a person before the law; the right to an effective judicial remedy; freedom from arbitrary arrest, detention or exile; the right to a fair trial and public hearing by an independent and impartial tribunal; the right to be presumed innocent until proved guilty; freedom from arbitrary interference with privacy, family, home or correspondence; freedom of movement and residence; the right of asylum; the right to a nationality; the right to marry and to found a family; the right to own property; freedom of thought, conscience and religion; freedom of opinion and expression; the right to peaceful assembly and association; and the right to take part in the government of one's country and to equal access to public service in one's country.

Article 22, the second cornerstone of the Declaration, introduces articles 23 to 27, in which economic, social and cultural rights-the rights to which everyone is entitled "as a member of society" -are set out. The article characterizes these rights as indispensable for human dignity and the free development of personality, and indicates that they are to be realized "through national effort and international cooperation". At the same time, it points out the limitations of realization, the extent of which depends on the resources of each State.

The economic, social and cultural rights recognized in articles 22 to 27 include the right to social security; the right to work; the right to equal pay for equal work; the right to rest and leisure; the right to a standard of living adequate for health and well-being; the right to education; and the right to participate in the cultural life of the community.

The concluding articles, articles 28 to 30, recognize that everyone is entitled to a social and international order in which the human rights and fundamental freedoms set forth in the

Declaration may be fully realized, and stress the duties and responsibilities which each individual owes to his community. Article 29 states that "in the exercise of his rights and freedoms, everyone shall be subject only to such limitations as are determined by law solely for the purpose of securing due recognition and respect for the rights and freedoms of others and of meeting the just requirements of morality, public order and the general welfare in a democratic society". It adds that in no case may human rights and fundamental freedoms be exercised contrary to the purposes and principles of the United Nations. Article 30 emphasizes that no State, group or person may claim any right, under the Declaration, "to engage in any activity or to perform any act aimed at the destruction of any of the rights and freedoms set forth" in the Declaration.

Importance and Influence of the Declaration

Conceived as "a common standard of achievement for all people and all nations", the Universal Declaration of Human Rights has become just that : a yardstick by which to measure the degree of respect for, and compliance with, international human rights standards.

Since 1948 it has been and rightly continues to be the most important and far-reaching of all United Nations declarations, and a fundamental source of inspiration for national and international efforts to promote and protect human rights and fundamental freedoms. It has set the direction for all subsequent work in the field of human rights and has provided the basic philosophy for many legally binding international instruments designed to protect the rights and freedoms which it proclaims.

In the Proclamation of Teheran, adopted by the International Conference on Human Rights held in Iran in 1968, the Conference agreed that "the Universal Declaration of Human Rights states a common understanding of the peoples of the world concerning the inalienable and inviolable rights of all members of the human family and constitutes an obligation for the members of the international community".

The Conference affirmed its faith in the principles set forth in the Declaration, and urged all people and Governments "to dedicate themselves to [those] principles . . . and to redouble their efforts to provide for all human beings a life consonant with freedom and dignity and conducive to physical, mental, social and spiritual welfare".[42a]

In recent years, there has been a growing tendency for United Nations organs, in preparing international instruments in the filed of human rights, to refer not only to the Universal Declaration, but also to other parts of the International Bill of Human Rights.

THE 1966 COVENANTS AND THE IMPLEMENTATION MACHINERY

The covenant on civil and political Rights,[43] hereafter stated as the civil covenant, incorporates more comprehensive provisions on implementation. The state party to the covenant "undertakes to respect and to ensure to all individuals within its territory... the rights recognized in the present covenant, without distinction" of any kind and "to take the necessary steps, in accordance with its constitution process and with tie provisions of the present covenant to adopt such legislative and other measures as may be necessary to give effect to the rights recognized in the covenant"[44]. The reporting procedure is the primary method of implementation provided under the civil covenant. The state parties to the civil covenant have the duty to submit reports on measures adopted by them giving effect to the rights recognized in the covenant and on the progress made in the enjoyment of those rights.[45] Reporting is common to both the International Covenant on Civil and Political Rights and the International covenant on Economic, Social and Cultural rights. However there is the difference, of procedure: under the Economic Covenant, the UN Secretary General shall transmit the reports to the Economic and Social Council,[46] and the later may transmit the reports to the Commission of Human Rights.[47] On the other hand under the Civil and Political Rights Covenant the secretary general shall transmit the reports to the Human Rights Committee for consideration,[48] and the later shall study the reports and shall transmit these with such general comments as it may consider appropriate to the states parties.[49]

Although reporting is common to both covenants, complaints by a state party against another which is alleged to have not given effect to the provisions of the covenant and by an individual claiming to be a victim of a violation by state action, are peculiar to the Civil Covenant.[50]

These periodic reporting mechanisms under both covenants remain unsatisfactory as far as the review of the activities of United Nations in the field of human rights is concerned. Regarding the efficiency of the reporting procedure the "Committee on Periodic Reports"[51] concluded that the reports continued to be uneven in presentation and information were lacking in self-criticism or evaluatian.[52] Furthermore, the same committee confirmed the continuing unsatisfactory nature of the reports and regretted that "in some cases (the reports) sounded and note of optimism which had little justification in reality".[53] Therefore, it is possible to conclude that there is unwillingness on the part of Member States to submit genuine reports. This is the main problem in both covenants.

It is also pointed out and rightly too, that although under the Civil Covenant there is an obligation of the State parties to submit reports, there is no express obligation to comply with the reports and comments of the Human Rights Committee. Article 40 para 5 lays down that the state parties may submit to the Committee observations on the comments of the committee. It is not clear as to what will happen thereafter. This is a very serious omission in the covenant. Clear provisions should have been made that if the committee does not accept the observation of the state parties concerned, the reports and comments of the committee would be binding on the state parties.[54]

In addition to the aforementioned reporting mechanism, the Civil Covenant provides for the *Inter-state communication system* on the application of the covenant and conciliation. The thing to be noted here is that this system is applicable only if a state party declares that it recognizes the competence of the

Human Rights Committee to receive and to consider communications.[55] According to Art. 41 (1) (a) of the civil covenant the reference to the Human Rights Committee should be preceded by the communication by the communicating state to another state party which is alleged to have not given effect to the provisions of the covenant. Within three months after the receipt of the communication the receiving state shall afford the state which sent the communication on explanation or any other statement in writing clarifying the matters, which should include, reference to domestic procedures and remedies taken, pending or available in the matter. Paragraph (b) of the same article stipulates that if the matter is not adjusted six months after the initial communication referred to in paragraph (1), either state shall have the right to refer the matter to the committee.

The Human Rights Committee can deal with a matter in relation to the inter-state communications only if it ascertain that all domestic remedies have been invoked and exhausted in the matter, in conformity with the generally recognized principles of international law. However, this rule is not applicable in a case where the application of the remedies is unreasonably prolonged.[56] The authority the Committee is squarely limited to offering its services to the State involved with a view to achieving a "friendly solution of the matter"[57] and if the dispute is not resolved the Committee can do no more than to record "a brief statement of the facts" and convey the report to the concerned States.[58] On the other way, if the parties to the dispute agree, the committee may continue its conciliatory role by appointing an adhoc Conciliation Commission.[59] The main function of the Conciliation Commission is to make its good offices available to the State parties concerned with a view to an amicable solution of the matter on the basis of respect for the civil covenant. If no amicable solution to the matter is reached, the conciliation commission shall confine its report to a brief statement of the facts and of the solution reached.[60]

If such a solution is not reached the Conciliation Commission's report shall embody its findings on all questions of fact relevant to the issues between the state parties concerned, as well as its views on the possibilities of amicable solutions of the matter.[61]

When we come to evaluate the efficiency of the interstate Communication mechanism it handing furnish an adequate guarantee for the effective observance of human rights.[62] Due to political ambition and other factors a government would not normally make a complaint against a State with which it is on friendly terms. Apart from the inadequacy of the system, it has been stated that the inter state complaints are greatly harmful to the peaceful relations between states as by politicizing disputes they would foster unfriendly relations.[63] Commenting generally on inter-state proceedings in international human rights Law, Professor John P. Humphrey was provoked to say:

> To give a state that the right to Complain that another state is violating human rights is one of the weakest techniques for enforcing human rights Law... The individual whose rights have been violated has no guarantee that any state will in fact sponsor his case. Indeed, it is unlikely that unless there is some political motivation for doing so. States will interfere with what is happening in other countries, particularly if their relations with them are friendy.[64]

The civil covenant established the Human Rights committee as the principal international organ of its implementation. It was established on September 1976 by the States parties to the Covenant. The Committee is composed of 18 members who are the nationals of the State parties to the Covenant.[65]

The role of the committee is very limited, that is, it is confined to making avaialble to State Parties concerned its good offices. It is not empowered to pass comments on the communication regarding the non-observance of the rights recognized under the covenant. Secondly a state party may withdraw its declaration at any time by notification to Secretary General: Lastly, inter state communication mechanism stated in Article 41 has not even once been utlized and this procedure lacks teeth.

The Third method of implementation of Human rights is conciliation method or procedure. The Human Rights Committee may, with the prior consent of the state parties concerned, appoint an ad hoc conciliation commission so as to make available to the state parties concerned the good offices of the commission with a view to make an amicable solution of the matter on the basis with respect for the present covenant.[66]

The Commission shall consist of five persons acceptable to the State parties Concerned. In case od disagreement between the parties the members of the commission are elected by a two-third majority vote of the committee from among its members.[67] It is to be clarified here that the concliation commission shall elect its own chairman and adopt its own rules of procedure.[68] The information received and collected by the committee shall be made available to the commission. After considering the matter by the commission, it shall submit to the chairman of the comittee a report for communication to the state parties concerned. If an amicable solution in reached, the commission shall confine its report to a brief statement of the facts of the solution reached. But if solution is not reachod the commission's report shall contain its findings on all questions of act relevant to the issues between the parties concerned, and its opinion on the possibilities of an amicable solution of the matter. In such a case the state parties concerned shall, within three months of the receipt of the report, notify the chairman of the committee whether or not they accept the contents of the report of the commission.[69]

It is submitted that the concliation meachism may be used only if a matter referred to the commitee in accordance with Article 41 is not resolved, this makes the scope of this procedure as very limited. In this mechaism solution on a subject referred to the commission depends upon the consent of the parties in respect of everything, even the appointment depends upon the consensus of the parties. The commission makes available to the state parties its good offices with a view to reach at an amicable solution of the subject referred. The commission's report or the opinion has no binding effect.

First Optional Protocol

The first Optional Protocol to the International Covenant on Civil and Political Rights enables the Human Rights Committee, set up under that Covenant, to receive and consider communications from individuals claiming to be victims of violations of any of the rights set forth in the Covenant.

Under article I of the Optional Protocol, a State party to the Covenant that becomes a party to the Protocol recognizes the competence of the Human Rights Committee to receive and consider communications from individuals subject to its jurisdiction who claim to be victims of a violation by that State of any of the rights set forth in the Covenant. Individuals who make such a claim, and who have exhausted all available domestic remedies, are entitled to submit a written communication to the Committee (Art. 2).

Such communications as are determined to be admissible by the Committee (in addition to article 2, articles 3 and 5 (2) lay down conditions for admissibility) are brought to the attention of the State party alleged to be violating a provision of the Covenant. Within six months, that State must submit to the Committee written explanations or statements clarifying the matter and indicating the remedy, if any, that it may have applied (Art. 4).

The Human Rights Committee considers the admissible communications, at closed meetings, in the light of all written information made available to it by the individual and the State party concerned. It then forwards its views to the State party and to the individual (Art. 5).

A summary of the Committee's activities under the Optional Protocol is included in the report which it submits annually to the General Assembly through the Economic and Social Council (Art. 6).

The committee has considered a number of communications of individuals who alleged the infringement of rights embodied in the covenant. Some of the cases are cited here. In Ambrosini case[70] the complaint was filed by a Uruguayan national, resident of Mexico. She contended that she was detained in uruguag on April 25, 1975 and tortured physically and physchologically. She was not produced before a Magistrate and was released on May 3, 1975. Similarly, her husband, step father and mother were arrested on April 3, 1975, October 22, 1975 and January 20, 1976, respectively and all were subjected to various kinds of tortures. The committee considered the complaint (communcication) and after examining the facts declared that the Government Uruguayan had violated the provisions of the covenant. It expressed the opinion that it was the duty of the Uruguayan as a state party to the optional protocol to take prompt steps to ensure compliance of the provisions contained in the covenant and also to make it definite that similar infringement of rights do not take place in the future and to grant appropriate and effective remedies to the civtim.

In Netto Case[71] the communication was submitted by Anna Maria Garcia Lanza de Netto alleging that her aunt and uncle had been arrested without any cause and were detained for three years and they were subjected to torture. The Uruguayan Government argued that the remedies, under Urguayan law had not been exhausted and the action was taken under the prompt security measures made under the state law. Urguayan Government did not make any submission of fact or law, this fact did not prevent the committee to proceeds with the case and giving its decision. The committee decided that the Government has violaled the rights enshrined in Article 7 and 10(1), because of torture; of Article 9(3) because they were not produced immediately after the arrest before a Judge and they were not put to trial within a reasonable time; of Article 9(4) beccause they had no effective access to legal assistance.

In another case[72] the complaint was filed by Ewardo Dante Santullo valcada, mentioning that he was arrested on September 8, 1976 and was subjected to various forms of torture by the officers of investigation and intelligence department. During the detention he was not allowed to avail the services of a legal practionor. After Considering the statements of complainant and the state party, the committee declared that the state party had failed to observe its obligations under the covenant. The committee has also entertained individual's communication from Mauritius,[73] Finalnd[74] and Canada.[75]

It is submitted that the Human Rights Committee has rendered a signal service in the redressal of grievance of the Human Rights of the individual under the individual's communication system although it is able to devote very little time because most of its time and energies are devoted to the consideration of state reports. Due to its pre-occupation with state reports, number of communications alleging violation of human rights remain pending. However, whatever little its has done in the filed to individual's communication system, it has already made an impact. It has helped development of a body of case of the committee on such matters as equality of treatment between sexes,[76] minorities[77] freedom from religion,[78] torture, detention and fair trial[79] etc. It is also significant to note that there has also been complaince with the decisions of the comittee : Canada, Finland and Mauritius in compliance with the decision of the comittee amended their national law.[80]

Second Optional Protocol

The Second Optional Protocol to the International Covenant on Civil and Political Rights, aiming at the abolition of the death penalty, was adopted by the General Assembly by its resolution 44/128 of 15th December 1989. Under its article 1, no one within the jurisdiction of a State party to the Protocol may be executed.

Article 2 of the protocol provides that no reservation is admissible to the second optional protocol, except for a reservation made at the time of ratification or accession that provides for the application of death penalty in time of war pursuant to a conviction for most serious crime of a military nature committed during war time.

Under article 3 of the Protocol, States parties must include in the reports which they submit to the Human Rights Committee information on measures taken to give effect to the Protocol.

Article 5 of the Second Optional Protocol provides that, with respect to any State party to the first Optional Protocol, the competence of the Human Rights Committee to receive and consider communications from individuals subject to that State's jurisdiction shall extend to the provisions of the Second Optional Protocol, unless the State party concerned has made a statement to the contrary at the moment of ratification or accession.

Under article 6, the provisions of the Second Optional Protocol apply as additional provisions to the Covenant.

The Second optional protocol provides three ways of implementation, namely the reporting system, Inter-state Communication system and Individual's Communication System. Similar to Civil Covenant under this protocol also, state parties are under obligation to send reports to the Human Rights Committee regarding the measures taken by them to implement the protocol. Article 3 lays down that the state parties to the protocol shall include in the reports which they submit to the Human Rights Committee in accordance with Article 40 of the Covenant information on the measures that they have adopted to give effect the present protocol. The protocol also provides inter-state communication procedure of implementation of the rights recognized in the protocol. A state party to the covenant who has made a declaration under Article 41 may file a complaint before the committee that another state party who has also made a declaration under Article 41, is not fulfilling its obligation, namely, to abolish death penalty or executing persons within its jurisdiction. This protocol also empowers an individual to present communications to the committee on the ground that their rights under the protocol are being violated. This procedure of implementation is available only to those individuals whose state are parties to the civil covenant, First optional protocol and to the second protocol.

Entry into Force of the Covenants and the Optional Protocols

The International Covenant on Economic, Social and Cultural Rights entered into force on 3 January 1976, three months after the date of deposit with the Secretary-General of the thirty-fifth instrument of ratification or accession, as provided in article 27. As at 30 September 1995, the Covenant had been ratified or acceded to by 132 States:

The International Covenant on Civil and Political Rights entered into force on 23 March 1976, three months after the date of deposit with the Secretary-General of the thirty-fifth instrument of ratification or accession, as provided in article 49. As at 30 September 2002, the Covenant had been ratified or acceded to by 140 States:

Afghanistan, Albania, Algeria, Angola, Argentina, Armenia, Australia, Austria, Azerbaijan, Barbados, Belarus, Belgium, Benin, Bolivia, Bosnia and Herzegovina, Brazil, Bulgaria, Burundi, Cambodia, Cameroon, Canada, Cape Verde, Central African Republic, Chad, Chile, Colombia, Congo, Costa Rica, Côte d'Ivoire, Croatia, Cyprus, Czech Republic, Democratic People's Republic of Korea, Denmark, Dominica, Dominican Republic, Ecuador, Egypt, El Salvador, Equatorial Guinea, Estonia, Ethiopia, Finland, France, Gabon, Gambia, Georgia, Germany, Grenada, Guatemala, Guinea, Guyana, Haiti, Hungary, Iceland, India, Iran (Islamic Republic of), Iraq, Ireland, Israel, Italy, Jamaica, Japan, Jordan, Kenya, Kyrgyzstan, Latvia, Lebanon, Lesotho, Libyan Arab Jamahiriya, Lithuania, Luxembourg, Madagascar, Malawi, Mali, Malta, Mauritius, Mexico, Mongolia, Morocco, Mozambique, Namibia, Nepal, Netherlands, New Zealand, Nicaragua, Niger, Nigeria, Norway, Panama, Paraguay, Peru, Philippines, Poland, Portugal, Republic of Korea, Republic of Moldova, Romania, Russian Federation, Rwanda, Saint Vincent and the Grenadines, San Marino, Senegal, Seychelles, Slovakia, Slovenia, Somalia, Spain, Sri Lanka, Sudan, Suriname, Sweden, Switzerland, Syrian Arab Republic, The former Yugoslav Republic of Macedonia, Togo, Trinidad and Tobago, Tunisia, Uganda, Ukraine, United Kingdom, United Republic of Tanzania, United States of America, Uruguay, Uzbekistan, Venezuela, Viet Nam, Yemen, Yugoslavia, Zaire, Zambia and Zimbabwe.

As at the same date, 44 States parties to the International Covenant on Civil and Political Rights had made the declaration under its article 41, recognizing the competence of the Human Rights Committee "to receive and consider communications to the effect that a State Party claims that another State Party is not fulfilling its obligations" under the Covenant. The provisions of article 41 entered into force on 28 March 1979 in accordance with paragraph 2 of that article.

The first Optional Protocol to the International Covenant on Civil and Political Rights entered into force simultaneously with the Covenant, having received the minimum 10 ratifications or accessions required. As at 30th September, 2002, 92 States parties to the Covenant had also become parties to the first Optional Protocol:

Algeria, Angola, Argentina, Armenia, Australia, Austria, Barbados, Belarus, Belgium, Benin, Bolivia, Bosnia and Herzegovina, Bulgaria, Cameroon, Canada, Central African Republic, Chad, Chile, Colombia, Congo, Costa Rica, Cyprus, Czech Republic, Denmark, Dominican Republic, Ecuador, El Salvador, Equatorial Guinea, Estonia, Finland, France, Gambia, Georgia, Germany, Guinea, Guyana, Hungary, Iceland, Ireland, Italy, Jamaica, Kyrgyzstan, Latvia, Libyan Arab Jamahiriya, Lithuania, Luxembourg, Madagascar, Malta, Mauritius, Mongolia, Namibia, Nepal, Netherlands, New Zealand, Nicaragua, Niger, Norway, Panama, Paraguay, Peru, Philippines, Poland, Portugal, Republic of Korea, Romania, Russian Federation, Saint Vincent and the Grenadines, San Marino, Senegal, Seychelles, Slovakia, Slovenia, Somalia, Spain, Suriname, Sweden, The former Yugoslav Republic of Macedonia, Togo, Trinidad and Tobago, Ukraine, Uruguay, Uzbekistan, Venezuela, Zaire and Zambia.

The Second Optional Protocol to the International Covenant on Civil and Political Rights, aiming at the abolition of the death penalty, entered into force on 11 July 1991, having received the minimum 10 ratifications or accessions required. As at 30 September 1995, the Protocol had been ratified or acceded to by 28 States:

Australia, Austria, Denmark, Ecuador, Finland, Germany, Hungary, Iceland, Ireland, Italy, Luxembourg, Malta, Mozambique, Namibia, Netherlands, New Zealand, Norway, Panama, Portugal, Romania, Seychelles, Slovenia, Spain, Sweden, Switzerland, The former Yugoslav Republic of Macedonia, Uruguay and Venezuela.

The question whether the idea of international implementation of human rights violates Article 2, paragraph 7 of the United Nations Charter attracted the attention of many for a long time. The USSR and its allies have always maintained that the establishment of an international organ for the implementation of human rights violated Article 2, parapgraph 7 of the Charter and it is purely a domestic matter. This argument was advanced on various occasions. Kelsen seems to be of the view that the question of assuring or protecting human rights is a matter which is essentially within the domestic Jurisdiction of a State and consequently within the prohibition of Article 2, paragraph 7.[81] This view was also shared, among others, by some members of the American Bar Association including one of its past president.[82]

The above viewpoint seems to have ignored the far-reaching changes that have taken place in international law as regards human rights. Resort to international techniques in the promotion of human rights is justified because of the following reasons : firstly, international efforts are essential to the search for world peace which in turn has an intrinsic link with the protection of human rights; secondly, in today's world which is interdependent, successful efforts to promote human rights, particualrly in the area of economic and social rights may require physical resources, technology, and expertise beyond a society's internal capabilities and, therefore, in such cases only international assistance can permit real progress; and thirdly, to the extent that many human rights denials result from the action or incation of government themselves, internal pressures for reform having proved ineffective and, therefore, the only hope for change in such circumstances may lie in international persuasion or pressure.[83] Now it is universally agreed that human rights are proper subjects of international concern. It has been affirmative assumed by the United Nations charter, international conventions, declarations and more than three decades of international practice.[84] Many eminent authorities like Lauterpacht, Jessup, Quincy Wright, Myres McDougal and Paul oppenheim also share the view that human rights are no longer within the domestic jurisdiction prohibition. The existing and the future international measures for the protection of human rights are, therefore, justified.

It has earlier been pointed out that the Civil and Political Rights Covenant; the Economic, Social and cultural Rights Covenant and the Optional Protocol of the former are the crux of the international efforts aimed at the protection of human rights. The Covenant on Civil and Political Rights establishes as the principal international organ of its implementation, the 'Human Rights Committee' which consists of eighteen persons of high moral character and recognized competence in the field of human rights, consideration being given to the usefulness of the participation of some persons having legal experience, sensing in their personal capacity.[85] According to the draft of the Commission on Human Rights, the members of the Human Rights Committee should be elected by the International Court of Justice but the Covenant envisages that the members of the Committee shall be elected by the State parties.[86] In the election of the Committee, consideration shall be given to equitable geographical distribution of membership and to the representation of the different forms of civilization as well as of the principal legal systems.[87]

THE COVENANT ON ECONOMIC, SOCIAL AND CULTURAL RIGHTS, 1966

Similar to the civil Covenant the implementation of the Economic Covenant consists of a system of reporting. States parties to the Economic covenant have undertaken the obligation to submit reports on measures adopted by them and the progress made in achieving the observance of the rights contained in the Covenant.[88] These reports are sent to the Economic and social council for consideration through the Secretary General.[89] According to Art. 16(2) (b) of the Economic covenant, the Secretary-General of the United Nations shall also transmit to the specialized agencies copies of the reports in regard to matters falling within their respective responsibilities.

The Economic and Social Council may submit from time to time to the General Assembly reports with recommendations of a general nature and a summary of the information received by it on the measures taken and the progress made in achieving general observance of the rights recognized in the Covenant.[90] The State parties to the Economic Covenant agree that the international action for the achievement of the rights recognized under the Economic Covenant includes such methods as the conclusion of convention, the adoption of recommendations and furnishing of technical assistance and the holding of regional meetings for consultation and study.[91]

To sum up the covenant on Economic, Social and Cultural Rights carries an elementary form of implementation in recognition of the fact that these rights are in a state of progressive development in many countries and can only be achieved progressively.[92]

The Economic covenant does not provide more implementation machinery other than an obligation to submit periodic reports to the Economic and Social Council on the measures adopted and the progress achieved towards the realization of these rights.

REGIONAL IMPLEMENTATION

The concern of international community for the protection and implementation of human rights norms is not merely left to the United Nations and other international organizations. There are also regional international systems relating to the development of the norms of human rights and regional mechanisms of implementation. Among these regional systems there are three properly established institutions whose role will be discussed under this section. They are: the European convention on Human Rights, the American convention of Human Rights and the African charter on Human and peoples rights.

The European Convention on Human Rights

The post world war II situation in Europe is characterized by two directions of developments. Firstly, the struggle to European integration on a level to serve not only technical needs and economic interests, but also to embody a system of liberal values which crystallize centuries of political development. Secondly, there is a concern in relations between states both within and beyond Europe, for the protection of human rights.[93] The European Convention for the Protection of Human Rights and Fundamental Freedoms is known not only for its successful system of international law for the protection of human rights, but also it is one of the most advanced forms of any kind of international legal process.

The European Convention on Human rights, hereafter referred as European convention, was drafted in the council of Europe during 1949 and 1950. The convention was signed on 4th November 1950, and came into force on 3rd September 1953, after its ratification by eight countries.

The council of Europe was established in 1949 with a view "to achieve a greater unity between its members for the purpose of safeguarding and realizing the ideals and principles, which are their common heritage and facilitating their economic and social progress", and this aim was to be pursued "through the organs of the council by discussion of questions of common concern and by agreements and common action in economic, social, cultural, scientific, legal and administrative matters and in the maintenance and further realization of human rights and fundamental freedoms.[94]

Emanating from the aforesaid objective, there are some incomparable features associated with the council of Europe. For example, according to Article 3 of the Statute every member state must accept the principles of the rule of law and of the enjoyments by all persons within its jurisdiction of human rights and fundamental freedoms. Also a member state which has seriously violated Article 3 of the statute may be suspended and requested by the committee of ministers to withdraw from the council of Europe and, if it does not comply, may be expelled.[95]

It has been stated that "the creation the council of Europe and the adoption of the convention on human rights are an acknowledgement that the protection of human rights cannot be separated from the very existence of independent European States."[96]

When we come to the implementation machinery under the European convention, the convention demands the High Contracting parties to secure to every individual within their jurisdiction the rights and freedoms defined in the convention.[97] The other implementation machinery under the convention is that it created two organs "to ensure the observance of the engagements undertaken by the High Contracting parties": the European commission of Human Rights and the European Court of Human Rights.[98]

The European Commission of Human Rights consists of a number of members equal to the number of High Contracting Parties and no two members of the Commission may be nationals of the same State[99] As a result, each High Contracting Party is likely to be represented on the Commission by one of its nationals, though the possibility of nationals of non-member States being appointed is not excluded. The members of the Commission are elected by the Committee of Ministers from a list of names prepared by the Assembly. The principal function of the Commission is to investigate alleged breaches of the Convention and to secure, if possible, a friendly settlement of the matter.[100] As the whole Commission will consist of fifteen members, its function of friendly settlement is performed by a sub-Commission of seven, of whom each of the parties concerned may appoint one, the remainder being chosen by lot.[101] If a friendly settlement is achieved, a brief report is prepared and published.[102] If the attempt at friendly settlement fails, the Commission as a whole draws up a report and states its opinion as to whether the facts disclose a breach of its obligations by the State concerned. In order to encourage frank discussion and facilitate the search for truth, the Commission meets in Camera,[103] and individual opinions may be stated in the report.[104]

Article 31 provides that, when negotiations fail, the Commission should forward its report to the Committee of Ministers, making such proposals as it thinks fit. In default of a reference within a period of three months to the Court of Human Rights, it is then for the Committee of Ministers to decide, on the basis of the Commission's report, whether a violation of the Convention has been committed, and, if so, what measures shall be taken, the High Contracting Parties undertake in advance to regard as binding any decision of the committee of Ministers in this respect.[105] It is of particular interest that such decisions of the Committee of Ministers under the Convention are binding and taken by a two-thirds majority, since under Article 15 and 20 of the Statute, the powers of the Committee, when discharging its ordinary business, are only to make recommèndations to governments, and for all important decisions a unanimous vote is required.

A serious difference of opinion, however, arose on the fundamental question whether a European Court of Human Rights should be created at all. A compromise solution was then adopted involving the principle of optional jurisdiction: the Court would have jurisdiction only in respect of those States which expressly accepted it. Such acceptance may also take place in different ways. Under Article 46 any High Contracting Party may at any time declare that it recognises as compulsory ipsofacto and without special agreement the jurisdiction of the Court in all matters concerning the interpretation and application of the present Convention. Such dęclarations may be made unconditionally or on condition of reciprocity. Independently of this, however, any State may consent to the jurisdiction of the Court in a particular case, either as plaintiff or defendant.

Two individual cases that were declared admissible were Lawless against Ireland and De Becker against Belgium.[106] The former related to the detention without trial of an alleged member of the Irish Republic Army and the latter to a prohibition pronounced on a wartime collaborator against exercising his profession of journalist. These cases were examined by a Sub-Commission, which was unable to reach a friendly settlement, with the result that reports were drawn up by the Commission and submitted to the Committee of Ministers early in 1960.

Within the following three months, the Commission decided to transmit these two cases to the Court. It considered that they raised important questions of principle which were more suitable for judicial decision by the Court than for decision by the Committee of Ministers, which is an essentially political organ. In this way, the Court of Human Rights was seized of its first business. The first case that came up for hearing *Lawles v. Ireland* and Irish Government raised a number of preliminary objections which involved important points of procedure relating to the respective functions of the Commission and the Court.

The Commission of Human Rights was unanimous in holding that the arrest and detention were not in accordance with Article 5 of the Convention, providing for the right to liberty and security of person and freedom from arbitrary arrest. However, Article 15 of the Convention provides:

> In time of war or other public emergency threatening the life of the nation any High Contracting Party may take measures derogating from its obligations under this Convention to the extent strictly required by the exigencies of the situation, provided that such measures are not inconsistent with its other obligations under international law.

The Commission concluded, by a majority of nine votes to five, that in making a determination of 5th July 1957 that there existed in the Republic of Ireland a public emergency threatening the life of the nation, the Respondent Government did not go beyond the proper margin of discretion allowed to it under Article 15, paragraph 1. This decision then led to consideration of further question: whether the arrest and detention of person without trial was a measure 'strictly required by the exigencies of the situation'. This question the Commission also answered in the affirmative, by a majority of eight votes to six, so that the conclusion of the Commission on the issue as a whole was that the facts found did not disclose a breach of the Convention by the Irish Government.

The Commission transmitted its report to the Committee of Ministers, setting out this conclusion, on I February 1960. On following I April, it decided to submit the case to the Court of Human Rights. Pleadings were exchanged during the following months, during the course of which the Irish

Government raised certain preliminary objections; oral hearings thereon took place on 3rd and 4th October and on 14th November the Court delivered its first judgement, relating to the preliminary objections.

The essence of the problem was the relationship which should be established between the individual applicant and the Court. Under the term of the Constitution an individual can bring an application before the Commission as Lawless did in this case but. under Article 44. only States and the Commission can bring a case before the Court. The difficulty arises after the case is referred to the Court by Commission. How an individual should be heard?

Elementary principles ofjustice. therefore, require that the other party should also be heard. But how is this to be done, since the individual applicant has no locus standi?

The Commission, therefore, sought another means of permitting the applicant's Rule 76 of its Rules of Procedure providing that, when such a case is referred to the Court, the Commission's Report shall be communicated to the applicant, who may then submit to the Commission his written observations thereon. This was duly done in the Lawless case, the applicant being informed that the document must be kept secret. The Commission then asked the Court to give leave for it to submit, as one of the documents in the case, the applicant's observations on the Report. The Irish Government objected both to the communication of the report to the applicant and to the proposal that his comments should be submitted to the Court.

As regards the publication of the report, the Government argued that Article 31 of the Convention clearly provides that, if the attempt at friendly settlement fails, the Commission's report shall be transmitted to the Committee of Ministers and to the Governments concerned, which shall not be at liberty to publish it. It was thus clearly with the intention that the report should be kept secret and, therefore, that it should not be communicated to the applicant. Furthermore, it was argued, the Government continued to be bound by the obligation of secrecy even after the case had been referred to the Court; it was inconceivable that a State should be in a position of inferiority to the Commission as regards the obligation of secrecy. The Government, therefore, asked the Court to hold that the publication of the report by the Commission to the applicant was in contravention of the Convention and that Rule 76 was ultra vires.

The Commission, in reply, expressed the view that the obligation of secrecy under Article 31 of the Convention was limited in two respects. It was clearly absolute as regards publication to the press or to third parties, but not as regards the applicant, who was a party to the proceedings; secondly, it was intended to ensure the secrecy of the report while the matter was pending before the Committee of Ministers, whose proceedings are confidential, but not at a time when the case has been referred to the Court, whose proceedings are of course, open to the public.

As regards the submission to the Court of the applicant's comments on the Commission's report, the Government pointed out that the Convention made it clear that an individual could not be a party to proceedings before the Court, and argued that the procedure proposed by the Commission amounted to a subterfuge which would in effect produce that result. If it were permitted, the applicant Would be permitted to do indirectly what was clearly prohibited if done directly. The President of the Commission submitted that the individual and the Government were on a footing of equality before the Commission; the Commission's report was a new factor in the case now before the Court; the Government would have every opportunity of challenging the contents of this report in the proceedings before the Court; the individual must be given, by some means or the other, a similar opportunity.

The Court's judgement considered first of all the question: Is Rule 76 of the Rules of Procedure of the Commission in general contrary to the terms of the Convention? The Court here was very cautious. It pointed out that the Commission and the Court were independent organs set up by the Convention, each with its own functions and responsibilities; and that the Court had no general power to interpret the

Convention in an abstract manner but only to decide particular cases referred to it in accordance with Articles 45 and 47. From these considerations, it concluded that:

The Court is not competent enough to take decisions such as that to delete a rule from the Commission's Rules of Procedure—a step which would affect all parties to the Convention—since this would amount to having power to make rulings on matters of procedure or to render advisory opinions; that accordingly the Court has no power to consider the point raised in a general manner by the Commission and the Irish Government.

The Court then turned from the general to the particular, namely to the communication of the Commission's Report in this case to Mr. Lawless. It recognises the need for secrecy in the proceedings before the Commission and the Committee of Ministers; but it re-affirmed the public character of the hearings before the Court. After pointing out that this public character attached only to oral proceedings and the judgement, but not to the document in the case (except when authorized by the Court), it went on to distinguish between publication in general and communications to the person directly concerned subject to injunctions of secrecy. This distinction led to the conclusion that the court is of the opinion that the Commission is unable under the Convention to communicate, to the applicant, with the proviso that it must not publish, the whole or part of the report or a summary thereof, whenever such communication seems appropriate; therefore, in the present case, the Commission, in communicating its report to G.R. Lawless, the Applicant, did not exceed its powers.

Finally, the Court considered the Commission's request for leave to communicate to the Court the applicant's observations on its own report and on other points which might arise during the proceedings. After reviewing the arguments on both sides, it drew attention to the fact that it is in the interests of the proper administration of justice that the Court should have knowledge of and, if need be take into consideration, the applicant's point of view. It went on to point out that there already existed three ways in which this could be done; in the Commission's report, in the statements of the delegates of the Commission before the Court and by bringing the applicant as a witness. Its conclusion, then, was that having been unable as yet to examine the merits of the case, it was not in a position to reach a decision on the Commission's report and reserved its right to do so at a later date.

While the Court considers that it was outside its competence to give a ruling on the general question whether Article 76 of the Commission's Rules of Procedure was in conformity with the Convention, it implicitly validated the rule, since the rule exists and is applied and the only body that could conceivably have invalidated it has declined to do so. Moreover, the Court held that, in this particular case, the communication of the report to Mr. Lawless, with the proviso that he should not publish it, was in order; this would, therefore, seem to be a clear precedent for the future.

The Court, thus, rejected both the objections of the Irish Government and upheld the procedure followed by the Commission. On the merits, the Court held that the complainant's arrest and detention without trial were justified by a public emergency threatening the life of the respondent country, Ireland, within the meaning of Article 15 of the European Convention, and that this emergency had been duly notified under this Article to the Secretary General of the Council of Europe.[107]

The De Becker case resulted in a change of legislation namely amendments to the Belgium Penal Code. So also as a consequence of the Belgium vagrancy cases (1966-72) Belgian law was amended, revising the former rules under which vagrants might be imprisoned without right of appeal.

The principle of exhaustion of local remedies and the provision of torture in the European Convention on Human Rights came up for scrutiny before European Court of Human Rights in a number of cases. In *Ireland v. United Kingdom*,[108] Ireland lodged various applications against the United Kingdom. Following an increase in Irish Republican Army's activities. United Kingdom Government detained without trial several persons suspected of serious activities. Ireland alleged that United Kingdom had adopted 'five techniques' to torture the detainees and thus violated Article 3 of the Convention. Article 3 of the Convention reads as follows:

No one shall be subjected to torture or to inhuman or degrading treatment or punishment.

The British Government adopted five techniques in the interrogation of the detainees These techniques consisted of:

1. *Wall Standing:* Forcing the detainee to remain for periods of some hours in a stess position, described by those who underwent it as being spread-eagled against the wall, with their fingers put high above the head against the wall, the legs spread apart and the face back, causing them to stand on their toes with the weight of the body mainly on the fingers;
2. *Hooding:* Putting a black or navy coloured bag over the detainees heads and, at least intially, keeping them there all the time except during interrogation;
3. *Subjection to Noise:* Pending their interrogations, holding the detainees in a room where there was continuous loud and hissing noise;
4. *Deprivation of Sleep:* Pending their interrogations, depriving the detainees of sleep;
5. *Deprivation of Food and Drink:* Subjecting the detainees to a reduced diet during their stay at the centre and pending interrogations.

In its judgement, the Court approved the rule that has been developed in the Commission's jurisprudence by which local remedies need not be exhausted in a State where the act or acts claimed to be in breach of the Convention is or are shown to be in consequence of an administrative practice and where the practice is being challenged as such. In Court's opinion, if there was an administrative practice of torture or ill-treatment, judicial remedies prescribed would tend to be rendered ineffective by the difficulty of securing probative evidence, and administrative enquiries would either be not instituted or, if they were, would be likely to be halfhearted and incomplete. The Court finally held that the use of five techniques by United

Kingdom Government in August and October 1971 constituted a practice of inhuman and degrading treatment in breach of Article 3 of the Convention. Although, the Court further added that the use of said five techniques did not constitute a practice of torture within the meaning of Article 3 of the Convention.

In *Donnelly v. United Kingdom,*[109] the European Commission of Human Rights held that the rule of exhaustion of local remedies extended to individual applications as well as State applications so that local remedies do not have to be exhausted where the applicant is a victim of a violation of the Convention attributable to an administrative practice and the existence of the practice has rendered local remedies ineffective.

In *Tyrer v. United Kingdom*[110] the Court held that infliction of corporeal punishment by birching of the Isle of Man amounted to degrading punishment violative of Article 3 of the Convention.

Dudgeon Case is quite interesting.[111] The applicant, a thirty-five-year old United Kingdom citizen resident in the Northern Ireland, was a homosexual. In 1976, the police seized evidence concerning his homosexual activities from his flat while searching it lawfully for drugs. He was taken to a police station and questioned about his sexual life. Later it was decided not to prosecute and his papers were returned. The applicant complained that the existence of the law in Northern Ireland making buggery (offences against the Personal Act, 1861) and 'gross indecency' (Criminal Law Amendment Act 1885) between consenting males a criminal offence was a breach of his right to privacy embodied in Article 8 of the Convention. The Court acknowledged the legitimate necessity in a democratic society for some degree of control over homosexual conduct notably in order to provide safeguards against the exploitation and corruption of those who are specially vulnerable by reason, for example, their youth. However, it falls in the first instance to the national authorities to decide on the appropriate safeguards of this kind required for the defence of morals in their society and, in practice, to fix the age under which young people should have the protection of criminal law. Therefore, the Court added a caveat to the effect that the restrictions imposed on the right to privacy must be justified by the necessities of the situation. The present case, the Court observed, concerned a most serious aspect of private life and, therefore, very serious reasons must exist for imposing restrictions. In Court's view, the impugned legislation constituted a continuing interference with the applicant's right to respect for his private life (which includes his sexual life) within the meaning of Article 8 of the Convention either he respects the law and refrains from engaging—even in private with consenting male partners—in prohibited sexual acts to which he is disposed by reason of his homosexual tendencies, or he commits such acts and thereby becomes liable to criminal prosecution. Finally, the Court held the impugned legislation breaches Article 8 of the Convention.

In *Young James and Webster*[112] cases in 1975, the British Rail entered into a closed shop agreement with three rail trade unions, by which membership of one of them was a condition of employment. The three applicants, who were British Rail employees before the agreement was negotiated, refused to become members and were dismissed. All three objected to membership on the ground that no one should be compelled to join a trade union. The European Commission of Human Rights was of the opinion that the applicant's freedom of association embodied in Article 11 of the Convention had been infringed and referred the case to the Court. The court also affirmed the Commission's opinion and held that Article 11 of the Convention had been violated.

The European Convention on Human Rights has been invoked against Turkey by a large number of citizens ofKurdish origin claiming to be victims of violation by the security forces in the emergency region of South-East Turkey since 1993. Under the European Convention, Turkey has so far been confronted with a total of some 800 individual complaints.

The monitoring aspect of the European Convention is achieved principally through the filing of complaints either by one or more states against another state, called inter-state procedure under Article 24 or by individuals under Article 25.

Individual complaints procedure is envisaged for dealing with the grievances of the individuals. Individuals are required to establish that they are victims of the alleged violations.

However, the situation has changed after the amendment of the European Convention in 1994 by Protocol No. II. After this amendment, the Court is the only machinery available for effective implementation of human rights. The new Court is a permanent and has one step process making the system of protection quicker and more efficient. Individuals have direct access to the Court.

Protocol No. 11 restructured the implementation machinery. The European Court started its work on 1st November, 1998. The European Commission continued to work for one year to finish off the cases declared admissible before 1st November, 1998. The Commission was finally dissolved in November 1999.

Generally, it is sound to conclude that there are effective implementation machineries under the European convention on human rights. The key to the effectiveness of the system lies on the facts that the member states are like-minded and tied with common cultural and social heritage and the system is kept outside the field of politics.[113]

EVALUATION

It is submitted that the European Convention for protection of Human Rights and fundamental freedoms (1950) is the first important regional Convention on human rights, which goes beyond the Universal Declaration of Human Rights and gives effect to civil and political rights contained therein by binding commitments. Secondly, it precisely defines civil and political rights and clarifies the contents of these rights by incorporating exceptions, restricitions or limitations to which such rights are subject to. Thirdly, it includes implementation machinery for human rights, which were, comission and the Court. On 31st October, 1998 the provision for the commission was deleted by Protocol XI. Fourthly, the jurisdiction of the court is very wider, which is mainly of two types: Contentious and advisory. Fifthly, the judgement of the court has binding effect. Article

46 of the Eurpoean Convention says that the state parties have undertaken to abide by the final judgement of the court in any case to which they are parties.[114] Lastly, the execution of the final verdict is supervised by the committee of ministers. It has been observed that when the law of the state party differs from the convention, the law of the state party, that is, national law is amended accordingto the convention. In *Dreland v. United Kingdom,*[115] the five methods of extracting confessions were held as inhuman. The U.K. immediately amended the law so that the decision of the Court may be given effect. It has been noted that several state parties have incorporated the European convention of Human Rights into their domestic law, then it is regarded as a part of their own law.

The American Convention on Human Rights

The American convention on human rights of 1969 is the other regional instrument under which protection and implementation of international human rights is duly reflected. The convention provides protection of human rights on a regional basis by countries in North, Central and South America. The convention entered into force on 18th July, 1978 after eleven states have deposited their instruments of ratification or adherence.

In their agreement the state parties to the convention have confirmed that the essential rights of man are not derived from one's being a national of a certain state but are based upon attributes of the human personality.[116] Also the parties to the convention considered those principles which have been set forth in the charter of the organization of American States, in the American Declaration of the Rights and Duties of Man, and in the Universal Declaration of Human Rights. Moreover, the convention proclaims that in accordance with the Universal Declaration of Human Rights, ideal of free man enjoying freedom from fear and want can be achieved only if conditions are created whereby everyone may enjoy his economic, social and cultural rights as well as his civil and political rights, and set out detailed provisions on civil and political rights, economic, social and cultural rights, and the means of protecting those rights.

The American convention provides for two organs competence with respect to matters relating to the fulfillment of the commitments made by states parties to the convention the Inter-American Commission on Human Rights and the Inter-American Court of Human Rights. Detailed discussion on the composition, power and function of the commission has been done under chapter III of the research work.

The Inter-American court of human rights, hereafter referred as court, consists of seven judges elected for a period of six years. The judges can be elected in their personal capacity from among jurists of the highest moral authority and of recognized competence in the field of human rights and no two judges may be nationals of the same state. During election of judges each of the states parties may propose up to three candidates among which at least one shall be a national of a state other than the proposing state.[117]

According to Article 55 of the convention states party to the dispute before the court have a right to have a judge of their nationality on the bench when their case is being heard. For this purpose even they may propose an ad hoc judge also. However, if several states parties to the convention should have the same interest in a case, they can be considered as a single party only for the purpose of Article 55. Similar to the European convention, only states parties and the commission have the right to submit a case to the court.[118]

The court can render the consultation service for the member states[119] and it shall submit a report on its work to the General Assembly of the organization of American states in each regular session.[120] The decision of the court is final and not subject to appeal, however, if there, is disagreement as to the meaning or scope of the judgement, the court shall interpret it at the request of any of the parties, provided the request is made within ninety days from the date of notification of the judgement.

The court may order provisional measures if the situation so demands, and order that the injured party be ensured the enjoyment of his right or freedom that was violated and if necessary the situation shall be remedied and that fair compensation has to be paid to the injured party.[121]

The other implementation mechanism under the American convention is reporting. Accordingly, the states parties to the convention are required to provide the commission with such information as it may request of them as to the manner in which their domestic law ensures the effective application of any provisions of the convention.[122]

The American Convention provides for the interstate complaint procedure also. The state party to the convention can bring its allegation of a violation of human rights set forth in the convention by another Member State only if it recognizes the competenace of the commission to receive and examine such communications.[123] This makes the inter-state complaint procedure optional contingent. The researcher is of the view that such requirement is not justifiable. The right to individual petition is the compulsory procedure under the convention whereby any person, or group of persons or any non-governmental entity legally recognized in one or more member states of the organization may lodge petitions with the commission.[124] Generally, it is possible to conclude that the American Convention is closely modelled on its European Counterpart.

The African Charter on human and Peoples' Rights

The African Charter on Human and Peoples' Rights of 1981, which may be also cited as the Banjul Charter on Human and Peoples' Rights because it was drafted in Banjul, Gambia. It is the third regional instrument, in terms of time, to come into existence. The African charter is unique in several ways.[125]

1. it deals with Civil and Political rights as well as with economic, social and cultural rights in a single document;
2. it sets out the obligations of human beings as well as their rights; and
3. it deals with the rights of people as well as those of individuals.

The African charter was adopted on 28th June, 1981 by the Heads of State and Government of the Organization of African Unity (18th Assembly) in Nairobi, Kenya and entered into force on 21st October, 1986 after being ratified by a majority of the OAU (Organization of African Unity) members States.[126] As stated earlier the African Charter is unique vis-a-vis other similar regional and international conventions. What are the reasons for this? It is obvious that the concept and practice of human rights in Africa have been conditioned by the continent's past, its culture, traditions, values, its contemporary political and economic development as well as the political concern of its leaders. It has been stated that "Africa's contemporary political realities and the heritage of its colonial past have influenced the African conception of human rights.

The underdeveloped economic condition in most of the African Countries is the other factor which contributed to social and political difficulties with the result of violations of human rights by governments.[127]

The pre and post Charter era of Africa is reflected by the struggle to adopt distinct and unique regional instrument from other conventions already adopted in other regions. For example the former president of Senegal, Leopold Sedar Senghor, Charged the African legal experts, assembled in Dakar in late November 1979 to draft the African Charter on Human and Peoples' Rights, to take Cognizance of African history, cultures realities and aspirations. He argued:

> Europe and America have constructed their system of rights and liberties with reference to a common civilization, to respective people and to some specific aspirations. It is not for us Africans either to copy them or to seek originality for originality's sake. It is for us to manifest both imagination and skill. Those of our traditions that are beautiful and positive may inspire us. You should therefore constantly keep in mind our values and the real needs of Africa.[128]

Moreover, since independence, there has been a very strong ambition to develop "Africanism" in Africa. Africans do not want to between as merely imitating or copying other regions.[129] For example in 1963 when Organization of African Unity (OAU) was created, African leaders rejected a suggestion to name the new institution an "Organization of African States" partly because there was already an Organization of American States.

The establishment of the OAU was basically for activating the goals of self determination for all Africans and the elimination of colonialism and apartheid. In its Charter of 1963, the OAU declared its main purposes to be:

1. the advancement of African Unity.
2. the achievement of an improved standard of living for the people of Africa.
3. the eradication of all forms of colonialism from Africa.
4. the promotion of international participation and respect for the charter of the United Nation and the Universal Declaration of Human Rights.[130]

The African Charter focuses on collective and group rights. Justifications for this approach has been stated by Ojo as Follows:

The African tradition lays more stress on the collective, the group or the community. If does not allow that the individual has any claims which may override that of society.[131]

When we see the provisions of the Charter we can ensure that the OAU's objectives are re-explained under the African Charter's preamble. Moreover state parties to the Charter pay a particular attention to the right to development and they warned that civil and political rights may have to suffer until they can satisfy economic, social and cultural rights.[132] Moreover, the state parties convinced to achieve the total liberation of Africa, the people of which are still struggling for their dignity and genuine independence, and undertaking to eliminate colonialism, neo-colonialism, apartheid, Zionism and ...... all forms of discrimination, particularly those based on race, ethnic group, colour, sex, language, religion or political opinions. It is from the aforesaid objectives that the unique nature of the African Charter is derivated. Articles 19-24 of the Charter exhaustively enumerated the peoples' rights and Articles 27-29 deals with the duties of the individuals toward the community. To see some of the peoples' Rights: Peoples have the right to get assistance of the States parties to the Charter in their liberation struggle against foreign domination, be it political, economic or cultural.[133] Article 20 stresses "the unquestionable and inalienable right" of people to self-determination. Also States parties to the Charter are expected to eliminate all forms' of Foreign economic exploitation particularly that practiced by international monopolies so as to enable their people to fully benefit from the advantages derived from their national resources.[134] To sum up it is possible to say that the rights recognized and the duties imposed under the African Charter are derivations from the African past history and traditions. The researcher thinks that this must not be interpreted and understood to affect he universality principle of human rights. When we see the implementation machinery under the charter it establishes the African Commission on Human and Peoples' Rights to follow up the proper implementation of human rights envisaged under the charter. Detailed discussion as to the role and function of the Commission has been done under the forthcoming chapter of this work.

EVALUATION

One of the defects of the African Charter is its failure to establish human rights court as compared to the previous discussed its counterparts i.e. the European and the American Conventions. It is the result of the African leaders unwillingness to do so. The African leaders found course to tradition and culture to stop the floodgate of interference into what they regard as their internal affairs, namely the issue of how states treat their own citizens.[135] For example before the adoption of the charter in 1961 African Jurists meeting in Lagos suggested in African Human Rights Charter under which a court, to which individual or groups of individuals may have recourse, would be created. Similar proposal was made by a conference in Dakar of Jurists from francophone African States in 1967.

However African leaders were not in a position to accept this recommendation while adopting the Charter.

The optional Protocol of 1998 has now provided for the establishment of an African Human Rights Court which when it comes into existence after achieving required ratifications will remove one of the major shortcoming of the African system and will give a boost to this regional mechanism.

NOTES

1. For example, the Convention on the Elimination of All Forms of Discrimination Against Women, the Convention on the Rights of the Child, as well as the international Convenant on Civil and Political Rights and the International Covenant on Economic, Social and Cultural Rights.
2. Claire Archbold, "The incorporation of civic and Social Rights in Domestic Law" in Globalization of Human Rights ed. by Jean Marc, colcared, Michael W. Doyee and Anne Mari Gardner,(2004), pp. 56-58.
3. Despite decision such as *R v. Drybones* (1970) SCR 282, DLR, 3D, 473, the courts' narrow interpreation of the rights may be seen in cases such as *Canada v. Lavell* (1974) SCR 1349, 38 DLR, 3D, 481 and *Bliss v. Attorney General Canada* (1979) 1 SCR 183 93 DLR, 3D, 417.

3a. Claire Archbold, "Incorporation of Rights in Domestic Law" in Globalization of Human Rights', edited by Jean Marc, Coiacud, Michal W. Doyee Annie Mari Gardner (2004) at pp. 58-65.

4. (1973) 128 CLR 557 at 582-583.
5. *Koowarta v. Bjelke-Petersen* (1983) 153 CLR 168 at 224-225.
6. (1996) 185 CLR 259.
7. Section 22AA read with the definition of refugee contained in Sec. 4(1).
8. (1989) 169 CLR 379.
9. (1999) AJHR 27.
10. (1997) 190 CLR 225.
11. (1997) 190 CLR 225 at p. 232.
12. (1996) 187 CLR 640.
13. *De L. v. Director General, NSW Department of Community Services* (1997) 190 CLR 207.

14. (1997) 191 CLR 119.
15. Michal Kirby, "Domestic Implementation of International Human Rights Norms." (1999) AJHR 27.
16. (1998) 72 ALJR 841 (HC).
17. Section 9(3) of the Air Services Act, 1995; Section 28(C) of Australian Postal Corporation Act, 1989; Sections 22 and 95 of Chemical Weapons (Prohibition) Act, 1994; Section 11 of Civil Aviation Act, 1988; Section 70(1) Nuclear Non-Proliferation (Safeguards) Act, 1987; Section 45(5) of OZone Projection Act, 1989; Section 366 of Tele Communication Act, 1997.
18. *Qantas Airways Ltd. v. Christie* (1998) 193 CLR 280.
19. (1996) 70 ALJR 541 (HC). decided by Michal Karby J.
20. (1996) 70 ALJR 541 at 542.
21. See also *Limbo v. Little* (1989) 98 FLR 421; Re Limbo (1989) 64 ALJR 241 (HC); *Linden v. Commonwealth* (1995) 70 ALJR 145.
22. (1997) 71 ALJR 767 (HC). The plaintiff invoked the Genocide Convention introduced into domestic jurisdiction by the Genocide Convention Act 1949 (Cth) (at 772-773); see also Akhavan, 'Enforcement of the Genocide Convention Through the Advisory Opinion Jurisdiction of the International Court of Justice' (1991) 12 *Human Rights Law Journal*, 285 at 296.
23. (1997) 71 ALJR 767 at 769.
24. See also Re Ditford; Ex parte Deputy Commissioner of Taxation (1988) 19 FCR 347 at 368-369 per Gummow J.
25. (1997) 71 ALJR 767 at 779 (HC).
26. See *Chicago and Southern Airlines Inc. v. Waterman Steamship Corporation* 323 US 103 at 111 (1948) and *Crockett v. Reagan* 658 F Supp 893 (1982).
27. UNCIO Documents, vol. 1, p. 717.
28. H.O.Aggrawal, "International Law & Human Rights"; 12th ed. (2005) p. 706-707
29. Ser Re Drummond Wren, 4 Ontario Reports, 778; A.D. 12 (1943-45) No. 50; *Oyanu v. California,* (1948) 332 U.S. 633; A.D. 16 (1949), No. 49.
30. See *Kemp v. Rubin,* A.D. 14 (1947), No. 37; *Fujii v. State of California,* ILR 19 (1952) p. 312.

31. See Re Noble and Wolf where both the High Court of Ontario and the Ontario Court of Appeal declined to follow Re Drummond Wren on the ground that the obligations set out in the United Nations Charter on the subject had not been made part of the law of Canada (A.D. 15 (1949) No. 100.

32. See *Sipes v. Mcghee,* A.D. 14 (1947) No. 35; *Hurd v. Hodge,* A.D. 14 (1947) No. 36.

33. David P. Forsythe, p. 57.

34. Instances of Working Groups are: (a) Working Groupon. Communications (1503) Resolution receiving individual complaints; (b) Working Group on Contemporary forms of Slavery; (c) Working Group on Minorities; (d) Working Group on.

35. The Commission, after receipt of the communication, sends it to the government concerned and summarizes it in a monthly confidential list. The government is given twelve weeks time to reply. The Commission considers the situations in closed session. Resolution 1503 empowers the Commission to make a 'thorough study' or institute an investigation by an ad hoc committee.

36. H.O. Aggrawal, "International Law & Human Rights"; 12th ed. (2005) p. 704-710.

36a. See Appendix 'A'

37. See Report of the Preparatory Commission of the United Nations, Document PC/20 (23 December 1945) 28, 36.

38. S.L. Bhalla, Human Rights and Institutional Frame Work for Imblementation, 1991, p. 10.

39. Economic and Social Council, Resolution 9(11), 21 June 1946.

40. General Assembly Resolution 217 A(III) 10 December 1948. Vote was Forty eight in favour, none against with eight abstentions.

41. Paras Diwan, Human Rights and the Law, 1998, p. 32.

42. J.E.S. Fawcelt, The Law of Nations (1968), p. 156: See also Percy Corbett, The Growth of World law (1971), pp. 181-182.

42a. Fact Sheet No. 2 (Rev. 1)—International Bill of Human Rights: Office of the High Commissioner for Human Rights, at pp. 3-4.

43. See Appendix 'B'

44. International Covenant on Civil and Political Rights, Article 2, Clauses 1 and two.

45. Art. 40 of the Civil Covenant.
46. The Covenant on Economic, Social and Cultural Rights, Art. 16.
47. Art. 19 of the Covenant.
48. Civil Covenant, Supra note 19, Art. 40(2).
49. Art. 40(4).
50. Bhall, Human Rights and Institutional Frame Work for imblementation, 1991, p. 41.
51. Commission on Human Rights, Resolution 3 (XVII) 14 March, 1961. For report of the Committee on Periodic Reports see UN Document E/CN. 4/831 (23 March 1962) 45 pp.
52. See UN Document E/3616/Rev. 1 (n.d. 1962) 10-11.
53. S.L. Bhalla, Human Rights and Institutional Frame Work for imblementation, 1991, p. 43.
54. Dr. S. K. Kappor, 'International Law and Human Rights', 14th ed. p. 787.
55. Civil Covenant Art. 41.
56. Civil Covenant Art. 41 (1) (c).
57. Civil Covenant Art. 41 (1) (e).
58. Civil Covenant Art. 41 (1) (h).
59. Civil Covenant Art. 42 (1).
60. Civil Covenant Art. 42 (7) (a).
61. Civil Covenant Art. 42 (7) (b).
62. U.N. Doc. E/CN. 4/53 (10 December 1947) 41.
63. U.N. Doc. E/CN/ 4/SR 115 (9 June 1949) 5-9.
64. P.R. Ghandhi "The Human Rights Committee and the Right of Individual communication", The British year Book of International Law, 1987.
65. Civil Covenant Art. 39.
66. Article 42(1)(a)
67. Article 42(1)(b)
68. Article 42(3)
69. Article 42(7)
70. It was considered by the Committee during its IX Session i.e. July 30 August 17, 1979.

71. 35 UN GAOR Supp. (No. 40) 111,Report of the Human Rights, Commitee.
72. Considered during October 15 to 26, 1979.
73. Maurition Women's Case,1981 Report of Human Rights Committee, p. 134.
74. 1985 Report of the Human Rights Committee, p. 249 (Vuolana v. Finland).
75. Lovelace Case, 1981 Report of the Human Rights Committeee, at p. 166.
76. Maurition Women's Case, 1981 Report of Human Rights Committee, p. 134.
77. Lovelace Case, 1981 Report of the Human Rights Committeee, at p. 166.
78. 1985 Report of the Human Rights Committee, p. 249 (Vuolana v. Finland)
79. Netto Case, Ambrosini Case and Ewardo Dante Case cited above.
80. Dr. S. K. Kappor, 'International Law and Human Rights', 14th ed. p. 904-805.
81. Hans Kelsen, The Law of the United Nations, New York, 1950, pp. 29 and 179.
82. Frank E. Holman, An International Bill of Rights; Proposals have Dangerous Implications for USA, ABAJ, pp. 984-86 and pp. 107-81 (1948).
83. Gurdip Singh, 'International Law', (2003) p. 514.
84. Richard B. Bilder, 'Rethinking International Human Rights: Some Basic Questions', *Human Rights Journal*, 2, 1969, p. 567
85. The Covenant on Civil and Political Rights, Article 28.
86. Article 29 and 30 of the Covenant.
87. Article 31 of the Covenant.
88. The Covenant on Economic, Social and Cultural Rights, Art. 16.
89. *Ibid.*
90. The Covenant on Economic, Social and Cultural Rights, Art. 21.
91. *Ibid.* Art. 23.
92. *Ibid.* Art. 2(1)

93. Jacobs and White, The European Convention on Human Rights, 2nd ed. 1996, p. 2.
94. Manual of the Council of Europe, its Structure Functions and Achievements, (London, 1970) Art. 1 (a) (b).
95. Manual of the Council of Europe, its Structure Functions and Achievements, (London, 1970) Art 7 and 8.
96. Jacobs and White Supra note 49, p.5.
97. European convention on Human Rights, Section I, Articles 2-12 and protocols, 1-4.
98. *Ibid.* Art 19.
99. European Convention of Human Rights, Article 28 of the Convention.
100. European Convention of Human Rights, Article 29 of the Convention.
101. European Convention of Human Rights, Article 30 of the Convention.
102. European Convention of Human Rights, Article 33 of the Convention.
103. European Convention of Human Rights, Article 32 of the Convention.
104. European Convention of Human Rights, Article 32 of the Convention.
105. European Convention of Human Rights, Article 46 of the Convention.
106. *Lawless v. Ireland, American Journal of International Law*, 56, 1962, 187-210; *De Becker v. Belgium*, Yearbook of European Convention on Human Rights, 1962, pp. 320-37.
107. Gurdip Singh, "International Law", (2003) pp. 534-540.
108. *Ireland v. United Kingdom*, European Court of Human Rights, Series A, Judgement of 18 January, 1978; also see D.J. Harris, Cases and Materials on International Law, 1983, p. 483.
109. *Donnelly v. United Kingdom*, Yearbook of European Convention of Human Rights, 16, 1973, Paras 212, 262; and Yearbook of European Convention on Human Rights, 19, 1975.94.
110. *Tyrer v. United Kingdom*, European Court of Human Rights, Series A, Vol. 26, 25 April 1978.

111. Dudgeon Case, European Court of Human Rights, Series A, Vol. 45, Judgement of 22 October, 1981; also see D.J. Harris, Supra Note 77, p. 513.
112. Young James and Webster cases, European Court of Human Rights, Series A, Vol. 44, 13 August 1981.
113. A.H. Robertson (ed). Human Rights in National and International Law (1968) p. 333.
114. Dr. S.K. Kappor, International Law and Human Rights, 14th ed. p. 824.
115. (1978) EHCR, See. A. Vol. 25.
116. See the Preamble of the American Convention on Human Rights (1969).
117. Art 53 of the American Convention on Human Rights
118. Art. 61of the American Convention on Human Rights
119. Art. 64 of the American Convention on Human Rights
120. Art. 65 of the American Convention on Human Rights
121. Art. 63 of the American Convention on Human Rights
122. Art. 43 of the American Convention on Human Rights
123. Art. 45 of the American Convention on Human Rights
124. Art. 44 of the American Convention on Human Rights
125. OAU Dco. CAB/LEG/67/3/Rev. 5.
126. Oiusola Ojo, "Understanding Human Rights in Africa", Human Rights in Pluralist World: Individuals and Collectivities (Jàn. Berting *et. al.* (ed) 1990, p. 116.
127. Oiusola Ojo, "Understanding Human Rights in Africa", Human Rights in Pluralist World: Individuals and Collectivities (Jan. Berting *et. al.* (ed) 1990, p. 116.
128. *Ibid.* See Note No.1.
129. Oiusola Ojo, "Understanding Human Rights in Africa", Human Rights in Pluralist World: Individuals and Collectivities (Jan. Berting *et. al.* (ed) 1990, p. 117.
130. John K. Ebiasah "In Africa Black Dictatorships have Demonstrated a Talent for Oppression Equal to that of the White", American Bar Assoication, Vol. 8, No. 2, 1970, p. 12.
131. Ojo, "Understanding Human Rights in Africa", Human Rights in Pluralist World Jan Berting *et al* (ed.) 1990 p. 116

132. See the Preamble of African Charter on Human and People's Rights of 1981.

133. Art. 20(3) of the African Charter.

134. Art. 21(5) of the African Charter.

135. Ojo, "Understanding Human Rights in Africa", Human Rights in Pluralist World Jan Berting *et. al.* (ed.) 1990 p. 116

3

IMPLEMENTATION OF HUMAN RIGHTS NORMS AND THE ROLE OF THE U. N. AND REGIONAL HUMAN RIGHTS COMMISSIONS

This Chapter aims to evaluate the roles of the universal and regional Human Rights Commissions in the protection and promotion of human rights. There are four basic transactional human right commissions which operate on a universal or regional basis. These are:

1. The UN Commission on Human Rights, authorized by Article 68 of the United Nations Charter.
2. The European Commission on Human Rights, which functions on a regional basis within the framework of the council of Europe.
3. The Inter-American Commission on Human Rights which functions on a regional basis within the framework of the Organization of American States, and
4. The African Commission on Human and Peoples Rights, which functions on a regional basis within the framework of the Organization of African Unity.

THE UN COMMISSION ON HUMAN RIGHTS

Nature and Composition

The UN Commission on human rights was established in 1946, according to Art. 68 of UN Charter, as one of the functional Commissions under the Economic and Social council (ECOSOC). The Economic and Social Council, inter alia, has power to set a Commission for human rights according to Art. 62 of the Charter.

The main function of the human rights commission is to assist the economic and Social Council in carrying out its responsibilities for promotion and observance of human rights. Now a days the commission has firmly established itself as the single most important UN organ in the human rights field.[1]

Members of the Commission are selected from the UN member States based on the equitable geographical principles. Because of the increasing UN membership the Composition of the Commission was also enlarged from the initial 18 members to 22 in 1961, 32 in 1966, 43 in 1979 and 53 in 1990. The members are elected for a term of three years by secret ballot by ECOSOC. Since the members of the Commission are nominees of government of the States selected to serve on the Commission, it has been generally commented that its decisions are often influenced by political considerations.[2] Regarding the capacity of members of the Commission there was on issue as to whether to nominate persons as government representatives or as experts in individual capacity. Majority of the ECOSOC members favoured that the members of the Commission should serve as non-governmental representatives. The then U.S.S.R., however, disagreed and requested the members to be representatives of governments, In its Resolutions, 9(11) and 12(11) of 21 June 1946 the Council decided that the governments elected to membership had the option to nominate persons either as government representatives or as experts in individual capacity. The Commission meets for six weeks every year in February and March at Geneva.

Terms of Reference

By 'terms of reference' to mean that the power and function of the Commission. Therefore attention must be given to the functioning of the Commission as well as to its evolving roles, including its activities in terms of Standardsetting and implementation.

The main issue to be noted in relation to the terms of reference of the commission is whether its mandate is limited or not. In the UN establishment conference, the San Francisco Conference of 1945, it was envisaged that the major task of the Commission would be drafting of an International Bill of Rights.[3] This was a clear reflection that there was strong priority for a limited promotional role of concentrating primarily on Standard-Setting rather than an open-ended protection role.

The terms of reference of the Commission as approved by the ECOSOC resolution 5(1) of 16th February, 1946 (Subsequently amended by ECOSOC resolutions 9(ii) of 21st June, 1946), which set up the Commission shall be directed towards submitting proposals, recommendations and reports to ECOSOC regarding:

(a) formulation of an international bill of rights;

(b) formulation of recommendations for an international declaration or convention on such matters as civil liberties, status of women, freedom of information;

(c) protection of minorities;

(d) prevention of discrimination on grounds of race, sex, languages, or religion; and

(e) any matters, within the field of human rights considered likely to impair the general welfare or friendly relations among nations.

In 1979, the ECOSOC (through resolution E/1979/36) added the following provision to these terms of reference: "The Commission shall assist the Economic and Social Council in the Coordination of activities concerning human rights in the UN system." In addition to paragraph (e) above, this proposal reflected a general mandate of the Commission.[4]

Functions of the Commission

Norm Creating Function

The UN Commission on Human Rights plays a continuous role of drafting of international instruments in the field of human rights. During its first two sessions, i.e. in 1947 and 1948, the Commission completed a comprehensive draft of the universal declaration, which was proclaimed by the General Assembly on Dec. 10, 1948, Moreover, the Commission drafted two Covenants i.e. the International Covenant on civil and political rights, and the international Covenant on cultural, social and economic rights, in 1954 and the General Assembly circulated the same to member states for soliciting their views. However, number of controversial political issues were raised during the commissions drafting of the covenants. The issues include:

1. whether there would be two covenants rather than one;
2. whether the right of self determination would be included in the covenants; and
3. Whether a territorial or colonial clause would be included.[5]

The other controversy was as to whether the Covenant should have only the traditional human rights, viz; only civil and political rights, or whether it should also include economic, social and cultural rights. In its Fifth Session (1950), the General Assembly expressed the view that both sets of rights were interrelated and independent, and directed the Human Rights Commission to include both. In its next session, the General Assembly reconsidered the matter and expressed the view that there should be two separate covenants. In addition to the covenants, an optional protocol on civil and political rights was adopted.[6]

Although the covenants were adopted by the General Assembly on December 16, 1966, it was after almost one decade they come into force. So slow were the states in ratifying the covenants that the covenant on Economic, social and cultural rights could come into force only on January 3, 1975 and the other covenant together with its protocol come into force on March 23, 1976.

The other problem the commission faced during and after its draft of the covenants was the strong opposition from USA, which is the most influential member of the United Nations for the reason that USA increasingly opposed to the principle of making human rights a matter of enforceable treaty obligations. For example in 1951 a "sense of the senate" resolution was proposed by senator breaker and others that condemned the draft covenants as being prejudicial to the rights already protected in the US Bill of rights and urged the US government to withdraw from further negotiations with respect to the covenant on human rights and all other covenants, treaties and conventions which seek to prescribe restrictions on individual liberty .... However this US measure did not affect the commission from completing its work on covenants by 1954, it put an impact on other normcreating activities during the late 1950's.

In 1950's the commission was concerned with the draft declaration on the rights of the child. It had received a completed draft from the UN Social Commission in 1951 but it was adopted in 1959 by the General Assembly. In 1950 the commission undertook conventions relating to discrimination in employment and in education. These undertakings were left to ILO and UNESCO to take the necessary steps. Accordingly ILO convention (No 111) concerning discrimination in respect of employment and occupation of 1958 and the convention against discrimination in education adopted by UNESCO in 1960.[7]

The period between 1961 and 1976 was characterised by the diminishing of the role of the commission in relation to drafting of international human right instruments. However starting 1977 the commission's standard-setting role entered a new, and ultimately very productive phase. In 1977 the General Assembly chosen the commission as the preferred forum for drafting of the declaration against torture which was adopted in 1984 and a convention on children's Rights which was adopted in 1989. Similarly the commission worked effectively in generating new international human right norms in the subsequent years.

One can imagine the various problems of the commission while drafting international instruments since states members to the commission as well as in the General Assembly pursue various political-economic and the like interests. Similar to USA, the then influential country, USSR was objecting to the creation of instruments. For example Soviet Union objected the universal declaration that it was weak and in many ways, absolutely unsatisfactory. Similarly the draft convention against apartheid was approved despite opposition by many western states. In spite of such objections the commission is accomplishing its task of creating of international human right norms quite efficiently and needs appreciation.

However there are some criticisms directed at the commission's performance in relation to the drafting of international human right norms. These can be summarised as follows.[8]

1. Its failure to indicate some sense of priorities in terms of standard-setting;
2. Its complete neglect of human rights standards drafted by organs other than by itself or its sub-commission;
3. The lack of any procedures designed to promote efficiency and the availability of the necessary expertise during the drafting process; and
4. The lack of any substantive role, at least since the 1960s, for the secretariat, thus leaving research etc. to the vagaries of the interests of individual delegations or interest groups.

The above mentioned criticisms must be noted by the commission in order to be more effective in its role of norm creation.

Dealing with Violations

This is the area where the role of the UN commission on human rights would be evaluated in respect of implementation of international human right norms. However, the commission failed to concern itself with problems of human rights violations for the first twenty years of its existence. Issues related to what are the reasons, the .historical perspectives of its power, sources of the commission's authority to deal with specific human right violations and the recent developments will be discussed below.

As far as the historical perspective of the commission's power to deal with specific human right violations is considered there have been three very distinctive phases:

1. 1946-66, during which the commission was not prepared to address the issue of specific violations at all;
2. 1967-78, when the commission struggled to evolve procedures which were initially designed to respond only to problems associated with racism and colonialism; and
3. 1979 to the present, when the procedures developed earlier have been applied in an increasingly creative and tailored fashion to an ever-widening range of countries and types of vioiations.[9]

During the first phase, i.e. 1946-66 the position of the commission was that it had "no power to take any action in regard to any complaints concerning human rights". However attempt has been made by the secretariat in 1947 to include the right of petition to the declaration of human rights, that provision was deleted by the commission's drafting committee and failed to appear in the declarations adapted by the general assembly in Dec. 1948.[10] The secretariat warnes the situation that "to lower the prestige and authority not only of the commission but of the United Nations as a whole. The opposition to the measure taken by the commission's drafting committee was expressed by the British Jurist Hersch Louter Pacht as an 'extra ordinary degree of ... abdications' of the UN's proper functions.

The absence of procedure for dealing with the specific human right violations during the period of 1946-66 doesn't mean there were no communications as to violations. For example in 1951-52 the commission received more than 25,000 communications, but none of them had been entertained.[11]

The issue to be noted here is what are the reasons for the failure of the commission to deal with problems of human right violations for the first twenty years of its existence? As pointed out by Zuijdwijk[12] there are some reasons. Firstly, the western block, which had a comfortable majority in the United Nations, was anxious to ensure that the United Nations would not begin examining alleged violations, given the certainty that western states would, and probably sooner rather than later, become the focus of such procedures. For example USA was worried about the certainty of complaints alleging racial discrimination while the UK, France, Belgium, Portugal and the other colonial powers feared complaints about conditions and practices in their colonies. Secondly, the commission itself was repeatedly proclaiming that it had no power to act on violations, its superior organs, the General Assembly and ECOSOC were deeply immersed in a wide range of highly controversial human rights issues.[13] Thirdly, another reason sometimes cited to justify the commission's inaction was that the covenants, when adopted would provide the desired avenue for redress.[14]

Generally because of various reasons the commission's role to deal with specific human right violations was curtailed during the year 1946-66 and it contributed significantly to a loss of credibility by the UN in human rights matters.

During the second phase, i.e. 1967-1978 there was a gradual assumption of responsibility by the commission. This period was characterised by the influx of new members to the UN, specially from the newly independent Asian and African states.

These new third world states showed willingness to develop new procedures in relation to the specific human right violations. The adoption of the convention on the elimination of all forms of racial discrimination (CERD) in 1966, which included provision in Art 14, for the submission of complaints by individual or groups against states which accepted the procedure, contributed more for the willingness of third world states.

In addition to the support of the third world countries and eastern European states as to the establishment of petition procedures, it was on the initiative of the special committee on decolonization in 1966, that the attention of the commission was drawn to petitions alleging human rights violations in South Africa. In 1966 the ECOSOC, by its resolution number 1102 (XL) of 1966, invited the commission to consider urgently the question of the violation of human rights, including policies of racial discrimination and segregation of apartheid in all countries, with particular reference to colonial and other dependent countries and territories, and to submit its recommendations on measures to hit those violations. However it was only after the General Assembly Resolution Number 2144A (XXI) of 1966, the commission's mandate to this issue become applicable to violations of human rights wherever they may occur.

It is after this that the two separate procedures were adopted by the ECOSOC. These are the procedures established over ECOSOC Resolution 123 (XLII) which established the principle that violations could be examined and responded to, and provided the necessary authorisation for the commission to engage in pubic debate on the issue each year; and the procedure under ECOSOC resolution 1503 (XLVIII) which provided a procedure by which the individuals may submit their petition as to the violation of human rights by states.

The third phase of the historical perspective of the commissions role in responding specific human rights violations is the period from 1979 to the present. This phase is termed as Evolution towards an effective response.

It is worthmentioning to see some of the progressive changes achieved under the 1503 confidential procedure. After the adoption of this procedure till annual figure of number of complaints increased from time to time. For example, from the time when the 1503 procedure began functioning (1972) until the mid 1980's an average of 25,000 complaints were received annually. In 1988 and 1989 the numbers rose to 200,000 and 300,000 respectively.

Similar to resolution 1503, the ECOSOC resolution 1235 of June 1967 which established the procedure on the basis of which the commission holds an annual public debate focusing on gross violations of human rights, has showed progress during this last phase.[15]

In putting into practice of resolution 1235 the commission lay in the struggle against racism in general and apartheid in particular. The agenda of the commission in relation to this issue was based on the "Question of the violation of human rights and fundamental freedoms, including policies of racial discrimination and segregation and of apartheid, in all countries, with particular reference to colonial and other dependent countries and territories.[16] It is very simple to estimate how the then political motive of the developed nations would object the application of this procedure. It was summarised that: "the third world wanted action against violations in southern Africa and other colonial situations. The eastern Europeans were happy with that focus since they had no colonies and were equally happy for racism in the west to be targeted. The west, well aware that it did not have numbers to block action..."

In the application of the resolution 1235 procedure the role played by NGO's such as Amnesty International and others has been very essential in a sense that they had created a far better informed public opinion and governments were beginning to be subjected to domestic pressure to do something about human rights.[17]

Generally the role of the commission as to the responding of specific violations of human rights has been developed due to the gradual struggle of the commission from time to time. One can imagine the effectiveness of such a procedure in ensuring the proper implementation of international human right norms.

SOURCES OF AUTHORITY

The issue to be noted here is what are the sources of authority of the commission to deal with specific violations of human rights by states? In order to answer this issue it is proper to see some relevant provisions of the charter and resolutions.

At the 180th meeting of the Human Rights Commission it was decided to request the secretariat to submit a legal opinion on the question as to whether the commission had the right to request the secretary-general to address enquiry's to governments.

Based on the question legal opinion asked from the legal department of the secretariat and the same department submitted its legal opinion dated 12th May, 1950. The conclusions were:

- the commission on human rights was established by the council under Art 68 of the charter which required the setting up of a commission "to promote human rights". Apart from this, the charter is silent on the question of the commission's powers and functions. Consequently, the rights of the commission can only be determined on the basis of authority delegated to it by the ECOSOC.
- There is no doubt that the economic and social council may itself address enquiries to governments for the purpose of obtaining information on questions with its competence. This right, which has frequently been exercised, rests on the power granted in Art 62, paragraph 1 of the charter authorizing the council to "make or initiate studies and reports with international economic, social, cultural, educational, health and related matters". With respect to human rights, this authority is also based in part upon paragraph 2 of Art. 62 under which the council may make recommendations for the purpose of promoting respect for, and observance of human rights and fundamental freedoms for all.
- With respect to the council's powers under Art. 62, it is clear that the council may delegate to its commissions the right to make studies reports and recommendations on matters falling within the competence of the commission.
- It may be concluded that under its broad terms of reference the commission on human rights has been

> authorized by the council to submit enquiries to governments where such enquiries are deemed necessary or useful in the preparation of the reports and proposals to be submitted to the council.[18]

From the aforesaid legal opinion one can deduce that still the competence of the commission to deal with the violations of human rights has been abridged since it could not deal with such a violation without delegation from the Economic and Social Council.

Nevertheless it is after 1966 that the competence of the commission to deal with all violations of human rights has been put in black and white. This competence emanates from council resolution 1102 (XI), 1164 (LXI), General Assembly resolution 2144 (XXI) and Commission on Human Rights Resolutions 2 (XXII), 8 and 9 (XXIII). It is necessary to discuss these resolutions briefly.

The economic and social council adopted resolution 1102 (XL) of 4th March, 1966. Under this resolution the council invited the commission on human rights to consider as a matter of importance and urgency the question of the violation of human rights and fundamental freedoms, including policies of racial discrimination and segregation and of apartheid in all countries, with particular reference to colonial and other dependent countries and territories and to submit to the council its recommendations on measures to halt such violation.

On its part, the commission on human rights adopted resolution 2 (XXII) of 25 March 1966 In response to the resolution 1102 (XL) of the ECOSOC. In its resolution 2 (XXII) the commission instructed the sub-commission on prevention of discrimination and protection of minorities "to examine all relevant United Nationsmaterials", and to submit to the commission such recommendations or comments as it considered appropriate. In part B. para 1 of the same resolution, the commission informed the ECOSOC that, in order to deal completely with the question of violations of human rights and fundamental freedoms in all countries, it will be necessary for the commission to consider fully the means by which it may be more "fully informed" of violations of human rights. The

ECOSOC decision of the commission under revolution 1164 (LXI) of 5th August 1966.

Based on the recommendation of the economic and social council, the General assembly adopted resolution 2144 (XXI) of 26 October 1966 in which it invited the ECOSOC and the commission to give immediate consideration to ways and means of "improving the capacity of the UN" to put a stop to violations of human rights wherever they might occur.

To sum up it was after 1966 that wide competence of the commission has been assumed and the commission became capable of dealing with violations of human rights and fundamental freedoms.

The Shortcomings of 1235 Procedure and the Thematic Procedures

There are some weaknesses related to the application of the 1235 procedure. Among them the commission's once in a year meeting is one in a sense that it resulted the slow, cumbersome situation. There is no effective and immediate sanction under this procedure.[19]

The ineffectiveness of the 1235 procedure partly resulted in 1970's the evolution of various "thematic procedures. These procedures were various in forms depending on the nature of the mission. The working group on informed or involuntary disappearances, was established in 1980 to deal with the then situation in Argentina and Chile. In 1982 special rapporteur on summary or arbitrary executions was appointed.[20]

In 1985, after the convention against torture has been adopted a special rapporteur on torture[21] aid the special rapporteur on religious intolerance was appointed in 1916, and so on.

It has been said that "the commission's special rapporteurs, working groups and other "thematic mechanisms can significantly affect states behaviour, making them the commission's most important tools.[22]

In 1995 there have been notable reports' mentioning of which is necessary here. These are:

- The report of the special rapporteur on torture (Nigel Rodley) on his visits to prisons in Russia at the invitation of Russian authorities, which highlights extreme overcrowding and other harsh conditions.[23]

- The report of the working group on arbitrary detention (chaired by Louis Joinet) on its visit to Vietnam, working group's first such site visits, which followed Vietnam's first invitation to a UN human rights mechanism.[24]
- A joint report by the special rapporteurs on torture and summary or arbitrary executions (Bacre Waly Ndiaye) on Colombia[25],and
- A special report on a mission to Indonesia and east Timor by the special rapporteur on summary and arbitrary executions.[26]

Moreover, the commission in 1995 prolonged the mandates of several important thematic mechanisms for further three year terms. These included the special rapporteurs on religions intolerance (Abdelfattor Amor) on torture, on summary and arbitrary executions, on the sore of children, the working group and disappearances and the secretary generals representative on internally displaced persons.[27]

As compared to the 1503 and 1235 procedures the thematic procedures have been effective regarding the fact-finding function the large number of visit being done enabled the commission to have more necessary informations. The mechanism under the thematic procedure is better developed and more advanced than the country-specific procedures under resolution 1235. The mission of the special groups and rappourters have been "well prepared, their co-operation with NGO's and other sources more comparative and they have demonstrated a greater willingness to tackle some of the structural dimensions of the problems with which they are dealing. However, the procedure does not escape from criticism for there remain many other important issues that are not being accorded comparable attention and they do not succeed in putting much pressure upon individual countries.[28]

The efficiency of the thematic procedures in selected countries does not mean there is fair and unbiased scrutiny.

The commission has been challenged for its failure to see all countries, especially the powerful nations, in the process of identifying countries that deserve to be targeted under the 1235 as well as the thematic procedures. This problem was raised during the commission's fifty-first session which was held from January 30 to March 10, 1995 and the session addressed situations involving three permanent members of the security council (China, Russia and USA).[29]

To sum up, the UN commission on human rights role in relation to dealing with specific human rights violations has been developing from time to time. Although the commission failed to assume this role during the first phase i.e. 1946-1966, now it reached to the present scenario under which the thematic procedures play a significant role in relation to the violation of human right in various countries of the world.

Other Functions of the Commission

The role of the commission is developing from time to time to meet the evolving contemporary questions of human rights. Among them the advisory function to the assembly as well as ECOSOC, carrying out educational programs as to human rights, providing public informations etc are available.

In some cases the commission contributes as a technical advisory body to the General Assembly as well as member states on a limited range of issues. This includes assistance to governments in promoting and safeguarding the rights of women, in eliminating racial discrimination, in protecting minorities, and in promoting freedom of information. Several forms of assistance are authorized under the program: seminars, regional training courses, fellowships and the advisory services of experts.[30]

Sponsoring studies and seminars on specific human rights topics is the other meaningful contribution of the commission. Among the more recent of the seminars, two in particular stand out as having significant contributions. They are the 1978 Geneva world-wide seminar on National and Local Institutions for the promotion and protection of human rights, which gave a major push to initiatives to establish human rights commissions and the like at the country level, and the 1979 Monrovia regional seminar on the establishment of regional commissions with special reference to Africa, which eventually led to the adoption of the African Charter on human and people's Rights.

Generally, the UN commission on human rights has a great contribution on the implementation if international human right norms.

> The commission is the nearest approach to permanent machinery for the supervision of the problem of protection of human rights.[31] The Commission can be treated as universal because the scope of the remedy available under it is wider than that available under optional protocot to International Covenant on Civil and Political rights. The individual communication system mentioned in the Human Rights Commission is available to individuals of all meamber states of the U.N. While under optional Protocal it is available only to the individuals of state parties of the civil covenant which are parties to optional protocol.

THE EUROPEAN COMMISSION OF HUMAN RIGHTS

The European Convention on Human Rights of 1950, which is named as formally entitled Convention for the protection of Human Rights and fundamental freedoms, sets up the European commission of Human rights alongside the European Court of human rights.[32]

The commission has an intermediate position in the system of European human rights law because it acts both as a protector of the judicial function and is an international institution directly accessible to individuals in their complaint of human rights violations.[33]

The commission accomplishes the functions of considering the admissibility of applications. It also attempt to facilitate a friendly settlement of the complaints it declares admissible and it presents a report and transfer the complaints to the court or Committee of Ministers if no friendly settlement is reached.

Furthermore, providing delegates for hearings before the court is the act to be observed by it.[34]

This part of the chapter is meant to see the various roles of the European Commission of Human rights in implementation of international as well as regional human right norms.

Composition of the Commission

According to Art. 20 of European convention on human rights, here after referred ECHR, the commission consists of a number of members equal to that of the contracting parties. The members of the commission are elected by the committee of Ministers by an absolute majority of votes, from a list of names drawn up by the Bureau of the consultative Assembly.[35] Candidates are needed to be of high-moral character and must possess the qualifications required for appointment to high judicial office or be persons of necessary competence in national or international law.[36] The members of the commission are elected for a period of six years. They may be re-elected.[37]

Members of the commission shall sit on the commission in their individual capacity.[38] As far as the practice is concerned the election of government officials has generally not been regarded as appropriate and most members of the commission hold independent judicial or academic legal appointments in their own countries.[39] This ensures the autonomy and neutrality, to some extent, of the commission from the government intervention. No two members of the commission may be nationals of the same state.[40]

The commission meets regularly ordinarily for periodic two weeks sessions. According to rule 15 of the Rules of procedure, it must meet for at least sixteen weeks in each year. For examples in 1992, with the press of considerable business, the commission held eight sessions.[41] Also in 1994 it held eight sessions amounting in total to sixteen session week and 9, 968 individual communications were received among which 2, 944 were registered and 2, 173 were disposed of.[42]

The work of the commission is part-time. Because of this part-time work and its heavy case load, important role is vested upon the commission's secretariat. According to Art. 37 of the convention secretariat, of the commission is provided by the Secretary General of the Council of Europe. Many of the commissioners are law professors and others are already retired from government, judicial or university employment. For example in 1994 the Commission was assisted by an establishment of 49 lawyers 36 administrative assistants and four translators.

The secretariat is bestowed with the main functions of conducting correspondence with applicants and governments, organizing the commissions sessions, preparing cases for examination, advising the commission on questions of national law and the law of the Convention, and assisting members of the commission in the drafting of its decisions and reports.[43]

According to Art. 20, as amended by protocol 8 of March 19, 1955, the commission may set up chambers composed of at least seven members to examine the admissibility of individual application which can be dealt with on the basis of established case-law or which raise no serious question of interpretation or application of the convention. According to Rule 49 of the Rules of Procedure of the European Commission of Human rights the members of the commission elected in respect of the respondent state is entitled to be a member of a chamber to which the individual application is referred.

According to the above protocol (Protocol 8) the commission may also set up committees composed of at least three members which can, if unanimous, declare application to be inadmissible or strike such applications from its list of cases. A chamber or a committee may at any time relinquish jurisdiction in favour of the plenary Commission. The plenary Commission has power to refer cases to either a chamber or a committee. There has been two chambers and six committees established and their efficient functioning is indispensable as a means of managing the over burden work of the commission.

Procedures before the Commission

Complaints about violations of the human rights protected by the convention are sent first to the commission. Art. 24 of the convention states: "Any High Contracting Party may refer to the Commission through the Secretary General of the Council of Europe, any alleged breach of the provisions of the convention by another High Contracting Party" from Art. 24 of the convention it is clear that it is only the States can refer to the commission, the existence of alleged violations of the provisions of the convention.

It is obvious that the object of the agreement is to protect not states but individuals who are the real party in interest. This is not taken into account, or purposely ignored during the signature of the convention. The reality is that during the negotiations a difference of opinion arise as to the desirability of including the right of individual petition, and the contracting parties expressed their fear that this might easily lead to abuse, particularly in the interest of subversive propaganda.[44] To avoid this danger express provisions were added to the effect that the commission would not entertain petitions which were anonymous manifestly ill-founded, or an abuse of the right of petition.[45] But as to objections to the right of individual petition the Committee of Ministers in August 1950 was unable to reach agreement in the right of individuals to seek a direct remedy. As a compromise solution agreed to make the right optional, that is to say, subject to an express declaration on the part of the government concerned that it recognizes the competence of the commission to receive petitions from individuals. Even for this procedure to be applied it was laid down that this procedure would only come into effect when six governments had made such declarations. Accordingly this number was achieved by 5th July, 1995, when the declarations have been made by Sweden, Ireland, Denmark, Iceland, the Federal Republic of Germany and Belgium.[46]

As far as the reference of petitions is concerned it will be worthmentioning to see Art. 25 of the Convention. Art. 25 sates:

1. The commission may receive petitions addressed to the Secretary General of the Council of Europe from any person, non-governmental organization or group

of individuals claiming to be the victim of a violation by one of the high contracting parties of the rights set forth in this convention, provided that the high contracting party against which the complaint has been lodged has declared that it recognizes the competence of the commission to receive such petitions. Those of the high contracting parties which have such a declaration undertake not to hinder in any way the effective exercise of this right.

2. Such declarations may be made for a specific period.
3. The declarations shall be deposited with the secretary general of the council of Europe who shall transmit copies thereof to the high contracting parties and publish them.
4. The commission shall only exercise the powers provided for in this article when at least six high contracting parties are bound by declarations made in accordance with the preceding paragraphs.

The commission became legally competent to receive individual petitions in accordance with Art 25 in 1955. By 25 July, 1994, all 30 of the then parties to the convention has agreed to recognize the admissibility of private petitions. Art 25 should be understood as excluding from the right of petition only to governmental bodies. Their rights of petition are protected only in case of infringement by other states under Art 24 which permits any contracting state to complaint about the conduct of any other contracting states, regardless of the nationality of the injured individual unlike to the ICS there is no requirement that a private party only be protected by that person's own national state.[47]

Art. 25 of the European convention "demonstrate beyond any shadow of doubt that international law has developed to a point where an individual not only has rights under international law but can himself bring a case before an international organ, even against his own government."[48] From this one can envisage the effective implementation of human right norms under the European convention.

Admissibility of Petition

In order to understand the conditions of admissibility of an application to the commission it is pertinent to see some provisions from the convention.

Exhaustion of Domestic Remedy

According to Art. 26 the commission may only deal with the matter after all domestic remedies have been exhausted, according to the generally recognized rules of international law, and within a period of six months from the date on which the final decision was taken.

Exhaustion of the effective local remedies available has its origin under general international law in claims brought by a state for wrongs to its nationals. Under the general principles of international law there are certain principles formulated regarding the local remedies rule. These are:

(a) A local remedy is not to be regarded as adequate and need not be resorted to if the municipal courts are not in a position to award compensation or damages;

(b) A claimant is not required to exhaust justice if there is no justice to exhaust; for example, where the supreme judicial tribunal is under the control of the executive organ responsible for the illegal act, or where an act of the legislative organ has caused the injury suffered;

(c) Where the injury is due to an executive act of the government as such, which is clearly not subject to the jurisdiction of the municipal courts, the injured foreign citizens are not required to exhaust local remedies;

(d) States may waive the condition that local remedies should be exhausted, although it is not clear whether an agreement between the disputant states to arbitrate the relevant issues will of itself operate as implied waiver.[49]

Taking into consideration the local remedies rule the commission has stated that the rule requiring the exhaustion of domestic remedies as a condition of the presentation of an international claim is founded upon the principle that the respondent state must first have an opportunity to redress by its own means within the frame work of its own domestic legal system the wrong alleged to have been done to the individual.[50] Also the main object of the rule is to protect the domestic legal system of the contracting states.

In one case[51] it has been stated that the domestic remedies rule applies also to inter-state applications under Art. 24, however the commission has recognized that the rule has only a limited application in inter-state cases. It applies where the case is concerned with violations of the rights of particular individuals. The rule of exhaustion of domestic remedies does not apply where the nature of the application is to determine the compatibility with the convention of legislative measures and administrative practices in general. In such a case the applicant government is required only to show by means of substantial evidence that the treatment complained of constitutes an administrative practice.

The commission has extended the above principles established in the inter-state cases to applications from individuals, if the complaint is regarding violations of the convention arising from administrative practices. In such cases the applicant is not expected to exhaust domestic remedies, because any judicial action in the national courts may not be effective and adequate to challenge the administrative practice. In one case[52] the commission concluded at the admissibility phase that the applicants who complained of ill-treatment while detained in Northern Ireland were victims of administrative practices and need not exhaust domestic remedies. The commission said:

> The domestic remedies rule does not apply to this part of the present applications – the commission finds that the applicants' complaint in this respect raises issues of law and fact whose determination should depend upon an examination of the merits of the case.[53]

The domestic remedies rule requires that the complaint should have been brought before the appropriate judicial or administrative authorities and should have been taken to the highest instance available. Moreover it is not sufficient that applicants take their cases before the domestic courts of appeal or other authorities. They must have raised before them, the particular complaints which they wish to raise before the commission. If they raise only some of their complaints, only those will be admissible.[54]

The other procedural rule prescribed under Art 26 is a period of limitation i.e. an application is inadmissible if it is not brought within six months from the date on which the final decision was taken. In one case[55] the commission stated that:

> "the two rules contained in Art. 26 ... are closely interrelated, since not only are they combined in the same Article but they are also expressed in a single sentence whose grammatical construction implies such correlation;...the term 'final decision', therefore in Art 26 refers exclusively to the final decision concerned in the exhaustion of all domestic remedies ... so that the six months period is operative only in this context."

In relation to this rule of a strict period of limitation there are some principles developed by the practice of the commission. It is the introduction of the application rather than its formal registration as an application under Art 25 which must occur within the six months.[56]

The time starts running from the moment when the applicant is aware of the act or decision of which he or she complains[57] Where no domestic remedies are available the six months period runs from the date of the act alleged to constitute the violation of the convention. Where it concerns a continuing situation, time runs from the end of the situation, but as long as the situation continues, the six months rule cannot bite.[58] Where domestic remedies are available, the period of six months runs from the date of the final domestic decision after effective and sufficient domestic remedies have been used.[59]

Incompatible and Ill-founded Complaints

Article 27(2) of the convention (Art 35(3) as modified by protocol II) declares that "the court shall declare inadmissible any individual applications submitted under Art. 34 which it considers incompatible with the provisions of the convention or the protocols thereto, manifestly (1) founded, or an abuse of the right of application".

This admissibility requirement is to limit that the commission cannot deal with complaints concerning rights not covered by the convention. It is not allowed to the commission to deal with a complaint, which is beyond the subject-matter covered by the convention.

On the other hand, Art 27(2) of the convention (Art 35(3)) as modified by protocol ii) requires the commission to reject as inadmissible an application which is 'manifestly illfounded'.

It has been said that the requirement that an application should not be manifestly ill-founded differs from all other conditions of admissibility in that it relates not to form but to substance; it goes to the merits of the case. Here it is necessary to create a distinction between 'manifestly ill-founded' and 'incompatibility'. A complaint is incompatible if it is altogether outside the scope of the convention, so that there is no possibility of going into the merits of the case. A complaint is manifestly ill-found if a preliminary examination of the merits shows that there is no need for any further such examination.[60] However there is no logical criterion for distinguishing the two.

The term "ill-founded" is also very difficult to put in a clear manner. This may be left to the discretionary power of the commission. In *Pataki v. Austria*[61] the commission stated the principle that "an application should be declared inadmissible as being manifestly ill-founded only when a preliminary examination does not disclose any appearance of a violation of the convention"; but its application of this principle has not always been satisfactory. The other possible problem is that the commission may not go in detail into the merits and the result will be devastating for the complainant.

Other Requirements

As far as the admissibility requirement is concerned there are other points to be seen in order to allow the admissibility. To list these remaining conditions: the respondent government must be a high contracting party-it is clear from articles 24 and 25 that an application may be brought only against a state which has ratified the convention, and in the case of Art. 25 which has recognized the competence of the commission. Applications must be directed against states or agents of states; there is no right of action under the convention against individuals acting in their personal capacities. Secondly, the application must not be brought before-Art. 27(l)(b) provides that an application under Art. 25 is inadmissible if it "is substantially the same as a matter which has already been examined by the commission or has already been submitted to another procedure of international investigation or settlement and if it contains no relevant new information". Thirdly, the application must be duly signed-Art. 27(1)(a) requires that applicants are identified and anonymous applications cannot be entertained. Lastly, there must not be abuse of the right of petition-Art. 27(2) clearly prohibits the admissibility of application because of an abuse of the right of application. Abuse of the right of petition may arise where the applicant makes improper use of the procedural rights under Art. 25 to bring the complaint before the commission.

The above mentioned points are procedural requirements to determine the admissibility of the petition. From the number of cases brought before the commission one can appreciate the important role being played by the commission in relation to implementation of human right norms. For example, in 1983 the commission opened some 3,150 provisional files' among them 499 formally registered, 407 dismissed and 29 applications merely declared admissible.[62] By 1989 the number of provisional files had grown to 4,900 while the number of registered applications reached 1,445; the cases declared inadmissible or struck off the list were .1,243- and those declared were in total 95.[63]

In its first 35 years from 1955 to 1989, the commission registered some 15,911 applications, of which only 12 come from states, the balance being submitted by individuals, and declared some 670 applications admissible.[64]

Generally, however strict procedural requirements are being followed by the commission, it is working as an efficient organ under the European convention.

Procedures After Admissibility

The procedures to be taken by the commission after admissibility of the case can be divided into three main parts. i.e. interim measures of protection; examination of the merits, and friendly settlement. Apart from these three matters the rest will be the duty of the European court of Human Rights, if no friendly settlement has been reached and the case is referred to the court.

Interim Measures of Protection

It is obvious that investigation of the merits of the case and determination of the application may take long period of time. During this time the applicant may be in danger. To avoid such a problem there must be some immediate protection to the individual. Unfortunately the European convention is silent about such interim measures of protection that the loophole has been created.

> In order to fill this lacuna., the commission has included a provision in its Rules of Procedure. Rule 36 provides:
>
> The commission or, where it is not in session, the president may indicate to the parties any interim measures the adoption of which seems, desirable in the interest of the parties or the proper conduct of the proceedings before it.

The thing to be noted here is that this rule is procedural, not part of the substantive provisions of the convention so that some states do not give due emphasis to it. For example in Cruz Varas V. Sweden[65] the commission requested Sweden under rule 36 to take certain interim measures but Sweden ignored the request and deported the applicant to Chile. When dealing the case, the court was requested to rule this as a violation of the convention, but the court did not accept this request.

Generally, the interim measure of the commission can orders effective only when they are accepted by the states. Refusal to comply is only a procedural irregularity not violation of the convention. Therefore, there must be amendment to the effect that can impose mandatory obligation over the high contracting parties to accept the interim measures order by the commission.

Examination of the Merits

If the commission accepts a petition, it will proceed, under Art. 28, to an examination of merits of the case. Art. 28(l)(a) of the convention provides: "it shall, with a view to ascertaining the facts, undertake together with the representatives of the parties an examination of the petition and if need be, an investigation, for the effective conduct of which the states concerned shall furnish all necessary facilities, after an exchange of views with the commission".

During examination of the case the task of fact-finding by the commission is very important because it is also necessary for the later decision of both the court and the committee of ministries. For this purpose the commission can carry out all procedural matters like exchange of written pleadings and oral arguments, calling witnesses, or any other measures which it considers necessary.

Friendly Settlement

Article 28(1)(b) of the convention provides: "it shall place itself at the disposal of the parties concerned with a view to securing a friendly settlement of the matter on the basis of respect for human rights as defined in this convention".[66]

This provision is supportive of Art. 33(l) of the United Nations Charter which puts conciliation as one of the traditional methods of peaceful settlement of international disputes. A friendly settlement of dispute under Art. 28(l)(b) depends on the agreement between the parties and on the basis of respect for human rights as defined in the covention.

If the commission succeeds in effecting a friendly settlement, it shall prepare a report and send it to the states concerned, to the committee of Ministers and to the secretary general of the council of Europe for publication.[67] On the contrary, if no solution is reached the commission prepares a report which specifies the facts and opinions of the commission to the committee of Ministers and to the state; concerned.[68]

The commission can refer the case to the European court of human rights.[69] If the case is not referred to the court within a period of three months from the date of the transmission of the report to the committee of ministers, the same shall decide by a two thirds majority whether there has been a violation of the convention.[70]

Generally, the European commission on human rights is an efficient organ in implementation of human right principles under the convention. From the above discussion one can clearly see how this multinational institution is operating properly and working efficiently.

INTER-AMERICAN COMMISSION ON HUMAN RIGHTS

New world provides another regional instrument where meaningful action on human rights is being pursued under the auspices of the Organisation of American States (O.A.S.) which operates under a Charter signed at Bagota on 30th April, 1948 which came in force on 13th December, 1951. Although the Declaration of Rights and Duties of man was adopted in 1948 by the Organisation of American States, it is on 22th November, 1969 that the American Convention on Human Rights adopted by the OAS in the Inter-American Specialised Conference on Human Rights. The Convention provides for two organs-the Commission and the Court.

The Inter-American Commission on Human Rights of the Organization of American States was established in 1959. The commission is vested with certain powers and functions regarding protection of human rights enshrined under the international instruments and in the American Convention on Human Rights. The function of the commission include investigation, conciliation, the making of recommendations, and the issuance of reports setting out its findings and conclusions.

Composition

The Inter-American commission on Human Rights is composed of seven members elected from persons of high moral character and recognized competence in the field of human rights.[71] The members are elected in their personal capacity by the General Assembly of the Organization from a candidates proposed by the member States.[72] Each member state may propose up to three candidates from which at least one of the candidates must be a national of a State other than the proposing State.[73]

A term of office for members of the commission is four years. Members may be re-elected only once. No two nationals of the same state may be members of the commission.[74] If vacancies may occur for the reasons other than the normal expiration of term, it shall be assigned by the permanent council of the Organization in accordance with the provisions of the statute of the commission.[75]

Powers of the Commission

Under the American Convention on Human Rights, which entered into force on 18th July, 1978, the commission is authorized:

(a) to develop an awareness of human rights among the people of America;

(b) to make recommendations to the government of the member States for the adoption of progressive measures in favour of human rights;

(c) to prepare studies and reports;

(d) to request the governments of member states to supply it with information on the measures adopted by them in matters of human rights;

(e) to respond, through the General Secretariat of the Organization of American States, to inquiries made by the member States on matters related to human rights and, within the limits of its possibilities, to provide these States with the advisory services they request;

(f) to take action on petitions and other communications under the provisions of the convention: and

(g) to submit an annual report to the General Assembly of the Organization of American States.[76]

- From the above powers there is no clear authorization to examine petitions. However, the commission conducts detailed investigations and publicizes serious violations, thus pressuring member states to respect the human rights set forth in the American Declaration.[77]
- The mandate of the inter-American Human rights commission expanded after 1966 when the second special Inter-American Conference (Second SIAC), which was held in RIO de Janerio, Brazil, passed Resolution XXII, After the same resolution for the first time the Commission was officially empowered to examine petitions submitted to it. Moreover, the resolution increased the commission's authority to seek information from and make recommendations to member governments.
- On the other hand the Second Special Inter-American Conference imposed certain restrictions on the commission. It directed the commission:

1. to attend primarily to political rights, thereby diminishing the Commissions mandate to protect economic, social and cultural rights. Here paragraph two of resolution XXII directs the Commission to give special attention to the following rights specified in the American Declaration:
   - Life, liberty and personal security,
   - Equality before the law,
   - Religious freedom, freedom of investigation, opinion, expression, and dissemination, fair trial, protection from arbitrary arrest and due process of law.

2. to ascertain, before examining petitions, whether domestic remedies had been fully exhausted.[78]

   - The 1967 revision of the OAS Charter made the commission an organ of the Organization of American States and directed the commission for the first time to "protect" as well as "promote" human rights.[79] The Commission has jurisdiction over all member states, whether or not they ratify the American Convention on Human Rights Generally, the power and function of the Commission has been strengthen after the 1965 second Special Inter-American Conference and reached to the present situation.

Procedure of Implementation

- According to Article 42 of the Convention, States parties transmit to the commission copies of the reports that they submit annually to the Executive Committee of the Inter-American Economic and Social Council and the Inter-American Council for Education, Science and Culture. The role of the Commission with respect to such reports is to "watch over the promotion of human rights implicit in the economic, social, educational, scientific and cultural standards set forth in the charter of the organization of American States.[80]
- In case of inter-state complaints, any state party to the Convention may declare its acceptance of the jurisdiction of the commission to receive and examine communications in which a State Party alleges that another state party has committed a violation of human rights incorporated in the convention. Also such communication must satisfy certain conditions before it is examined by the commission, e.g., local remedies have been exhausted, has been filed within six months of the notification of final judgment, and the matter is not pending before another international procedure for settlement.[81]
- According to Article 44 of the convention the right to individual petition is a compulsory technique whereby any

person, or group of persons or any non-governmental entity legally recognized in one or more member states of the Organization may lodge petitions with the commission. The petition must contain the name, nationality, profession domicile and signature of the petitoner.

The conditions for the inadmissibility of the petition stated under the American convention on Human Rights are some quite similar to that of the European Convention. In the American case conditions of exhaustion of local remedies and filing of petition within six months of final judgement will not apply when the domestic legislation of the state party does not afford due process or access to remedies or there has been unwarranted delay in rendering final judgment.[82]

Article 46 of the American Convention on Human Rights specify the conditions of admissibility as follows:

(1) Admission by the commission of a petition or communication lodged in accordance with Articles 44 or 45 shall be subject to the following requirements:

(a) that the remedies under domestic law have been pursued and exhausted in accordance with generally recognized principles of international law;

(b) that the petition or communication is lodged within a period of six months from the date on which the party alleging violation of his rights was notified of the final judgment.

(c) that the subject of the petition or communication is not pending in another international proceeding for settlement; and

(d) that, in the case of Art. 44, the petition contains the, name, nationality, profession, domicile, and signature of the person or persons or of the legal representative of the entity lodging the petition.

(2) The provisions of paragraphs 1.a and 1.b of this article shall not be applicable when:

(a) the domestic legislation of the state concerned does not afford due process of law for the protection of the right or rights that have allegedly been violated;

(b) the party alleging violation of his rights has been denied access to the remedies under domestic law or has been prevented from exhausting them; or

(c) there has been unwarranted delay in rendering a final judgment under the aforementioned remedies.

Art. 46 (2) qualifies the requirement of exhaustion of domestic remedies. This makes the American Convention more progressive than the European Convention since the later has no this kind of provision which can protect the individual from the unnecessary procedure of domestic law.

Once the commission declares the inter-state communication or the individual petition admissible, it requests information from the concerned government and shall furnish that government a transcript of the pertinent portions of the petition or communication. After receiving the information it shall examine the case as to whether the grounds for the petition or communication still exist and, if they do not, the commission shall order the record to be closed. If no record has been closed, it shall examine the matter set forth in the petition or communication in order to varify the facts. If necessary it can also carry out investigation for effective conduct of which it has requested and the states concerned shall furnish to it, all necessary facilities. After this the commission shall place itself at the disposal of the parties concerned with a view to reaching a friendly settlement of the matter.[83]

- If the Commission succeeds in securing a friendly settlement, it shall draw up a report, which shall be transmitted to the petitioner, to the states parties to the convention and to the Secretary General of the Organization of American States for Publication.[84] Here the publication is important to create public awareness to the matter.

If a friendly settlement is not reached, the commission shall draw up a report setting forth the facts and stating its conclusions to the states concerned.[85] If, within a period of three months from the date of the transmittal of the report of the commission to the states concerned, the matter has not either been settled or submitted by the commission or by the state concerned to the court, the commission may set forth its opinion and conclusions concerning the question submitted for its consideration. Furthermore, the commission shall make pertinent recommendations and shall prescribe a period within which the state is to take the measures. On expiry of this period, the commission reviews the steps taken by the state and decides whether to publish its report or not.[86]

A perusal of the above provisions shows that that the commission performs two main functions: (i) the general education function i.e. to develop an awareness of human rights among the people of America; and (ii) the administrative-cum-judicial functions, namely to make recommendations to the governments of member states, to prepare reports, making requesting governments to furnish information, rendering advisory services, considering and deciding individual petitions and to submit annual report to the General Assembly.[87]

To sum up the power given and functions bestowed on the Inter-American Commission on Human Rights to implement the Human Rights norms enshrined under the Convention must be exercised in a manner to ensure the mandatory technique of individual petitions. The powers given to the commission to examine the complaints by the states parties or the individuals are the manifestation of the confidence of states over the commission. More work is expected from this three decades old commission.

AFRICAN COMMISSION ON HUMAN AND PEOPLES' RIGHTS

The African Charter on Human and Peoples' Rights of 1981 established, an African Commission on Human and Peoples' Rights, hereinafter called the Commission, within the Organization of African Unity to promote human and peoples' rights and ensure their protection in Africa.

Intensified and elevated human right violation is common in most African Countries. Therefore the need for effective mechanism for the promotion and protection of human rights is not questionable.

The African Charter on Human and Peoples' Rights, hereinafter called the African Charter, also claims for the establishment of national human rights institutions, as envisaged by Article 26 of the African Charter. Art. 26 provides.

> States parties to the present Charter shall have the duty to guarantee the independence of the Courts and shall allow the establishment and improvement of appropriate national institutions entrusted with the promotion and protection of the rights and freedoms guaranteed by the present Charter.

In Africa the period of 1980's has been characterized as the time when official bodies charged with promoting or protecting human rights have been established in Zimbabwe, Swaziland, Uganda, Togo, Zaire, Benin, The Gambia, Namibia, Equatorial Guinea, Cameroon and Gabon. These institutions are different in their operation. For example, the Zimbabwean Ombudsman cannot investigate alleged human rights violations by the security forces, whereas the Ugandan Inspector General of Government can. The Human Rights institutions in Africa generally follow one of three different models[88].

> (i) "Ombudsman – The model of the Swedish Ombudsman has been the one most widely used in Commonwealth Africa. However, African Ombudsman differ in important respects from the Swedish original; for example, most are answerable to the head of state rather than to the legislature. There are also significant differences between them. Tanzania, Nigeria and Zambia have multi-member institutions, while Ghana, Mauritius, and Zimbabwe have individuals, the institutions in Uganda and Namibia have broader mandates and investigative powers than many of their counterparts. The function of Ombudsman is almost exclusively investigative, they have little or no role in human rights promotion."

(ii) "National Commission—Togo, Benin and Cameroon have all adopted a similar model of a multi-member national commission with a mandate to investigate allegations of human rights abuse, advise the government on human right matters and promote awareness of human rights in the country at large."

(iii) "Government Department—The Department des Droits et des libert'es du citoyen in Zaire provides the modes for this. Gabon appears to be following a similar path. The role of the Zairian Department, headed by a State Commissioner, has been to investigate allegations of abuse, but also to represent the government at international human rights forums."

Composition of the African Commission on Human and Peoples' Rights

- The Commission is composed of eleven members chosen from amongst African personalities of the highest reputation, high morality, integrity, impartiality and competence in matters of human and peoples' rights; due emphasis is given to persons having legal experience. The members serve in their personal capacity not in a representative capacity.[88a] Moreover, no two or more nationals of the same state may be a member of the Commission at a time.[89]

The manner of election is that by secret ballot by the Assembly of Heads of state and Government, from a list of persons nominated by the member States of the Charter.[90] Each high contracting party can nominate not more than two candidates of which one may not be a national of the state nominating.[91]

The term of office of the members is six year period and the member is eligible for re-election.[92] In case of death or resignation of a member of the commission, the Chairman of the Commission shall inform the Secretary General of the OAU and the later declares the Seat Vacant from the date of death or resignation. The seat can be also vacant if a member has stopped discharging his duties for only reason other than a temporary absence by the unanimous opinion of other members of the Commission. In the case of the above mentioned vacancies the Assembly of Heads of State and Government shall replace the member whose seat become vacant.[93]

The secretary of the commission is appointed by the Secretary General of the Organization of African Unity[94] whereas the Chairman and Vice Chairman shall be elected by the Commission for a period of two years and they are eligible for re-election.[95] Members of the Commission have the right to enjoy diplomatic privileges and immunities provided for in the General Convention on the Privileges and Immunities of the Organization of African Unity.[96] This contributes for the effective and fearless work of the Commission. Generally the Charter deals with detail provisions regarding the composition of the commission than the previous two Convention i.e. the European Convention and the Inter-American Convention on Human Rights.

Power and Functions

1. The commission is basically bestowed with the power of promoting educational activities and facilitating human right protections in Africa. Articles 45 of the African Charter provides as follows:
   (a) to collect documents, undertake studies and researches on African problems in the field of human and peoples' rights, organize seminars, symposia and conferences, disseminate information, encourage national and local institutions concerned with human and peoples' rights and should the case arise, give its views or make recommendations to Governments.
   (b) to formulate and lay down, principles and rules aimed at solving legal problems relating to human and peoples' rights and fundamental freedoms upon which African Governments may base their legislations.
   (c) to co-operate with other African and international institutions concerned with the promotion and protection of human and peoples' rights.

2. Ensure the protection of human and peoples' rights under conditions laid down by the present Charter.
3. Interpret all the provisions of the present charter at the request of a state party, an institution of the OAU or an African Organization recognized by the OAU.
4. Perform any other tasks which may be entrusted to it by the Assembly of Heads of State and Government.

According to Art. 45 (3) the Commission is authorized to interpret all provisions of the African charter. It seems the absence of the court structure under the charter that necessitated to give this power to the Commission. As we have seen in previous sections both the Inter-American and the European Conventions established the human rights court structure but not the African one.

Procedure of Implementation

The main procedures of communication to the commission under the charter can be divided into two i.e. Communication From States and Other Communication.

In case of communication from states a High contracting party which believes that the other party has violated the provisions of the Charter may submit a written communication to the violating state. This communication should be addressed to the Secretary General of the OAU and to the Chairman of the Commission and the state of which the communication is addressed shall respond within three months of the receipt of the communication shall give written explanation or statement elucidating the matter.[97] If no issue is settled within three months to the satisfaction of the two states involved either state have the right to submit the matter to the commsioni.[98] Before dealing with the matter the commission must be sure that all existing local remedies have been exhausted, unless it is obvious to the commission that the procedure of achieving these remedies would be prolonged.[99] After obtaining all necessary and sufficient information and after having tried all appropriate means to securing a friendly settlement the commission shall prepare a report stating the facts and its findings to the states concerned and to the Assembly of Heads of states and Government.[100] Doing this the commission may make such recommendations as it deems useful.[101] Apart from submitting its activity report to each ordinary session of the Assembly of Heads of State and Governments, it has not the right to publish its findings unless it is authorized by the Assembly of Heads of State and Government. This, possibly, can reduce the Public awareness of the existence of human right violation. Therefore, there must be amendment to this effect and the commission shall publish its findings without the authorization of the Heads of States and Governments.

In case of other Communications, under article 55-59 of the Charter, the Commission receives before each session a list of communications other than those from States Parties and decides which of them to consider. Such communications are considered if a simple majority of members of the commission decide to do so.[102] There are some requirements to be fulfilled before consideration of the communication other than those of states parties to the charter. To this effect Art. 56 states that such communications shall be considered if they:

1. indicate their authors even if the latter request anonymity;
2. are compatible with the charter of the Organization of African Unity or with the Charter;
3. are not written in disparaging or insulting language;
4. are not based exclusively on news disseminated through the mass media;
5. are sent after exhausting local remedies, if any, unless it is obvious that this procedure is unduly prolonged;
6. are submitted within a reasonable period of time;
7. do not deal with cases which have been settled by these states involved.

After communication if there are special cases which reveals the existence of a continuous violations of human and peoples rights, the commission draws the attention of the Assembly of Heads of State and Government to these special cases.[103] Whatever measures taken shall remain confidential unless otherwise is decided by the Assembly of Heads of State and Governmet.[104] Even the report can be published upon the decision and if it has been considered by the Assembly of Heads of State and Government.

A prominent characteristics of the African Charter which differentates it from other regional convention is that it embodies a number of duties. Enumeration of duties is an appreciable step but there is no specific provision for their enforcement. Secondly, the implementation machinery of human rights under the African charter is weak when we compare to the European Convention and the Inter-American Convention. This is not to undermine the role that is being played by the African Commission on human and peoples' right. It has great contribution for the protection and promotion of Human Rights in Africa. It is to be noted that European Convention is the most effective in promoting and implementing international human rights norms.

NOTES

1. Philip Alston (ed), The UN and Human Rights: A Critical Appraisal (1995) p. 126.
2. Abdulrahim P. Vijapur, The UN at Fifty: Studies in Human Rights, (1996) p. 64.
3. US Dept. of State, *Bulletin* (1946), XIII 5.
4. Alston, 'The U.N. and Human Rights' A Critical Appraisal (1995) p. 128.
5. f.n. at p. 131
6. Paras Diwan, Human Rights and the Law: Universal and Indian (1998), p. 31.
7. Alston, 'The U.N. and Human Rights' (1995) p. 132-134
8. Alston, 'The U.N. and Human Rights' (1995) p. 128.
9. Philip, 'The UN and Human Rights: A Critical Apparisal', (1995) p. 139.
10. Louterpach, International Law and Human Rights (1950) p. 244-51.

11. Schwetb and Alstan "The Principal Institutions and other Bodies Founded under the Charter", in Vasak and Alston (eds), International Dimensions of Human Rights, (1982), p. 271-72.
12. Zijdwijk, Petitioning the United Nations. P. 14.
13. Alston (ed) Supra note 1, p. 141.
14. Zuijdwijk, Petitioning the United Nations, p. 4
15. Philip, 'The UN and Human Rights: A Critical Apparisal', (1995) p. 143-145.
16. CHR Res. 8 (XXIII) (1967).
17. Alston, 'The U.N. and Human Rights' (1995) p. 157-159
18. B.G. Ramcharon, The Principles of legality in International Human Rights Institutions: Selected Legal Opinions (1997) p. 23-26.
19. Alston, 'The U.N. and Human Rights' (1995) p. 173.
20. Reports UN. Doc. E/CN. 4/1983/16; E/CN. 4/1984/29 upto E/CN. 4/1991/36.
21. Reports UN. Doc. E/CN. 4/1986/15 upto E/CN. 4/1991/17.
22. John R. Crook "The Fifty-First Session of the UN Commission on Human Rights", *American Journal of International Law,* Vol. 90, No 1, p. 127.
23. UN Doc. E//CN. 4/1995/34/Add. 1.
24. UN Doc. E//CN. 4/1995/31/Add. 4.
25. UN Doc. E//CN. 4/1995/III.
26. UN Doc. E//CN. 4/1995/61/Add. 1.
27. Crook, p. 129.
28. Alston, p. 180-181.
29. Crook, p. 128.
30. Edward Lawson (ed) Encyclopedia of Human Rights (2nd ed), (1969) p. 1484.
31. Jan Brownlie, "Principles of Public International Law" 2nd ed. (1973) p. 554.
32. The European convention on Human Rights, 1950 Art. 19.
33. Kay and Bradley, European Human Rights Law: Text and Materials, (1995), p. 30.

34. Luke Clements, European Human Rights: Taking a case under the convention, (1994), p. 6-7.
35. European Convention, Art. 21.
36. Art. 21 (3) of the European Convention.
37. Art. 22 (1) of the European Convention.
38. Art. 23 of the European Convention.
39. Jacobs and White, The European Convention on Human Rights, 2nd ed. (1996) p. 341.
40. European Convention, Art. 20 (1).
41. Kay and Brodley, European Human Rights Law: Text and Materials, (1995) p. 31.
42. Jacobs and White, The European Convention on Human Rights, (1996) p. 341.
43. See Rule 13 of Rules of procedure of ECHRS.
44. A.H. Robertson, The Law of International Institutions in Europe, (1961), p. 73.
45. European Convention, Art. 27.
46. Robertson, The Law of International Institutions in Europe, (1961) p. 73.
47. Kay and Bradley, European Human Rights Law (1995) p. 33.
48. Robertson, The Law of International Institutions in Europe, (1961) p. 68.
49. J.G. Starke, Introduction to International Law, 10th ed (1989), p. 311.
50. Jacobs and White, Supra note 54, p. 354.
51. App. 788/60, P funders case, Austria v. Italy, 11 Jan, 1961 (1961) 4 year book 116, 146-50.
52. *Donnelly and others v. United Kingdom,* Joined App S. 5577-83/72, 5 Apr. 1973, 16 year book 212.
53. *Donnelly and others v. U.K.,* 43 Collection of decisions, 122 (1973).
54. Kontakt-Information-*Theropie and Hagen v. Austria,* App. 11921/86, 12 Oct. 1988, 57 DR. 81.
55. *De Backer v. Belgium,* App. 214/56, 9 June, 1958 2 year book 214, 242.

56. *X and Y v. Ireland,* App. 8299/78 (1980).
57. *Hilton v. United Kingdom,* App. 12015/86, (1988).
58. *Tite v. France,* App. 11123/84, (1987).
59. *Baier V. Sweden,* App. 11763/85, 1989.
60. Jacobs and White, The European Convention on Human Rights, 2nd ed. (1996) p. 365.
61. App. 569/59(1960)
62. Stock-Taking on the European Convention on Human Rights. The first Thirty Years (1984) p. 312.
63. 1989 Year book of the Europen Convention on Human Rights, 19(1993)
64. 1989 year book at 23, 21.
65. *Cruz Varas v/s. Sweden,* 201 (1992) 14 EHRR 1
66. 201 (1992) 14 EHRR 1
67. European Convention, Art. 30.
68. Art. 31 of the Convention.
69. Art 44 and 48 of the Convention.
70. Art 32 of the Convention.
71. The Inter-American Convention on Human Right of 1969, Art. 34.
72. Art. 35 of the Convention.
73. Art. 36 of the Convention.
74. Art. 37 of the Convention.
75. Art. 38 of the Convention.
76. Lowson, 'Encylopedia of Human Rights' (1969) p. 790-91.
77. Jane A Peddicord, "The American convention on Human Rights: potential Defects and Remedies", *Texas International Law Journal,* Vol. 19, No. 2, p. 141.
78. Jane A Peddicord, "The American convention on Human Rights: potential Defects and Remedies", *Texas International Law Journal,* Vol. 19, No. 2, p. 141.
79. Charter of the Organization of American States, Art. 30, 1948, Art. 112.
80. Lowson, 'Encylopedia of Human Rights' (1969) P. 791.

81. American Convention, Art. 43.
82. Art. 46, of the American Convention.
83. Art. 48 of the American Convention.
84. Art. 49 of the American Convention.
85. Art. 50 of the American Convention.
86. Art. 51 of the American Convention.
87. V.S. Mani, "Regional approaches to the implementation of Human Rights", *IJIL*, Vol. 21 No. 1 (1981) p. 105.
88. Carver and Hunt *"National Human Rights Institutions in Africa"* Official document presented on International Conference on the Establishment of the Ethiopian Human Rights Commission and the Institution of Ombudsman. P. (iv).

88a. *The African Convention and Human and People' Rights*, 1984, Art. 31.

89. Art. 32 of the African Convention.
90. Art. 33 of the African Convention.
91. Art. 34 of the African Convention.
92. Art. 36 of the African Convention.
93. Art. 39 of the African Convention.
94. Art. 41 of the African Convention.
95. African Convention, Art. 42.
96. Art. 43 of the African Convention.
97. Art. 47 of the Convention.
98. Art. 48of the Convention.
99. Art. 50of the Convention.
100. Art. 52of the Convention.
101. Art. 53of the Convention.
102. Art. 55 (2) of the Convention.
103. Art. 58 of the Convention.
104. Art. 59 of the Convention.

4

NATIONAL HUMAN RIGHTS COMMISSION IN INDIA

During the struggle for independence, our freedom fighters raised voices against human rights violations and deprivation of basic civil, political and economic rights at the hands of the foreign ruler. When free India set about the task of preparing a Constitution for self governance, one area on which there was complete unanimity was the subject of fundamental rights. With history of strife emanating from social evils of casteism and communalism, and a large chunk of population engaged in struggle for existence amidst extreme poverty, deprivation, hunger, illiteracy, unemployment and all consequent miseries, it was clear that respect for human rights, not merely in theory, but in practice from the stand point of good governance could be the only lasting solution for guaranteeing peace, tranquillity and equitable development.

Taking cue from the Universal Declaration of Human Rights that became part of the firmament of International law in 1948, as indeed from Constitutions of other great democracies of the World, India adopted her Constitution that assured one and all that it would be a Democratic Republic aiming to secure to all its citizens Justice, Liberty and Equality while promoting dignity of the individual. The Constitution assured Justice not merely in abstract but Justice of broad spectrum covering social, economic and political rights. The liberty guaranteed to the citizens of India has promised to be inclusive of liberty in the matter of thought, expression, belief, faith and worship. Similarly, if not more importantly, the right to equality, grafted as a basic precept of the State Policy, was intended to be not merely of status but of opportunity.

Human Rights movement in the free world reached a landmark when UN General Assembly adopted a resolution in December 1993 to endorse "Paris Principles of 1991" that mooted the idea of establishing institutions designed to provide "guidance and directions" for affording better protection of human rights. In the wake of those developments, India committed to "respect for international law and treaty obligations in the dealings of organized people with one another", enacted the Protection of Human Rights Act, 1993 with a view to bring about greater accountability and strengthen the domino of human rights in the Country.

This Chapter aims to evaluate the role played by the National Human Rights Commission of India, in promoting the human rights. Accordingly, the chapter has been divided into following heads:

1. International Origin of the National Human Rights Commission.
2. Nature of National Human Rights Commission.
3. Protection of Human Rights Act, 1993.
4. Illustrative Cases.
5. Evaluation of the Working of NHRC.

INTERNATIONAL ORIGIN OF THE NATIONAL HUMAN RIGHTS COMMISSION

It is a well known maxim that independent domestic institutions play an important role in ensuring effective implementation of international human rights standards at the national level. National and domestic human rights mechanism can take many forms. They comprise courts, Ombdusman and human rights commissions. The effective protection of human rights requires flexible mechanism that cannot entirely be undertaken within the traditional complaint-oriented court system. Therefore, national Human Rights Commission, with their "complimentary mechanisms" have lately become the much needed "third force" for the protection and promotion of human rights at the national level. Although these institution are created at the state/country level, it is interesting that the United Nations has defined their normative framework, primarily because strengthened institutions can influence national agendas and enhance the effectiveness of the international system for the promotion and protection of the Human Rights. While there has been a recent growth of human rights commission, the United Nations focused attention on them as early as 1946.[1]

During 1960s to 1970s, norms setting in the field of human rights gained momentum. In 1978, the United Nations Commission on Human Rights decided to organise a seminar in order to lay down guidelines for the anatomy and functioning of national institutions. Accordingly a seminar was held in Geneva in September 1978 which approved a set of guidlines with regarding the structure were as under:

(i) They (The institutions) should reflect in their composition wide cross sections of the nation, thereby bringing all parts of the population into the decision making process in regard to human rights.

(ii) They should (in appropriate Cases) have local or regional advisory organs to assist them in discharging their functions.

The guidelines suggested that the functions of these institutions should be:

(i) to act as a source of human rights information for the government and people of the country.

(ii) to assist in educating formation of public opinion and promoting awareness of and respect for human rights.

(iii) to consider, deliberate upon and make recommendations regarding any particular state of affairs that may exist nationally and which the government may wish to refer to them,

(iv) to advise on the questions regarding human rights matter referred to them by the government,

(v) to study and keep under review the status of legislation, judicial decisions and administrative arrangements for the promotion of human rights, and to prepare reports on these matters to the appropriate authorities;

(vi) to perform any other function which the government may wish them to carry out in connection with the duties of the state under those international instruments in the field of human rights to which it is a party.

Subsequently the guidelines were accepted by the commission on Human Rights as well as by the General Assembly. The assembly invited the states to take suitable steps for the establishment of the national institutions for the promotion and protection of human rights, and requested the Secretary-General to submit a detailed report on existing national institution. In 1990, the Commission on Human Rights called for a workshop to be convened which was held in Paris from October 7 to October 9, 1991. It was a significant event in the establishment of the normative framework of national rights institutions. The 'Paris Principles'-"principles relating to the status and functioning of national institutions for the protection and promotion of human rights." Subsequently, the United Nations Commission on Human Rights, the United Nations General Assembly and the Vienna Conference in 1993 endorsed many of the Paris Principles. According to these principles, a national institution should have the following functions:

(i) to submit recommendations, proposals and reports on any matter relating to human rights including legislative and administrative provisions and any situation of violation of human rights to the government, parliament and any other competent body;

(ii) to promote confirmity of national laws and practices with international human rights standards;

(iii) to contribute to the reporting procedure under international instruments;

(iv) to assist in formulating and executing human rights teaching and research programmes and to increase public awareness of human rights through information and education.

(v) to co-operate with the United Nations, regional institutions and national institutions of other countries.

Amnesty International has also come out with guidlines on human rights commission. While Amnesty International emphasizes the important role human rights commission can play in protecting human rights, it rightly points out that these institutions cannot take and must not replace the traditional legal edifice provided by an independent and impartial judiciary.

On the lines of above stated international norms a number of human rights commission have been set up in different parts of the world. These institutions have a very unique role in translating international human rights standards into reality, and giving them a local flavour and acceptability without diluting their essential universal characteristics.[2]

NATURE OF THE NATIONAL HUMAN RIGHTS COMMISSION

The scope of the Paris Principles encompasses a range of forms that national human rights institutions can take. These forms include, but are not limited to, ombudsman and national human rights commissions. Since the work of the ombudsman form of national human rights institutions is restricted to oversight over public officials, in recent years the promotional work of the United Nations as well as the overall international trend of development has concentrated on national human rights commissions. These functions of these institutions include not only providing governments with advice and counsel, but also promoting human rights awareness and advocacy among the general public.

A national human rights commission is a "supplementary national institution" to the already-existing legislative, executive and judicial branches of the government. Given rise in constitutional forms of government among modern states, the normal functioning of the legislative, executive and judicial branches should now include the promotion and protection of human rights as a core objective. Nonetheless, a supplementary human rights institution might also be needed, because in the postwar development of human rights, the rights to which a person was entitled were no longer confined to citizens' rights as guaranteed in national constitutions. The rights of the individual have been extended to the universal rights guaranteed by international human rights law and treaty law. In other words, human rights no longer belong to one country–they are no longer simply a domestic matter, but now the subject of concern and oversight by the international community. The "supplementary" function of national human rights commissions was designed in response to this postwar development, and thus it has both domestic and international aspects.

The Paris Principles stress that national human rights commissions should be both independent and pluralistic. Independence means guarantees of freedom from interference in terms of budget, personnel, and performance of their duties, within the limits set by the constitution and laws of the country. Pluralism means that the composition of national human rights commissions has to reflect the diverse social forces of civil society.

The functions of national human rights commissions include: First, to present ideas, proposals, suggestions and reports to the government, the legislature, and other entities as designated by law; Second, to promote bringing domestic law and its application into accord with international human rights standards; Third, to promote ratification and implementation of international human rights standards; Fourth, to assist in (but not directly participate in the drafting of) national human rights reports required by international human rights conventions; Fifth, to assist in the planning and practice of human rights education and research programs, and work through the media to promote the general public's awareness of human rights issues; Sixth, to cooperate with the United Nations, regional organizations, and other national human rights institutions on human rights issues; Seventh, in cases of human rights violations, to exercise a supplementary quasi-judicial competence in conducting investigations and negotiations.

The above stated functions may be divided into three categories consultative, investigatory and educational. These responsibilites are discharged in a way that is "supplementary" to those discharged by pre-existing government institutions, and that the great majority of work of protecting human rights will be carried out by the legislative, executive, and judicial branches as provided for in the constitution. In a democratic constitutional order, the executive, legislative, and judicial branches should already be carrying out their constitutionally mandated responsibility of protecting human rights, and thus the national human rights commission should perform only a supplementary role. Even so, with the contemporary universalization of human rights, it was not only countries which were still developing in democratic, constitutional terms for which the establishing of a national human rights commission was an urgent necessity in order to protect human rights. Advanced countries as well felt the need to narrow the gap between domestic implementation and international standards by establishing their own national human rights commissions.[3] This is why the number of countries which have already established or which are preparing to establish national human rights commissions is continuing to increase.

PROTECTION OF HUMAN RIGHTS ACT, 1993[3a]

The India has growing concern in issues relating to human rights and devising more effective methods of implementation of human rights norms enshrined under the constitution and other international instruments for which India is a party.

It is worth noting to see why Human Rights Commission is needed in India. Violation of human rights by government forces such as police, the armed and Paramilitary forces, etc. is common in India. As a result various Human rights activists, lawyers, and non-governmental organizations were demanding for the establishment of independent and non-governmental commission of human rights for better protection of human rights. The other reason, as stated in the Act on discussion here, is that there has been growing concern in the country and abroad about issues relating to human rights. Also the changing social realities and emerging trends in the nature of crime and violence necessitated the Government to deal with the situation. When the government of India moved to suppress, liquidate and eliminate sweeping terrorism in certain parts of the country, some human rights activists and agencies in India and abroad, particularly the Amnesty International, raised hue and cry and virtually launched a movement against the Government for its alleged acts of suppression of human rights. Different kinds of discussions were held at various forums regarding the human rights situation in the country. Therefore, taking into account the aforesaid matters the Government of India passed the Protection of Human Rights Act of 1993.

The Protection of Human Rights Act, 1993 provides for the establishment of three basic institutions, i.e. the National Human Rights Commission, State Human Rights Commission and Human Rights Courts for better protection of human rights and for the matters connected with their functioning. However, this study will only deal with the National Human Rights Commission. The study traces on the matters related to structural organization, inquiry into complaints and the procedure thereof, and other related functions of the commission.

There are some loopholes under the Act, which perhaps affect the autonomous functioning of the commission as well as the effective protection for human rights by the commission as stated under the Act. Attempt has been made to see the loopholes and recommend the possible changes to the provisions.

Protection of Human Rights Act, 1993

Purpose and Reasons

The Protection of Human Rights Act, 1993 (No 10 of 1994), which established the National Human Rights Commission of

India and provided for the establishment of the State Human Rights Commissions, Human Rights Court and Special Public Prosecutor, was intended to achieve different objectives. According to the Act the objects and reasons are[4]:

1. India is a party to the International Covenant on Civil and Political and the International Covenant on Economic, Social and Cultural Rights, adopted by the General Assembly of the United Nations on the 16th December 1966. The Human Rights embodied in the previously mentioned Covenants stand substantially protected by the Constitution.
2. However, there has been growing concern in the country and abroad about issues relating to Human Rights. Having regard to this, changing social realities and the emerging trends in the nature of crime and violence. Government has been reviewing the existing laws procedures and system of administration of justice, with a view to bring about further accountability and transparency in them, and devising efficient and effective methods of dealing with the situation.
3. Wide-ranging discussions were held at various fora such as the Chief Ministers' Conference on Human Rights, seminars organized in various parts of the country and meeting with leaders of various political parties. Taking into account the views expressed in these discussions, the Human Rights Commission Bill, 1993, was introduced in the Lok Sabha on 14th May 1993. The Bill was referred by the Speaker to the Standing Committee of Parliament on Home Affairs. In view of the urgency of the matter, the protection of Human Rights Ordinance, 1993, promulgated by the President on 28th September 1993, after incorporating certain amendments having regard to the discussions in the said Standing Committee.

However, the three institutions, viz. The National Human Rights Commission, State Human Rights Commission and Human Rights Courts, have been established for the better protection of Human Rights, this study will only deal with the role of the National Human Rights Commission in implementing the Human Rights norms stipulated under the Indian Constitution and other International instruments.

Structural Organization of the National Human Rights Commission (NHRC)

According to section, 3(2) of the Act the Commission shall consist of:

(a) a Chairperson who has been a Chief Justice of the Supreme Court;

(b) one member who is, or has been a Judge of the Supreme Court;

(e) one member who is, or has been, the Chief Justice of a High Court.

(d) two members to be appointed from amongst persons having knowledge of, or practical experience in, matters relating to Human Rights.

According to Section 3(3) of the Act, the Chairpersons of the National Commission for Minorities, the National Commission for the Scheduled Castes and the National Commission for Scheduled Tribes and the National Commission for Women shal! be deemed to be Members of the Commission for the discharge of functions specified in clauses (b) to (j) of Section 12.[5]

The Act also makes provision for a Secretary-General who shall be the chief executive officer of the commission and shall exercise such powers and discharge such functions of the commission as it may delegate to him.

In *Paramjit Kaur v. State of Punjab,*[6] the Supreme Court held that the Chairman of the Commission in his capacity as a Judge of the High Court and then as a Judge of the Supreme Court and also as Chief Justice of India, and so also two other members who have held high judicial offices as Chief Justice of HighCourts, have throughout their tenure, considered, expounded and enforced the Fundamental Right and are, in their own way, experts in the field. TheCommission is truly an expert body to which a reference can be made by the Supreme Court under Article 32 and once such a reference has been made no prohibition under the Protection of Human Rights Act will affet the jurisdiction of the Commission to investigate a case referred to it by the Supreme Court.

Appointment of Chairperson and other Members

The Chairperson and other Members are appointed by the President by warrant under his hand and seal after obtaining the recommendations of Committee consisting of:

(a) Prime Minister -- Chair person

(b) Speaker of the House of People – Member

(c) Minister in Charge of Ministry of Home Affairs in the Government of India – Member

(d) Leader of the Opposition in the House of the People – Member

(e) Leader of the Opposition in the Council of State – Member

(f) Deputy Chairman of the Council of State – Member

A Sitting Judge of the Supreme Court or Sitting Chief Justice of a High Court can be appointed only after consultion with the Chief Justice of India.[7]

It is further provided that no appintment of a Chairperson or a Member shall be invalid by reason of any vacancy in the above Committee headed by the Prime Minister.[8]

Term of Office of Members

A person appointed as chairperson shall hold office for a term of five years from the date on which he enters upon his office or until he attains the age of seventy years, whichever is earlier.[9] A person appointed as a member shall also hold office for a term of five years from the date on which he enters upon his office and shall be eligible for re-appointment for another term of five years. This is however, subject to the condition that no Members shall hold office after he has attained the age of seventy years.[10] Further, on ceasing to hold office, a Chairperson or a Member shall be ineligible for further employment under the Government of India or the Government of any State.[11]

Removal of a Memeber of the Commission

The Chairperson or any other Member of the Commission can be removed from his office by order of the President on the ground of proved misbehaviour or incapacity after the Supreme Court, on reference being made to it by the President, has, on inquiry held in accordance with the procedure prescribed in that behalf by the Supreme Court, reported that the Chairperson or such other Member, as the case may be, ought on any such ground be removed.[12] But despite this provision or notwithstanding this provision the president may by order remove from office the Chairperson or any other Member if the Chairperson or such other person, as the case may be:

(a) is adjudged an insolvent; or
(b) engages during his term of office in any paid employment outside the duties of his officer; or
(c) is unfit to continue in office by reason of infirmity of mind or body; or
(d) is of unsound mind and stands so declared by a competent Court; or
(e) is convicted and sent to imprisonment for an offence which in the opinion of the president involves moral turpitude.[13]

In the above cases, it will not be necessary for the President to refer the matter to the Supreme Court and obtain its report before ordering the removal of a Chairperson or a Member.

Headquarters of the Commission

The headquarters of the National Human Rights Commission (NHRC) is located at Delhi. The Commission may, however, with the previous approval of the Central Government establish offices at other places in India.[14] The Commission shall ordinarily hold its meetings and sittings in its offices located at Delhi.[15] However, it may, in its discretion, hold its meeting at any other place in India if it considers it necessary and expedient.[16] The Commission or some of the Members may transact business at places outside its headquarters as and when previously approved by the Chairperson, provided that if the parties are to be heard in connection with an equiry under the Act at least two Members shall constitute the bench of the Commission for such purpose.[17]

Officers and other Staff of the Commission

Section 11 of the Act reads as follows:

1. The Central Government shall make available to the Commission
   (a) an Officer of the rank of Secretary to the Government of India who shall be the secretary general of the Commission and
   (b) Such police and investigative staff under an Officer not below the rank of a Director General of Police and such other Officer and staff as may be necessary for the efficient performance of the functions of the Commission.
2. Subject to such rules as may be made by the Central Government in this behalf the Commission may appoint such other administrative technical and Scientific staff as it may consider necessary.
3. The salary, allowances and conditions of service of the officers and other staff appointed under sub Section (2) shall be such as may be prescribed.

Procedure of the Commission

The Commission shall meet at such time and place as the Chairperson may think fit.[18] The Commission shall regulate its own procedure.[19] All orders and decisions of the commission shall be authenticated by the Secretary-General or any other officer of the comission duly authorised by the chairperson in this behalf.[20]

Function of the Commission

The Indian National Human Rights Commission is established to have an effective mechanism for the promotion and implementation of various human rights norms in this country. To this effect there are many roles and functions vested with the commission under the Act. The Commission shall perform all or any of the following functions, namely:

(a) inquire, *suo motu* or on a petition persented to it by a victim or any other person on his behalf, [or on a direction or order of any Court] into complaint of:

   (i) violation of human rights or abetment thereof; or

   (ii) negligence in the prevention of such violation by a public servant;

(b) intervene in any proceeding involving any allegation of violation of human rights pending before a court with the approval.of such court;

(c) visit under intimation to the State Government any jail or any other institution under the control of the State Government, where persons are detained or lodged for purposes of treatment, reformation or protection to study the living conditions of inmates and make recommendations therein;

(d) review the safeguards provided by or under the Constitution or any law for the time being in force for the protection of human rights and recommend measures for their effective implementation.

(e) review the factors, including acts of terrorism, that inhibit the enjoyment of human rights and recommend appropriate remedial measures study treaties and other international instruments on human rights and make recommendations for their effective implementation.

(g) undertake and promote research in the field of human rights.

(h) spread human rights literacy among various sections of the society and promote awareness of the guards available for the protection of these rights through publications, the media, seminars and other available means.

(i) encourage the efforts-of non-governmental organisations and institutions working in the field of human rights; and

(j) such other functions as it may consider necessary for the promotion of human rights.[21]

But there are certain matters which are not subject to the jurisdiction of the Commission. The Commission cannot enquire into any matter which is pending before a State Commission or any other Commission duly constituted under any law for the time being in force.[22] Besides this, the Commission or the State Commission shall not enquire into any matter after the expiry of one year from the date on which the act constituting violation of human rights is alleged to have been committed.[23] In *Paramjit Kaur v. State of Punjab,*[24] the question arose before the apex court was whether the prohibition contained in clause (2) of Section 36 would apply in a matter referred by the apex Court under Article 32 of the Constitution, relating to violation of human rights, to the Commission?

The Commission pointed out that the shackles and limitations under the Act would not apply in a matter referred to it by the Supreme Court because in such matters the commission does not function under the provisions of the Act but under the directions of the court. The provisions contained in the Act do not limit the powers of the Supreme Court Conferred by Article 32 of the Constitution. It is, therefore, reasonable to hold that the Supreme Court designated, the commission as a body sui generis to carry out the functions and determine issues entrusted to it by the Supreme Court. To read otherwise is to render it otiose.[25]

The Supreme Court confirmed the above view taken by the commission and observed that, "the power and jurisdiction of the Supreme Court under Article 32 of the Constitution cannot be curtailed by any statutory limitation including those contained in Section 36 (2) of the Act. If the Supreme Court can exercise that power unaffected by the prohibition contained in Section 36 (2), there is no reason why the Commission, at the request of the Supreme Court, cannot investigate or look into the violations of human rights even though the period of limitation indicated in Section 36(2) might have expired. In such a situation, the Commission will not be affected by the bar contained in Section 36(2) and it will be well within its rights to investigate the matter referred to it by the Supreme Court. Further, in deciding the matters referred by the Supreme Court, National Human Rights Commission is given a freehand and is not circumscribed by any conditions. Therefore, the jurisdiction exercised by the National Human Rights Commission in these matters is of special nature not covered by enactment or law, and thus acts sui generis. The Commission is also a body sui juris created under an Act made by Parliament for examining and investigating the questions and complaints relating to violation of human rights, as also the negligence on the part of any public servant in preventing such violations.[26]

Inquiry Into Complaint

Section 12(a) of the Act gives the Commission the power to inquire, suomoto or on a petition presented to it by a victim or any person on his behalf into the complaint of (i) violation of Human Rights or abatement thereof; or (ii) negligence in the prevention of such violation, by a public servant;

Therefore, the Commission can only inquire into the complaint of violation of Human Rights or abatement thereof or negligence in the prevention of such violation by the public servants. It is clear that apart from public servants there are other violators of Human Rights in the society. For example landlords, factory owners, extremists, terrorists and so on. Who can inquire violations by such persons? However, it is difficult to the Commission to inquire into the violations committed particularly by the terrorist and extremists. This provision should be amended to incorporate violations by private individuals. The researcher is of the opinion that thinking the Government organs as the only violators of Human Rights is the traditional approach where the Human Rights were considered as forms of denial of power to the Government. Now a days what we have to focus should be the violation in any forms, not only violations by Government organs.

Before proceeding to the practical power of inquiry exercised by the Commission, let us see the statutory powers of inquiry. According to Section 13 (1) of the Act, the Commission has all the powers of a civil Court trying a suit under the Code of Civil Procedure, 1908, and particularly in respect of the following matters:

1. summoning and enforcing the attendance of witnesses and examining them on oath;
2. discovery and production of any document;
3. receiving evidence on affidavits;
4. requisitioning any public record or copy thereof from any Court or office;
5. issuing Commission for the examination of witnesses or documents; and
6. any other matter which may be prescribed.

Another notable thing in relation to this Section is that the Commission, in its first annual report, 1993-94 has recommended the amendment of this Section as to include the following paragraph:

> "Exercise, the power to compel the attendance of any person to whom summons have been issued, under Section 32 of the code."

However, this proposed amendment, inter alia, by the Commission in its first, second and third report has not yet been taken to give effect by the Government This matter was pursued by the Chairperson with the Minister of Home Affairs who, after consultations with the Ministries of Law and Finance, stated in reply that:

> "We need to gain more experience in the working of the National Human Rights Commission before we assess the actual need for changes in the already carefully worked out provisions of the statute."[27]

From this, one can understand how the Government is reluctant to accept the proposed amendments of the Commission.

The Commission also has the power to require any persons subject to any privilege which may be claimed by that person under any law for the time being in force, to furnish information on such points or matters as in the opinion of the Commission may be useful for, or relevant to, the subject matter of the inquiry and any person so required shall be deemed to be legally bound to furnish such information within the meaning of Section 176 and 177 of the Indian Penal Code. The Commission may authorize any officer, not below the rank of a Gazetted Officer to enter into any building or place where the Commission has reason to believe that any document relating to the subject matter of the inquiry may be found, and may seize any such document or take extracts or copies there from.[28]

The Commission shall be deemed to be a civil Court and when any offence as it is described in Section 175 (omission to produce document to public servants by person legally bound to produce it,) Section 178 (Refusing Oath or affirmation when duly required by public servant to make it), Section 179 (Refusing to answer public servant authorized to question). Section 180 (Refusing to sign Statement) or Section 228 A (Disclosure of identity of the victim of certain offences) of the Indian penal code is committed in the view, or presence of, the Commission , may after recording the facts constituting the offence and the Statement of the accused as provided for in the code of Criminal Procedure, 1973, forward the case to a Magistrate having jurisdiction to try the same and the magistrate to whom any such case is forwarded shall proceed to hear the complaint against the accused as if the case has been forwarded to him under Section 346 of the Code of Criminal Procedure.[29]

Further, every proceeding before the commission shall be deemed to be a judicial proceeding within the meaning of sections 193 and 228, and for the purposes of section 196 of the Indian Penal Code, and the commission shall be deemed to be a civil court for all the purposes of Section 195 and Chatper XXVI of the code of Criminal Procedure, 1973.[30]

Investigation: The Commission may for the purpose of conducting any investigation pertaining to the inquiry, utilise the services of any officer or investigation agency of the Central Government or any State Government with the concurrence of the Central Government or the State Government, as the case may be.[31] For the purpose of investigating into any matter pertaining to the inquiry, any officer or agency whose services are utilised under Section 14(1) noted above, may, subject to the direction and control of the Commission:

(a) summon and enforce attendance of any person and examine him;

(b) require the discovery and production of any document;

(c) requisition any public record or copy thereof from any office.[32]

But it may be noted here that no statement made by a person in the course of giving evidence before the Commission shall subject him to, or be used against him in, any civil or criminal proceeding except a prosecution for giving false evidence by such statement.

This is however, subject to the proviso that if the statement:

(a) is made in reply to a question which he is required by the Commission to answer, or

(b) is relevant to the subject-matter of the inquiry, then it may be used against him in any civil or criminal proceeding.[33]

The officer or agency whose services are utilized under Section 14(1) noted above, shall investigate into any matter pertaining to the inquiry and submit a report thereon to the Commission within such period as may be specified by the Commission in this behalf.[34] The Commission shall satisfy about the correctness and the facts stated and the conclusion, if arrived at, the said report submitted by the officer or agency and for this purpose the Commission may make such inquiry (including the examination of the person or persons who conducted or assisted in the investigation), as it thinks fit.[35]

Procedure for Dealing with Complaints: Regulation 8 of the National Human Rights Commission (Procedure) Regulations, 1994[36] lays down the following procedure for dealing with complaints of alleged violation of 'human rights':

(1) All complaints in whatever form received by the Commission shall be registered and assigned a number and placed for admission before a Bench of two Members constituted for the purpose not later than two weeks of receipt thereof. Ordinarily complaints of the following nature are not entertainable by the Commission:

  (a) in regard to events which happened more than one year before the making of complaints;[37]

  (b) with regard to matters which are subjudice;

  (c) which are vague, anonymous or pseudonymous;

  (d) which are of frivolous nature; or

  (e) those which are outside the purview of the Commission.[38]

(2) No fee is chargeable on complaints.

(3) Every attempt should be made to disclose a complete picture of the matter leading to the complaint and the same may be made in English or Hindi to enable the Commission to take immediate action. To facilitate the filing of the complaints, the Commission shall, however, entertain complaints in any language included in Eighth Schedule of the Constitution. It shall be open to the Commission to ask for further information and affidavits to be filed in support of allegations whenever considered necessary.

(4) The Commission may, in its discretion, accept telegraphic complaints and complaints conveyed through Fax.

(5) The Commission shall have the power to dismiss a complaint in limine.

(6) Upon admission of a complaint the Chairperson/ Commission shall direct whether the matter would be set down for inquiry by it or should be investigated into.

(7) On every complaint on which a decision is taken by the Chairperson/Commission to either hold an inquiry or investigation, the Secretariat shall call for report/ comments from the concerned Government/authority giving the latter a reasonable time therefore.

(8) On receipt of the comments of the concerned authority, a detailed note on the Merits of the case shall be prepared for consideration of the Commission.

(9) The directions and recommendations of the Commission shall be communicated to "the concerned Government/authority and the petitioner as provided for in Sections 18 and 19 of the Act.

(10) The Commission may, in its discretion afford a personal hearing to the petitioner or any other person on his behalf and such other person or persons as in the opinon of the Commission should be heard, for appropriate disposal of the matter before it and where necessary call for records and examine witnesses in connection with it. The Commission shall afford a reasonable hearing, including opportunity of cross-examining witnesses, if any, in support of the complaint and leading of evidence in support of his stand to a person whose conduct is enquired into by it or where in its opinion the reputation of such person is likely to be prejudicially affected.

(11) Where investigation is undertaken by the team of the Commission or by any other person under its discretion, the report shall be submitted within a week of its. completion or such further time as the Commission may allow. The Commission may, in its discretion, direct further investigation in a given case if it is of the opinion

that investigation has not been proper or the latter requires further investigation for as certaining the truth or enabling it to properly dispose of the matter. On receipt of the report, the Commission on its own motion, or if moved in the matter, may direct inquiry to be carried by it and receive evidence in course of such inquiry.

(12) The Commission or any of its Members when requested by the Chair person may undertake visits for an on-the-spot study and where such study is undertaken by one or more Members, a report thereon shall be furnished to the Commission as early as possible.

Steps after inquiry: After the inquiry under the Act is complete the Commission may take any of the following steps:

(1) Where the enquiry discloses the commission of violation of human rights, or negligence in the prevention of violation of human rights by a public servant, it may recommend to. the concerned Government or authority the initiation of proceedings for prosecution or such other action as the Commission may deem fit against the concerned person or persons.

(2) Approach the Supreme Court or the High Court concerned for such directions, orders or writs as that court may deem necessary.

(3) Recommend to the concerned Government or authority for the grant of such immediate interim relief to the victim or the members of his family as the Commission may consider necessary.

(4) Subject to the provision of clause (5) provide a copy of the inquiry report to the petitioner or his representative.

(5) The Commission shall send a copy of its enquiry report together with its recommedations to the concerned Government or authority and the concerned, Government or authority shall, within a period of one

month, or such further time as the Commission may allow, forward its comments on the report, including the action taken or proposed to be taken thereon, to the Commission.

(6) The Commission shall publish its enquiry report together with the comments of the concerned Government or authority, if any, and the action taken or proposed to be taken by the concerned Government or authority on the recommendations of the Commission.[39]

Regulation 11 of the National Human Rights Commission (Procedure) Regulations, 1994 further provides that report of follow-up action shall be submitted to the Commission at every subsequent sitting indicating therein the present stage of action on each 'item on which the Commission had taken a decision in any of its earlier meeting, excepting the items on which no further action is called for:

Procedure with Respect to Armed Forces: Section 19 of Protection of Human Rights Act, 1993 provides:

(1) Notwithstanding anything contained in this Act, while dealing with complaints of violation of human rights by members of armed forces, the Commission shall adopt the following procedure namely:

(a) it may, either on its own motion or on receipt of a petition, seek a report from the Central Government;

(b) after the receipt of the report, it may, either not proceed with the complaint or, as the case may be, make its recommendations to that Government.

(2) The Central Government shall inform the Commission of the action taken on the recommendations within three months or such further time as the commission may allow'.

(3) The Commission shall publish-its report together with its recommendations made to the Central Government and the action taken by that Government on such recommendations.

(4) The Commission shall provide a copy of the report published under sub-section (3) to the petitioner or his representatives.

Annual and Special Reports of the Commission: The National Human Rights Commission is required .to submit an annual report to the Central Government and to the State Government concerned and may at any time submit special reports on any matter which, in its opinion, is of such urgency or importance that it should not be deferred till submission of the annual report.[40] After the annual report is submitted by the Commission, the Central Government and the State Government, as the case may be, shall cause the annual and special reports of the Commission to be laid before each House of Parliament or the State Legislature respectively, as the case may be, along with a memorandum of action taken or proposed to be taken on the recommendations of the Commission and the reasons for non-acceptance of the recommendations, if any.

OTHER FUNCTIONS: RECOMMENDATION TO IMPROVE JAIL CONDITIONS

Section 12(C) of the Act entrusts to the Commission the responsibility "to visit, any jail or any other institution under the control of the State Government, where persons are detained or lodged for purposes of treatment, reformation or protection, to study the living conditions of the inmates and make recommendations thereon".

The Commission is deeply concerned with the appalling condition of over-crowding, lack of sanitation, poor medical facilities, inadequate diet and the like in most of the jails in the country. In order to combat such a situation the Commission has taken two approaches: First, to study the factors responsible for over-crowding in jails and the steps needed to reduce that over-crowding; second, to encourage such measures as may be necessary to develop or improve the skills of inmates, with a view to enabling their re-orientation and facilitating their reintegration into society upon release from Jail.[41] However, the situation is not changed and the Commission concluded that the prison system is seriously in need of reform. The contribution of the century old Indian prison Act of 1894 is very high in this regard. Therefore, the Commission recommended upon the drafting of a new Bill. In order to achieve this objective the Commission gathered comprehensive information from all States and Union Territories. Then it collected the data and presented to a National Conference of Directors General of Police, Inspectors General of Prisons and Home Secretaries that was called by the Commission on 14th November 1995. At that conference, a core group was set-up to draft a Model Prison Bill to replace the prisons Act of 1894.[42] However, the Commission urged all states to have appropriate resolution passed in their respective legislatures, no immediate action has been taken and the serious problems relating to the prison are going on without change in most parts of the country.[43] Absence of custodial premises for women, absence of balanced diet, overcrowding, the lack of adequate knowledge and of training of prison staff of different ranks and so on are common to all prisons. The Commission is taking possible measures in co-operation with the concerned bodies for system reform of Prison and other centres of detention.[44]

Review of Laws, Implementation ofTreaties and Other Instruments of Human Rights

Sub Section (d) and (f) of Section 12 of the Act respectively empower the Commission to review the safeguard provided by or under the constitution or any law for the time being in force, and study treaties and other international instruments on Human Rights with a view to making recommendations for their effective implementation. There are various measures taken by the Commission in this regard which are as under:

Review of Terrorist and Disruptive Activities (Prevention) Act (TADA, 1987

The role played by the Commission in the campaign against TADA is worthmentioning. The Commission has paid its attention to this Act since it touches on three most sensitive areas: the Constitution, India's treaty obligation, and the determination of the nation to preserve and protect Human Rights despite the destructive impact of terrorism, which is the mortal enemy of the society.

The Union Government had decided to extend the Act, a temporary legislation, beyond 23rd May 1995 when it was due to expire. The Commission considered the Act "incompatible with our culture traditions, legal history and treaty obligations". The effective stand taken by the Commission made it difficult and the Act lapsed on 23 May 1995, and even a substitute legislation could not be declared by the Parliament.[45]

Review of Armed Forces (Special Powers) Act, 1958

The representation against the Armed Forces (Special powers) Act, 1958 has been brought to the knowledge of the Commission when it visited Nagaland in April 1995. The representation asserted that the provisions of the Act gave virtually unlimited powers to personnel of the security Forces to conduct searches and to arrest without warrant, to detain and even shoot to kill, on grounds of committing or on suspicion of Committing certain offences.[46] Therefore, the Commission was of the opinion that the powers given under the Act are too vast and sweeping and pose a grave threat to the fundamental rights and liberties of the people under the area covered by the Act.

The Commission has begun a process of examining the Act and presented its recommendation to the Ministry of Defence. Moreover, the Commission is taking appropriate measures as to the amendment of the Act.

Police Reform

As indicated in the Annual Report of the Commission for the year 1995-96, "an efficient, honest police force is the principal bulwark of the nation against violations of Human Rights. A police force that is often overworked and ill-equipped, whose condition of service are inadequate and whose integrity is repeatedly questioned, itself becomes part of the problem".

One can understand from the annual reports of the Commission that majority of the complaints that the Commission has received relate to the conduct of the police. Among them the custodial death, rape and torture, killing under firing and "fake encounters" by police are some of the common violations. In his recent call, Justice M.N. Venkatachaliah, the NHRC Chairperson, confirmed that sixty per-cent of all arrest made by the police in India are "Unnecessary and unjustifiable", and these accounted for 43 per-cent of the total expenditure in current by prisons. He added, "the majority of the complaints reaching NHRC relate to the police".[47]

The Second Report of the Police Reforms Commission, which, as long back as 1979, proposed a number of reforms to be taken. Particularly, that report calls for full respect for the Supreme Court Judgment in the case of *Abhinandan Jha and others Vs. Dinesh Mishra,*[48] which directed that the investigative tasks of the police should be placed beyond any kind of intervention by the executive or non-executive.

The NHRC has been taking repeated exchanges of views with the Central Government over the past year. As a result, the Union Home Minister addressed to all Chief Ministers on 3rd April, 1997, on the subject of Police Reforms and Restructuring.

In its recent recommendation, the Commission has recommended the setting up of a Police Security and Integrated Commission (PSIC), a non-statutory advisory Authority to improve the quality of policing in the country. It has highlighted the need for "insulating" the investigation wings of the police "from external and political pressures".[49] The Commission proposed the setting up of non-statutory "district police complaints authorities" to examine people's grievances against police excesses, arbitrary detention and arrests, false implication in Criminal cases and custodial violence. The Commission is of the opinion that "public pressure can be more compelling than statutory functions" as a moral force for the success of their recommendations.[50]

Review of Laws Relating to Persons with Disabilities

In the previous annual report, the Commission examined the functioning of th Persons with Disabilities (Equal Opportunities, Protection of Rights and Full Participation Act 1995 and its impact. Subsequently, a comprehensive set of recommendations wa communicated to authorities in the Central and State Governments specifying their obligation under the Persons with Disabilities Act and the action they were expected to take. During the period under review, (1-4-03 to 31-3-04) a preliminary analysis of family laws and civil and criminal procedures have been undertaken, which indicates a certain degree of bias against persons with psychiatric and intellectual disabilities and also those suffering from epilepsy. For instance, "The Hindu Marriage Act of 1955", Section 5(2)(a), (b), (c), while specifying the conditions for a valid Hindu Marriage states, "(a) at the time of the marriage, neither party is incapable of giving a valid consent of it in consequence of unsoundness of mind (b) though capable of giving a valid consent has been suffering from mental disorder of such a kind or to such an extent as to be unfit for marriage and the procreation of children (c) has been subject to recurrent attacks of insanity or epilepsy". In Section 12(1), the Act lays down conditions of a voidable marriage, which inter alia includes conditions specified in Section 5(2)(a), (b), (c), referred in the previous para. The Commission is deeply concerned over the possible misuse of such provisions in the law depriving persons affected by temporary mental illness of their right to enter into marital relations and/or to maintenance. Similarly, the Hindu Adoption and Maintenance Act of 1956 Section 7 and 8 prohibit a person from adopting a child unless the adopter has attained majority and is of sound mind. The provision of giving children away in adoption on grounds of unsoundness of the mind of the parent under this act needs to be carefully examined in the light of the definition of disability provided in Section 2(1) of the Persons with Disabilities (Equal Opportunities, Protection of Rights and Full Participation) Act, 1995 which stipulates that, "person with disability means a person suffering from not less than forty percent of any disability as certified by a medical authority." Here the compatibility of Hindu Adoption and Maintenance Act 1956 Section 9(4), with Section 2(1) of Persons with Disabilities (Equal Opportunities, Protection of Rights and Full Participation) Act, 1995 needs careful examination since both the Acts have designated separate authorities to decide on the issue of unsoundness of the mind. Likewise, the Indian Contract Act of 1872 absolved any person of unsound mind from contractual liability. Since a majority of people having mild to moderate degree of psychiatric and intellectual disability can manage the responsibilities of day-to-day life, this provision needs to be re-examined.[51]

REVIEW OF LAWS

Child Marriage Restraint Act, 1929

It is a well known fact that child marriages are still prevalent in certain parts of the country, especially in Rajasthan, Chhattisgarh, Madhya Pradesh. Jharkhand, Bihar and Uttar Pradesh. It is on Akshya Trtiya, popularly known as Akha Teej, when hundreds of child marriages are openly performed despite the fact that the Child Marriage Restraint Act was enacted in 1929 and later amended in 1978. Given the ramifications it has on the rights of children, particularly girl children, the Commission, since its inception, has continued to focus its attention towards eradication of this problem. In its preceding annual reports, the Commission had reported that the draft Child Marriage Restraint Bill recommending substantial changes in the Child Marriage Restraint Act, 1929 was sent to the Department of Women and Child Development. Ministry of Human Resource Development. Government of India for consideration. A copy of the draft Bill was also forwarded for information to the Ministry of Home Affairs and Ministry of Law and Justice, Government of India. The draft Bill was also sent to all the State Governments and Union Territories inviting suggestions/objections, if any.[52]

In order to discuss the amendments/recommendations made in the draft Bill, the Commission convened a meeting on

22-02-2005 under the chairmanship of Dr. Justice A.S. Anand, Chairperson of the Commission. Meanwhile, the Legislative Department, Ministry of Law and Justice, Government of India informed that they had introduced a new Bill entitled 'The Prevention of Child Marriage Bill, 2004' in the Rajya Sabha on 20-12-2004. This Bill, the Legislative Department stated, would repeal the Child Marriage Restraint Act, 1929.[53]

The meeting appreciated the Legislative Department for their efforts in introducing the new Bill in the Rajya Sabha as well as for taking into consideration almost all the amendments/recommendations proposed by the Commission in the new Bill. The meeting was attended, inter alia by the Secretary and the Joint Secretary, Legislative Department, Ministry of Law and Justice; the Joint Secretary, Department of Women and Child Development, Ministry of Human Resource Development; the Joint Secretary and the Senior Research Officer, National Commission for Women and Director (Human Rights), Ministry of Home Affairs. In this meeting, a general discussion also took place on the new Bill introduced in Parliament and the provisions incorporated therein. After a detailed discussion, it was pointed out that:

- there was need to bring the definition of child in the proposed Bill in consonance with the definition prescribed for the child in the Convention on the Rights of the Child' that had been ratified by the Government of India;
- there was need to make a statutory provision on compulsory registration of marriages as this would deter communities from indulging in child marriages; and
- keeping in view the best interest of the child, there was need to modify Section 14 of the proposed Bill.[54]

Protection from Domestic Violence Bill, 2002

There is no denial of the fact that domestic violence is a universal phenomenon that cuts across culture, religion, class and ethnicity. Despite this widespread prevalence, such violence is not customarily acknowledged and has remained invisible. The social construction of the divide between the public and private domain underlies the hidden nature of domestic violence against women. Legal jurisprudence has historically considered the domain of the house to be within the control and unquestionable authority of the male head of household. Thus, acts of violence against members of the household, whether wife or child, have generally been perceived as discipline, essential for maintaining the rule of authority within the family. In the last two decades, apart from the Indian women's movement that has contributed largely to a growing public awareness of violence against women, international conventions also have been equally explicit in acknowledging the State's responsibility for human rights violations by private actors in both the public and private spheres. The Vienna Accord of 1993 and the Beijing Platform of 1995 together crystallized the principle that women's rights are human rights. Keeping this in view, the Department of Women and Child Development in consultation with the Ministry of Law, Justice and Company Affairs drafted a Bill on the Protection from Domestic Violence that was also introduced in the Parliament on 8-03-2002. As reported in the preceding annual report, the said Bill was referred to the Standing Committee of the Parliament pertaining to the Ministry of Human Resource Development for further examination and for suggesting changes, if any, required in the draft Bill. After the Standing Committee submitted its report, the Department of Women and Child Development sent a copy of the draft Bill, along with a copy of the report of the Standing Committee, to the Commission for its comments. Both these documents were carefully examined by the Commission and comments/modifications suggested by it were later forwarded to the Department of Women and Child Development. The comments/modifications suggested by the Commission have already been reported by it in its annual report for the year 2002-03. In the Memorandum of Action Taken on the Annual Report of National Human Rights Commission for the year 2002-03, the Ministry of Home Affairs has stated that the aforesaid draft Bill was circulated by the Department of Women and Child Development to all the concerned Ministries/Departments for their comments and views. Further, it added that the Bill would be Finalized after the views are received.[55]

It is to be noted here that due to efforts of NHRC Domestic violence Bill has been passed by the Parliament and has come into force.

Protection of Human Rights Act, 1993

The Commission had referred a proposal to the Government, in March, 2000, for amendments to the statute. As reiterated, over the years, the Commission is of the considered view that the amendments, as proposed by the Commission, are necessary to ensure the independence and effectiveness of the Commission in the fulfillment of its mandate. Despite the long passage of time, no progress has been made despite efforts made to expedite the amendments.[56]

Food Safety and Standard Bill, 2005

The Commission expressed its concern regarding the reported repeal of the Infant Milk Substitute, Feeding Bottle and Infant Foods Act (IMS Act.) as proposed by its inclusion in Schedule one of the Food Safety and Standard Bill 2005.

The Hon'ble Chairperson in his letter dated 15-03-2005 to the Minister of State, Ministry of Food Processing Industries conveyed the concern of the Commission in this regard. In particular, he pointed out that the IMS Act is not a routine food law, nor does it have anything in common witn the other Acts in the repeal list. It is a special Act to protect, promote and support breastfeeding and it focuses on marketing practices and other practices which interfere with breastfeeding, and thereby jeopardize the well being of baby and mother. The Commission observed that the protection of breastfeeding is vital for saving the lives of millions of children in India every year. The Commission urged to keep the above facts in view and to take appropriate action in order to protect the "best interests" of children–the IMS Act should not be repealed.[57]

IMPLEMENTATION OF TREATIES AND OTHER INTERNATIONAL INSTRUMENTS

Convention Against Torture

Torture and other cruel, inhuman or degrading treatment or punishment are particularly serious violation of human rights and, as such, arc strictly condemned by International Law. Based upon the recognition that such practices are outlawed, the Convention against Torture and other Cruel, Inhuman or Degrading Treatment or Punishment (the Convention) strengthens the existing prohibition by a number of supporting measures. The Right against Torture has been judicially recognized by the Apex court as a Fundamental Right. The Commission has been requesting the Government of India to ratify the 'Convention against Torture and other forms of Cruel Inhuman and Degrading Punishment or Treatment', which was signed by India on 14-10-1997 on the recommendation of the Commission. The Convention entered into force on 26-06-1987 (Article 27).

In October, 2003 the Government of India informed the Commission that the draft cabinet note for ratification of convention against torture is under examination. The Commission has been reminding the Government to expedite action regarding this. The Ministry of Home Affairs has in its letter dated 10-09-2005 informed that the Ministry of External Affairs has constituted an Inter-Ministerial Group under the Chairmanship of AS (UN), comprising of representatives from the MHA. Ministry of Law and L&T Division of the MEA to go into the question of early ratification and steps required for this purpose. The MHA has informed that the action on ratification of the Convention could be taken only after the receipt of the recommendations of the group. The Commission would therefore, again like to reiterate for early notification of the UN Convention against Torture.[58]

The 1977 Protocol additional to the Geneva Convention of 1949

India ratified the four Geneva Conventions of 1949 in 1959 and enacted the Indian Geneva Conventions Act in 1960 incorporating them in the Indian legal system. The four Geneva Conventions of 1949 were considerably supplemented by two additional protocols adopted in 1977. Protocol I contains new rules on international armed conflicts while Protocol II develops the rules on international humanitarian law governing non-international armed conflicts. These protocols contain elaborate norms and provisions concerning protection of human rights in times of armed conflicts - both international as well as national. The Ministry of External Affairs has. vide letter dated 29-12-2003. stated that "... all matters relating to International Humanitarian Law (IHL) including Geneva Conventions were extensively discussed during the recent Conference of the Partis to the Red Cross Movement and the Geneva Conventions in Geneva. The changing nature of armed conflict in the contemporary period (Afghanistan. Iraq. conflicts in Africa, etc.). their impact on IHL and the Geneva Conventions and the related issues are under review at the international level. In the light of these developments, it is felt that the concerned Ministries and Agencies of the Government including Ministry of Defence, Ministry of Home Affairs. Ministry' of External Affairs and Ministry of Law should take stock of the current realities and of our response."[59]

The Commission persued the reply received from the Ministry of External Affairs and desired to know from the Ministry the specific responses on its part regarding signing of the two additional protocols to the Geneva Convention 1949. The Ministry of External Affairs has further informed that a thorough examination of substantive aspects of these protocols is needed and their Ministry is consulting the concerned agencies. In this regard Inter-Ministerial Meeting was convened by MEA on 22-07-2004. The Ministry of Home Affairs and the Ministry of Defence were requested to study the subject. The issue of accession to the Geneva Convention was discussed in the meeting of the Commission and the Commission has desired that issue should be addressed after a joint meeting of MEA, MHA and Ministry of Defence. The Ministry of Home Affairs in the Action Taken Report on the Annual Report of the Commission for the year 2002-2003 has mentioned that the consultation process is going on in the Government of India in order to take stock of the current realities.[60]

Optional Protocols to the Convention on the Rights of the Child

Protection and promotion of the rights of children has always been a central issue on the agenda of the National Human Rights Commission. India is a home to more than four hundred million children and these children undoubtedly are the supreme asset of the nation. Recognizing the rights of children and our duties towards them, the Constitution of India, first and foremost, has protected their rights. Having ratified the UN Convention on the Rights of the Child, the Government of India has committed itself inter alia towards all round development of children, including reducing inequalities among them; protecting them from violence and exploitation: and creating an overall environment that will nurture them to bloom into robust citizens who will be the pride of the nation. In the Commission's earlier annual reports, the Commission had recommended that the Government of India examine and become a party to Optional Protocols I and 2 to the Convention on the Rights of the Child, dealing with the involvement of children in armed conflict and the sale of children, child prostitution and child pornography. The Memorandum of Action Taken on the Annual Report of the National Human Rights Commission for the year 2002-03 also mentions that the Government has approved the signing and ratification of the aforesaid two Optional Protocols to the Convention on the Rights of the Child. The Ministry of External Affairs has communicated to the Commission that the Government of India had signed the above two Optional Protocols on 15-11-2004. These, however, are yet to be ratified. The Commission trusts that the Government of India would ratify the two Optional Protocols to the Convention on the Rights of the Child in the best interest of our children.[61]

PROMOTION OF HUMAN RIGHTS LITERACY AND AWARENESS

One of the mandates of the Commission under Section 12 (h) of the Protection of Human Rights Act, 1993 is the Promotion of Human Rights Literacy and Awareness. The Commission has been endeavouring to achieve the objectives with its own resources. The entire range of activities of the Commission is aimed at creating an environment in which rights can be better promoted and protected. The decisions taken by the Commission in respect of complaints, the programmes and projects undertaken, seminars and workshops held and its publications and discourses, all aim to create a culture of human rights in the country.[62]

National Action Plan on Human Rights Education

The Commission has decided to take up the task of development of the National Action Plan and has set up a group of experts comprising representatives from Government Departments, legal experts, and representatives from NGOs and civil society.[63]

UN Decade of HR Education and the National Action Plan of Human Rights Education

The period 1995-2004 was declared as the United Nations Decade for Human Rights Education by the United Nations. The National Human Rights Commission pursued with the Government to develop a National Action Plan for Human Rights Education and as mentioned in the previous annual report the National Action Plan of Human Rights Education was Finalized and circulated by the Government in 2001. As per the action plan. Government has taken steps to reorient the syllabus so as introduce elements of human rights in school education as well as in Universities. According to the information with the Commission, so far 35 Universities/ Colleges have introduced Certificate, Diploma and PG courses on Human Rights with Financial assistance from the University Grants Commission. With a view to assess the level of Human Rights Education at the School level, the Commission took up an in-house study to prepare a Status Paper on Human Rights Education at School in 2004-2005. The textbooks prescribed for schools brought out by the NCERT and the SCERT were analyzed with regard to the human rights component being taught in schools with possible suggestions to enhance the quality of human rights education in schools. The study revealed that Human Rights Education is not taught as a separate subject. However, the NCERT and the SCERT, Delhi have integrated human rights concepts in various subjects from the primary level to the higher secondary level. The Study also revealed that wide ranges of issues related to Human Rights are covered in the school curriculum. The focus needs to be on the methodology of imparting the concepts to the students and an analysis of the perception and understanding of the human rights issues by the students. In order to assess the position prevailing in the various states in the field of human rights education a questionnaire was also sent to all the States/Union Territories to indicate the steps being taken by them to promote Human Rights Education in Schools. The information has been received from 17 States and is under compilation.[64]

Human Rights Education for Youth

With a view to spreading an awareness of human rights issues among university students, the Commission conducts internship programmes during summer and winter vacations every year. During the internship, the students are apprised of the working of the Commission. They arc also made aware of the provisions of the Constitution and the main institutions and international instruments relevant to an understanding of human rights. The interns are provided an opportunity to interact with NGOs working in the field of human rights and are also taken to field visits. In addition the students are assigned research topics to work on.[65]

Human Rights Training

The Commission is deeply concerned about human rights awareness, literacy and sensitization, which is one of the mandates of the Commission under Sec 12(h) of Human Rights Act, 1993. One of the main endeavours of the Commission is to promote citizens' increasing and persistent demand for dignity, respect, justice and prevent violations of their human rights by public servants. For this, it is essential that the public servants should be sensitized through training, to meet the human rights challenges that they encounter in their work sphere or else violations will continue to escalate and flourish. Simultaneously, the Commission is required to encourage the NGOs and other institutions working in the field of human rights as partners. The training programme involved civil administrators, law enforcement agencies, para-military forces, lawyers, academicians judicial officers, NGOs, prison officers and other stakeholders. This programme proved to be useful in enhancing the professional knowledge, human rights awareness, skills and perception of the participants.

When the Commission talks about Human Rights Education, it must be understood that a context specific broad and dynamic human rights education is being referred to. Advancing this trend, the Commission organized a programme of Human Rights Education from a disability perspective in four distinct phases to empower the Law schools and departments with the capacity to deliver an optional paper in 'Human Rights, Disability and Law' and simultaneously help them address disability throughout the programme of legal studies. Phase I included face-to-face training at NLSIU, Bangalore in July 2004 attended by 30 participants comprising law faculties and disability and human rights advocates. In Phase II the participants undertook individual studies using desk research and field investigations. Phase III included a seminar in which participants shared findings of their studies and in Phase IV, the participants facilitated five training workshops for a group of Law Faculties, Disability Rights and Human Rights advocates.[66]

During the period 2004-05, twenty six training programmes were conducted in the form of workshop/seminar/training courses, on a wide range of human rights issues and subjects. These programmes were organized in collaboration with State Human Rights Commission, Universities. Institutes, Academies. Law Schools. United Nations High Commission for Refugees, UNICEF and NGOs. Further, the target groups/participants of these training programmes were Civil Servants, Police Officers, Judicial Officers, Prison Officers, Lawyers, NGOs,

Journalists, Academicians, Teachers and Social Activists. The above training programmes focus on the issues of Human Rights Awareness and Sensitization, Human Rights Investigations, Legal Literacy, Dalits Rights and related issues. These training programmes were conducted in four regions i.e. North, East, South and West of the country. Besides giving Financial support, the Commission has provided Resource Persons and Human Rights Training materials for the training programmes. Three in-house training programmes were also conducted for officers and staff of the Commission, so as to orient them to human rights principles, philosophy, practices, values and culture, necessary to deal with matters handled by them in the Commission. United Nations agencies like. UNHCR, UNICEF arranged day long briefing session for our officials, to specially focus on issues of Refugees and Child Rights, respectively.[67]

Para Military and Armed Forces

The para-military and armed forces are often called upon to maintain peace and law and order in areas affected by terrorism or insurgency. Pursuant to the commission's efforts, the subject of human rights is now included in all of their training courses at all levels. To encourage interaction and experience-sharing between personnel of para-military forces and the Commission, holding of an annual debate competition, both in Hindi and English, was started in 1998. With every passing year this debate competition has been attracting growing and enthusiastic participation of the personnel of para-military forces, competing in both languages. Human rights education is also included in training courses for Para Military and Armed Forces so as to create better awareness among officers and staff on human rights.[68]

National Institute of Human Rights

The National Institute of Human Rights (NIHR) which was set up in the National Law School of India University Bangalore, had been a resource extensively used by the Commission in the past. The Commission approved a project

'Review of the Status of Human Rights Education in India at the University level' submitted by the NIHR. However, the project report is yet to be received.[69]

The Media and Legal Issues of Freedom of the Press

The Commission has shared a special relationship with the media. Based on reciprocity in highlighting issues of human rights, the Commission has found a key ally in the media in generating public awareness. The Commission has frequently taken cognizance of human rights violations on the basis of media reports. It has benefited substantially from the editorials, letters and articles that feature in the media. The media has indeed acted as a watchdog for the Commission on many occasions. The diverse opinions across the country and the world find a voice through the media and it is this, which has prompted the Commission on a daily basis to scan 24 newspapers—regional, national and international.[70]

ILLUSTRATIVE CASES

Alleged Custodial Death of Shenskhem Kharasaiot Followed by Death of Two in Police Firing in Meghalaya

The Commission took notice of a case broadcasted over all Indian Radio and requested the proper measure to be taken by the Meghalaya State. Accordingly, the next kin of the deceased was given Rs. 25,000 to meet Funeral expenses and the ex-gratia assistance of Rs. 50,000 has been given to the next Kin of the deceased and a near .relatives of the deceased had been given an appointment in Government on compassionate ground.[71]

Death of Kheshiho Sumi in Custody of the Armed Forces (Assam Rifles) in Nagaland

In this case, upon the intervention of the Commission, the Ministry of Defence has sanctioned a sum of Rs. 1.00 Lakh to the next of kin of Kheshiho Sumi, who died in the custody of Assam Rifles.[72]

Custodial Death of Shri Bundoo in Uttar Pradesh

In this case the Commission ordered the compensation to be paid to the next kin of the deceased and recommended a compensation of Rs. 1.00 Lakh.[73]

Death in Police Custody of Shri Udayan in Kerala

This case was brought to the notice of the Commission by Dr. Xavier Paul who alleged that Udayan died in police custody in the Lock-up in Manharghat police station on 20 January 1994. Amnesty International also reported this incident in a publication brought out by it in March 1994. On the basis of evidence obtained, the Commission was of the view that the torture to which Udayana was subjected by the police in the lock-up contributed to his committing suicide. The Commission recommended that a case should be registered against the police officials responsible for torturing Udayan and payment of compensation of at least Rs. 1,00,000/- to the family of Udayan. The same has been done by the State Government of Kerala.[74]

Rape of T. Uma in Police Custody in Tamil Nadu

On receipt of a report from the collector, Kamaraja District, Tamil Nadu, about the custodial rape of T. Uma by the Head Constable of Alangulam police station, the Commission called for a report. Later it was confirmed that Uma was raped by the Head Constable and in addition to Criminal prosecution and simultaneous departmental action against the Head constable and other policemen who were involved in this incident, the State Government also sanctioned Rs.1,00,000 as compensation to Uma.[75]

Alleged Death of Korra Satya Rao a tribal in Visakhapatnam District

After receiving a complaint about the alleged death of Korra Satya Rao in the areaofVissakhapatnam district by police officials the Commission ordered inquiries to be conducted and it was confirmed that the sub-inspector and three police constables were in complicity to the death of Korra Satya Rao.

The Commission recommended that the police official's concerned be prosecuted undersection 304 of the Indian Penal Code and that Rs 1.00 Lakh be paid in compensation to the next Kin of the deceased. The Government of Andra Pradesh subsequently confirmed compliance with the Commission's directidn.[76]

Alleged Death of 125 children in Phubani District

Under this case it was proved that 125 children below the age of 10 years died as a result of acute malnutrition, accompanied by repeated attacks of malaria, chickenpox and various water-born diseases. The Commission commented that adequate and satisfactory arrangement had not been made to prevent the calamity. The Commission therefore recommended the State Government to pay a sum amounting to Rs 6,52,000 to the 125 tribal families whose children had died.[77]

Recent Attacks on Members of the Christian Community

The Commission took suo-motu cognizance of recent attacks on member of the Christian community in Madhya Pradesh, Gujarat and Orissa. In relation to this recent shocking situation the Commission issued notice to the Chief secretaries of the States of Madhaya Pradesh, Gujarat and Orissa and also to the Union Home Secretary to take immediate measures to control and prevent such events, to investigate and bring to book those who have been responsible for the events occurring in these States; to provide immediate relief and assistance to the victims and the next of Kin of those who have died, to take all necessary measures and to report to the Commission on the steps taken within two weeks.[78]

Mass Killings in Gujarat after Godhra Scandal

In reaction to Godhara Scandal, the burning of Hindus in boggies of Railway (27th Feb., 2002) in Gujarat there were attacks on members of a particular community. The NHRC[79] took suo motu cognizance. In this matter proceeding on the situation in Gujarat were recorded in continuation of earlier

Proceedings of the Commission dated 1 and 6 March 2002. They also follow upon a visit of the Chairperson of the Commission to Gujarat between 19-22 March 2002, during which mission he was accompanied by the Secretary-General of the Commission, Shri P.C. Sen, the Special Rapporteur of the Commission, Shri Chaman Lal, and his Private Secretary, Shri Y.S. Murthy. During the course of that mission, the team visited Ahmedabad, Vadodara and Godhra and held intensive discussions, inter alia, with the Chief Minister, Chief Secretary and senior officers of the State, eminent citizens, including retired Chief Justices and Judges of High Courts, former civil servants, leaders of political parties, representatives of NGOs and the business community, numerous private citizens and, most importantly, those who were the victims of the recent acts of violence.

The Commission observed that the tragic events that have occurred have serious implications for the country as a whole, affecting both its sense of self-esteem and the esteem in which it is held in the comity of nations. Grave questions arise of fidelity to the Constitution and to treaty obligations. There are obvious implications in respect of the protection of civil and political rights, as well as of economic, social and cultural rights in the State of Gujarat as also the country more widely; there are implications for trade, investment, tourism and employment. Not without reason have both the President and the Prime Minister of the country expressed their deep anguish at what has occurred, describing the events as a matter of national shame. But most of all, the recent events have resulted in the violation of the Fundamental Rights to life, liberty, equality and the dignity of citizens of India as guaranteed in the Constitution. And that, above all, is the reason for the continuing concern of the Commission.

(i) The Statute of the Commission, as contained in the Protection of Human Rights Act, 1993, requires the Commission under the provisions of Section 12, to perform all or any of the following functions, namely:

"(a) inquire, suo motu or on a petition presented to it by a victim or any person on his behalf, into complaint of

(i) Violation of human rights or abetment thereof; or

(ii) Negligence in the prevention of such violation, by a public servant;

(b) review the safeguards provided by or under the Constitution or any law for the time being in force for the protection of human rights and recommend measures for their effective implementation;

(c) study treaties and other international instruments on human rights and make recommendations for their effective implementation;

(d) such other functions as it may consider necessary for the promotion of human rights."

The term 'human rights' is defined to mean the right relating to life, liberty, equality and dignity of the individual guaranteed by the Constitution or embodied in the International Covenants and enforceable by courts in India (Section 2(1)(d)), and the International Covenants are defined as the "International Covenant on Civil and Political Rights and the International Covenant on Economic, Social and Cultural Rights adopted by the General Assembly of the United Nations on 16th December 1966" (Section 2(1)(f)).

(ii) It is therefore in the light of this Statute that the Commission must examine whether violations of human rights were committed, or were abetted, or resulted from negligence in the prevention of such violation. It must also examine whether the acts that occurred infringed the rights guaranteed by the Constitution or those that were embodied in the two great International Covenants cited above.

(iii) The Commission would like to observe at this stage that it is the primary and inescapable responsibility of the State to protect the right to life, liberty, equality and dignity of all of those who constitute it. It is also the responsibility of the State to ensure that such rights are not violated either through overt acts, or through abetment or negligence. It is a clear and emerging principle of human rights jurisprudence that the State is responsible not only for the acts of its own agents, but also for the acts of non-State players acting within its jurisdiction. The State is, in addition, responsible for any inaction that may cause or facilitate the violation of human rights.

(iv) The first question that arises therefore is whether the State has discharged its responsibilities appropriately in accordance with the above. It has been stated in the Report of the State Government that the attack on kar sevaks in Godhra occurred in the absence of "specific information about the return of kar sevaks from Ayodhya" (p. 12 of the Report). It is also asserted that while there were intelligence inputs pertaining to the movement of kar sevaks to Ayodhya between 10-15 March 2002, there were no such in-puts concerning their return either from the State Intelligence Branch or the Central Intelligence Agencies (p. 5) and that the "only message" about the return of kar sevaks, provided by the Uttar Pradesh police, was received in Gujarat on 28 February 2002 i.e., after the tragic incident of 27 February 2002 and even that did not relate to a possible attack on the Sabarmati Express.

(v) The Commission is deeply concerned to be informed of this. It would appear to constitute an extraordinary lack of appreciation of the potential dangers of the situation, both by the Central and State intelligence agencies. This is the more so given the history of communal violence in Gujarat. The Report of the State Government itself states:

"The State of Gujarat has a long history of communal riots. Major riots have been occurring periodically in the State since 1969. Two Commissions of Inquiry viz., the Jagmohan Reddy Commission of Inquiry, 1969, and the Dave Commission of Inquiry, 1985, were constituted to go into the widespread communal violence that erupted in the State from time to time. Subsequently, major communal incidents all over the State have taken place in 1990 and in 1992-93 following the Babri Masjid episode. In fact, between 1970 and 2002, Gujarat has witnessed 443 major communal incidents. Even minor altercations, over trivial matters like kite flying have led to communal violence." (p. 127).

The Report adds that the Godhra incident occurred at a time when the environment was already surcharged due to developments in Ayodhya and related events (also p. 127).

Indeed, it has been reported to the Commission that, in intelligence parlance, several places of the State have been classified as communally sensitive or hyper-sensitive and that, in many cities of the State, including Ahmedabad, Vadodara and Godhra, members of both the majority and minority communities are constantly in a state of preparedness to face the perceived danger of communal violence. In such circumstances, the police are reported to be normally well prepared to handle such dangers and it is reported to be standard practice to alert police stations down the line when sensitive situations are likely to develop.

(vi) Given the above, the Commission is constrained to observe that a serious failure of intelligence and action by the State Government marked the events leading to the Godhra tragedy and the subsequent deaths and destruction that occurred. On the face of it, in the light of the history of communal violence in Gujarat, recalled in the Report of the State Government itself, the question must arise whether the principle of 'res ipsa loquitur' ('the affair speaking for itself') should not apply in this case in assessing the degree of State responsibility in the failure to protect the life, liberty, equality and dignity of the people of Gujarat. The Commission accordingly requests the response of the Central and State Governments on this matter, it being the primary and inescapable responsibility of the State to protect such rights and to be responsible for the acts not only of its own agents, but also for the acts of non-State players within its jurisdiction and any inaction that may cause or facilitate the violation of human rights. Unless rebutted by the State Government, the adverse inference arising against it would render it accountable. The burden is therefore now on the State Government to rebut this presumption.

(vii) An ancilliary question that arises is whether there was adequate anticipation in regard to the measures to be taken, and whether these measures were indeed taken, to ensure that the tragic events in Godhra would not occur and would not lead to serious repercussions elsewhere. The Commission has noted that many instances are recorded in the Report of prompt and courageous action by District Collectors, Commissioners and Superintendents of Police and other officers to control the violence and to deal with its consequences through appropriate preventive measures and, thereafter, through rescue, relief and rehabilitation measures. The Commission cannot but note, however, that the Report itself reveals that while some communally-prone districts succeeded in controlling the violence, other districts-sometimes less prone to such violence-succumbed to it. In the same vein, the Report further indicates that while the factors underlining the danger of communal violence spreading were common to all districts, and that, "in the wake of the call for the 'Gujarat Bandh' and the possible fall-out of the Godhra incident, the State Government took all possible precautions" (p. 128), some districts withstood the dangers far more firmly than did others. Such a development clearly points to local factors and players overwhelming the district officers in certain instances, but not in others. Given the widespread reports and allegations of groups of well-organized persons, armed with mobile telephones and addresses, singling out certain homes and properties for death and destruction in certain districts-sometimes within view of police stations and personnel-the further question arises as to what the factors were, and who the players were in the situations that went out of control. The Commission requests the comments of the State Government on these matters.

(viii) The Commission has noted that while the Report states that the Godhra incident was "premeditated" (p. 5), the Report does not clarify as to who precisely was responsible for this incident. Considering its gruesome nature and catastrophic consequences, the team of the Commission that visited Godhra on 22 March 2002 was concerned to note from the comments of the Special IGP, CID Crime that while two cases had been registered, they were being investigated by an SDPO of the Western Railway and that no major progress had been made until then. In the light of fact that numerous allegations have been made both in the media and to the team of the Commission to the effect that FIRs in various instances were being distorted or poorly recorded, and that senior political personalities were seeking to 'influence' the working of police stations by their presence within them, the Commission is constrained to observe that there is a widespread lack of faith in the integrity of the investigating process and the ability of those conducting investigations. The Commission notes, for instance, that in Ahmedabad, in most cases, looting was "reported in well-to-do localities by relatively rich people" (p. 130). Yet the Report does not identify who these persons were. The conclusion cannot but be drawn that there is need for greater transparency and integrity to investigate the instances of death and destruction appropriately and to instil confidence in the public mind.

(ix) The Report takes the view that "the major incidents of violence were contained within the first 72 hours." It asserts, however, that "on account of widespread reporting both in the visual as well as the electronic media, incidents of violence on a large-scale started occurring in Ahmedabad, Baroda cities and some towns of Panchmahals, Sabarkantha, Mehsana, etc." in spite of "all possible precautions having been taken" (p. 128-129). The Report also adds that various comments attributed to the Chief Minister and Commissioner of Police, Ahmedabad, among others, were torn out of context by the media, or entirely without foundation.

(x) As indicated earlier in these Proceedings, the Commission considers it would be naïve for it to subscribe to the view that the situation was brought under control within the first 72 hours. Violence continues in Gujarat as of the time of writing these Proceedings. There was a pervasive sense of insecurity prevailing in the State at the time of the team's visit to Gujarat. This was most acute among the victims of the successive tragedies, but it extended to all segments of society, including to two Judges of the High Court of Gujarat, one sitting and the other retired who were compelled to leave their own homes because of the vitiated atmosphere. There could be no clearer evidence of the failure to control the situation.

(xi) The Commission has, however, taken note of the views of the State Government in respect of the media. The Commission firmly believes that it is essential to uphold the Right to Freedom of Speech and Expression articulated in Article 19(1)(a) of the Constitution, which finds comparable provision in Article 19 of the Universal Declaration of Human Rights, 1948 and Article 19 of the International Covenant on Civil and Political Rights, 1966. It is therefore clearly in favour of a courageous and investigative role for the media. At the same time, the Commission is of the view that there is need for all concerned to reflect further on possible guidelines that the media should adopt, on a 'self-policing' basis, to govern its conduct in volatile situations, including those of inter-communal violence, with a view to ensuring that passions are not inflamed and further violence perpetrated. It has to be noted that the right under Article 19(1)(a) is subject to reasonable restrictions under Article 19(2) of the Constitution.

(xii) The Commission has noted the contents of the Report on two matters that raised serious questions of discriminatory treatment and led to most adverse comment both within the country and abroad. The first related to the announcement of Rs. 2 lakhs as compensation to the next-of-kin of those who perished in the attack on the Sabarmati Express, and of Rs. 1 lakh for those who died in the subsequent violence. The second related to the application of POTO to the first incident, but not to those involved in the subsequent violence. On the question of compensation, the Commission has noted from the Report that Rs. 1 lakh will be paid in all instances, "thus establishing parity." It has also noted that, according to the Report, this decision was taken on 9 March 2002, after a letter was received by the Chief Minister, "on behalf of the kar sevaks," saying "that they would welcome the financial help of Rs. 1 lakh instead of Rs. 2 lakhs to the bereaved families of Godhra massacre" (see p. 115). This decision, in the view of the Commission, should have been taken on the initiative of the Government itself, as the issue raised impinged seriously on the provisions of the Constitution contained in Articles 14 and 15, dealing respectively with equality before the law and equal protection of the laws within the territory of India, and the prohibition of discrimination on grounds of religion, race, caste, sex or place of birth. The Commission has also noted the contents of the Report which state that "No guidelines were given by the Home Department regarding the type of cases in which POTO should or should not be used" and that, subsequent to the initial decision to apply POTO in respect of individual cases in Godhra, the Government received legal advice to defer "the applicability of POTO till the investigation is completed" (pp. 66-67). The Commission intends to monitor this matter further, POTO having since been enacted as a law.

(xiii) The Commission has taken good note of the "Rescue, Relief and Rehabilitation Measures" undertaken by the State Government. In many instances, strenuous efforts have been made by Collectors and other district officers, often acting on their own initiative. The Commission was informed, however, during the course of its visit, that many of the largest camps, including Shah-e-Alam in

Ahmedabad, had not received visits at a high political or administrative level till the visit of the Chairperson of this Commission. This was viewed by the inmates as being indicative of a deeper malaise, that was discriminatory in origin and character. Unfortunately, too, numerous complaints were received by the team of the Commission regarding the lack of facilities in the camps. The Commission has noted the range of activities and measures taken by the State Government to pursue the relief and rehabilitation of those who have suffered. It appreciates the positive steps that have been taken and commends those officials and NGOs that have worked to ameliorate the suffering of the victims. The Commission, however, considers it essential to monitor the on-going implementation of the decisions taken since a great deal still needs to be done. The Commission has already indicated to the Chief Minister that a follow-up mission will be made on behalf of the Commission at an appropriate time and it appreciates the response of the Chief Minister that such a visit will be welcome and that every effort will be made to restore complete normalcy expeditiously.

(xiv) In the light of the above, the Commission is duty bound to continue to follow developments in Gujarat consequent to the tragic incidents that occurred in Godhra and elsewhere. Under its Statute, it is required to monitor the compliance of the State with the rule of law and its human rights obligations. This will be a continuing duty of the Commission which must be fulfilled, Parliament having established the Commission with the objective of ensuring the "better protection" of human rights in the country, expecting thereby that the efforts of the Commission would be additional to those of existing agencies and institutions. In this task, the Commission will continue to count on receiving the cooperation of the Government of Gujarat, a cooperation of which the Chief Minister has stated that it can be assured.

The National Human Rights Commission made following Recommendations

Law and Order

(i) In view of the widespread allegations that FIRs have been poorly or wrongly recorded and that investigations are being 'influenced' by extraneous considerations or players, the Commission is of the view that the integrity of the process has to be restored. It therefore recommends the entrusting of certain critical cases to the CBI. These include the cases relating to the

- Godhra incident, which is at present being investigated by the GRP;
- Chamanpura (Gulbarga Society) incident;
- Naroda Patiya incident;
- Best Bakery case in Vadodara; and the
- Sadarpura case in Mehsana district.

(ii) The Commission recommends that Special Courts should try these cases on a day-to-day basis, the Judges being handpicked by the Chief Justice of the High Court of Gujarat. Special Prosecutors should be appointed as needed. Procedures should be adopted for the conduct of the proceedings in such a manner that the traumatized condition of many of the victims, particularly women and children, is not aggravated and they are protected from further trauma or threat. A particular effort should be made to depute sensitive officers, particularly officers who are women, to assist in the handling of such cases.

(iii) Special Cells should be constituted under the concerned District Magistrates to follow the progress of the investigation of cases not entrusted to the CBI; these should be monitored by the Additional Director-General (Crime).

(iv) Specific time-frames should be fixed for the thorough and expeditious completion of investigations.

(v) Police desks should be set-up in the relief camps to receive complaints, record FIRs and forward them to Police Stations having jurisdiction.

(vi) Material collected by NGOs such as Citizen's Initiative, PUCL and others should also be used.

(vii) Provocative statements made by persons to the electronic or print media should be examined and acted upon, and the burden of proof shifted to such persons to explain or contradict their statements.

(viii) Given the wide variation in the performance of public servants in the discharge of their statutory responsibilities, action should be initiated to identify and proceed against those who have failed to act appropriately to control the violence in its incipient stages, or to prevent its escalation thereafter. By the same token, officers who have performed their duties well, should be commended.

Camps

(i) Visits to camps by senior political leaders and officers should be organized in a systematic way in order to restore confidence among those who have been victimized. NGOs should be involved in the process and the management and running of the camps should be marked by transparency and accountability

(ii) Senior officers of the rank of Secretary and above should be given specific responsibility in respect of groups of camps.

(iii) Special facilities/camps should be set-up for the processing of insurance and compensation claims. The Chief Minister of the State had requested the Commission to issue an appropriate request to insurance companies for the expeditious settlement of claims of those who had suffered in the riots. The Commission will readily do so and recommends that the State Government send to it the necessary details at an early date in order to facilitate such supportive action.

(iv) Inmates should not be asked to leave the camps until appropriate relief and rehabilitation measures are in place for them and they feel assured, on security grounds, that they can indeed leave the camps.

Rehabilitation

(i) The Commission recommends that places of worship that have been destroyed be repaired expeditiously. Assistance should be provided, as appropriate, inter alia by the State.

(ii) Adequate compensation should be provided to those who have suffered. This will require an augmentation of the funds allocated thus far, through cooperative arrangements involving both the State and Central Governments. Efforts should be made to involve HUDCO, HFDC and international financial and other agencies ànd programmes in this process.

(iii) The private sector, including the pharmaceutical industry, should also be requested to participate in the relief and rehabilitation process and proper coordinating arrangements established.

(iv) The role of NGOs should be encouraged and be an intrinsic part of the overall effort to restore normalcy, as was the case in the coordinated effort after the earthquake. The Gujarat Disaster Management Authority, which was also deeply engaged in the post-earthquake measures, should be requested to assist in the present circumstances as well.

(v) Special efforts will need to be made to identify and assist destitute women and orphans, and those subjected to rape. The Women and Child Development Department, Government of India and concerned international agencies/programmes should be requested to help. Particular care will need to be taken to mobilize psychiatric and counselling services to help the traumatized victims. Special efforts will need to be made to identify and depute competent personnel for this purpose.

(vi) The media should be requested to cooperate fully in this endeavour, including radio, which is often under-utilized in such circumstances.

Police Reform

(i) The Commission would like to draw attention to the deeper question of Police Reform, on which recommendations of the National Police Commission and of the National Human Rights Commission have been pending despite repeated efforts to have them acted upon. The Commission is of the view that recent events in Gujarat and, indeed, in other States of the country, underline the need to proceed without delay to implement the reforms that have already been recommended in order to preserve the integrity of the investigating process and to insulate it from extraneous influences.

In continuation of previous proceedings[80] the commission in its proceedings dated My 31, 2002 pointed out, the tragic event in Gujarat starting with the Godhra incident and continuing with the violence that rocked the State for over two months, have greatly saddened the nation. There is no doubt, in the opinion of this Commission, that there was a comprehensive failure on the part of the State Government to control the persistent violation of the rights to life, liberty, equality and dignity of the people of the State. It is, of course, essential to heal the wounds and to look to a future of peace and harmony. But the pursuit of these high objectives must be based on justice and the upholding of the values of the Constitution of the Republic and the laws of the land. That is why it remains of fundamental importance that the measures that require to be taken to bring the violators of human rights to book are indeed taken.

It is to be noted that there has been a decline in the incidents of violence in the past three weeks and that certain positive developments have taken place since the start of May 2002. However, as these Proceedings indicate, much remains to be done, and the integrity of the administration must be restored and sustained if those who have suffered are to be fully restored in their rights and dignity. The Commission will therefore continue to monitor the situation with care, and it calls upon the Government of Gujarat to report to it again, by 30 June 2002, on all of the matters covered in the Comments and Recommendations contained in these Proceedings, including the Confidential Report of 1 April 2002 transmitted to it earlier.

The Commission in the last quoted the thoughts of Mahatama Gandhi, Sardar Vallabhbhai Patel who, born in Gujarat, illuminated the life of the country with their wisdom, foresight and courage.

Gandhiji once observed: "It has always been a mystery to me how men can feel themselves honoured by the humiliation of their fellow beings."

He also said: "Peace will not come out of a clash of arms but out of justice lived and done."

And the comments of Sardar Patel, who chaired the Advisory Committee of the Constituent Assembly charged with the drafting of the articles on Fundamental Rights, are also of the deepest significance. The issue then was this: in the years preceding Independence, detractors of the National Movement, including elements of the retreating colonial power, repeatedly claimed that the minorities of India could not possibly find justice at the hands of other Indians. Sardar Patel was determined to refute this politically motivated assessment of the character of the country. Accordingly, on 27 February 1947, at the very first meeting of the Advisory Committee of the Constituent Assembly on Fundamental Rights, Minorities and Tribals and Excluded areas, Sardar Patel asserted:

"It is for us to prove that it is a bogus claim, a false claim, and that nobody can be more interested than us, in India, in the protection of our minorities. Our mission is to satisfy every one of them..... Let us prove we can rule ourselves and we have no ambition to rule others."

So it was that the Constitution of the Republic included a series of articles having a bearing on the rights of minorities-some of general applicability, others of greater specificity. The most notable were those relating to the Right to Equality (particularly articles 14, 15, 16 and 17), the Right to Freedom of Religion (articles 25, 26, 27 and 28), Cultural and Educational Rights (particularly articles 29 and 30) and, upholding them all, the Right to Constitutional Remedies (in particular article 32).

Critical and cruel as the communal dimension was to the tragedy of Gujarat, what was at stake, additionally, was respect for the rights of all Indians-irrespective of community-that are guaranteed by the Constitution. That Constitution assures the Fundamental Rights of all who dwell in this country, on a non-discriminatory basis, regardless of religion, race, caste, sex or place of birth. It was this guarantee that was challenged by the events in Gujarat. It is for this reason that the Commission has followed developments in that State closely, and that it will continue to monitor the situation for as long as is needed.

Terrorist attack at Akshardham Temple in Gandhinagar[81]

The Commission[82] shared the nation's shock and grief, strongly condemned the terrorist attack on innocent civilians at the Akshardham temple in Gandhinagar on Sept. 24, 2002. The Commission observed that such criminal acts are in any circumstances unjustifiable, they are violative of every conceivable human right. It further stated that the full force of the law must be brought to bear in dealing with such acts of terrorism and bringing to justice those who perpetrate or abet them.

Procedings to Protect Victims and Witnesses[83]

The Commission[84] in its proceedings dated 16th June, 2003 pointed out that the right to fair trial is a constitutional imperative and fairness of a trial includes, proper protection of the rights of the accused as also the capacity of witness to come forth to make true and faithful statement in respect of matters within their knowledge, without any fear or favour and further that fair trial envisages a fair deal to the victims also. The commission, therefore, asked to Director General of Police, Gujarat to take measures to protect the safety, physical and psychological well-being, dignity and privacy of victims and witness who have to depose either in court or before the commission of enquiry (Nanavati Commission). The DGP assured the commission that all the Superintendents of Police and Commissioners of Police have been instructed to give due protection to witnesses or victims who makes a request for the same.

Best-Bakery Case[85]

The Commission[86] on consideration of the report of its team which was sent to Vadodara filed a special leave petition under Article 136 of the Constitution in the Supreme Court with a prayer to set aside the judgement of the trial court in the Best Bakery Case and sought direction for further investigation by an independent agency and retrial of the case in a competent court located outside the state of Gujarat. The commission contended in the special leave petition that:

(i) The Concept of fair trial is a constitutional imperative and is explicity recognized as such in the specific provisions of the Constitution including Article 14, 19, 21, 22 and 39A of the Constitution as well as the various provisions of the code of Criminal Procedure, 1973.

(ii) The right to fair trial is also explicitly recognized as a human right in terms of Article 14 of the International covenant on civil and Political rights which has been ratified by India and which now forms part of the statutory legal regime explicity recognized as such under Section 2(1)(d) of the Protection of Human Rights Act, 1993.

(iii) Violation of a right to fair trial is not only a violation of fundamental right under our Constitution but also violative of the internationally recognized human rights as spelt out in the ICCPR to which India is a party.

(iv) Whenever a criminal goes unpunished, it is the society at large which suffers because the victims become demoralized and criminals encouraged. It therefore, becomes duty of the Court to use all its powers to unearth the truther and render justice so that the crime is punished.

(v) It is, therefore, imperative in the interests of justice for the Hon'ble Supreme Court, in exercise of the powers under Article 142 of the Constitution, to lay down guidelines and directions in relation to protection of witnesses and victims of crime in criminal trials which can be adhered to both by the prosecuting and law enforcement agencies as well as the subordinate judiciary. This is essential in order to enhance the efficacy of the criminal justice delivery system.

The Commission also filed separate application under Section 406 Cr.P.C. before the Supreme Court for transfer of four cases[87] for their trial outside the State of Gujarat.

Militants Attack 'Langer'—7Vaishno Devi Pilgrims Killed, Jammu & Kashmir[88]

The Commission took suo-motu cognizance of media reports on the outrageous terrorist attack of Langer at Ban Ganga Near Katra, Distt. Udhampur, J&K on their way to the Vaishnoi Devi Shrine on 21 July 2003, killing seven devotees, including a child and injuring many innocent civilians. The commission had consistently taken the position that such criminal acts were wholly unjustified and were violative of every conceivable human right. The commission therefore called upon the authorities to ensure that the full force of the law must be brought to bear in dealing with such acts of terrorism and bringing to justice those who perpetrate or abet them. The commission extended its deepest condolences to the families of those who had lost their lives or been onjured in the terrorist attack.

In response the report received from the Director General of Police, Jammu & Kashmir indicated that two grenades were hurled by suspected anti-national elements into the open compound of 'Langar' at Banganga which resulted in the death of Six persons and injuries to fifty others. At the time of the attack, CRPF personnel along with local policemen were deployed on the track near langar on Aug. 10, 2003 Mr. Hohd. Yousuf alias Mithu resident of Bagani Basantgarh was apprehended and during sustained interrogation, he admitted that he along with two militants, namely satal of Pakistan and Mohd. Abdullah of Doda was responsible for the explosion. The report further stated that in view of the increased rush of pilgrims on account of Amarnath Yatra, the security arrangements were reinforced by deputing on Trg. Coy of on consideration of the report the commission dirged DG (P), J&K to indicate whether any compensation/Exgratia or otherwise has been paid to the next of kin of those killed at Vaishno Devi in the terrorist attack.

Pursuant to the Commission's direction the DG (P) J&K had sent a report stating that ex-gratia relief @ Rs. 1 Lakh each has been sanctioned one paid to the next of Kin of 6 deceased killed in the Bomb blast on 21st July 03. Since action had been taken by the State Govt. the commission decided that no further action was called for in this case and acordingly closed the case.

Custodial Death of Haji Mohd. Nabuji Tentwala in Police Custody in Ahmedabad, Gujarat[89]

The Commission on 19.1.1996 received an intimation dated 18.1.1996 from the Commissioner of Police, Ahmedabad City, Glijarat regarding death of Haji Mohd. Nabuji Tentwala in police custody on 12.7.1995. It was stated that he was arrested in connection with Cr.Case No. 106/95 u/s 302/342/34 IPC and S. 135 B.P. Act. by the police who tied him with rope, beat him with sticks. Fists and kicks to death. The report further indicated that two of the accused police persons namely PSI J.V. Surela &. PC Bharatkumar were arrested and bailed out on 31.10.1995 and 2.1.1996 respectively. In response to the notice issued by the Commission, the Commissioner of Police, Ahmedabad City submitted the post-mortem, inquest and magisterial inquiry reports. As per the post mortem report the body of the deceased was having 23 ante-mortern injuries and the cause of death was indicated as "due to shock as a result of injuries present on the body". The inquest report conducted by the Sub-Divisional Magistrate, Ahmedabad City indicated that there were signs of blunt weapon blows on various parts of the body. The magisterial inquiry conducted by the Sub-Divisional Magistrate. Ahmedabad City blamed the PSI Surela and ACP Brahm Bhatt and other police personnel for the death of Haji Mohd. Tentwala and recommended investigation to pin point the responsibility of the death and to ascertain the actual culprits from the police staff. A separate report dated 20.7.1996 submitted by the District Magistrate, Ahmedabad. Gujarat indicated that a case No. 19/95 u/s 302/123/04/114, IPC had been registered by the Crime Branch against PSI Surela and 4-5 police personnel and another case No. 20/95 was registered u/s 330/342 against the main accused PSI Surela. PCs Navnect. Bharat Rathore, Raju and ACP Brahm Bhutt and four other police personnel. On consideration of the records of the case, the Commission held that the deceased was wrongfully arrested by the police for interrogation in a criminal case and was brutally thrashed to extract confession. Consequently, he suffered as many as 23 injuries, which resulted in his death. It is a case of gross violation of human rights. Accordingly, the Commission directed to issue notice to the Chief Secretary. Government of Gujarat to show cause as to why the Commission should not recommend payment of interim relief u/s 18(3) of the Protection of Human Rights Act, 1993 to the next of kin of the deceased.In response to the show cause notice, the Secretary, Home Department, Government of Gujarat, vide letter dated 19.6.2004 submitted that criminal offences had been registered against the police personnel responsible for beating up the accused and departmental action had also been initiated and are pending final outcome. It was acknowledged that human rights violation had taken place and the State Government had taken appropriate action against the concerned accused police personnel. The report further mentioned that for the violation of human rights, both criminal and departmental proceedings had already been initiated and awaiting final outcome. To the circumstances the Home Secretary requested that the show cause notice may be withdrawn and further action may be considered after the outcome of the criminal proceedings pending before the Court. The Commission considered the response received from the

State Government on 22.9.2004. While referring to the observations of the Hon'ble Supreme Court of India in the case of Neelbati Behra vs. State of Orissa, 1993 (2) SCC 746. it observed and ordered as under:

(a) This Commission has taken a consistent stand that the obligation of the State to ensure safety of persons while in its custody is strict and absolute and admits of no exception. The indefeasible right to life of every citizen, including convicts, prisoners or underrials, cannot be taken away except in accordance with the procedure established by law, while the citizen is in the custody of the State. Violation of that right renders the State vicariously liable for its acts of commission and omission and such liability is not contingent upon determination of the ultimate guilt of the offenders in a criminal court. Besides, death in police custody as a result of torture is perhaps the worst type of crime in civilized society.

(b) It is now an established law that the failure of the State to take all possible steps to protect the life of the citizens while in its custody makes the State vicariously liable for its action/omission.

(c) Immediate interim relief envisaged in Section 18 (3) of the Act has to be correlated to the injury/loss which the victim or members of his family have suffered owing to the violation of human rights by public servants. By no stretch of imagination can it be argued that award of this immediate interim has to be dependent upon the strict establishment of criminal liability after a full dress court trial. If this view is accepted, the relief will then neither be immediate nor interim. A meaningful and harmonious construction of this clause would leave no doubt that the Commission is entitled to invoke its benevolent sweep on a prima-facie view of the matter irrespective of whether there is any litigation civil or criminal relating to the matter.

(d) The idea of immediate interim relief does not therefore, presuppose the establishment of criminal liability of the offender in a court of law as a precondition for the grant of the relief nor does it depend on whether any civil litigation is either pending or prospective. A welfare state must recognize its obligation to afford relief to its citizens in distress, particularly those who are victims of violations of their human rights by public servants. The limiting of such statutory relief only to cases in which criminal liability of the offending public servant is established in a court of law beyond reasonable doubt is, to thwart an otherwise civilized piece of legislation by importing totally irrelevant limitations. The Commission desires to point out that the ground urged by the Government in this case, when it has been acknowledged by the State itself that there has been violation of human rights of the citizen, is misconceived.

Accordingly, the Commission recommended to the State Government ofGujarat to pay a sum of Rupees One lakh by way of interim relief to the next of kin of the deceased and to submit compliance report to the Commission within four weeks.

Torture and Gang Rape bv Police Officers in Tripura[90]

The Commission received a complaint from Shri Suhas Chakma, Director, Asian Centre for Human Rights, New Delhi alleging that Ms. Reang, a 17 year old girl was tortured and gang raped by a group of three Special Police Officers of the State Government of Tripura on 26/5/ 2003. The victim girl's family complained to the police station naming the three guilty SPOs but their complaint was not recorded. In response to the notice, a report received from the DGP, Tripura indicated that a case No. 6/2003 u/s 366 (A), 376, 326 and 34 IPC was registered in Police Station Raishyabari against the three named persons on 28/5/2003. The medical report confirmed that the victim, aged 17 years was sexually assaulted and raped. The three SPOs had been discharged from the service, arrested and sent to jail. In view of the gravity of the allegation of sexual brutality committed on a hapless girl by the three SPOS, the Commission directed to issue a notice to the Chief Secretary, Government of Tripura to show cause as to why interim relief not be granted to the victim. The Government of Tripura informed the Commission that it had paid an amount of Rs. 15,000/- as compensation to the victim Ms. Mithirung Reang. However, the Commission observed that the offence of rape not only amounts to violation of the human rights of the victim, but it also tends to violate the mind and scar the psyche of a person permanently. Besides, it carries a social stigma for the victim and her family. The Commission, therefore, directed the Government of Tripura to pay an amount of Rupees Fifty thousand as immediate interim relief to the victim after adjusting Rupees Fifteen thousand already paid. As the State Government submitted its compliance report in respect of payment of an amount of Rupees Thirty five thousand, the case was closed on 10/1/2005.

Sexual Harassment at Work Place[91]

The Commission took cognizance of a complaint, dated 12-3-2004 referred by Ms. K. Geeta, Programme Coordinator of SAKSHI, an NGO alleging sexual harassment of Ms. Asha Rajora, Technical Assistant in the Herbal Research and Development Institute, Gopeshwar, Uttaranchal by the Director of the Institute. Allegations of further harassment by way of non-renewal of her job contract with effect from 1-5-2004 were also levelled. The Commission directed the Chief Secretary, Uttaranchal and District Magistrate, Dehradun to submit their reports in the matter. The Commission also directed the State Authorities to inform (i) whether the Vishakha Guidelines are being followed in letter and spirit, while holding the inquiry; and (ii) whether any protection has been given to the complainant in the meanwhile. An interim report received from the Chief Secretary, Government of Uttaranchal indicated that the Commissioner, Garhwal Circle, has been requested to inquire into the matter as he was heading the Divisional Vigilance Committee. The interim report was however silent about the constitution of Divisional Vigilance Committee and whether it is in conformity with the guidelines laid down by the Supreme Court of India in Vishakha's case, which requires that the Complaints Committee should be headed by a woman and not less than half of its members should be women. Further, to prevent the possibility of any undue pressure or influence from senior levels such Complaints Committee should involve a third party, either NGO or other body who is familiar with the issue of sexual harassment. The Chief Secretary, Uttaranchal was therefore requested to clarify as to whether the Divisional Vigilance Committee is in conformity with Vishakha Guidelines. The Principal Secretary, Government of Uttaranchal informed the Commission that on the basis of the recommendations made by the Vigilance Committee, which was constituted in accordance with the guidelines in Vishakha case, the services of Dr. J. S. Rawat, Director, HRDI, Gopeshwar were terminated with effect from 4.10.2004. Since action had been taken by the Government in the case of sexual harassment the case was closed on 17-1-2005.

Water Supply to Slum Clusters and Resettlement Colonies[92]

The National Human Rights Commission has sought the comments of the Delhi Administration on a newspaper report that the water supplied to slum clusters and resettlement colonies in the city is full of filth and aerms. Taking suo-motu cognizance of a report, the Commission has given Chief Secretary, NCT and the Chairman, Delhi Jal Board four weeks time for their response.

The report published on December 28, 2006 in The Hindustan Times said that according to a study carried out by the NGO Hazard Centre 92% of water samoles collected from five slum clusters and six resettlement colonies were not fit for human consumption due to an alarming presence of a variety of pollutants including biological wastes. The report further added that the same authorities provide better quality of water to the affluent parts of the city.

The Commission, after going through the contents of the report said if true, they raise a serious issue of violation of Human Right to Health of the citizens.

Abandoned Boy's Case[93]

The National Human Rights Commission has sought a report from the District Collector, Gautam Budh Nagar about a media report which said a boy who was abandoned in a sedated condition by an unidentified man a week ago, was being looked after by a tea stall owner.

The report covered by NDTV on December 28, 2006 said that, the police was called in but when the boy could not tell anything about his parents, they left him at the tea stall. The report further said that police and the administrative authorities were not available for comments on the rehabilitation and protection of the boy named Jitendra. The media report also suggested that it is not clear how the boy will be handed over to the right authority as Uttar Pradesh does not have a specified Govt. body to protect such children.

After going through the contents of the report, the Commission said if they are true, they raise serious issue of violation of human rights of children. The Commission has sought a factual report from the District Collector within two weeks.

Necessary Steps Taken for Refugees[94]

The United Nation High Commissioner for Refugees Mr. Antonio Guterres called on the Acting Chairperson of NHRC, Dr. Justice Shivaraj V. Patil. Later, an interactive meeting was held, which was attended by Members Justice Y. Bhaskar Rao, Shri R.S. Kalha, Shri P.C. Sharma, Secretary General Shri R. K. Bhargava, Joint Secretary Smt. Aruna Sharma and the Chief Coordinator (Trg.) Shri PMV Siromony,

Dr. Justice Patil welcomed Mr. Guterres and briefed the visiting dignitaries on the thirteen years of the Commission. He referred to the various issues being dealt by the Commission including the issue of refugees. He also highlighted that the Commission had visited the refugee camps in Tamil Nadu and surveyed the conditions there. He pointed out that India has been providing shelter to quite many refugees displaced from their countries. Dr. Patil said that the Commission has felt the need for a Nationa Legislation to deal with the problem of refugees in India and has recommended the same to the Indian Government. He said the Government in principle has accepted the same. The Acting Chairperson stressed that there has to be a clear definition of refugees so that it is not confused with other forms of migrant population. He further expressed his concern on the issue of inability to distinguish between the bona-fide refugees from illegal immigrants and the other foreigners. Dr. Patil said that this issue needs to be addressed, so that the benefits percolate to the bona-fide refugees.

Mr. Antonio Guterres praised the Indian Government's generosity in granting protection to a number of refugees. He supported the idea of a solid National Legislation and said that the UNHCR will extend all cooperation for such a Legislation. He assured that his organization would cooperate with the Commission and the Indian Government to provide assistance including training exchange of practices and discussions in the problem areas concerning refugees.

Visually Impaired Venkataiah Case[95]

The NHRC which took Suo-Motu cognizance of a news report published in the Telugu Daily "Enadu" on September, 16, 2005 had asked the Secretary, Education Department, Andhra Pradesh to look into the matter and send comments. The news report had sai'd that Mr. Venkataiah, who had participated in National Chess Competitions in 2002 and won bronze medal, had scored 818 marks out of 1000 in class XII examination and secured 21222nd rank in DIET CET , wanted admission in Teacher Training Course. The report said the State Education Department Officers had given admission to those candidates who had scored lower rank than Mr. Venkataiah and bluntly refused his admission on the ground that he was visually impaired. On repeated requests, the officers assured that his case might be considered under the Disabled Welfare Quota of sports authority. The report highlighted that the office of

DIET CET, however informed that no seat was available. Pursuant to two other directions of the Commission, the Secretary, Education Department, Andhra Pradesh submitted his report in October, 2006. The report said according to the Convener, DIET CET-05, three candidates had been admitted based on the priority assigned by the officials of Sports Authority of Andhra Pradesh. The officials from the Authority had stated that Mr. Venkataiah was not eligible for admission into DIET and also informed that handicapped persons are not eligible for reservation under sports quota for admission. The report submitted also mentioned that the State Govt. had examined the matter and permitted the Director of School Education, Andhra Pradesh to allot a seat to Mr. Venkataiah in any DIETs in the State, during the academic year 2006-07 as a Special Case.

Relief to Injured Pupil and Illegally Detained Woman[96]

The National Human Rights Commission has sent a notice to the District Collector, Ghaziabad on a news report which said that a teacher of a Junior High School at Nahal, had beaten up a student of class-III and injured his right eye. The news report published in the "Times of India" on December 22, 2006 said the teacher, Mr. Rashid had beaten the student for noncompletion of homework. The report also said that the child underwent an emergency surgery at All India Institute of Medical Sciences where his father was told that normal vision in the right eye can never be restored. The report further highlighted the the teacher always carried a stick and often used it in the class.

After going through the press report, the Commission said if the contents are true, they raise serious issue of violation of human rights of the students. The Commission has directed that the press report be forwarded to the District Collector, Ghaziabad for a factual report within two weeks.

The Commission also came across a distressing news published in "Indian Express" on December 23, 2006 under the captio) "Cops mix up identity, jail woman for 14 days". As per the report, a Head Constable of UT of Chandigarh arrested a woman named Santosh from Karnal and brought her to Chandigarh presuming that she was the proclaimed offender in a liquor smuggling case. The report also said that the police neither verified her husband's name nor matched her photograph with that of the real accused who had already been arrested six years ago. According to the report, the real accused who also belong to the same colony.

After going through the press report, the Commission said if the contents are true, they raise serious issue of violation of human rights of women. The Commission directed that a copy of the newspaper report be transmitted to the Administrator, Union Territory of Chandigarh for a factual report within four weeks.

Recent Happenings in Nithari Village in Noida[97]

The National Human Rights Commission has sent notice to the Chief Secretary and DGP, Uttar Pradesh following media reports regarding sexual abuse of children and their murder by two people in Nithari Village in Noida. Taking Suo-Motu cognizance of reports appearing both in electronic media and newspapers, the Commission said if the contents of the reports are true, they reveal gross violation of human rights of the citizens and in particular the children because of certain acts of omissions on the part of public servants, who did not take timely action in the matter. The reports which appeared in the media said that at least 38 children from Nithari Village, near Noida's Sector-31 went missing over a period of 30 months but only 19 police complaints were registered, though 5 of these 19 children returned home. The recent discovery of skeletons and body parts in the area suggest that more than those registered as missing have been killed. The report appearing in the press had said that employer-servant duo of Mohinder Singh and Surinder has confessed to sexual abuse, mutilation and killings of not only young boys and girls but also grown-up women and dumping the remains of those murdered in the drain behind the house The reports further revealed that their barbaric act came to light not because the police were investigating the disappearance of children but by sheer chance as they nabbed Surinder who was in possession of a cell phone belonging to a missing women Payal who was also murdered. Showing distress at the happenings in Nithari village, one of the editorials highlighted that the drain where the skeletons were found was neither cleaned nor inspected throughout the period of these horrifying happenings. It highlighted the negligence of the State Administration and said those who are guilty of and responsible for such prolonged negligence of even routine investigation and civil function should be sacked forthwith. The reports also said the same. Keeping in mind the seriousness of the matter, the Commission has directed that related press clippings be sent to the Chief Secretary and DGP, UP for factual report within two weeks.

Evaluation of the Working of National Human Rights Commission of India

The first three annual report (1993-1996) were named as one step forward, one more step and another step respectively. Analysing the fourth report[98] it was pointed out that this report seems like a step in the right direction, it is precisely because it reflects with foresight, its concern to cretate an effective, efficiaious and self standing institution of governance.[99] The Commission in its fourth report notes,[100]

"There has been an increasing emphasis, during the year under report, on the investigation of cases by the Commission's Investigation division. As against 876 cases investigated or monitored by that Division during the year 1995-96, 1047 complaints were taken up for investigation or monitoring during the year 1996-97 of these 296 were investigated by the Commission's own staff and the remaining 751, which were sent to other agencies such as the state Police, were closely monitored. Out of these Cases, 256 were closed after processing. In certain instances the investigating officers of the commissions worked in concert with representatives of Non-Governmental Organisations (NGOs). Such as association with the NGOs in the investigation of case was not limited to obtaining detailed information on cases, but, on occassions, also the interviewing of victims, particularly in cases of violation against women. 26 cases were sent to the state of UP, the commission felt that in such cases the investigation of the District Police was slipshod and cursory.[101]

The issue of Human Rights in areas of terrorism and insurgency is riddled with complexities resulting in downward compromise inimicals to human rights. The commission is right to treat fake encouner' reports with the utmost seriousness and to work out an information system that it is to be kept informed of all alleged violations. Apart from its dealing with complaints under Section 12(1) PHRA, 1993, the strategy of the commission is to seek effect to the normative standards that exist in various judgements, international Conventions and Law Commission reports. In this, the commission has taken significant steps to implement the importatnt Supreme Court decisions in D.K. Basu[102] and Joginder Singh[103] and is right in its observation that "upswing in reported deaths in custody is the result of its repeated instructions that information regards such tragic occurrences must not be suppressed. Equally, in this part of the reports, it does not obfuscate the issue and outrightly condemns atrocity death and rape by the armed forces when they are called in aid of the civil power. Following the Vishaka[104] and PUCC[105] decisions, the commission was right to place a premium on its persuading the government to acede to the Anti-Torture Convention of 1984 and taking steps to implement it. Under Section 12(b) the commission is obliged to, study treaties and other International instruments on human rights and make recommendations for their effective implementation. Pursuant to its interpretation of its statuotry function, the Commission feels that it has been enriched in its own work by invoking international treaty norms and has, therefore, decided to press for their implantations:

Suffice is to say, that three and a half year after it was established, the commission's daily reliance on these treaties and instruments in the examination of issues before it, has led to the increasing relaization that, in various Sections of government, and at various levels of it, that India's Commitments are to be honoured not in their breach but in their practice.[106] In so far as this represents the policy of the commission, this is unexceptional. In so far, as it represents as affirmative statement of the receptivity of international human rights obligations in governmental circles, we only wish it were true.[107]

Commenting upon fifth report (1997-98) Rajeev Dhavan observed, just as the commission has prioritised its civil liberties concerns over custodial crimes and atrocities, it has rightly concerned itself with the rights of the mentally disabled and those in protective homes, albeit it in a less systematic way. In both these areas, it has partly been drawn into these areas by the Supreme Court. Its involvement in getting rid of manual scavenging and meeting the awesome challange of the AIDS disease are as praiseworthy as they have proved to be inexact. The real problem with the commission's perception of economic and social rights has been that it has not succeeded in involving an incisive view of what needs to be done. The commission in relating to application of international covenant in domestic law asked the National Law School to undertake a more systematic analysis of India's treaty obligations generally. More pointedly, the commission is also pushing the Indian Government to join the refugee convention which is necessary for a refugee prone country such as India even though the government continues to shuffle its fact on this issue. Dhavan further suggests that we must await a more concrete plan from the commission on the subject of India's international law obligations in respect of human rights and its liason with other countries.[108]

The NHRC in its annual report (2003-04) pointed out, 'National Human Rights institutions play a crucial role in translating international human rights norms and standards into practical action. However, their active participation in the elaboration of an International treaty is a new development. Emphasizing the involvement of National institutions, the United Nations High Commissioner for Human Rights in April 2002 stated that, "it will be of at most importance that not only States but also National Human rights Institutions are able to contribute their experience to the elaboration of the new conventions on the rights of persons with disabilities". The

NHRC jointly hosted an International workshop of National Institutions from the Asia Pacific Region and Commonwealth countries at New Delhi between 26th to 29th May, 2003 in collaboration with the Asia Pacific orum of National Human Rights Institutions, the United Nations Office of the High Commissioner for Human Rights and the British Council. The Participation of the workshop:

(a) Strongly affirmed the need for the development of a comprehensive and integral convention.

(b) Stressed that the convention should be a 'rights based' instrument, built on international human rights norms and standards and social justice. It should be informed by the overaching principle that all persons with disabilities, without exception, are entitled to the full benefit and enjoyment of all fundamental human rights and freedoms on the basis of equality, dignity and without discrimination.

(c) Further stressed that the situation of all disability groups and the diverse conditions relates to gender, race colour, age, ethnicity and other considerations must be taken into account which elaborating the convention.

In its Twelfth annual report,[109] the NHRC observed that 'the commission is of the firm view that though nothing justifies Terrorism, far too many people live in conditions where it can breed. It is common Knlowedge that systematic human rights violations for long periods of time are often the root cause of conflicts and terrorism. It can not be denied that disillusionment with a society where there is exploitation and massive inequalities and whose systems fails to provide any hope for justice are fertile breeding grounds for terrorism, which more often than not thrives in environments where human rights and more particularly Economic, Social and Cultural rights are denied by the State and political rights are violated with impunity both by the State and non-state actors. Any worthwhile strategy to resolve conflicts and terrorism will have to ensure enjoyment of as regards the death which occured in the police custody in the course of the year 2004-05, the report indiciated that there was a noticeable decline in such cases *vis-a-vis* the previous year in the State of Bihar, Gujarat, Maharashtra, Uttar Pradesh, Assam, Rajasthan, Tamil Nadu and West Bengal. During the year, the commission came across a large number of cases complaining of avoidane on the part of the police station officers to register complaints of a cognizable offence or a tendency to minimise the gravity of the offence while registering a case. The commission considered it a violation of statutory obligations imposed on the police station incharge by the provisions of chapter XII code of Criminal Procedure, in particular. Section 154 Cr.P.C. Such deviant act on the part of the police officers, in the opinion of the commission, does have an adverse effect on criminal Justice delivery system. Accordingly, the commission recommended that Central Government, all State Governments and all the Government of UTs should issue necessary instructions to all the concerned police officers to meticulously adhere to provision of Section 154 Cr.P.C. in the matter relating to registeration of cases. The report also included the human rights of the mentally ill prisoners, rights of the disabled, right to health, public hearing on right to health case practice of female foeticide and infanticide, trafficking in women and children, rights of children and the rights of vulnerable etc.

A close scrutiny of annual reports of 2003-04 and 2004-05 shows the anxiety of the NHRC in matters relating to custodial deaths, custodial torture, police harassment, illegal detention and torture in police custody. The commission has rightly held that the liability of the state to ensure safety of persons while they are in custody is strict and absolute and there are no exceptions to it. It is submitted here that the annual report (2005-06) has been sent by the National Human Rights Commission to the Parliament and due to its non-availability of it, it could not be discussed here.

C. Raj Kumar, an eminent scholar points out that over the years, the NHRC has developed a good reputation both nationally and internationally with regard to intervention on human rights matters NHRC's opinions on numerous matters are inconsistent with the Indian Government's position. The NHRC also engages state Governments on various human rights and law reform matters, the most important of which is ensuring that legislation conforms to the human rights obligations in the Indian Constitution and other laws. The NHRC's moral legitimacy is based on its members' impartiality and integrity and not on its institutional independence or its guaranteed powers in the protection of Human Rights Act of 1993. While it is difficult to evaluate whether the NHRC has successfully reduced human rights violations, it has certaininly attempted to develop a human right culture in India. In addition, there have been serious attempts to create accountability mechanisms for human rights violations in different levels of the Indian Government to ensure that human rights remain the central focus of Indian political and government discourse. The NHRC remains a forum in which people can seek justice for human rights violations.[110]

NOTES

1. Vijayashri, Sripat (2000), "India's National Human Rights Commission: A Shackled Commission", 18 B.U. Int'. L.J.1.
2. Arun Roy (ed.), (2004), "National Human Rights Commission of India", p. 74.
3. A Handbook on the establishment and strengthening of national institutions for the promotion and protection of human rights, Professional Training Sereis No. 4 United Nations, 1995.

3a. See Appendix.

4. Introductory Statement of the Protection of Human Rights Act, 1993.
5. See Section 3(2) of the Act.
6. AIR 1999 SC 340, 340.
7. Section 4(1) of Protection of Human Rights Act, 1993.
8. Section 4(2) of the Act.
9. Section 6(1).
10. Section 6 (2).
11. Section 6 (3).

12. Section 5(1).
13. Section 5(2).
14. Section 3(5).
15. Regulation 3, The National Human Rights Commssion (Procedure) Reguation, 1994.
16. Regulation 4, The National Human Rights Commssion (Procedure) Reguation, 1994.
17. Regulation 12, The National Human Rights Commssion (Procedure) Reguation, 1994.
18. Section 10(1) of the Act.
19. Section 10(2) of the Act.
20. Section 10(3) of the Act.
21. Section 12.
22. Section 36(1).
23. Section 36 (2).
24. AIR 1999 SC 340.
25. AIR 1999 SC 340, at P. 342.
26. AIR 1999 SC 343-344.
27. NHRC Annual Report for the Year 1995-96.
28. Section 13(3) of the Act.
29. Section 13(4) of the Act.
30. Section 13(5) of the Act.
31. Section 14 (1).
32. Section 14(2).
33. Section 15.
34. Section 14 (4).
35. Section 14(5).
36. These Regulations were made by the National Human Rights Commission in exercise of the powers conferred on it by sub-section (2) of Section 10 of the Protection of Human Rights Act, 1993 (No. 10-of 1994).
37. See Section 36 (2) of the Act.
38. See also Sectton 36(1)of the Act.

39. Section 20 (1).
40. Section 20(2).
41 Paragraph 6.3.
42 *Ibid.*
43 Paragraph 3.33.
44 Paragraph 3.49.
45 Paras Diwan (1998), Human Rights and the Law: Universal and Indian, p. 546.
46 Supranote 11, Paragraph 4.3
47 *The Times of India,* Saturday March 13, 1999, p. 1.
48 AIR 1963 Supreme Court 117 (V5 Supreme Court 32).
49 *The Times of India,* Thursday March 18, 1999, p. 7.
50 *Ibid.*
51. National Human Rights Commission, Annual Report 2003-04, para 5.23 - 5.28.
52. National Human Rights Commission, Annual Report 2004-05, Para 17.1
53. National Human Rights Commission, Annual Report 2004-05, Para 17.2
54. National Human Rights Commission, Annual Report 2004-05, para 17.3
55. National Human rights Commission, Annual Report 2004-05, para 17.10
56. At the time of writing this report, the Commission has come across the copy of the Protection of Human Rights Act (Amendment) Bill, 2005, which is proposed to be introduced by the Government in the Rajya Sabha. The amendments proposed in the Bill are under examination in the Commission. However, it is noted that the Bill does not reflect the amendments as proposed by the Commission The Act has been amended by the Protection of Human Rights (Amendment Act, 2006-No. 43 of 2006)
57. National Human Rights Commission, Annual Report 2004-05, para 17.13.
58. National Human Rights Commission, Annual Report 2004-05, para 17.14 to 17.18.

59. National Human Rights Commission, Annual Report 2004-05, para 17.19 & 17.20.
60. National Human Rights Commission, Annual Report 2004-05, para 17.21 to 17.24.
61. National Human Rights Commission, Annual Report 2004-05, para 17.25 to 26.
62. National Human Rights Commission, Annual Report 2004-05, para 13.1.
63. National Human Rights Commission, Annual Report 2004-05, para 13.2.
64. National Human Rights Commission, Annual Report 2004-05, para 13.3 to 13.6.
65 National Human Rights Commission, Annual Report 2004-05, para 13.7 & 13.8.
66. National Human Rights Commission, Annual Report 2004-05, para 13.9 & 13.10.
67. National Human Rights Commission, Annual Report 2004-05, para 13.14 to 13.16.
68. National Human Rights Commission, Annual Report 2004-05, para 13.20 to 13.28.
69. National Human Rights Commission, Annual Report 2004-05, para 13.29.
70. National Human Rights Commission, Annual Report 2004-05, para 13.30.
71. NHRC Annual Report 1993-94, Illustrative Cases.
72. NHRC Annual Report 1995-96.
73. NHRC Annual Report 1996-97.
74. NHRC Annual Report 1996-97.
75. NHRC Annual Report 1996-97.
76. Illustrative Cases- 1993-94 report of NHRC.
77. NHRC Annual Report 1993-94.
78. Human Rights Newsletter (NHRC), Feb. 1999 Vol.6, No.2.
79. Case No. 1150/6/2001-02 dated 1.4..2002; Coram—J.S. Verma J. Chairperson, Smt. Sujata v. Manohar and Sh. Virendra Dayal J.J., Members.

80. March 1,6,2002, April 1 and May 1, 2002.
81. Suo motu Complaint, Case no. 1150/6/2001-02, dated 25th Sept., 2002.
82. Consisting of J.S. Verma J. Chairperson, Mr. S. Sujata V. Manohar and Virendra Dayal J.J., Members.
83. Suo Motu Complaint, Case no. 1150/6/2001-02, dated 16th June, 2003.
84. Consisting of Dr. Justice A.S. Anand, Chairperson and Justice Mrs. Sujata V. Manohar, Member.
85. Suo Motu Complaint, Case no. 1150/6/2001-02, dated July 11 and 21, 2003.
86. Consisting of Dr. Justice A.S. Anand, Chairperson and Justice Mrs. Sujata V. Manohar, Member.
87. Godhra Incident, Chamanpura Incident, Naroda Patia incident and the Sadarpura Case in Mehsana district.
88. Case No. 58/9/2003-2004
89. Case No. 7586/95-96/NHRC
90. Case No. 5/23/2003-2004WC
91. Case No. 1775/35/2003-2004-WC
92. Cognizance on news paper item. Proceeding dated 5th Jan., 2006.
93. NHRC proceedings dated Jan. 5, 2006
94. December 27, 2006.
95. Suo motu cognizance, proceedings of NHRC dated 9th January, 2007.
96. Proceedings of NHRC dated 9th January, 2007.
97. Suo motu cognizance, proceedings of NHRC dated 2nd January, 2007.
98. 1996-97
99. R. Dhavan, "The Lesser Evil? Judges and Indian Democracy", (PIL SARC Working Paper No. 152).
100. Relating to order to investigate. See 11(1)(b) of POHRA, 1993 lays down that the Central Government shall make available to the Commission such police and investigative staff under an officer not below the rank of a Director General of Police and such other officers and staff as may be necessary for the efficient performance

of the commission. While Sec. 11(2) says commission may appoint such other administrative, technical and scientific staff as it may consider necessary.

101. NHRC Annual Report 85, Para 9-10 (1996-97).

102. *D.K. Basu v. State of West Bengal,* (1997) 1 SCC 416.

103. *Joginder Singh v. State of Uttar Pradesh,* (1994) 4 SCC 260.

104. *Vishaka v. State of Rajasthan,* (1997) 6 SCC 241.

105. *People Union for Civil Liberties v. Union of India,* (1997) 1 SCC 301.

106. NHRC Annual Report Para 4.11 (1996-97).

107. Rajeev Dhawn, Step by Step : 4th Annual Report of NHRC: 1996-97 41 J.I.: L.I. (1999) p. 193-194.

108. 43:4 J.I.L.I. (2001) 497, 498

109. Annual Report 2004-2005 (Covering the period April 1, 2004 to March 31, 2005).

110. C. Raj Kumar, "Human Rights Implications of National Security Laws in India: Combating Terrorism while preserving Civil Liberties", 33 Denv. J. Int'l. L. & Pol'y, 195 (2005).

5

NON-GOVERNMENTAL ORGANISATIONS AND IMPLEMENTATION OF HUMAN RIGHTS

Besides the International and National institutions, there are a number of Non-Governmental Organisations (NGOs) actively engaged in the field of human rights. Today, there exist a myriad of these non-governmental human rights organizations throughout the world. Some specialize in only one subject such as human rights, health,or environmental matters; others focus either on more general interests and agendas or on particular issues of a given speciality. Whether or not they have a formal affiliation with an intergovernmental organization, the NGOs resemble domestic pressure groups or lobbies.[1] NGOs have emerged as agents of information, initiators of development and proposals, in the area of protection of human rights. They are at the origin of most of the norms and are indispensable for forming public opinion there by ensuring actual implementation of proposals and plans relating to prfotection and implementation of human rights. The three documents constituting the international human rights Charter were possible by the elaboration, proposals and untiring work of the NGOs. Accordingly, in this chapter an attempt has been made to study the non-governmental organisations and implementation of Human rights. For this purpose, the present study has been divided under following heads:

1. NGOs at the International Level and in Different Countries.
2. Kinds of Human Rights Orgnisations.
3. Role of NGOs in Indian Perspective.
4. NGOs, voluntary Organisations and Public Interest Litigation.

NGOs AT THE INTERNATIONAL LEVEL AND IN DIFFERENT COUNTRIES

Human rights NGOs functions differ depending upon the purpose for which they were established their resources, the geographic regions in which they operate and the nature of their membership. There are NGOs which are interested in the world-wide promotion of human rights. Others limit their activities to human rights problems in specific regions or sub-regions or to specific countries or issues.[2]

Human rights NGOs have played a particularly important role in the evolution of the international system for the protection of human rights and in trying to make it work. Governments which violate human rights are always eager to make sure that the applicable international human rights norms institutions and procedures remain weak and ineffective. The human rights NGOs provide a needed counterpoint to these governmental attitudes and deserve much of the credit for the progress that has been made in recent decades.[3]

Amnesty International, the Lawyers Committee for Human Rights, the International League for Human Rights, the International Commission of Jurists, the Watch Committees, to cite but a few well-known NGOs, have world-wide interests. The Andean Commission of Jurists and the Washington Office for Latin America (WOLA), for example, are organizations with regional and sub-regional agendas.[4]

NGOs employ different methods in the pursuit of their goals. Some choose to resort to only one or a limited number of techniques or activities, be it the preparation of reports, the filing of complaints with international organizations, the promotion of international legislation, lobbying before national and international bodies, and so on.[5]

Main human rights NGOs have consultative status of one form or another with the UN, the Council of Europe, the Organization of American States, UNESCO and other regional or specialized intergovernmental Organisations. This status permits their representatives, subject to certain conditions and restrictions, to present committees and commissions and, in certain cases, to affect the agendas of these bodies. Many contemporary human rights instruments can be traced to proposals and,or drafts prepared by NGOs.[6]

Some NGOs have also contributed significantly to the strengthening of the reporting systems that have been established under various human rights treaties. Thus, for example, the International Covenants on Human Rights and the International Convention on the Elimination of all Forms of Racial Discrimination require the States Parties to file periodic reports indicating what action they have taken to comply with their obligations under these treaties. These reports are examined by special committees which these conventions created.[7]

The NGOs have on various occasions succeeded in getting the UN Commission on Human Rights, its Sub-Commission for the Prevention of Discrimination and Protection of Minorities and other UN bodies to focus on specific human rights violations, which they would otherwise not have done. The NGOs also deserve a great deal of credit for the creation by the UN and its Specialized Agencies of institutions and procedures for dealing with human rights violations. This has been accomplished by NGOs through their written and oral interventions in the proceedings of these bodies and by lobbying key representatives and delegations.[8]

As a rule, these committees lack the power to investigate the veracity of the claims made in the reports which the states submit. They are usually also not empowered to hear witnesses or to request information from sources other than the state representatives, who are heard when their country's report is discussed by the committee. On that occasion committee members are permitted to ask the state representatives questions about the contents of their reports. The restraints under which these committees operate make reliable fact-finding difficult. This has prompted a number of NGOs to prepare their own country reports. Their findings are then passed on to any interested committee members prior to its meetings with the representatives of the reporting state. The information supplied by the NGOs enables the members to probe the veracity of the state reports and to get material into the record that does not appear in the state reports.[9]

Some intergovernmental organizations have established legal mechanisms that permit individuals, groups and Non-governmental organizations to file human rights complaints, over the past five decades. NGOs have filed many complaints with the Inter-American Commission on Human Rights, both under the American Convention and under the OAS Charter-based petition system.[10] Human rights NGOs have pioneered the practice of using distinguished foreign lawyers or judges as observers at trials of individuals who have been charged with or appear to be tried for political offences. Amnesty International and the International Commission of Jurists try to make frequent use of trial observers in order to ensure due process of law for the accused.[11]

Human rights NGOs devote a great deal of time and resources to activities designed to influence the human rights policies and diplomacy of various countries. In the United States, for example, human rights NGOs are very active in promoting US ratification of international human rights instruments.[12]

There has also been, in many parts of the Third World the explosive emergence of NGOs as a major collective actor in development activities and on the public agenda in general.[13] One particular kind of third World NGO—poor people's organizations—have become internally more sophisticated and thus have increased their militancy and mobilization capabilities. While most of the Third World NGOs have not started with an explicit human rights agenda, they have tended to come rather quickly to activities involving the promotional and assertion of human rights.

AFRICA

The Organization of African Unity attributed the African crises to historical legacies. Africa's dependence on foreign markets, and deteriorating terms of trade and sketched a general strategy to escape these constraints by building self-reliant, local and regional economies, despite analysis of the crises and prescriptive solutions, however, the situation faced in most African Countries is unrelentingly grim. Most African Countries are confronted with:

(a) Dependency on a few primary export commodities and deteriorating terms of trade;

(b) Decline in agricultural production, often of cash crops and almost everywhere of basic food crops;

(c) Failure of import-substitution industrial development strategies;

(d) Deteriorating infrastructures for small holder agriculture;

(e) Recurrent weaknesses in the design or administration of programs of rural and agricultural development.[14]

A number of international reports of the World Bank, UNDP, UNICEF, FAO, etc., depict critical situation confronting most African countries: crises produced by a conjuncture of exogenous shocks, failures of national development strategies; and flaws and pathologies in development administration.[15]

Africa must confront a bewilderingly large number of deepening crises, some of them are as under:

(1) The apartheid crisis overshadows most of the other crises. A lawless regime in Pretoria continues to violate most shamelessly the most basic human rights of the people of South Africa. It also continues, through armed intervention as well as blatant economic intervention, to violate the sovereignty of neighboring countries and the rights of their people.

(2) The food crisis is constantly worsening as man-made famines combine with natural disasters to cause unparalleled human starvation and suffering.

(3) The ecological crisis has reached chronic, almost non-resolvable proportions and exacerbates the already severe food crisis.

(4) The debt crisis sees the poor in several countries of Africa reeling under austerity measures and cuts in social services programs resulting from the imposition of severe structural adjustment policies by the international financial institutions.

(5) The health crisis, reflected in dismal Infant and child mortality rates and in malnutrition figures, has been further exacerabated by the scourge of the AIDS epidemic.

(6) The refugee crisis remains severe, as wars rage unabated in several parts of the continent.

African NGOs have adopted their agendas for action in response to such crises and the rural poor figure prominently in such agendas.[16]

There are many reasons why both developmental and human rights NGOs in Africa are focusing on strategies for the rural poor.

In the first place, there now seems to be wide agreement that the productivity and well-being of peasant smallholders must be a central focus of concern in the countries which comprise this region. The need to boost deteriorating production of both food and other crops, and to arrest massive migrations to urban areas, and to create local markets, domestic industries and more equitable distributions of income and employment opportunity combine to produce this new emphasis.

Secondly, for reasons' grounded in both pragmatic assessments of the pathologies of development administration in rural areas and in human rights considerations, it seems vital that peasant smallholders must no longer be perceived as the passive objects of state-directed efforts at rural development, but rather as the active subjects of these efforts.[17]

The above discussion may be summarized as follows:

(1) Although there has not yet been, in Africa, the explosive emergence of NGOs as a collective actor such

as has occurred in Asia and Latin America, there has been a steady increase of NGO activity, proceeding usually in a more discreet manner.[18]

(2) African NGOs have tended to adopt much less confrontational stances against power elites. While they have advocated the approach of mobilizing and organizing groups of victims for their own self-help, such approach has not been vocalized as having empowerment as its prime objective. African NGOs have tended to be less overtly ideological. Thus, while liberation theology and dependencia theories might indeed influence their thinking, they have tended to rely oil more pragmatic justifications for their activities.

(3) African governments have tended to adopt a dualilstic relationship towards their NGOs. On the one hand, they welcome NGO activity in service providing areas to relieve pressure on the governments own programs in this regard. But on the other hand, given the severely scarce resource constraints that most African bureaucracies operate under, they would be resource constraints that most African bureaucracies operate under, they would be resentful were NGOs seen to be operating under conditions of plentiful resources.[19]

LATIN AMERICA

Latin America is a region with the longest history of the colonial experience. Ancient civilizations, like Aztecs, Mayas and Incas, were destroyed. Millions of natives died in the mines and land exploitations and in some places, spherically Islands, they totally disappeared.

Three centuries of colonial rule took away every piece of gold and silver Latin America could produce to be sent to Europe to finance first wars, and later the industrial revolution.

The sub-continent is now with indigenous people: blacks, majority of half breeds, and also with white Creoles and immigrants that came from Mediterranean countries including some sazon enclaves and even Japanies. The value, logics and structure of contrasted civilizations our imposed West the forced Africa—live together a wide melting pot.

War is present in many countries of the region (Central America, Columbia, Peru) and military intervention has been practiced in the Malvinas and Grenada. Chile, Haiti, Panama, Honduras, have open or concealed military regims, dictatorships or manipulated civil democracies. Cuba continues to be an isolataed island. The renaissance of fragile democracies in the southern countries (Argentina, Uruguay Brazil, Bolivia, Peru) after decades of military dictatorships.

The role of the so-called Non-governmental Organizations in this convulsive region is extremely important. Specially those concerned with human rights and development issues, social emergencies, grassroots movements, revolutionary or reformist instances, and other social forces like churches, universities, international cooperation agencies, etc.[20]

Latin America NGOs, appear to have passed through four main roles:

(1) *Intergradation:* Numerous programs were developed in the 50s having as their target training. The objective of these programs was to render assistance to the poor in order that they may be integrated into the rest of the society.[21]

(2) *Reform:* After the triumph of the Cuban Revolution in 1959, awareness was heightened among Latin American NGOs regarding the deep-rooted social problems which called for fundamental social transformations. In order to counter such transformations and the replications of Cuba, the U.S. created ALPRO (the Alliance for Progress) and provided support for trade unions, cooperatives, peasant leagues, enterprise associations, and liberal political parties all with the ideology of the free market and representative democracy.[22]

(3) *Revolution:* Repression and dictatorships marked the 1970s decade in many countries of Latin America

(Argentina, Urguay, Brazil, Chile, Paragray, even of violent reaction should be considered in all social initiatives trying to reach causes and structures. The aim to accumulate power and to cooperate with political parties and movements was present in many NGOs.

(4) *Civilization:* Many NGOs in the 1980s are becoming aware that orthodox schemes for development and even for revolution bring heavy costs to our people. Many paradigms of our action in the last 30 years have been imported, adopted, adapted, but not proper.[23]

In this perspective, the Latin American NGOs are trapped in a dilemma. Are they introducing the values, mechanics, targets and policies of the industrialized and post-industrialized societies with their own powerful NGOs channeling money in large amounts creating centralized and pyramidal enclaves, coopting the best local human resources, multiplying dependency through projects? Or are they people-rooted; underscoring the proper resources; mobilized by war or hunger suffered by people?

This kind of NGOs puts the accent more in participation than in representation and more on social productivity than concentration of economic or political power. They are based on voluntary work more than in remunertive work. They are generating a proper model of knowledge accumulation through the method of Participatory Action Research (PAR) awakening the people's memory and creating a generator perspective.

ASIA

Every country in Asia, to greater or lesser extent, we witness today 'several alarming and intolerable trends.Some of them are the following:

(1) The growing incidence of malnutrition, hunger and starvation and growing permanent degradation of the physical environment for the production of food and the meeting of survival needs.

(2) The glowing impoverishment, exploitation and powerlessness of a majority of the rural and urban population.

(3) The worsening of already intolerable conditions of those subject to multiple oppression and exploitation such as women, children and religious or ethnic minorities.

(4) The routinization of the debasement of human beings leading to very devaluation of human life.

(5) The increasing adoption, by the elites in such countries, of a life-style whose affluence can only be sustained by the pauperization and exploitation of others.

(6) The growth of fundamentalist trends in religious revivalism making religion a divisive rather than a cohesive force.

(7) The growth of material and moral corruption among the bureaucracy and their virtually total lack of accountability.

(8) The growing militarization of developing countries achieved through government expenditure on arms at the expense of programs to alleviate poverty.

(9) The increasingly authoritarian nature of political institutions despite their virtually total lack of accountability.[24]

The above has led to the emergence of three strands within the Asian human rights movement:

(1) Responding to extremely oppressive conditions and repressive regimes, a category of human rights NGOs emerged at local, grassroots level to mobilize local communities for protracted political struggles. Often inspired by liberation theology, these NGOs saw the human rights struggle as being, initially, a struggle against the present political regime.[25]

(2) Responding to the ineffectual nature of government programs to deliver basic services to the rural poor, a second set of NGOs attempted to deliver such services

themselves while also embarking upon education activities to develop the communities capacities to meet their own needs in the future. Such NGOs turned to human rights to assert entitlements of local impoverished communities to resources from the state to meet such needs.

(3) A third strand of the human rights movement in Asia arose out of the disillusionment of significant sections of the educated middle-classes with the results and the direction of the development model adopted by the country. Thus human rights organizations who were concerned about subjecting national development projects and developmental decision takers to accountability under international human rights law began to emerge.[26]

Both NGOs and grassroots organizations of the rural poor are turning to human rights as a means to:

(1) Empowerment: It is increasingly felt that human rights can play a significant role in the empowerment of the impoverished. The oppressed can become more self-reliant through an understanding of their rights. Indeed, the right to organize and rights of association are vital to impoverished groups seeking to mobilize and organize themselves and thus develop counterrvailing power.

(2) Securing accountability: Human rights can also play a significant role in securing the accountability of those who wield power and control resources essential to the satisfaction of basic human needs. Rights to secure mandamus or prohibition are important checks on abuse of power. Rights of access to information, rights to a public hearing and freedom of speech and of the press are crucial in checking governmental lawlessness and abuse of discretion or powers by bureaucraatic and government officials.

(3) Participation: Human rights have an important role to play in combating exclusion as well as in asserting

the right to participate in key decisions affecting resource allocation or relating to technology choice.

(4) Assert values: Human rights are also being increasingly viewed as a means to express and reinforce social value and ethical principle which should underlie the much-needed restructuring of social orders.[27]

The professional and intellectuals in the Third World have attempted to reach out to human rights activists through a variety of intellectual and professional movements:

(1) The Regional Studies and Development Studies Movement in many Third World countries has helped reorient lawyers and social scientists to special problems of development and underdevelopment and to the human rights implications of such process. This has helped forge a new sense of identity and solidarity around Third World issues and has helped sensitize them to processes of impoverishment, exploitation, exclusion, and dependency and to the roles of human rights theory and activism in fighting against such processes.

(2) The Critical Studies Movement has called attention to deep-rooted pathologies that exist in law and the legal profession in most Third World countries. The Movement has been iconoclastic: debunking legal sacred cows and myths by calling attention to the wide gap that exists between the law on the books and the law in action; between law and justice the movement has worked towards securing fundamental changes in the legal system to make it more accessible, more indigenous, more just and more supportive of social change.

(3) The Alternatives Movement has challenged the development models adopted by Third World countries models emphasizing modernizataion, industrialization, economic growth, and integration into the global capitalist system. The movement

stimulate human rights activism in support of the victims of development policies and projects and has also stimulated activism centered around formulating arid implementing policies and programs of alternative development which are built and the adoption of alternatives to Western consumer-oriented life-styles.

(4) Participator Action research: The concept of participatory action research (PAR) originated in Latin America but soon gained acceptance in Asia and Africa. PAR emphasizes the importance of participatory development of knowledge, action strategies and human rights through closes interaction with grassroots communities. PAR has fundamentally changed human rights thinking and activism in the Third World by broadening the base of human rights actors to include those we are victims of human rights violations.[28]

Most social activists adopted an attitude of legal nilhilism; the less contact with the legal system as their work on grassroots conscientization and organization gathered momentum. They soon began to shed such an attitude. Contact between activists and intellectuals and professionals increased within the context of specific action strategies which necessitated new forms of association and organization:

(1) *Campaigns:* such as the Infant formula Campaign.

(2) *Coalition:* such as the International Coalition for Justice in Bhopal.

(3) *Solidarity and protest organizations:* such as Greenpeace.

(4) *Lobby groups:* such as the Asia Pacific Forum for Woven, Law and Development.

(5) *Regional networks:* such as the Asian Regional council on Human rights.

(6) *Social movements:* such as the consumer movement, the women's movement and the environmental movement.[29]

Intellectual movements, social movements, and pragmatic-action strategies and campaigns have brought the main human rights actors in the third World – victims, activists, intellectuals, and professions – together in variety of situations of infraction. As a result, human rights organization in the third World have become more interdisciplinary in nature and more broad-based in composition.

A few Third World NGOs wear the label of human rights. But the vast majority of Third World NGOs, concerned primarily with education, or development, or delivery of support and services, have adopted human rights into their agendas and programs of action. A broad definition of human rights organization in the Third World would have to include all these non-specialist NGOs which are undertaking significant human rights activities.[31]

KINDS OF HUMAN RIGHTS ORGANISATIONS

On the basis of functions which the human rights organisations perform, there may be following kinds:

(1) *International, Regional, National, Local:* In Asia, where the governments have firmly rejected any regional intergovernmental human rights organization, a number of regional non-governmental organization have sprung up.

(2) *Governmental, Non-governmental, Intergovernmental:* While the majority of human rights organizations in the third World are non-governmental, there has been the recent trend to establish governmental human rights commissions.

(3) *On the Consideration of membership:* In Asia, a distinction is usually drawn between people-based organizations (PBOs) and participatory organization of the rural poor (PORPs) on the one hand which are primary-level organizations, and support groups which render services to PBOs and which are referred to as secondary-level organizations.

(4) *On the Consideration of target:* Some human rights organizations serve only single target groups. Distinctions are being made between human rights organizations performing, mobilizational roles, advocacy group; documentation center; forum; coalition; or campaign are used to describe a range of human rights organizations in the Third World.

(5) *According to category of human rights* specialization this Western categorization of groups focusing on civil and political rights and those focusing on economic, social, and cultural rights, is not much used in the Third World where organizations tend to focus on both categories of rights.[31]

Third World human rights organizations did not start as explicit human rights organizations at all and may have been emergency-aid organizations, philanthropic, developmental, or environmental organizations.

Third World human rights organizations are not a mirror image of their first World counterparts. Nevertheless, it is possible and useful to study Third world human rights organizations in terms of the conventional roles of human rights activism.[32]

(1) *Promotion:* Many third World human rights organizations do embark on typical human rights promotion activities employing locally appropriate devices such as comic books, folk theatre etc.

(2) *Standard setting:* third World human rights organization are increasingly recognizing the importance of participating in standard-setting work, both at, the international level as well as at the national level.

(3) *Monitoring:* Third World human rights groups have been actively monitoring implementation of national legislation and are beginning to be concerned with international human rights law.

(4) *Enforcement:* Impressive strides have been made here by third World human rights groups in assisting enforcement of rights through the courts.

(5) *Lobbying for law reform:* There has been a flurry of activity here especially in countries like the Philippines where parliamentary, legislative processes have been restored after a long lapse of time.

Human rights organizations in the third World have also played unique roles which result from their human rights activism originating in community and victim-group mobilization and organization.[33]

Thus Human rights organizations in the third World have acted:

(1) help to create, grassroots organizations and help their organizational development. They have helped organize people to make better use of their own local productive resources, to create new resources and services, to promote equity and alleviate poverty, to influence government actions towards the same objectives and to establish new institutional frameworks that will durably sustain humane people-powered development.

(2) help to act as an intermediary between local government and community organizations.

(3) help to, where circumstances warrant, raise funding and direct it to local community organizations.

(4) help to develop capacity for and strengthen community based resource management with an emphasis on participation, equality and equity. Human rights organization working in neglected rural areas have helped set up local production related organization such as water-user societies,pastoral-grazing associations, credit, production or consumer cooperatives, food processing cooperatives, farm equipment purchase or lease associations, tree grower associations, etc.

(5) help to create not only the means for community organizing but also for community self-defence.

(6) help to assert community rights and raise community awareness and expectations,

(7) help to protect activists against reprisals from high handed administrators.[34]

Thus, human rights organization in the Third World have had to constantly undergo a process of self-development. There has been a need for constant reflection based on praxis to reconceptualize human rights concepts and theory. There has also been a need for a professional unlearning and relearning process accompanied by the development of genuine professional humility.[35]

Third World human rights NGOs have tended to shy away from institutional relationships with one another. Attempts to coordinate have been received as attempts to control. NGOs cherish their autonomy, identity, and independence and there foe are willing to accept at most, loose coordination Within a membership organization. Other factors militating against formal institutional relationships involve turf; competition for scarce or limited resources; ethnic, religious, or other cultural diversity; different perceptions of mandate ranging from narrow civil libertarian to broad empowerment focused.[36]

Third World human rights NGOs are much more successful in their functional relationships. They have often come together in action campaigns. They have worked together on training programs, on fact-finding missions and on election monitoring. Such situations do not endanger each NGOs independent identity, hence functional relationships have proved much more effective than institutional relationships.

The role of NGOs cannot be underrated. For it is only through them many problem have been highlighted and brought to the notice of National and International organisations eg; Deforestation, Carpet factory, Match factory, Glass factory, Women abuse, Child labour and Hazardous industries.[37]

We appeal to human rights organisations to stress that life whether in the first or third world has equal value and must receive the same care and protection. The NGOs also have played in important role in the activities of the United Nations in the field of human rights. The human rights to healthy and safe environment was first recognised in the UN Universal declaration of human rights in 1948. The constitutional recognition of human rights to a safe and healthy environment by several countries has had minimal impact on the level of protection actually enjoyed by the most vulnerable individuals and groups.[38]

When foreign governments permit their individuals and corporations to export hazardous substances and technologies and the lack of capacity of the unknowing receiving countries to cope with unforeseeable consequences of such perverse development e.g., banned medicines dumped into developing country as charity. The Governments and Public Sectors which are bemused by the latest technologies and without giving a thought to the consequences import hazardous technologies in chemical and nuclear power, Cobalt scanners, cobalt X-ray machines at exorbitant prices.[39]

It is submitted that the Bangalore principles do not undermine the soverignty of national laws making institutions. They acknowledge that if those institutions have made a rule which is unambiguous and binding, no international human rights principle can undermine or overrule the applicable domestic law. To introduce such a principle requires the opportunity of a gap in the common law or of an ambiguity of a local statute. For form being a negation of soverignity, this is an application of it.[39a]

The technologies which have become obsolete in Developed countries and found to be hazardous are dumped into the 3rd world countries. Here again the NGOs which are unaffected financially and otherwise can without fear of repercussions come forward and enlighten the public and make them aware of the hazards and fight for the rights of innocent public.[41]

We are destroying our planet Earth non-violently but none the less relentlessly. It is increasing the rate of species extinction. Disposal of toxic and nuclear waste in vulnerable areas, loss of forest and of arable soil lit fill alarming rate will affect the survival of the present and future generations. It is again an NGO, CHIPKO movement and Sunderlal Bahuguna who brought it into limelight. There are universal Declaration of Human Rights of 1948. The Article 25 & Article 3 can also form the basis of it safe and healthy environment. The rights were reiterated in the 1972 Stockholm declaration at the UN Conference on Environment. But neither of these declarations are legally binding. The most recent pronouncement on human rights and environment is contained in resolution 1990,40 of 6th march 1990 adopted at 52nd meeting of the commission of human rights of UN Economic and social councils:

Calls upon all states approved UN bodies specialised agencies and intergovernmental and non-governmental organization to take necessary measures to ensure that the result of scientific and technological progress...are used for benefit of mankind and for promoting and encouraging universal respect for human rights and fundamental freedom and not abuse human values. The human rights movement is approximately 20 years old. Although a post World War II movement it is really in 1970s that it took its present characteristic i.e. a movement made up of independent national, regional and international NGOs. It is a highly diverse movement that has now spread into every continent.[42]

Health and happiness go hand in hand. Thus the right to good health is regarded as one of the basic human rights. The problems arising out of disability are varied and complex. Most of the problems encountered by the disabled stem from prejudices and ignorance on the part of the so called healthy persons. From the holistic point of view the definition of the term disability as given by the UN is quite exhaustive in its meaning. There are various types of disabilities namely; (1) visual disability (2) hearing disability (3) speech disability (4) mental retardation and (5) orthopedic disability.[43]

According to UN estimate more than 500 million people are physically or mentally disabled and the population of disabled is increasing every year by 15 million as a result of war, accident, malnutrition and disease. By 2010 the figure may surpass 700 million mark. 1/5th of these is women about 250 million. Thus such women are subjected to dual discrimination.

This colossal magnitude of the Problem need to be dealt with and fought on all fronts by government and voluntary organisations with concrete and bold efforts to provide rehabilitation. The help of NGOs becomes necessary since NGOs include nonprofit associations, foundations, groups and volunteers. They are very diverse in structure, composition and objective. Some deal with education, others are activists and yet others deal with technical projects.[44]

NGOs, first of all, locally based can recognise the vulnerable group and disseminate relevant information. Secondly, play an important role in the education of the citizen, a role which the authors of the universal declaration considered of prime importance. NGOs are tools by which human rights can be made known and respected. Last but not the least of the three functions of NGOs is that of catalyst encouraging official bodies to act. There are various non government organisations all over the world without whose help it will be impossible to sort out and solve the problem. Because of illiteracy and apathy towards such individuals even family members do not care properly They are considered a burden on the family and society. They can lead the vulnerable persons to proper organisation which will give guidance, training and rehabilitation to such individuals. NGOs can collect funds, run schools and find jobs. They can develop work potential for such persons by opening centers at places where easily approachable e.g. vocational training is given and work is generated. It requires lot of dedication and hard work and also sympathetic and psychological approach and of course personal involvement. Which is not possible by non human approach of government bodies who do it as only part of their job and not with a similar approach as a group of concerned citizens, development activists, social workers and child development experts would do.[45]

The rehabilitation process, involves basically three aspects. (1) physical rehabilitation, (2) vocational rehabilitation and (3) psycho-social integration. Thus linking of NGOs and government authorities is important. Various norms have been laid down by UN through its various resolutions and declarations.[46]

International NGOs have played a crucial role in raising private funds and channeling them to developing countries but there have been problems of NGO independence, geographical allocation of resources, interference in the NGOs own agenda, priorities and approach; and of NGO accountability.[47] Third world NGOs have helped work out for themselves some of the problems inevitable in a donor,recipient relationship and have even begun to articulate the elements that helpbuild up a good relationship: demandled, honesty, commitment to values and goals, relevance, flexibility, confidentiality, partnership, long-term collaboration. They have even been able to soften donor insistence upon projectizing activities and have earned recognition of the principle that not only project but also processes are deserving of donor support.[48]

Thus, over the years, Third World NGOs and donor agencies have been working seriously towards fashioning a truly rewarding partnership of equals. This partnership is presently in great peril with governments in countries like Indonesia and India placing severe constraints upon the NGOs freedom to receive foreign funding. These restraints have also been accompanied by a variety of other restrictive or corporative measures which place in jeopardy the effective survival of NGOs as autonomous and independent entities.[49]

The NGOs are fighting back against their own governments repressive policies. At this juncture their most vital need for external support is precisely support in their present struggle for survival. Donors can, and should, exert influence over recipient governments to ensure that the latter maintain public policy and legislative frameworks that safeguard the role of NGOs—a role they have fought so hard and so long to get recognized.[50]

Similarly, donor agencies must be vigilant to ensure that NGOs win their struggle not only against repression but also against cooptation. The current flood of rhetoric from governmental and international agencies alike, looking to NGOs to perform a variety of functions and play a variety of roles that governmental agencies themselves cannot, must be viewed with healthy scepticism as a potentially cooptative ploy.[51]

A number of specialised agencies, such as ILO, UNESCO, WHO, UNICEF, UNDP, FAO, UNIDO,UNCHER etc. besides these many NGOs like Rotary International, Lions International, Maitraiyi and many others are deeply engaged in rehabilitation task. It is the NGOs who are constantly in touch with the grass roots of the problems and carry on their activities with utmost dedication irrespective of governmental support and backing by authorities. The international bodies may only provide guidelines and set norms for the human rights, but the main task of integrating and implementing them remains that of the member nations.[52]

The NGOs can help the government authorities by implementing programmes to preserve the sense of well being and proper health of the vulnerable groups. The whole scheme of preventive measures requires immunization against infections and congenital diseases. It is an effective measure of preventing disability and death.[53]

WHO as part of its global efforts has launched its expanded programme of immunization (EPI) in 1974. Approximately 200 million lives are saved each year. Rotary International (a NGO) is busy with the programme with the local bodies. There are well known big NGOs who with local chapters and dedicated volunteers are also doing their best to help such problems.[54]

In the third world many nutritional disorders are endemic which lead to wise spread impairment and disability leading to drain of work capacity of the nation. To mention a few major ones Protein Energy Malnutrition (PEM), endemic goiter, xerophthalmia leading to blindness and nutritional anemia.[55]

The NGOs help by providing nutritional education for families and educating the farmers about crop rotation.proper storage, judicial use of pesticides and germicides. Magnitude of this requires no telling. Again many organisations like CARE, WHO, UNICEF are working hand in hand with the Government and local. NGOs to combat these problems by educating the people, improving food habits, providing supplementary feeding programmes like enriching the local foods by additives for example flour with B-Complex, edible fat with vitamin A&D, add Iodine to salt in goiter belts. 'Me magnitude of the projects is so big that it will become impossible without NGOs help, eg. Tata Salts, who are also advertising the use and benefit of iodised salt. Food adulteration is again a big problem in our country which has not been touched but is equally hazardous to the health and well being and can even cause permanent damage for example Lathyrism, Milk, cereals, pulses, spices and condiments arc copiously adulterated. Government makes laws and rules.[56]

FAO has also laid down guidelines regarding the content of foods and additives, but the implementation again is difficult. Only through non-profit voluntary organisations and judiciary can the culprits be brought to Justice. For government bodies In most places are corrupt and close their eyes and ears if their pockets are filled. The awareness of malpractice in food additives, spurious advertising and selling gimmicks has baffled the public.[57]

Some enlightened individuals have started consumer protection societies and forums in many cities and the idea is spreading. MRTP act is also helpful but only when people complain. When the public is made aware through mass media and local bodies can the consumer be protected.[58]

Diseases like AIDS spreading their tentacles, blighting the lives of hundreds of youth. In 1989 there were only 49 victims of AIDS in India but now the toll is above 1000 and unreported cases many times more. The teenage segment is a pathetic spectacle. Parents unable to cope send the children to prison due to lack of social organisations to provide crucial care. New Life—a central government Organisation has proved ineffective. Blood banks role in Bombay is scandalous and only NGOs which are incorruptible and dedicated can save the situation.[59]

Drug abuse needs a multi-dimensional and multi-faceted approach. It is a psychosocial and medico problem. Only detoxification does not solve the problem because it is necessary to understand that the addict is both physically and psychologically weakened. It is a social problem largely due to social conditions. A community based approach has to be adopted to counteract. Pre and post detoxification counseling for becoming drug free can be done at drug deaddiction centres by volunteers. As early as 1985-86 the significance to fight this growing problem came into notice of government. A scheme to rehabilitate drug addicts was prepared. By 1986-87 seven counseling centres came up in the voluntary sector. These centres began functioning' each with a team of very dedicated social workers, counselors and doctors. So far 86 counseling centres have been set up in the country.

Thus rehabilitation by accentuating the positive side, encouraging a hobby, nurturing friendship, providing information are important. The rehabilitation programme specialists say educate at home, show and tell and promote alternatives to the sufferer. The NGOs community has emerged as a potent force in catalyzing various actions through the mobilization of social forces and pressing government bodies to take needed action in all activities.

NGOs are emerging as agents of information, initiators of development and proposals, in the field of protection of human rights. They are at the origin of most of norms and are indispensable for forming public opinion there by ensuring actual implementation of proposals and plans. The three documents constituting the international human rights Charter were possible by the elaboration, proposals and untiring work of the NGOs.

The active part played by NGOs in the foundation of world organisation for human rights is exemplified by the fact that UN Charter provides that Economic and Social Council may make suitable arrangements for consultation with non-government organisations which are concerned with matters within their competence. In national and international bodies, law and practice are not always on the same wavelength, the gap between the fundamental needs of people and UN debates is widening and the NGOs are the only ones who can build bridges between these two realities.

ROLE OF NGOs IN INDIAN PERSPECTIVE

In India the present NGOs movement towards human rights activism has its origin to emergency era and inherently to some of the leading events such as the "increasing weakness in professional efficiency of the state apparatus and many of the democratic institutions like the bureaucracy, political parties, judiciary and the media, their social bias and political partisanship and the growing incredibility in popular perceptions which have a close bearing on India's quest for nation-building, economic development and social transformation. In addition to this, the brutalisation of state machinery, criminalisation of politics, use of money, muscle and mafia in electoral practices, misuse of preventive detention, intensification of the social and regional tensions in Kashmir, Assam, Punjab, Andhra Pradesh, Tamil Nadu and Karnataka, the demand for regional autonomy and the emergence of democratic groups like PUCL, PUDR, APCLC, etc., are also some of the results of this movement.[60] It is evident that many NGOs are working with stimulating zeal and sparkling style; with refreshing fearlessness and passion for socio- spiritual betterment; explores men and matters, issues and themes, displaying a deep commitment to humanity.[61]

V.R. Dasgupta suggests for human rights organisations as under[62]: (a) To work constantly for the improvement and evolution of a human rights culture which is in harmony with the genius of the Nation and in consonance with Bharatiya traditions, values and sense of justice and to make justice delivery system more and more efficient. (b) To strive towards excellence in all spheres of individual and collective activity so that the nation constantly rises to higher levels of endeavour and achievement. (c) The unity, integrity and sovereignty of the nation is the basic commitment of the parishad and it shall undertake, encourage and promote all activities whose object is to imbibe the spirit of unity and integrity and develop brotherhood amongest the children of Bharatmata. (d) To cultivate the science of law and to promote advance studies and research in law and its administration. (e) To promote the reform of administration of justice and of law and its healthy development suitable to the social, economic and other needs of the people. (f) To promote the diffusion of the knowledge of law and its administration and principles on which they are based. (g) To encourage and conduct investigations in legal and allied fields. (h) To promote excellence in legal education and to impart instructions in law and allied fields. (i) To publish studies, treations, books, periodicals, reports and other literature relating to law and allied fields. (j) To undertake documentation of important legal and allied materials. (k) To institute and maintain libraries. (l) To review the working of Indian constitution and laws from time to time and suggest such changes as may be required to make them effective instruments for service of the society. (m) To work for making legal remedies available to all, particularly the weaker sections of the society and to strive for proper implementation of law (n) To work for the improvement of the legal system with a view to making it more responsive to the needs of the community and that justice is delivered equal quickly and with the least expense to the litigent (o) To pursue advocates with a view of harnessing their intellect and energies organise and awaken the Bharatiya Samaj and to work for its welfare. (p) To co-operate with other societies, institutions and organisations, national and international in the pursuit of all or any of the above objects; and to affiliate with apex All India Body with similar objects. (q) To do all such things and to perform all such acts as may be, necessary or proper for the achievment of any or all of the above objects.[62]

In Indian context, a large number of NGOs have been coming forward to undertake the herculean task of promoting human rights at the grass-roots. For example, NGOs like Vigil India Movement (Banglore), Citizen for Democracy (Aligarh), Prayas (Delhi), Institute of Objective Studies (Delhi), Foundation for Legal Aid Environment and Social Action (Guntur, A.R), Human Rights Wing (Darbhanga, Bihar), Society for Rural Development and Action (Mandi, Himachal Pradesh), People's Union of Civil Liberties (Srinagar, J & K), Indian People's HRC (Bombay), Human Rights Education Movement of India (Madras, Tamilnadu) are some of the trustworthy and prominent institutions. There activities include publishing newsletters, research work, organising seminars, conferences, street-plays, folk dances at community level.

Moreover, World Vision (India) and the Society for the Promotion of Youth and Masses (SPYM) has been working on human rights in specific areas such as girl child rights, women's rights etc. In the field of promotion of human rights in the rural areas, pro-active commitments of some voluntary organisations and their dedicated workers are highly appreciable and of paramount importance.

NGOs Role Towards Legal Aid Programmes

'The voluntary organisations and social action groups must be encouraged 'and supported by the State in operating the legal aid programmes. It is now acknowledged throughout the country that the legal aid programme which is needed for the purpose of reaching social justice' to the people cannot afford to remain confined to the traditional or litigation oriented legal aid programme but it must, taking into account the socio-economic conditions prevailing in the country, adopt a more dynamic posture and take within its sweep what may be called strategic legal programmes consisting of promotion of legal literacy, organisation of legal aid camps, encouragement of public interest litigation and holding of Lok Adalats or Niti Melas for bringing about settlements of disputes whether pending in Court or outside.[63] 'Every voluntary organisation or social action group which receives support from the State Govt.. has to furnish whatever factual information is required by the Central Govt. State Government, or the Committee for implementing Aid Schemes' or the State Legal Aid and Advice Board, but such voluntary organisation or social action group must not be under the control or direction or supervision of the State Government or the State Legal Aid and Advice Board because voluntary organisations and social action groups operating these programmes should be totally free from any Governmental control.[64] The State Government undoubtedly has an obligation under Article 39-A of the Constitution, which embodies a Directive Principle of State Policy to set up a comprehensive and effective legal aid programme in order to, ensure that the operation of the legal system promotes justice on the basis of equality.[65]

In order to provide pre-litigation services, the voluntary organisations have been encouraged and boosted by financial support from the State. Legal aid clinics have been established in law colleges and law faculties in the Universities. The clinics have done commendable work in creating legal awareness among the rural masses of the society. Neither it was possible for the State nor for voluntary organisations to organise legal literacy camps in all the villages and slum areas of the city, therefore/a need was felt to create a force of para-legal agencies. Para legals are the persons who do not possess full knowledge of law but they have preliminary knowledge of it. Para-legals are the human resource that can enlighten the rural masses about their legal rights and duties. Most of the litigation is only due to the ignorance of the people about their legal rights and duties. Para-legals is the force that can go in the interior areas of the society and can provide preliminary help and assistance in the field of law, to the needy persons.[66]

To protect the weak against the strong is the modem interpretation of the maintenance of social order and, consequently, it is an essential function of the State.[67] It means that the policies of the government should be so determined and its laws so formulated that equal opportunity is provided to all to grow and expand and no one is denied his necessities. To express it in the words of Mr. Roosevelt, former President of U.S.A., the State should strive to establish a social order which should ensure "freedom from wants", and "freedom from fear" for all. These are welfare functions and a government that claims to be responsive to the needs of the people cannot afford to ignore them.[68]

But the present system of administration of justice is not favourable to the downtrodden and vulnerable masses of the community-It suffers from various defects more specifically those of delay and expense. People are priced out of judicial system not only by reason of its expensiveness but also because of the nature and the condition of the legal and judicial process-Judicial process has become cumbersome. Pleadings in it have become formal and thereby law itself has become alien to the majority of civic population. Judicial proceedings are so complicated that the poor people can hardly understand them. They sit in Court as helpless spectators in their own case.[69] They are completely mystified by the ceremonial formalities of Court Proceedings and this, to a large extent, alienates them from Law, the legal system and the judicial process. Thus, the courts are being used mostly for the purpose of vindicating the rights of the wealthy and affluent sections because they alone possess the golden key to unlock the doors of justice, while the rights of the poor go unprotected.[70]

There is a constitutional prescription of justice: social, political and right to equality, yet one can hardly expect equal justice under present legal system unless and until it provides additional support to weaker persons.[71] Indeed, the Courts are temples of justice but for the poor they are rather like five star hotels and one can hardly hope to have an easy access to them without having ample money in the pocket and spare time for completing unwanted judicial formalities.[72] The poverty has become one of the greatest obstacles, which restrains persons in seeking justice through these courts of law. The law has become a bewildering jungle of rules and a procedure, which confounds both judges and lawyers alike. In such circumstances, a poor fellow is not expected to conduct his case successfully without sufficient aid and assistance. The legal professionalism, monopolisation of the knowledge of law, exorbitant fees of lawyers are the factors which are coming in the way of a poor fellow in seeking justice in courts.[73] The poor fellow always cries for justice and sorely needs a helping hand for his survival and struggle for existence in the realm of law. Hon'ble Justice P.N. Bhagwati rightly warned that it is a highly dangerous and explosive situation and the earlier we realise its gravity, the better it is for all of us in this country.[74] Indeed, in the present legal system the poor are always exploited, harassed and they always face the painful side of law. Therefore, before their patience is exhausted something must be done- Law must not only speak justice but also behave justly to do justice and this can be done only by infusing legal aid in arteries of present Indian legal system.

Justice A. S. Anand, aptly explained the drawback in the present legal system in following words:

> "The poor, illiterate and weaker sections in our country suffer day in and day out in their struggle for survival and look to those who have promised them equality-social, political and economic. We, who are responsible for upholding the Rule of Law in the country, may not be in a position to solve all of their problems but we can certainly contribute our might to nourish and safeguard the constitutional goal of 'equal justice for all' to the extent possible. I am deeply pained when I notice that all over the country, a very large number of under-trial prisoners suffer prolonged incarceration even in petty criminal matters merely for the reason that they are not in a position, even in bailable offences, to furnish bail bonds and get released on bail. Many of them during such confinements only develop criminal traits and come out fully trained criminals."[75]

This requires wholesale reform and new reorientation of law. The existing law is not suitable in present day Indian context. It is required to be shaped in conformity with new economic conditions of human life. It must become a source of strength and comfort to the deprived and vulnerable sections of the community and an active dispenser of Justice.[76] The law must prove itself as a protector of weaker section and ensure social justice, which is its most important task in the present context. In this way the institution of legal aid becomes very essential to balance the interest of affluent class and the socio-economical backward segment of the society. Thus, legal aid seems to be a by-product of social dynamism that urges changes in law and initiates legal reform. It gives social interpretation to various principles and doctrines like equality, rule of law, social justice etc.[77]

The most important function of the welfare State is the creation of conditions that., assure social justice by removing social inequalities created by capitalism. Poverty has been a problem in all times and it did not become less acute with the advancement of civilisation. Hence, there is a great responsibility on the shoulders of socialistic State to assure social justice to the poor masses of the society. The eradication and control of poverty is essentially the function of modem Welfare Slate. This can be done by launching suitable socio-economic schemes by Government. But so long as it exists, it creates disabilities on the part of poor persons and they become unable to have the full benefits of legal and political rights. In this context, it is the paramount mission of the NGOs and voluntary organisations to undertake protective measures for the welfare of the weaker sections of the community and also to provide an additional support to the poor so that they may be able to reap the full benefit of the welfare legislation.[78]

Being a welfare state. India is also taking its long strides towards social justice. In order to mitigate economic inequalities and social disabilities incorporation of social justice becomes necessary in the administration of justice. Here the dynamic role of NGOs and voluntary organisations is important to enhance the cause of Legal Aid strategies. The Legal Aid is very essential for the survival of healthy democracy, which is founded on the equality, dignity and worth of the man. As such the brotherhood of man is the solid basis of a democratic society and all its members stand equal as common fraternal beings. A society riddled with social and economic inequalities cannot be regarded as democratic. Today political democracy has become a social democracy that aims at the welfare of all its classes. For want of appropriate system of administration of justice, social justice is not available to all and we cannot keep our political democracy on the path of social progress and economic development. Therefore, it is idle to speak of the blessing of democracy in which the poor though enjoys all the equal protection of law, yet suffer all the unjust social consequences. The society rots if one citizen is overpowered or undermined by another. A democratic government cannot succeed in such an undemocratic society.[79]

NGOs and voluntary organisations also provide on intellectual and moral leadership to propagate and support the dynamic concept of rule of law by their missionary campaign, common cause programmes and pressure action strategies. The rule of law without legal aid is nothing but a pseudo slogan and a jurist myth. Equal access to justice for the rich and the poor alike must be seen as an essential part of the maintenance of the rule of law. Rule of law does not mean that the protection of law must be made available only to the fortunate few, and that law should be allowed to be prostituted by vested interests for protecting and upholding the status-quo under the guise of enforcement of their civil and political rights. The poor too have civil and political rights and they are also the beneficiaries of the rule of law.[80] We cannot be said to live under the rule of law till all citizens are effectively allowed to assert and defend their legal rights. If it does not happen then the rule of law exists on paper and not in reality. The rule of law oppresses the poor and the rich men take advantage of the rule of the law. The principle of the rule of law is not an end in itself. Left to it, it has been said that it has got all the propensity of becoming quite an 'unruly horse' and has also the capacity of hitting the poor below the belt. Certainly this happens in the absence of legal aid or when a party is not adequately represented in a legal system.

The doctrine of rule of law in its social meaning cannot afford to rule out the insufficient and inadequate protection and enforcement of the right of all people in usual course. The rule of law in its real spirit by excluding arbitrariness must postulate that the people are under the rule of law and not under the rule of men. Gujarat Committee rightly observed[81] that there could be no rule of law unless the machinery of law is readily accessible to all. The poor must be placed in the same position as the rich by means of adequate legal aid.

The concept of legal aid is the very spirit of equality and its movement is dedicated to the principle of equal justice to the poor. Equal justice of fair treatment within the purview of judicial process implies an easy access to courts and other governmental agencies on the basis of equality. Equal justice requires a systematic approach in removing the prevailing inequalities and injustices in our society. Legal aid is a vital limb of our Constitution and becomes, for this reason, an interpretative doctrine reflecting the desired fulfilment of the basic objectives of equality. Equal justice is corrective of inequalities, which create social imbalance in society. If a large section of society is prevented from exercising its legal power for protection of their rights and security of an honourable existence, there can be neither equality nor justice in such society.[82]

NGOs and voluntary organisations with their pro-active approach and fact finding mission constantly reminds the state and law emforcing machinaries that equal justice for all is a cardinal principle on which our entire system of administration of justice is based. To be just is to equal and impartial to all. Justice and equality are the principles of righteousness and today they depend for their validity upon contingence of legal aid. Legal aid alone can hold the weaker sections to make their stand in the legal battle in the Courts of law where they are often defeated due to want of economic means. The denial of justice to needy person is nothing but a negation of equality. Equal representation before the law in a true democracy must be claimed as a matter of right. It cannot be granted as a matter of charity or favour. The poor suffer denial of redress and equal protection of law because of inability to pay for legal services-Thus, the old rule "Every person must bring his own suit upon his own bottom at his own expenses" operated very harshly against poor who have not enough money to meet out the cost of litigation. Hence, without legal aid there can be no equality in a true sense.[83]

NGOs movement in modern legal, political and social theory is organically related to the urge for social justice. This idea dawned upon human consciousness after the French Revolution and the declaration of liberty, equality and fraternity as the guiding principle of social and political life. The term social justice is comprehensive of social, economical and political facets of life and its aim is to remove imbalances prevailing in the society amongst people particularly in social and economical spheres, and to ensure a reasonably equal and conducive situation for all round development of all people. Social justice represents a great humanistic aspiration in the world and provides necessary help to those persons who are not getting justice. Ulpian, who describes justice, as "giving each man his due" must be properly understood. Functional and motivated theme of NGOs is based on the paramount mission that social Justice provides social due, and postulates that no person should be deprived of justice due to social inequalities. Poverty must not become disqualification for those who seek justice.[84]

Social justice is gravitational doctrine. It directs all other doctrines their progressive mutual fulfilment and realisation. It is a pole star by which all human activities are redirected. It is not a Utopian slogan but is a living concept and something, which is capable of a comprehensive human sympathy for those who need it urgently for making their life worth living. Legal aid provides equal opportunities in the administration of justice and to some extent removes social inequalities. In this way NGOs and voluntary organisations has become an important limb of social justice.[85]

Similarly one of the principles of natural justice i.e., audi alteram partem is in absence of legal aid may become a mere formality or procedural, requirement and can be used as a subtle device to hoodwink justice. The truth of the dicta that no one shall be condemned unheard is dependent upon adequate and proper legal representation to ensure proper hearing. The opportunity of being heard is not available to a large section of society on account of poverty. The right of being heard without a provision of vocal chord of legal aid is a sheer formality and an illusion devoid of reality.[86]

Like its elder sister equity, legal aid has arisen in the history of legal development to soften the rigours of law, to mitigate its hardship and to make it more just. Equity though related to legal aid is distinguishable from it. Equity is medieval in its origin and has antiquated itself whereas, legal aid is modern and more alive and potent to provide a new approach and evaluation of law and its worrying in society by looking to the practical social consequences and defects. Legal aid with all the potentiality has to become a programatic attack upon legal anomalies. It can provide stimulus for theoretical analysis and amplification of law and its doctrines.

The concept of legal aid should not be considered as extraneous and foreign to our legal system but as an essential part of it. It is neither a charitable sentiment nor an idle dream or a Utopian project. It is an organic and real function of the administration of justice. It is an effective mode of imparting social justice, which means real justice in society. This must be considered vital for the furtherance of social solidarity and national integration of different sections of Indian Community. It is to be seen as the legal commitment of the State to its citizens.

In formal sense legal aid is neither more nor less than the help given to a person concerned to maintain his or her right under the law.[87] At its minimum, it is a phrase which means giving to persons' of limited means gratis, or for nominal fees, legal advice and legal assistance in court in civil and criminal matters.[88] But the upholding of a man's right has to be seen in the light of social and economic conditions for this, the meaning of legal aid is to be re-understood. Legal aid reacts against inequitable conditions of life in society, which are maintained under the law. It is an anti-monopolistic, socialistic or collectivist device calling for the proper distribution of the services of law. Legal aid in its wider meaning equalises the fruits of justice in action in all social, economic and political fields. It makes imperative that no man shall be denied his right at law for lack of means.

Legal aid movement has become a social movement and its ultimate aim is to establish social righteousness by mitigating and ameliorating legal incapacity and hardships of weaker sections of the society. It is to be treated as a part of programme to secure social justice to the poor. It is also an indispensable part of equipment for streamlining and removing the defects of the working of present legal system.[89] Therefore, the scope of legal aid cannot be circumscribed to the limited skirmishes of exemption of court fee, process fee or making provision for providing counsel or legal assistance in court. But it will lead ultimately to a comprehensive and complete socialisation of legal process and conversion of legal doctrine into a welfare scheme to uplift the poor.[90]

Lord Denning rightly observed that after Second World War, the greatest, development in the field of law is legal aid. No country can progress until the administration of justice is strengthened. Nothing rankles more than the feeling of injustice. A person can live without food for a few days but he cannot tolerate injustice even for a few seconds Law and order can be maintained when the people have faith in the judiciary. When judicial system if failed, it may endanger the peaceful condition of a country. Honourable Justice P.N. Bhagwati rightly warned that before the people of country lose their temper we must do some for the pious cause poor. The indication made by Justice was towards legal aid to the poor. By providing a provision of legal aid we have opened the doors of courts for the poor- The Apex Court of our country is not easily accessible the poor masses of our society. By judicial activism legal aid scheme has been implemented more vigorously and the courts have become the courts of the poor also. The credit goes to the legal aid scheme and pro-active approach of NGOs due to that judiciary has been able to maintain its credit.[91]

The present system of administration of justice is very complicated and it has become very difficult for a common man to reap out of it. By expanding the scope of legal aid justice is made available at door steps of the down trodden masses of our society. Legal aid, by its strategic arms like PIL, Lok Adalat, Legal awareness programmes etc. has been successful in imparting justice to thousands of people who might have not gel justice otherwise. Thanks to the governmental and non-governmental agencies who have done tremendous work for the cause'of the poor- In India, legal aid movement has taken the course of its journey towards gaining social justice and it is becoming very popular. It has not still attained sufficient maturity of thought and action. It does not seem to be very embracing and effective. Much study, research and practical work has still to be done in order to make it living reality.

Voluntary Organisations and Legal Aid Programme

The Legal Aid Programme cannot be successfully implemented without the active co-operation of voluntary social organisations. The social workers can play active and useful role in providing necessary co-operation by becoming a link between the person seeking legal aid and the aid rendering social welfare agencies. The constant and intensive participation of voluntary organisations and contribute a lot in solving legal and social problems of the poor and can easily become inextricable parts of the State Legal Aid Programme. The involvement of people in solving the problems of the poor marks a welcome shift from the stark division, which hitherto separated the affluent from the poor. The Expert Committee on Legal Aid, has emphasised the necessity of voluntary organisations in the, following words;

"The object of legal aid is to bridge not only the gap between the rights which our people deserve and that which they have, but also the one between the rights conferred on them by law and the prospects of their enforcement. If legal aid is conceived not as an arithmetical total of instances and official assistance rendered in matters of law to the needs and indigent but as a movement aiming to ensure for the people their just right, the role of voluntary agencies in any such scheme will be largely self-evident."[92]

The voluntary Organisations can evolve a strategy to change socio-economic structure of the society, which is responsible for the creation, and perpetuation of poverty and denial of justice to the large masses of the people. They can make socio-legal investigations for identifying injustices to the vulnerable and deprived sections of the community and pursue judicial process for providing remedy to them. They can also net as watchdogs of people's interest and can encourage the poor people to mobilise themselves.[93] They may be able to locate the area where the application of law is harsh on the poor. In this regard, the Committee further observed:

"Wherein the law itself operates harshly on the poor or to promote public interest litigation, wherein it would not be worthwhile of any one individual to file a suit. A case of a public nuisance caused by smoking factory chimney in a working class area is an example in point. Such organisations can also help public-spirited lawyers to identify the areas wherein their special skills would be of great avail. Para-legal services can also be performed by voluntary agencies such as ascertaining the facts relevant to legal disputes and in appropriate case advising the parties to adopt non-legal remedies of settlement."[94]

[There are many organisations, which are working in the field of legal aid. Indeed, they require nurturing and nourishing by the State, State Bar Council, Social Workers, etc. Such organisations may be classified into two categories; lawyers groups and non-lawyer-' groups- Neither lawyer nor layman alone can do justice with in Legal Aid Scheme. Hence, there should be involvement of as the classes of persons in such organisations.[95] In addition to lawyers, other persons like businessmen, retired officers, social workers who are dedicated to serve the society may also be associated with such voluntary organisations.[96] The Committee for implementing Legal Aid Scheme. State Legal Aid and Advice Boards are supporting such organisations financially. These agencies have also organised seminars, workshops, para-legal training programmes, etc..

Although, there is no exhaustive list of organisations working in the field of legal aid, however, names of some agencies have published by CILAS- These are: (i) Chatisgarh Majdoor Sangh (Local Organisation of marginal farmers and landless labour) in Sarai Palli Tehsil of Raipur District. (M.P.) (ii) Banwasi Sewa Ashram, Mirzapur (U.P.) (iii) Antyodaya Chetna Mandal, Mayurbhanj (Orissa) (iv) Rural Litigation and Entitlement Centre. Dehradun (U.P.) (v) Indian Association of Lawyers (Kerala Chapter) (vi) Society for Community Organization Trust (T.N.) (vii) Rural Entitlement and Legal Aid Centre. Gandhi Bhawan, Bhopal (viii) Kashtakari Sanghatna, a mass organisation of marginal farmers and landless labourers working in Thana District of Maharashtra.

In the State of Rajasthan also many social workers individually or collectively are working for the cause of the poor and providing free legal aid and advice. The Rajasthan State Legal Aid and Advice Board is also maintaining the record of much social workers/organization. These are the following: (i) Rajasthan Legal Support and Social Action Centre. R.L.S.S.A.C; (ii) Sewa Mandir, Udaipur; (iii) Bhilwara Adult Education Association, Bhilwara; (iv) Rajasthan Kisan Sanghathan, Banswara; (v) Dalit Yuwa Morcha, Devgarh, District Chittorgarh; (vi) Shramik Vidyapith, Ajmer; (vii) Rajasthan Harijan Sevak Sangh, Bapunagar, Jaipur; (viii) Sangham Kshetra Yojana Samiti, Kimel. Bijowa, P.O. Rani, District Pali; (ix) Mahila Lok Jagrati Samiti, Jawahar Nagar Jaipur; (x) Social Work and Research Centre, P.O. Mada, Distt, Dungarpur (Raj.) and (xi) Social Works and Research Centre, Village Tilonia, District Ajmer (Rajasthan) etc.]

[Social Works and Research Centre, Tilonia, a Registered society since February, 1972, has been actively engaged in the work of upliftment of Scheduled Castes and Scheduled Tribes in different areas and particularly in and around Tilonia Village, District Ajmer. It has presented writ petition[97] in the Supreme Court in India for the purpose of remedying gross violation of the Minimum Wages Act. 1948.]

[Besides these, there are many voluntary organisations, which have contributed a lot in implementing legal aid scheme in India. The Bombay Legal Aid Society, Calcutta Legal Aid Society and Madras Legal Aid Society are providing free legal aid and advice since pre-independence of India. The Bombay Legal Aid Society, which was established in 1925, took first-initiative and pursuaded the Government to take step in the field of legal aid. Anand Niketan Ashram, Rangpur (Gujarat) is also an old organization which has launched the Lok Adalat System in modern perspectives.] Legal Aid also remained a subject of discussions amongst socio-political workers. Mr. Madhu Limaye, Member of Parliament submitted a draft bill on Legal Aid in Criminal Matter before Parliament in 1970, which was not passed.

Nirmala Niketan, Bombay had visited Bombay Central Jail and submitted its report regarding ill treatment and torture with Women Prisoners in the Police lock-up to the Supreme Court of India.[98] The People's Union for Democratic Right, New Delhi had highlighted violations of various labour laws doing some construction works in Asiad Games.[99] Some individuals like Mrs. Hingorani (advocate),[100] Sheela Barse (Social Worker)[101]. Arun Shouri (Journalist),[102] Upendra Baxi (Jurist),[103] etc, have also contributed a lot in enforcing the rights of poor masses in the society.

The public spirited persons are also advising the Supreme Court for the general interest of poor masses. For professors of Delhi University have written an open letter to the Supreme Court dated Sept. 16,1978 regarding the cases of *Tukaram v. State of Maharashtra.*[104] A young but orphan girl, Mathura was raped by Policemen, the Supreme Court heard that the' cries and alarms are, of course, a concoction on her part. In the said letter attention of the court was directed towards these questions. Why was she in the Police Station in the dead hours of night? Why were the lights put off and doors shut? Why was she not relieved after her statement was recorded? Ink has hardiv become dry on the decision in Nandini Satpati Case[105] when Supreme Court through K. Aiyer, condemned the practice of calling women to Police State in violation of Section 160(1) of Cr.P.C.

The test of performance of any organisations lies not in its membership but in its qualitative work and social duties and in its accomplishments. If these organisations are encouraged and supported by the State and other sensible citizens in various ways, then time will not be far when these agencies will serve as sword in enforcing the rights of the poor and as shield against their violation.

In *Bihar Legal Support Society. New Delhi v. Chief Justice of India and another*[106] the services of social action groups were highly hailed and recognised by the Supreme Court of India. This writ petition raises a question as to whether the State Government should support voluntary organisations or social action groups engaged in the legal aid programme and if so to what extent and under what conditions. There can be no doubt that if the legal aid programme is to succeed it must involve public participation. The State Government undoubtedly has an obligation under Article 39A of the Constitution, which embodies a directive principle of State policy, to set up a comprehensive and effective legal aid programme in order to, ensure that the operation of the legal system promotes Justice on the basis of equality. But we have no doubt that despite the sense of social commitment which animates many of our officers in the Administration, no legal aid programme can succeed in reaching the people if its operation remains confined in the hands of the Administration It is absolutely essential that people should be involved in the legal aid programme because the legal aid programme is not charity or bounty but it is a social entitlement of the people and those in need of legal assistance cannot be looked upon as mere beneficiaries of the legal aid programme but they should be regarded as participants in it. If we want to secure people's participation, and involvement in the legal aid programme, we think the best way of securing it is to operate through voluntary organisations and social action groups.[107] These organisations are working amongst the deprived and vulnerable sections of the community at the grass-root level and they know what are the problems and difficulties encountered by these neglected sections of Indian humanity. They have their ringer on the pulse of the people and they know from their own experience as to what are the unmet legal needs of the people, what are the sources of exploitation and injustice to the under-privileged segments of society and what measures are necessary to be taken for the purpose of ending such exploitation and injustice and reaching social or distributive justice to them. We are therefore definitely of the view that voluntary organisations and social action groups must be encouraged and supported by the State in operating the legal aid programme.[108]

It is now acknowledged throughout the country that the legal aid programme which is needed for the purpose of reaching social justice to the people cannot afford to remain confined to the traditional or litigation oriented legal aid programme but it must, taking into account the socio-economic conditions prevailing in the country, adopt a more dynamic, posture and take within its sweep what we may call strategic legal aid programme consisting of promotion of legal literacy, organisation of legal aid camps, encouragement of public interest litigation and holding of Lok Adalats or niti melas for bringing about settlements of disputes whether pending in Courts or outside.[109] The assistance of voluntary agencies and social action groups must therefore be taken by the State for the purpose of operating the legal aid programme in its widest and most comprehensive sense, and this is an obligation, which flows directly from Article 39A of the Constitution.[110]

But at the same time it is necessary to point out that the State cannot be asked to encourage and support any and every voluntary organisation or social action group because there are types and types of voluntary organisations and social action groups in the country and if the State were required to encourage and support other voluntary organisation or social action group for operating the legal aid programme and particularly the strategic programme comprising legal aid camps and lok adalats, the possibility of abuse of such encouragement or support cannot be ruled out. It is therefore necessary to lay down norms which should guide the State in lending its encouragement and support to voluntary organisations and social action groups in operating legal aid programmes and organising legal aid camps and lok adalats or niti melas. The Supreme Court is of the view that the following norms should provide sufficient guidance to the State in this behalf and we would .direct that the State Government shall, in compliance with its obligations under Article 39A of the Constitution extend its co-operation and support, to the following categories of voluntary organisations and social action groups in running the legal aid programme and organising legal aid camps and Lok Adalats or niti melas:

(1) Voluntary organisations and social action groups which are recognised by the Committee for Implementing Legal Aid Schemes set up by the Government of India or whose programme or programmes are supported by way of grant or otherwise by the Government of India or the State Government or the Committee for Implementing Legal Aid Schemes or the State Legal Aid and Advice Board.

(2) Voluntary organisations and social action groups which organise legal aid camps or lok adalats or niti melas in conjunction with or with the support of the Committee for Implementing Legal Aid Schemes or the Kerala State Legal Aid and Advice Board.

(3) Voluntary organisations and social action groups which are recognised by the State Government or the State Legal Aid and Advice Board on an application being made in that behalf.[111]

Every voluntary organisation or social action group falling within clauses (1), (2) or (3) above and to which co-operation and support are directed to be extended by the State Government shall furnish whatever factual information is required by the Central Government or the State Government or the Committee for Implementing Legal Aid Schemes or the State Legal Aid and Advice Board, but we may make it clear that such voluntary organisation or social action group shall not be under the control or direction or supervision of the State Government or the State Legal Aid and Advice Board because we take the view that voluntary organisations and social action groups operating these programmes should be totally free from any Governmental control.[112]

The voluntary organisations and social action groups must be encouraged and supported by the State in operating the legal aid programmes. It is now acknowledged throughout the country that the legal aid programme which is needed for the purpose of reaching social justice to the people cannot afford to remain confined to the traditional or litigation oriented legal aid programme but it must, taking into account the socio-economic conditions prevailing in the country, adopt a more dynamic posture and take within its sweep what may be called strategic legal programmes consisting of promotion of legal literacy, organisation of legal aid camps, encouragement of public interest litigation and holding of lok adalats or niti melas for bringing about settlements of disputes whether pending in Court or outside. Every voluntary organisation or social action group which receives support from the State Govt... has to furnish support; from the State Govt. has to furnish whatever factual information is required by the Central Govt- State Govt. or the Committee for implementing Aid Schemes or the State Legal Aid and Advice Board, but such voluntary organisation or social action, group must not be under the control or direction or supervision of the State Government or the State Legal Aid and Advice Board because voluntary organisations and social action groups operating these programmes should be totally free from any Governmental control.[113]

The State Government undoubtedly has an obligation under Article 39-A of the Constitution which embodies a Directive Principle of State Policy to set up a comprehensive and effective legal aid programme in order to ensure that the operation of the legal system promotes justice on the basis of equality.

In *Bihar Legal Support Society. New Delhi v. Chief Justice of India and another.*[114] The Supreme Court of India has emphasised upon the significance of the Social Action Groups and made important observation upon the aims and objectives of such groups.[115]

This writ petition has been filed by the Bihar Legal Support Society which is a registered Society having as its main aim and objective provision of legal support to the poor and disadvantaged sections of the community with a view to assisting them to fight for their constitutional and legal rights through the process of law. The occasion for tiling the writ petition is set out in para 2 where it has been slated that a Bench of this Court sat late at night on 5-9-1986 for considering the bail application of Shri Lalit Mohan Thapar and Shri Shyam Sunder Lal and that the same anxiety which was shown by this Court in taking up the bail application of these two gentlemen must "permeate the attitude and inclination of this Hon'ble Court in all matters where questions relating to the liberty of citizens, high or low, arise" and that the bail applications of "small men" must receive the same importance as the bail applications of "big industrialists". The petitioner, therefore, prays that special leave petitions against orders refusing bail or anticipatory bail should be taken up by this Court immediately in the same manner in which the special leave petition of these two "big industrialists" was taken up by the Court.

The Supreme Court has pointed out that so far as this Court is concerned, the special leave petitions of "small men" are as much entitled to consideration as special leave petitions of "big industrialists". In fact, this Court has always regarded the poor and the disadvantaged as entitled to preferential consideration than the rich and the affluent, the businessmen and the industrialists.[116] The reason is that the weaker sections of Indian humanity have been deprived of justice for long, long years: they have had no access to justice on account of their poverty, ignorance and illiteracy. They are not aware of the rights and benefits conferred upon them by the Constitution and the law. On account of their socially and economically disadvantaged position they lack the capacity to assert their rights and they do not have the material resources; with which to enforce their social and economic entitlements and combat exploitation and injustice.

The majority of the people of our country are subjected to this denial of access to justice and overtaken by despair and helplessness, they continue to remain victims of an exploitative society where economic power is concentrated in the hands of a few and it is used for perpetuation of domination over large masses of human beings. This Court has always, therefore, regarded it as its duty to come to the rescue of those deprived and vulnerable sections of Indian humanity in order to help them realise their economic and social entitlements and to bring to an end their oppression and exploitation.[117]

NGOs, VOLUNTARY ORGANISATION AND PUBLIC INTEREST LITIGATIONS

In India NGOs and the voluntary organisations have played significant role in responding the mass voice of weak, meek, poor, suppressed, downtrodden and exploited people and emerged as powerful protective shield of assistance in the field of legal battle to the needy persons. In this context, activised, sensitized, dynamic and dedicated approach of some prominent NGOs and the voluntary organisations is worthy to appreciate. For example, Bihar Legal Support Society, People Union for Democratic Rights [PUDR], Bandhua Mukti Morcha, Rural Litigation and Entitlement Kendera [RLEK], Common Cause A Registered Society [CCARS] etc. have invoked the judicial process by way of public interest litigation. Following are some illustrative cases instituted by these NGOs and voluntary organisations to accelerate the momentum of missionary cause of human rights:

In *Peoples Union for Democratic Rights v. Union of India,*[118] it was held that the Peoples Union for Democratic Rights and locus standi to file a petition for enforcement of various labour laws under which certain benefits are conferred on the workers. The Union brought this fact to the notice of the Court through a letter. The Court rejected the argument that such 'public interest litigation' would create arrears of cases and therefore they should not be encouraged. Bhagwati, J., (as he then was) declared, 'Wo State had the right to tell its citizens that because a large number of cases of the rich are pending in our courts we will not help the poor to come to the courts for seeking justice until the staggering load of cases of people who can afford rich lawyers is disposed off."

In *Bandhua Mukti Morcha v. Union of India,*[119] an organisation dedicated to the cause of release of bonded labours informed the Supreme Court through a letter that they conducted a survey of the stone-quarries situated in Faridabad District of the State of Haryana and found that there were a large number of labours working in these stone-quarries under "inhuman and intolerable conditions" and many of them were bonded labours. The petitioners prayed that a writ be issued for proper implementation of the various provisions of the Constitution and statutes with a view to ending the misery, suffering and helplessness of these labours, and release of bonded labourers. The Court treated the letter as a writ-petition, and appointed a Commission consisting of two advocates to visit these stone-quarries and make an inquiry and report to the Court about the existence of bonded labourers. Speaking for the majority Bhagwati, J. (as he then was) no behalf of himself and Pathak and Amarendra Nath Sen. JJ., held that where a public inteiest litigation alleging the existence of bonded labourers is filed it is nor proper oirthe part of the Government to raise preliminary objection. On the contrary, the Government should welcome an enquiry by the court so that if it is found that there are bonded labourers or workers living inhuman condition such a situation can be set right by the Government.

In *Bihar Legal Support Society, New Delhi v. The Chief Justice of India and others,*[120] a petition was filed by a social worker seeking release of children below 16 years detained in jails Supreme Court directed that the petitioner should have access to information and should be permitted to visit jails, children's homes, remand homes, observation homes, borstal schools and all institutions connected with housing delinquent or destitute children and that State Government should extend necessary assistance to the petitioner. It was also clarified that information collected by petitioner will be placed before the Court and will not be published otherwise.

The court observed that it a child is a national asset, it is the duty of the State to look after the child with a view to ensuring full evelopment of its personality. That is why all the statutes dealing with children provide that a child shall not be kept in jail. Even apart from this statutory prescription, it is elementary that a jail is hardly a place where a child should be kept. There can be no doubt that incarceration in jail would have the effect of dwarfing the development of the child, exposing him to baneful influences, coarsening his conscience and alienating him from the society. It is a matter of regret that despite statutory provisions and frequent exhortations by social scientists, there are still a large number of children in different jails in the country. It is no answer on the part of the State to say that it has not got enough number of remand homes or observation homes or other places where children can be kept and that is why they are lodged in jails. It is also no answer on the part of the State to urge that the ward in the jail where the children are kept is separate from the ward in which the other prisoners are detained. It is the atmosphere of the jail, which has a highly injurious effect on .the mind of the child, estranging him from the society and breeding in him aversion bordering on hatred against a system which keeps him in jail. The State Governments must set up necessary remand homes and observation homes where children accused of an offence can be lodged pending investigation and trial. Ore no account should the children be kept in jail and if a State Government has not got sufficient accommodation in its remand homes or observation homes, the children should be released on bail instead of being subjected to incarceration in jail. A.I.R. 1986 SC 1773.

In *Rural Litigation and Entitlement Kendera v. State of U.P.*,[121] the Supreme Court rightly remarked that though procedural laws do apply in PIL yet every technicality in the procedural law is not available as a defence when a matter of grave public importance is for consideration before the Court. Even if it is said that there was a final order, in a dispute regarding closure of mines causing environmental disorder in hill areas, the plea of res jitdicata could not be entertained in a subsequent public interest litigation to protect the environment. Undoubtedly, the Environment (Protection) Act/ 1986 (29 of 1986) has come into force with effect from 19th November 1986. Under this Act power is vested in the Central Government to take measures to protect and improve the environment. The instant writ petitions were filed as early as 1983, more than three years before the Act came into force. The Supreme Court appointed several Expert Committees, received their reports and on the basis of materials placed before it, made directions, partly final and partly interlocutory, in regard to certain mines in the area. The Court has made several directions from time to time. As many as four reportable orders have been given. The several parties and their counsel have been heard for days together on different issues during the three and a quarter year of the tendency of the proceedings. The Act does not purport to—and perhaps could not—take away the jurisdiction of the Supreme Court to deal with a case of this type. In consideration of these facts, there would be no justification to decline the exercise of jurisdiction at this stage. Ordinarily the Court would not entertain a dispute for the adjudication of which a special provision has been made by law but that rule is not attracted in the instant case. Besides it is a rule of practice and prudence and not one of jurisdiction.

In *Common Cause A Registered Society v. Union of India and others,*[122] the allotments of retail outlet for petroleum products (the petrol pumps), by Capt. Satish, Sharma, Minister of State for Petroleum and Natural Gas, exercising the powers of the Central Government, have been challenged in this public interest petition under Article 32 of the Constitution of India. The petition as originally filed was directed against corruption in various fields of public life. Mr. H. H. Shourie—Director "Common Cause"—appearing in person, invited his Court's attention to a news item dated August 11, 1995, on the front page of "Indian Express" under the caption "In Satish Sharma's Reign, Petrol and Patronage Flow Together". The solicitor general who was present in Court, took notice of the news item and stated that he would have the matter examined in the Ministry concerned and file an affidavit giving Ministry's response to the news item. The news item, inter alia/stated as under:

> "Not only the relatives of the most of the officials working for Captain Satish Sharma but even his own driver and the driver of his additional Private Secretary have been allotted petrol pump and gas agency respectively........We place on record our appreciation for Mr.'H. D. Shourie, who, very ably, assisted us in this matter. He shall be entitled to costs, which we quantify as rupees fifty thousand. The cost shall be paid by Capt. Satish Sharma personally."

In *Gaurav Jain v. Union of India and others*[123] there was a petition seeking improvement in plight of prostitutes/fallen women and their progeny. The Apex Court issued directions for prevention of induction of women, in various forms into prostitution; their rescue from the vile flesh trade; and rehabilitation through various welfare measures so as .to provide them with dignity of person, means of livelihood and socio-economic empowerment.

The court observed that it is the duty of the State and all voluntary NGOs and public spirited persons to come into their aid to retrieve them from prostitution, rehabilitate them with a helping hand to lead a life with dignity of person, self-employment through provisions of education, financial support,, developed marketing facilities as some of major avenues in this behalf. Marriage is another object to give them real status in society. Acceptance by the family is also another important input to rekindle the faith of self-respect and self-confidence. Housing, legal aid, free counselling assistance and all other similar aids and services are meaningful measures to ensure that unfortunate fallen women do not again fall into the trap of red light area contaminated with foul atmosphere.[124] Court observed and recognised that NGO is an effective armoury in its bow to steer clear the social malady, economic reorganisation as effective instruments to remove disunity, and to prevent frustration of the disadvantaged, deprived and denied social segments in the efficacy of law, and pragmatic direction pave way for social stability peace and order.

In Indian perspective the present NGOs movement towards human rights activism owes its origin to emergency era and inherently to some of the leading events such as the "increasing weakness in professional efficiency of the state apparatus and many of the democratic institutions like the bureaucracy, political parties, judiciary and the media, their social bias and political partisanship and the growing incredibility in popular perceptions which have a close bearing on India's quest for nation-building, economic development and social transformation. In addition to this, the brutalisation of state machinery, criminalisation of politics, use of money, muscle and mafia in electoral practices, misuse of preventive detention, intensification of the social and regional tensions in Kashmir, Assam, Punjab, Andhra Pradesh, Tamil Nadu and Karnataka, the demand for regional autonomy and the emergence of democratic groups like PUCL, PUDR, APCLC, etc., are also some of the results of this movement.[125] It is evident that many NGOs are working with stimulating zeal and sparkling style; with refreshing fearlessness and passion for socio- spiritual betterment; explores men and matters, issues and themes, displaying a deep commitment to humanity.[126]

In Indian context, NGOs have a delicate, sensitive, Challenging and Hurculean task to achieve the missionary cause of human rights culture. There is a great need for socio-legal protection to miserable, downtrodden and helpless people in Indian milieu.[127] No legal protection or social justice can be available to those who cannot organise themselves into violent pressure groups. It is precisely such sections of *The wretched of the earth* who need such protection and justice most like the victims of dowry-murders and other atrocities, the unfortunate women forced to become prostitutes, devadasis, women workers, working housewives, the divorcees, the eunuchs, the orphans, the innocent children working under callous employers; children kidnapped, maimed and used by professional goondas for begging, and the children of divorced persons; the Vanavasis deprived of their traditional rights in forest areas, victims of the conspiracy of contractors, conservators and politicians, and displaced on a large scale in the name of developmental projects like dams; the denotified communities or the ex-criminal tribes and all the nomadic and 'seminomadic tribes; the bonded labour; the dalits- and the backward classes; those affected by natural calamities, such as, floods, fire, droughts, earthquakes, epidemics, etc. or by extraneous factors, such as, terrorism, riots, wars, accidents, violence, sabotage etc.[128] All these unfortunate people are unable to organise, themselves into effective pressure groups. As representatives of the moral and social conscience of the society, the activists of the NGOs are expected to do the needful to provide appropriate relief to them.

The most important function of the welfare State is the creation of conditions that, assure social justice by removing social inequalities created by capitalism. Poverty has been a problem in all times and it did not become less acute with the advancement of civilisation. Hence, there is a great responsibility on the shoulders of socialistic State to assure social justice to the poor masses of the society. The eradication and control of poverty is essentially the function of modem Welfare Slate. This can be done by launching suitable socio-economic schemes by Government. But so long as it exists, it creates disabilities on the part of poor persons and they become unable to have the full benefits of legal and political rights. In this context, it is the paramount mission of the NGOs and voluntary organisations to undertake protective measures for the welfare of the weaker sections of the community and also to provide an additional support to the poor so that they may be able to reap the full benefit of the welfare legislation.[129]

NGOs and voluntary organisations also provide on intellectual and moral leadership to propagate and support the dynamic concept of rule of law by their missionary campaign, common cause programmes and pressure action strategies. The rule of taw without legal aid is nothing but a pseudo slogan and a jurist myth- Equal access to justice for the rich and the poor alike must be seen as an essential part of the maintenance of the rule of law- Rule of law does not mean that the protection of law must be made available only to the fortunate few, and that taw should be allowed to be prostituted by vested interests for protecting and upholding the status-quo under the guise of enforcement of their civil and political rights. The poor too have civil and political rights and they are also the beneficiaries of the rule of law.[130] We cannot be said to live under the rule of law till all citizens are effectively allowed to assert and defend their legal rights. If it does not happen then the rule of law exists on paper and not in reality. The rule of law oppresses the poor and the rich men take advantage of the rule of the law. The principle of the rule of law is not an end in itself. Left to it, it has been said that it has got all the propensity of becoming quite an 'unruly horse' and has also the capacity of hitting the poor below the belt. Certainly this happens in the absence of legal aid or when a party is not adequately represented in a legal system.

NGOs movement in modern legal, political and social theory is organically related to the urge for social justice. This idea dawned upon human consciousness after the French Revolution and the declaration of liberty, equality and fraternity as the guiding principle of social and political life. The term social justice is comprehensive of social, economical and political facets of life and its aim is to remove imbalances prevailing in the society amongst people particularly in social and economical spheres, and to ensure a reasonably equal and conducive situation for all round development of all people. Social justice represents a great humanistic aspiration in the world and provides necessary help to those persons who are not getting justice. Ulpian, who describes justice, as "giving each man his due" must be properly understood. Functional and motivated theme of NGOs is based on the paramount mission that social Justice provides social due, and postulates that no person should be deprived of justice due to social inequalities. Poverty must not become disqualification for those who seek justice.[131]

The Legal Aid Programme cannot be successfully implemented without the active co-operation of voluntary social organisations. The social workers can play active and useful role in providing necessary co-operation by becoming a link between the person seeking legal aid and the aid rendering social welfare agencies. The constant and intensive participation of voluntary organisations and contribute a lot in solving legal and social problems of the poor and can easily become inextricable parts of the State Legal Aid Programme. The involvement of people in solving the problems of the poor marks a welcome shift from the stark division, which hitherto separated the affluent from the poor. The Expert Committee on Legal Aid, has emphasised the necessity of voluntary organisations in the, following words:

"The object of legal aid is to bridge not only the gap between the rights which our people deserve and that which they have, but also the one between the rights conferred on them by law and the prospects of their enforcement. If legal aid is conceived not as an arithmetical total of instances and official assistance rendered in matters of law to the needs and indigent but as a movement aiming to ensure for the people their just right, the role of voluntary agencies in any such scheme will be largely self-evident."[132]

The voluntary Organisations can evolve a strategy to change socio-economic structure of the society, which is responsible for the creation, and perpetuation of poverty and denial of justice tu the large masses of the people. They can make socio-legal investigations for identifying injustices to the vulnerable and deprived sections of the community and pursue judicial process for providing remedy to them-They can also net as watchdogs of people's interest and can encourage the poor people to mobilise themselves.[133] They may be able to locate the area where the application of law is harsh on the poor.

In Indian perspective, NGOs and the voluntary organisations have done commendable work in responding the mass voice of weak, meek, poor, suppressed, downtrodden and exploited people and emerged as powerful protective shield of assistance in the field of legal battle to the needy persons. In this context, activised, sensitized, dynamic and dedicated approach of some prominent NGOs and the voluntary organisations is worthy to appreciate. For example, Bihar Legal Support Society, People Union for Democratic Rights [PUDR], Bandhua Mukti Morcha, Rural Litigation and Entitlement Kendera [RLEK], Common Cause A Registered Society [CCARS] etc. have invoked the judicial process by way of public interest litigation. There are many illustrative cases instituted by these NGOs and voluntary organisations to accelerate the momentum of missionary cause of human rights.[134]

In Indian context, a large number of NGOs have been coming forward to undertake the herculean task of promoting human rights at the grass-roots. For example, NGOs like Vigil India Movement (Banglore), Citizen for Democracy (Aligarh), Prayas (Delhi), Institute of Objective Studies (Delhi), Foundation for Legal Aid Environment and Social Action (Guntur, A.R), Human Rights Wing (Darbhanga, Bihar), Society for Rural Development and Action (Mandi, Himachal Pradesh), People's Union of Civil Liberties (Srinagar, J & K), Indian People's HRC (Bombay), Human Rights Education Movement of India (Madras, Tamilnadu) are some of the trustworthy and prominent institutions. There activities include publishing newsletters, research work, organising seminars, conferences, street-plays, folk dances at community level.

Moreover, World Vision (India) and the Society for the Promotion of Youth and Masses (SPYM) has been working on human rights in specific areas such as girl child rights, women's rights etc. In the field of promotion of human rights in the rural areas, pro-active commitments of some voluntary organisations and their dedicated workers are highly appreciable and of paramount importance.

From aforesaid discussion it becomes crystal clear that in recent years the human rights movements and activism have gained greater momentum and legitimacy in India. Development programmes of various national institutions and procedural safeguards for protection of human rights goes together with the proliferation of non-governmental national organisations working in human rights arena. NGO is an effective armoury in its bow to steer clear the social malady, economic reorganisation as effective instruments to remove disunity, and to prevent frustration of the disadvantaged, deprived and denied social segments in the efficacy of law, and pragmatic direction pave way for social stability peace and order. As a part of social engineering process these NGOs are providing a healing touch and protective shield to the victims of exploitation, adverse socio-economic circumstances, the commercial exploitation, custom oriented injustice, gender oriented vulnerability in social cybernatix.

NOTES

1. Ashish Chandra (2000), Human Rights Activism and Role of NGOs p. 4.
2. A.V. Raghwan (1997), Association of NGOs with the Human Rights Machinery, p. 112.
3. Ravi Nair (1988), Co-operation of Non-Governmental Organisations in Human Rights Perspective, p. 423.
4. Mohammad A. Ansari (1998), People's Movements and Protection of Human Rights at p. 41.
5. Surendra Pratap Rana (2001), Non-Governmental Bodies and Human Rigths Conspectus at p. 228.
6. Arun Mahajan (1999), The Role of NGOs in Implementing and Enforcing Human Rights Law at p. 148.

7. Priya Prakash, Functional Aspects of Non-Governmental Organisations and Institutions Towards Promotion of Human Rights, *The Times of India* 22, January, 2001.
8. N.V. Reddy (1995), Human Rights Organisations and Activists at p. 2.
9. Rachel Brett (1995),, The Role and Limits of Human Rights NGOs at the United Nations, *Political Studies*, Vol. XIII, at p. 96.
10. Charlotle Bunch (1997), NGOs: Cultural and Ideological Perspectives, *Human Rights Quarterly*, Volume IX, at p. 468.
11. Prabhakar Sharma (1999), NGOs and Human Rights Activists at p. 72.
12. Bharat H. Desai (1996), Expansion of NGOs Pro-Active Role: Credibility and Acceptance, *The Hindustan Times*, 18 August.
13. Tarun Bose (1997) , NGOs as Instruments of Humanitarian Mission at p. 22.
14. Jeremy Waldron (1992), Human Rights and the search for Community Conciousness, The Oxford Amnesty Lecturers, London.
15. Scott Davidson (2003), Human Rights, Open University Press, Buckingham, Philadelphia.
16. Peter H. Schuck (1997), Non-Governmental Organisations and Policy Process, *Public Administration Review*, New York, Vol. XI.
17. S. Lukes (1996), Human Rights NGOs in Third World at p. 128.
18. Jeremy Waldron (1992), Human Rights and the search for Community Conciousness, The Oxford Amnesty Lecturers, London.
19. Jeremy Waldron (1992), Human Rights and the search for Community Conciousness, The Oxford Amnesty Lecturers, London.
20. S. Lukes (1996), Human Rights NGOs in Third World at p. 85.
21. Jeremy Waldron (1992), Human Rights and the search for Community Conciousness, The Oxford Amnesty Lecturers, London.
22. T. Howard (1994), Globalisation and Latin America, Cambridge, OUP, Vol. III.
23. Will Kymlicka (1994), Multicultural Citizenship, Cambridge, OUP, Vol. IX.

24. S. Lukes (1996), Human Rights NGOs in Third World at p. 145.
25. S. Bandopadhyay (2000), Role of NGOs: Home and Abroad at p. 32.
26. P.R. Dasgupta (1996), The Significant Role of the NGOs in the Protection of Human Rights A Critical Perspective at p. 412.
27. Supra Note 38, at p. 148.
28. S. Lukes (1996), Human Rights NGOs in Third World at p. 166.
29. Rachel Brett (1995), The Role and Limits of Human Rights NGOs at the United Nations, *Political Studies*, Vol. XIII at p. 92.
30. Charlotle Bunch (1997), NGOs: Cultural and Ideological Perspectives, *Human Rights Quarterly*, Volume IX, at p. 423.
31. Supra Note 44.
32. Supra Note 47 at p. 445.
33. Supra Note 50 at p. 238.
34. Rachel Brett (1995), The Role and Limits of Human Rights NGOs at the United Nations, *Political Studies*, Vol. XIII, at p. 97.
35. Charlotle Bunch (1997), NGOs: Cultural and Ideological Perspectives, *Human Rights Quarterly*, Volume IX, at p. 470.
36. Sudarshan Sharma (2000), Socio-Political Genesis of Human Rights Organisations at p. 112
37. P. R. Dasgupta (1996), The Significant Role of the NGO's in the Protection of Human Rights: A critical Perspective at p. 224.
38. P.R. Dasgupta, The Significant Role of the NGO's in the Protection of Human Rights: A Critical Perspective (1996) at p. 225.
39. R.K. Gupta, Implementation of Human Rights: A Realistic Approach Needed to be adopted (2001) at p. 54.
40. Speech delivered by Michall Kirby J. at a conference on "Implementing International human Rights: Domestic Implementation of International Human Rights orms", 6th Dec., 1997.
41. *Ibid.* at p. 55.
42. R.K. Gupta (2001), Implementation of Human Rights: A Realistic Approach Needed to be adopted, at p.s 55-56.
43. P. Gopalaswamy (2000), Non-Governmental Organisations: A Challenging Perspective at p. 218.

44 *Ibid.* at p. 219.

45. P. Gopalaswamy (2000), Non-Governmental Organisations: A Challenging Perspective at p. 220.

46. R.C. Mishra (2001), NGOs and Human Rights Activism at p. 179.

47. Kumar Suresh (1999), Dialogue on Ancient Wrongs: NGOs Role at p. 231.

48. M.P. Rana (2002), Human Rights and Societal changes at p. 122.

49. R.M. Pal (1996), Social Welfare Programmes and Role of National Institutions at p. 27.

50. A.K. Merchant (1998), Atrocious Forms of Human Rights at p. 311.

51. VE. Moray (2001), Struggle for Human Rights and Community Consciousness at p. 318.

52. Mukundan K. (2002), NGOs and Human Rights Culture, at p. 113.

53. R. A. Diwaker (2000), Englightened Social Activists and Human Rights Perspective at p. 113-114.

54. V.B. Rawat (1999), Societal Aspects of the Protection and Promotion of Human Rights at p. 242.

55. P. Gopalaswamy (2000), Non-Governmental Organisations : A Challenging Perspective at p. 33.

56. Imtiaz Ahmed (1998), People's Movement and Role of NGOs: A Critical Overview at p. 177.

57. V.R. Dasgupta (2001), NGOs and Human Rights Activism: Continuing the Discussion at p. 263.

58 R. K. Gupta (2001), Implementation of Human Rights: A Realistic Approach Needed to be adopted at p. 164.

59. Pratibha Sharma (1999), Social Backwardness and Yeomen Service of NGOs at p. 65.

60. V.R. Dasgupta (2001), NGOs and Human Rights Activism: Continuing the Discussion at page 86.

61. P. Gopalaswamy (2000), Non-Governmental Organisations : A Challenging Perspective at page 134.

62. V.R. Dasgupta (2001), NGOs and Human Rights Activism: Continuing the Discussion at pages 221-223.

63. K.R. Narayana (1996), "Liberal Values and Human Rights", *Mainstream*, Vol. XXXIV, No. 21, February 24, p. 7-10.
64. M. Shiviah (1995), "Human Rights and the Third World: Towards a Reassessment of Ideological Dynamics", *Economic and Political Weekly*, Nov. 18, p. 2937-46.
65. *Ibid.*
66. M. Shiviah (1995), "Human Rights and the Third World: Towards a Reassessment of Ideological Dynamics", *Economic and Political Weekly*, Nov. 18, p. 2937-46.
67. A.C Kapur (1981), Principles of Political Science. S. Chand & Company Ltd., Ramnagar, New Delhi, p. 611.
68. Anand Mehta (1999), Right of Life and Personal Liberty, at page 281.
69. Blackstone (1982), Personal Liberty and other Human Rights: Community Expectations, at page 36-37
70. C.R. Parthsarthi (1999), Civil Liberties and Human Rights: A Challenging Issues, at page 144.
71. Badri Prasad Jalan (1995), Discrimination Against Women in Specific Areas: Some Momentous Socio-Legal Issues at page 21.
72. Attar Chand (1985) , Politics of Hainan Rights and Civil Liberties at page 248.
73. Chakradhar Jha (1993), Judicial Review of Legislative Acts at page 422.
74. See C.M. Lodha (1983), Judiciary-Fumes Flames and Fire. Unique Traders. Jaipur, p. vii
75. Nyaya Deep, Vol. U Oct.-Dec. (1999) page 47
76. Vijay Pal Arora (1996), Right to Life, Freedom and Equality at page 5.
77 A.M. Ahmadi (1995), Inagural Speech at a Workshop on "Judicial Process, Social Legitimacy and Institutional Viability", The Institute of Advanced Legal Studies, Pune, December 16.
78 A.P. Singh (1999), Human Rights and Protective Discrimination, the Academy Law Review, Vol. XXIII 209.
79. Vijay Pal Arora (1996), Right to Life, Freedom and Equality at page 26.
80. *PUDR vs.Union of India,* AIR 1982 SC 1173

81. Report of Gujarat Legal Aid Committee (1971) 107

82 C.V.N. Sastri J. (1999), Role of the Bench and the Bar in the Administration of Justice, A.I.R. *Journal* 155.

83 Ashok H. Desai (1997), Law Day Speech, November 26, 1996 in the Supreme Court Premises; 2 SCC *(Journal)* 10.

84. Venkataraman Chandrasekhran (1996), *Domestic Violence and Indian Social Structure,* at page 221.

85. P. N. Mishra (1995), Civilized Life and Human Dignity at page 32.

86. *See Powel vs. Alabana,* 287 U.S- 45 (1932)

87. Pollock (1974), The English Legal Aid System, Orient Longman Ltd. N. Delhi.

88. Madhva Menon (1973), Justice for the Poor: Rationale Retrospect and Prospect, in Law and Poverty edited by L.M. Singhvi, N.M. Tripalhi Pvl, Ltd. p. 218.

89. L. M. Singhvi (1973) , Law and Poverty, N.M. Tripathi Pvt. Ltd. 287.

90 A.S. Anand CJI (1999), Address at the 135th Anniversary of the Madras Bar Association, Chennai, April24, 1999, See The Times of India April 26.

91 Ansuman Singh (1999), Valedictory Address at the Golden Jubilee Celebrations of the Rajasthan High Court, Jaipur, on September 26, 1999 , *The Times of India,* Monday, September 27.

92. Report of the Expert Committee on Legal Aid-Processual Justice to the people (1973), 194.

93. Priya Prakash (2001) , NGOs Towards Redressing Societal Wrongs at page 36.

94. Report of the Expert Committee on Legal Aid-Processual Justice to the people (1973), 197.

95 P. Gopalaswamy (2000) , Non-Governmental Organisations: A Challenging Perspective, at page 4.

96 V. R. Dasgupta (2001), NGOs and Human Rights Activism: Continuing the Discussion at page 249.

97. *Sanjit Roy v. State of Rajasthan,* A.I.R. 1983 S.C. 328.

98. *For Example Sheela Barse v State of Maharashtra,* A.I.R. 1983 S.C. 378.

99. Per Justice Bhagwati in *People's Union for Democratic Rights v. U.O.I., A.I.R., 1983 S.C. 1473*

100. *Hussainara Khatoon v. State of Bihar* (1980) S C C. 81

101. For Example *Sheela Barse v State of Maharashtra,* A.I.R. 1983 S.C. 378.

102. M.S. Commu Kapoor Aswani Sarin, *A . Shouri v. State of U.P.*

103. *Upendra Baxi vs. U.O.I.* (1983) 2 S.C.C. 309.

104. (1979) 2 SCC 143.

105. (1978) 2 SCC 424.

106. AIR 1986 SC 1773.

107. Pratibha Sharma (1999), Social Backwardness and Yeomen Service of NGOs, at page 204.

108. Pratibha Sharma (1999), Social Backwardness and Yeomen Service of NGOs, at page 204.

109 S. Gopalaswamy (1998), Non-Governmental Organisations and Redressing Social Wrongs at page 372.

110. S. Gopalaswamy (1998), Non-Governmental Organisations and Redressing Social Wrongs at page 373.

111 R.K. Gupta (2001), Implementation of Human Rights: A Realistic Approach Needed to be adopted at page 92.

112. *Ibid* at pages 92-93.

113 R.K. Gupta (2001), Implementation of Human Rights: A Realistic Approach Needed to be adopted at pages 95-96

114. AIR 1986 SC 1773.

115. *Ibid.*

116. *Bihar Legal Support Society. New Delhi v. Chief Justice of India and another,* AIR 1986 SC 1773.

117. *Bihar Legal Support Society. New Delhi v. Chief Justice of India and another,* AIR 1986 SC 1773.

118. AIR 1983 SC 339.

119. AIR 1984 SC 803.

120. AIR 1986 SC 1773.

121. (2001) 4 SCC 577.

122. AIR 1996 SC 3538 (Para 28).

123. AIR 1997 SC 3021 para 28,60

124. *Ganrav Jain v. Union of India and others,* A.I.R. 1997 SC 3021 para 28,60.

125. V.R. Dasgupta (2001), NGOs and Human Rights Activism: Continuing the Discussion at page 86.

126. P. Gopalaswamy, Non-Governmental Organisations: A Challenging Perspective (2000) at page 134.

127. Priya Prakash (2001) , NGOs Towards Redressing Societal Wrongs at p. 432.

128. Mukundan K. (2002), NGOs and Human Rights Culture at p. 87.

129. A.P. Singh (1999), Human Rights and Protective Discrimination, the Academy Law Review, Vol. XXIII 209.

130. *PUDR vs.Union of India,* AIR 1982 SCH 73

131. Venkataraman Chandrasekhran (1996) , Domestic Violence and Indian Social Structure at p. 221.

132. Report of the Expert Committee on Legal Aid-Processual Justice to the People (1973), 194.

133. Priya Prakash (2001), NGOs Towards Redressing Societal Wrongs, at p. 36.

134. *See, Peoples Union for Democratic Rights v. Union of India* AIR 1983 SC 339; *Bandhua Mukti Morcha v. Union of India,* AIR 1984 SC 803; *Bihar Legal Support Society, New Delhi v. The Chief Justice of India and others,* A.I.R. 1986 SC 1773; *Rural Litigation and Entitlement Kendera v. State of U.P.,* (2001) 4 SCC 577; *Common Cause A Registered Society v. Union of India and others,* AIR 1996 SC 3538 (Para 28) etc.

6

CONSTITUTIONAL ETHOS AND JUDICIAL ACTIVISM TOWARDS HUMAN RIGHTS JURISPRUDENCE

After the end of the Second World War, movement for protecting human rights to all gained strength. The War, the great scourage on humanity, the atomic bombardment of Hiroshima and Nagasaki made man to realize that if something concrete and tangible would not be done man's doom were heralded. Efforts at securing human rights were intensified. Soon after the coming into force of the United Nations Charter, on December 10, 1948, the General Assembly of the United Nations adopted and proclaimed the Universal Declaration of Human Rights. Thereafter, two International Covenants, one on Economic, Social and Cultural Rights and the other on Civil and Political Rights were adopted by the General Assembly.

The Constitution of India came into force on 26th January, 1950. Part III and Part IV of the Constitution embodies Human rights jurisprudence having impact of Universal Declaration of Human Rights. India has acceded to both the covenants and deposited relevant document of accession with the United Nations.

This Chapter aims to explore the constitutional ethos and Human rights, pro-active judicial approach towards human rights perspective and Judicial Yeomen Service towards harmonising Municipal Law with International Law.

CONSTITUTIONAL ETHOS AND HUMAN RIGHTS

The Constitution of India which came into force in 1950 is an eloquent testimony of the nation's deep commitment to human rights. It proclaims basic human rights and fundamental freedoms and guarantees their enjoyment by all, irrespective of caste, colour, sect or religion. It has also created legal institutions to enforce the fundamental rights comprising liberty, equality and social justice.

Part III of the Constitution guarantees a comprehensive and impressive array of fundamental rights covering a wide range of civil, political, cultural, economic and social rights. These rights are subject to certain explicit exceptions that do not render them illusory. The range of human rights embodied in this part, Article 14 to Article 32, is very wide. Some of these rights are availbale to citizens as well as to aliens. These rights may be categorized as under:

Right to Equality

Article 14 to 18 contains the right to equality. Article 14 guarantees to every person right not to be denied equality before the law or the equal protection of laws.[1] Article 15 prohibits the state to discriminate against citizens on grounds only of religion, race, caste, sex, place of birth or any of them. But the state is empowered to make special provisions in favour of women, children and for the advancement of members of scheduled castes and tribes and socially and educationally backward classes of citizens.[2] Article 16 ensures equality of opportunity for all citizens in matters relating to employment or appointment to any office under the state. Discrimination in matters of public employment in any form such as religion, race, caste, sex, descent, place of birth and residence is strictly prohibited.[3] But the state can make a provision for the reservation of appointment or posts in favour of any backward classes of citizens which, in the opinion of the state are not adequately represented in the service under the

State.[4] The social evil of 'untouchability' rooted in the Indian society, has been abolished and its practice in any form has been forbidden.[5] Article 18 prohibits conferment of titles by the state, but military and academic distinction are exempted from the prohibition.

Right to Freedom

Article 19 of the Constitution confers on the citizens of India six vital freedoms, namely, "freedom of speech and expression," freedom to "assemble peaceably and without arms", to "form associations or unions", "to move freely throughout the territory of India", "to reside and settle in any part of the territory of India" and to "practise any profession, or to carry on any occupation, trade or business".[6] Originally this article guaranteed a right to property and to obtain compensation for the property acquired by law for a public purpose except in the crucial areas of agrarian reforms. The 44th constitutional Amendment, 1978 deleted this right and made it a legal right.[7] The right guaranteed by Article 19 are not absolute but are subject to reasonable restrictions on specific grounds mentioned in clause (2) to (6) of the same article.

Certain Safeguards to the Accused of Crime and Right to Life and Liberty

Impressive procedural rights are provided in Articles 20 to 22 of the Constitution of India. Art. 20 protects against ex-post facto laws, double jeopardy and self incrimination. Article 21 secures the most cherished human right in the tone, "No person shall be deprived of his life or personal liberty except according to procedure established by law". Accepting an American Jurist, Felix Frankfurter's sagacious advice, the framers of the Indian Constitution deliberately avoided the inclusion of 'due process' clause in Article 21. The resistance was not to due process as a requirement of fair procedure but to the substantive interpretation that could flow from it. The 'due process' was replaced with 'procedure established by law' a clause taken from the Japanese Constitution.[8] Article 22 provides protection against arrest and detention in certain cases. Clause (1) and (2) of this Article confer fourt rights upon a person who has been arrested. Firstly, he shall not be detained in custody without being informed, as soon as may be, of the grounds of his arrest. Secondly, he shall have the right to consult and to be represented by a lawyer of his own choice. Thirdly, right to be produced before a Magistrate within 24 hours of arrest. Fourthly, no detention beyond this period without the authority of the court, other clauses of Article 22 relates to preventive detention.

Right Against Exploitation

The framer's deep commitment to upholding the dignity of the individual is well reflected in Article 23 by prohibiting traffic in human beings and begar and other similar forms of forced labour. The employment of children below the age of fourteen years in any factory or mine or hazardous employment is also banned by Article 24.

Right to Freedom of Religion

Articles 25 to 28 contains various facets of religious freedom. Article 25 guarantees to all persons freedom of conscience and the right freely to profess, practise and propagate religion. The state is not only empowered to regulate this freedom in the interest of public order, morality, health, social welfare but also the economic, financial, political or other secular activity associated with religious practice may be regulated or restricted. Freedom to establish, maintain institution for religious and charitable purposes, managing their own affairs in matters of religion, own and acquiring of property and administration of such property according to law, is also guaranteed to every religious denomination. Article 27 prohibits the levying of a tax the proceeds of which are meant specifically for payment of expenses for the promotion or maintenance of any particular religion or religious denomination. Religious instruction in educational institutions wholly maintained out of state funds is prohibited.[9]

Cultural and Educational Rights

India is a multi-ethnic and multi-religious nation reflecting a rich diversity of castes, religion, language and cultures. In establishing a secular state founded on the principle of equality, the founding fathers were guided by the principle of enlightened accomodation of diverse faiths and religion. Accordingly, the Constitution contains special provision protecting the interests of minorities.[10] Accordingly clause (1) of Article 29 gives protection to every section of the citizens having a distinct language, script or culture by guaranteeing their right to conserve the same. Articles 30 gives all minorities, whether based on religion or language, the right to establish and administer educational institutions of their choice. Further, the state is enjoined not to discriminate in granting aid to educational institutions on the ground that the management of the institution is in the hands of a minority.[11]

Right to Property

Originally the Constitution guaranteed the right to property. But it was deleted from the list of fundamental rights by Constitution (Forty-fourth) Amendment Act, 1978.

Right to Constitutional Remedies

The right to constitutional remedies is the last but an important fundamental right. Unlike other rights, it is remedial and not substantive in nature. Article 32(1) says that the right to move the Supreme Court by appropriate proceedings for the enforcement of the rights conferred by Part III, i.e. fundamental rights is guaranteed. Clause (2) of the same Article empowers the Supreme Court to issue directions or orders or writs, including the writs in the nature of habeas corpus, mandamus, prohibition, quo-warranto and certiorari, Whichever may be appropriate for the enforcement of any of the rights conferred by Part III of the Constitution. This is a very significant provision in that it prevents part III from being reduced to mere chimerical constitutional claptrap.

These Human rights provisions were written in the Constitution with the hope that one day the tree of true liberty would bloom in India.[12] The express declaration of fundamental rights coupled from the introduction of judicial review in the Constitution marks a radical departure with the pivotal British constitutional doctrine of parliamentary supremacy.

The Indian Constitution was a product of the post world war II era—a seminal period in the development of human rights. Part III also reflects the inspirational impact of another great charter of liberties—the Universal Declaration of Human rights which was adopted by the General Assembly of united Nations in 1948. Many of the fundamental rights are included in both the Universal Declaration of Human Rights and The International Covenant of civil and Political Rights. The Indian Citizens has the good fortune to be constitutionally blessed with many of the International Covenat's rights twenty-one years before India become a signatory to it.[13] The chart below shows the rights embodied in Indian Constitution, UDHR and the ICCPR:

There are some rights in the International Covenant on civil and political rights such as right to speedy trial,[14] right to free legal services,[15] freedom from imprisonment on inability to fulfill a contractual obligation,[16] right to travel abroad[17] right to privacy,[18] freedom from torture, cruel, inhuman or other degrading treatment or punishment[19] and a right to compensation to the victim of unlawful arrest or detention,[20] which have not been explicitly included in the Constitution of India.

It is pointed out that the manner in which these rights will be available to the Indian citizens depends on the fashion in which international treaty law is given domestic legal effect in India. Suffice is to say at this point, India subscribes to the dualist view of international law, provisions of international treaty law can be given internal legal effect only through domestic legislation.[21] The Supreme Court took this view in *Jolly George Verghese v. Bank of Cochin.*[22]

PRO-ACTIVE JUDICIAL APPROACH TOWARDS HUMAN RIGHTS PERSPECTIVE

Human Rights have been made non-derogable by Article 13(2) of the Indian Constitution and their enforcement has been

Universal Declaration of Human Rights	*Int. Covenant on Civil and Political right*	*The Indian Constitution*	*Name of the Civil & Pol. Right/ Fundamental Right*
Article 4	Article 8(3)	Article 23	Freedom from Compulsory Labour.
Article 7	Article 14(1)	Article 14	Right to equality.
Article 2	Article 26	Article 15	Protection against discrimination on any ground.
Article 21(2)	Article 25(c)	Article 16	Right to have access to public Services.
Article 18,19	Article19(1)&(2)	Article 19(1)(a)	Freedom of speech and expression.
Article 20	Article 21	Article 19(1)(b)	The right of peaceful assembly.
Article 23(4)	Article 22(1)	Art. 19(1)(c)	Freedom of association.
Article 13(1)	Article 12(1)	Art. 19(1)(d) & (e)	Freedom of movement and freedom to Choose one's own residence.
Article 11(2)	Article 15(1)	Art. 20(1)	Freedom from expost facto legislation.
	Article 14(7)	Art. 20 (2)	Freedom from double Jeopardy
	Article 14(3)(g)	Art. 20(3)	Freedom from Self-incrimanation
Article 3	Art. 6(1)&9(1)	Art. 21	Right to life and personal liberty.
Article 9	Art. 9(2)(3)&(4)	Art. 22	Protection to arrested persons.
Article 18	Art. 18(1)	Art. 25	Freedom of thought, religion and Conscience.
	Article 27	Article 29	Right of minorities
Article 8		Article 32	Right to Constitutional remedy.

assigned to the Supreme Court. The fundamental right to move the court can therefore be appropriately described as the cornerstone of the democratic edifice raised by the Constitution. That is why it is natural that this court should regard itself as the protector and guarantor of the basic human rights and should declare that it cannot, consistently with the responsibility laid upon it, refuse to entertain applications seeking protection against infringement of such rights.[23] In the words of apex court, in discharging duties assigned to it, this court has to play the role of a 'sentinel on the quivive,[24] and it must always regard it as its solemn duty to protect the said fundamental rights 'zealously and vigilantly'.[25]

Over the last 57 years, the apex court of India has rendered invaluable service to the nation by upholding the Human Rights. A vast majority of the Constitutional Cases which came before the Supreme Court were those which helped to preserve and maintain the right of the common man against the state. In doing so, the court has acted judicially, uninfluenced by any philosophy other than the philosophy of the Constitution. The court has protected personal liberty against arbitrary encroachment by the state. The fundamental rights in our Constitution are entrernched with so many restrictions and that imposes a heavy duty on the judiciary to impose a check on the exercise of government powers in violation of these rights. The Supreme Court has stood to the need and has proved true to the aspirations of the people. In fact, the judicial attitude has changed with the need of the time and has ignored the traditional procedural obstructions. This has cretated the concept of juidical activism in the Indian legal system.[26]

The concept of equality in Article 14 and the menaing of the words 'life' 'liberty' and law in Article 21 have been considerably enlarged by judicial decisions. Anything which is not 'reasonable', just and fair' is not treated to be equal and is, therefore violative of Article 14. Rule of non-arbitrariness is a facet of equality in Article 14. Thus any arbitrary state action is struck-down as violative of Article 14. The word 'life' in Article 21 has been construed to, mean life with dignity and not mere physical existence; 'liberty' has been construed in the manner envisaged in the Preamble, that is, liberty consistent with social norms; and the word 'law' means a law which is fair in content and in procedure. It has been held that the validity of a law contemplated by Article 21 must satisfy the test of fairness,[27] consideration of every legitimate expectation[28] in decision making is necessary to satisfy the rule of non-arbitrariness; and absolute power in any individual is antidemocratic,[29] are judicially evolved principles which form part of the constitutional law 'Right to know' emanates from Article 19(1)(a) which guarantees freedom of speech and expression.[30] This provision also covers freedom of press, media including electronic media.[31]

Article 21 securing the right to life and personal liberty, has been applied and implemented with infinite potential as a result of which this provision has assumed the character of a reservior of legal norms to be drawn upon by the judiciary to sustain a wise range of claims and interests which has led to the development of a new human rights jurisprudence.

It is significant that even though, to begin with A.K. Gopalan,[32] the apex court of India ruled that a procedure duly enacted by the legislature was sufficient to deprive a citizen of the liberty. The procedure did not have to conform to the principles of natural justice, and it did not have to fulfill the tests of other fundamental rights. Rejecting the narrower view, in *Maneka Gandhi v. Union of India,*[33] the court articulated that Part III of the Constitution was designed to create conditions in which every human could develop his personality to the fullest extent. It was held that the procedure established by law must be right, just, fair and infused with the principles of natural justice, the procedure can not be arbitrary, fanciful and oppressive. Thus it can be said that the requirement of substantive and procedural fairness was held essential for the validity of a law contemplated by Article 21. The requirement of fairness for constitutional validity entrenched by decisions in Royappa[34] and Maneka Gandhi has its foundation in the opinion of Vivian Bose J. in Anwar Ali Sarkar Case.[35] Vijayshri Spripat[36] points out that procedural due process, which was crystallized in the Constitution and received a death blow in

Gopalan, was finally resurrected twenty-eight years after the commencement of the Constitution.

The Supreme Court has expanded the scope of Article 21, to include certain rights, which though are not specifically incorporated in the Constitution of India. Due to judicial activism the undermentioned rights emanate from the right to life and liberty:

Right to Travel Abroad

In *Satwant Singh Sawhney v. A.P.O., New Delhi,*[37] it was held that the right to travel abroad is included within the expression 'personal liberty' and, therefore, no person can be deprived of his right to travel except according to the procedure established by law. Since a passport is essential for the enjoyment of that right, denial of a passport amounts to deprivation of personal liberty. In the absence of any procedure prescribed by the law of land sustaining the refusal of a passport to a person, its refusal amount to an unauthorised deprivation of personal liberty guaranteed by Article 21. The decision was accepted by the parliament and the infirmity was set right by the enactment of the Passport Act, 1967. In Maneka Gandhi's Case,[38] it was made clear that any procedures which permits impairment of the constitutional right to go abroad without giving a reasonable opportunity to show cause cannot but be condemned as unfair and unjust.

Right to Privacy

In *Kharak Singh v. State of U.P.,*[39] Subba Rao, J. pointed out that right to privancy "is an essential ingredient of personal liberty" and that the right to personal liberty is a "right of an individual to be free from restrictions on encroachments on his person, whether those restrictions on encroachments are directly imposed or indirectly brought about by Calculated measures.[40] In *Govind v. State of M.P.,*[41] the court contemplated a right of privacy included in the right to personal liberty. In *State of Maharashtra v. Madukar Narayan,*[42] the court held that even a woman of easy virtue is entitled to privacy and no one can invade her privacy as and when he likes. Describing the right to privacy in *R. Raj Gopal v. State of T.N.*,[43] the court held that it is the rights to be let alone and a citizen has right to safegard the privacy of his own, his family, marriage, procreation, motherhood, child-bearing and education among other matters. Right to privacy also includes telephone conversation. Therefore, telephone-tapping amount to its violation unless it is permitted under procedure established by law.[44]

Right to Livelihood

Article 23(1) of Universal Declaration of Human Rights lays down that, "Everyone has the right to work and to protections against unemployment".

The right to 'livelihood' has not been specifically included in Part III of the Indian Constitution embodying fundamental rights, though it is a part of the Directive Principles of State policy.

In *People's Union for Democratic Rights v. Union of India*,[45] the court said that non-implementation of certain provision of labour laws by non-payment of minimum wages by contractors to the workers, amounted to denial of the right to live with human dignity and so it was violative of right to life guaranteed under Article 21 of the Constitution.

A wide connotation was given to the word 'life' in the olga Tellis Case. A public spirtied Journalist filed a petition on behalf of pavement dwellers alleging that their eviction without being given an alternative arrangement for accomodation amounted to violation of Article 21. It was held that an equally important facet of the right to life is the right to livelihood. If the right to lielihood is not treated as a part of the constitutional right to life, the easiest way of depriving a person of his right to life would be to deprive him of his right to livelihood. The court pointed out, 'that which alone makes is possible to live, leave aside what makes life livable, must be deemed to be integral component of the right to life, the motive force which proples their desertion of their earths and homes in the village in the struggle for survival, that is the struggle for life. So unimpeachable is the nexus between life and means of livelihood.[46]

Right to Legal Aid

Article 14(3)(d) of the covenant on Civil and Political Rights provides that, Every one shall be entitled to be tried in his presence, and to defend himself in person or through legal assistance of his own choosing and to be informed, if he does not have legal assitance, of this right, and to have legal assistance assigned to him in any case where the interests of justice so require and without payment by him in any such case, if he does not have sufficient means to pay.

The Constitution of India does not provide this right as a fundamental right. But the Supreme Court held that the right to free legal aid at the cost of the state to an accused who cannot afford legal services for reasons of poverty indigence, or incommunicado situation is part of fair, just and reasonable procedure under Article 21.[47] Not only that, the trial court is under an obligation to tell an accused who fails to afford legal representation that he is entitled to be represented by a lawyer at the cost of the State.[48] In case an accused is not told of this right and therefore he remains unrepresented by a lawyer, his trial is vitiated by constitutional infirmity and any conviction as a result of such trial is liable to be set aside.[49]

Right to Speedy Trial

Article 24(3)(c) of International covenant on Civil and Political Rights, 1996 says that in the determination of any criminal charge against him every one shall be entitled to the following minimum guarantees, in full equality—'to be tried without undue delay'. The Indian Constitution does not provide this right as a fundamental right. But in *Hussainara Khatoon v. Home Secy., Bihar,*[50] it was held that a procedure which keeps such large number of persons behind bars without trial so long cannot possibly be regarded reasonable, just or fair so as to be in conformity with the requirement of Article 21. Bhagwati J., pointed out that although the right to speedy trial is not specifically mentioned as a fundamental right, it is implicit in the broad sweep and content of Article 21.

Since Hussainara in a large number of cases involving accused charged with serious and non-serious offences, mentally retarded persons and others have come up before the court and it was held that all persons awaiting trial for long can approach to Supreme Court which will give necessary directions in the matter.[51] In *State of Bihar v. Ramdas Ahir,*[52] the court emphasized that by now the basic human right to speedy trial in all criminal prosecution has been expressly written as if with pen and ink in the constitutional right relating to life and liberty guaranteed under Article 21 of the Constitution. Again in *Kartar Singh v. State of Punjab,*[53] the Supreme Court pointed out that the concept of speedy trial is read into Article 21 as an essential part of fundamental right to life and liberty guaranteed and presented under our Constitution.

Right Against Cruel and Unusual Punishment

Article 5 of the Universal Declaration of Human Right says, "No one shall be subjected to torture or to cruel, inhuman or degrading treatment of punishment." Although, there is no specific prohibition of cruel or degrading treatment under the Constitution of India but the Supreme Court of India while giving a wider meaning to term 'life' and 'liberty' in Article 21 included the prohibition of cruel, in human and degrading treatment in this fundamental right.

In *Francis Corale v. A.D.M. Union Territory of India,*[54] it was laid down that any form of torture or degrading treatment would be offensive to human dignity and would therefore be violative of Article 21.

Regarding capital punishment Article 6(2) of the International covenant on Civil and Political Right, 1966 provides: "In countries which have not abolished the death penalty, the sentence of death may be imposed only for the most serious crimes in accordance with the law in force at the time of comission of the crime and not contrary to the provisions of the present covenant and to the convention on the prevention and punishment of the crime of genocide. This penalty can only be carried out pursuant to a final judgement rendered by a competent court".

In India death sentence can be imposed for serious crimes only and the procedure for imposing such sentence is provided in section 354(3) of Criminal Procedure Code. In *Jagmohan Singh v. State of U.P.*,[55] the constitutionality of imposing death penalty was challenged. The Supreme Court held that if the entire procedure of criminal trial under the Criminal Procedure Code for arriving at a sentence of death is valid then the imposition of death sentence in accordance with the procedure established by law cannot be said to be unconstitutional. This view was reiterated in subsequent cases.[56]

Right of Relase and Rehabilitation of Bonded Labour

International Covenant on Civil and Political Rights, 1966 provided that, "no one shall be required to perform forced or compulsory labour"[57] Accordingly, the Supreme Court of India, in *Bandhua Mukti Morcha v. Union of India*,[58] Article 21 read with the Directive Principles of State Policy enshrined in Articles 39, 41 and 42 as well as he Bonded Labour System (Abolition) Act, 1976 obliges the State to identify, release and suitably rehabilitate the bonded labourers. The bonded labourers also have the right to live with human dignity enshrined in Article 21.

Right to Know

The Supreme Court has also recognised the right to know in Article 21 as a necessary element of participatory democracy.[59]

Right to Compensation

Right to claim monetary compensation for the violation of the rights in Article 21 has also been recognised in several cases by the apex court of India.[60]

Right to Pollution Free Environment

The United Nations Conference on the Human Environment was held at Stockholm in June 1972. It lays down that:

(a) Man has the fundamental right to freedom, equality and adequate conditions of life, in an environment of quality that permits a life of dignity and well being, and

(b) Man bears a solemn responsibility to protect and improve the environment for present and future generations.[61]

The Constitution of India, did not orginally contain any direct provisions relating to the protection of natural environment. But by Constitution (Forty-Second Amendment) Act 1976, a fundamental duty 'to protect and improve the natural environment and to safeguard the forests and wild life of the country' was inserted.[62]

Due to judicial activism the right to pollution free environment has been included in Article 21. In *Rural Litigation and Entitlement Kendra, Dehradun v. State of U.P.,*[63] the Supreme Court orderd for closing the limestone quarries in Dehradun and Mussoorie. It was observed, "This would undoubtedly cause hardship to the lessees, but it is a price that has to be paid for protecting and safeguarding the right of the people to live in a healthy environment with minimal disturbance of ecological balance and without avoidable hazard to them and to their cattle, homes, agricultural land and undue affection of air, water and environment". Accordingly, it was held that Economic development should not be allowed to take place at the cost of ecology or by causing wide spread environmental destruction and violation.[64] Again in *Consumer Education and Research Society v. Union of India,*[65] it was pointed out that where an attempt has been made by the state legislature and state government to balance the need for environment protection and the need for economic development of backward area then it would not be proper to apply the principle of prohibition. It would be safer to apply the principles of protection, 'polluter pays' keeping in mind the principle of sustainable development. Similarly in *K.M. Chinnappa v. Union of India,*[66] it was held that while thinking of the development measures the needs of the present and the ability of the future to meet it own needs and requirement have to be kept in view. While thinking of the present the future should not be forgotten. In the case of *Essar Oil v. Halar Utkarsh Samiti,*[67] the apex court took a view that, "...But in a sense all development is an environmental threat. Indeed the very existence of humanity and the rapid increase in population together with the consequential demands to sustain the population has resulted in the concreting of open lands, cutting down of forests, filling of lakes and the pollution of water resources and the very air that we breathe..." Merely asserting an intention for development would not be enough to sanction the destruction of local ecological resources.[68] Accordingly it was held that the tanks are important part of environment of area and the governent as a trustee is responsible to protect and preserve historic tanks.

Thus the consistent view of the Apex Court of India is that right to unpolluted environment and preservation and protection of nature's gift is included in the ambit tof Article 21. This right encompasses wide variety of many other rights such as protection of wild life, forests, lakes, ancient monuments, fauna-flora, unpolluted air, protection from air, water and noise pollution and maintenance of ecological balance.[69]

An analysis of above different facets of the right shows that the fundamental right to life and liberty has been interpreted, by the Supreme Court and various High Courts in India, in a wide and comprehensive manner so as to invest it with significance and vitality which may enhance the dignity and worth of a human being. The aforesaid, decisions also reflect the Court's keen awareness of India's International obligations and the Court's predilection to use international human rights and environmental norms to inform Indian Constitution law.

JUDICIAL YEOMEN SERVICE TOWARDS HAR-MONISING MUNICIPAL LAW WITH INTERNATIONAL LAW

Theories on Relationship between International Law and Municipal Law

There are four main theories regarding the relationship between International law and municipal law. These are known as Monism, dualism, delegation theory and transformation or specific adoption theory.

MONISM

Kelsen, an Austrian jurist, is leader of monist school of thought.[70] Monists hold the view that international law and municipal law are concomitant aspects of one legal system. They contend that international law and municipal law not only resemble each other but, at the same time, spring from a single ground norm or standard which is the fountain head of all laws. According to them, international law and municipal law, mediately or immediately regulate the conduct of individuals.

DUALISM

Dualists hold that international law and municipal law are entirely distinct legal systems. International law, dualists contend, has a different character from that of municipnl law. In other words, international law and municipal law have no relation whatsoever with each other. In support of their stand, dualists give three reasons which are as follows:

(a) the origin of international law and municipal law are different in as much source of municipal law is the will of State itself whereas the source of international law is the common will (Gemeinwille) of States,

(b) the subjects of municipal law are individuals whereas the subjects of international law are States:

(c) international law and municipal law differ in regard to the substance of their law in as much as municipal law is a law of a sovereign over individuals whereas international law is a law, not above, but between sovereign States, and is, therefore, a weaker law.

The chief exponents of dualism are Triepel[71] and Anzilotti.[72] The dualistic doctrine attributes primacy to municipal law and considers it as superior legal system.

Delegation Theory

The delegation theory emphasizes that there is delegated to each State constitution by the rules of international law, the right to determine when the provisions of a treaty or convention are to come into force and the manner in which these are to be embodied in State law. The procedure and methods to be adopted for this purpose by the State are continuation of the process begun with the conclusion of the international treaty or convention. There is no transformation of international law into municipal law. There is not even fresh creation of the rules of municipal law. In fact, the process of creation of municipal law is prolongation of one single act of creation, i.e. creation of international norms. The theory of monism, therefore, attaches primacy to international law and treats international law as superior legal system.

Transformation or Specific Adoption Theory

Dualists contend that international law cannot be directly applied within the municipal sphere by State courts. Rules of international law become binding on municipal courts if, and only if, such rules are transformed into municipal legislation. In other words, municipal law strengthens international law and makes it operative by incorporating it into national law by legislation and thereby making international law bind municipal courts. Since, according to positivist theory, international law and municipal law constitute two strictly separate and structurally different systems, international law cannot impinge upon municipal law unless municipal law allows its constitutional machinery to be used for that purpose. According to transformation theory, there is a difference between international treaties which are of the nature of promises, and municipal statutes which are of the nature of commands. It, therefore, follows that transformation of international law into municipal law is formally and substantively indispensable.

Obviously, neither dualistic theory nor monistic theory represents the truth. These are diametrically opposite approaches. It. therefore, becomes necessary to study the practice of India to understand the relationship of international law with municipal law.

Indian Practice Regarding the Relationship between International Law & Municipal Law

International Custom: On International custom, India does not follow Blackstonian doctrine that law of nations is part of the law of the land. In fact, Blackstonian doctrine is subject to qualifications even in England. Article 51(c) of the Constitution of India is guiding stone as far as Indian practice on international custom is concerned. It states that the State shall endeavour to 'foster respect for international law and treaty obligations in the dealings of organized peoples with one another'. It may be said that the distinction in Article 51(c) between international law and treaty obligations is that the term 'international law' refers to international customary law. The acceptance of such an approach would mean that customary international law is not incorporated into Indian municipal law ipso facto. In league with this approach, is the contention that Article 51(c) reduces the position of international law in India to a mere directive principle.

Does it mean that the doors of Indian law have completely been shut to the incorporation of international customary law into Indian municipal law and corresponding enforcement of the international customary norms by the Indian courts[73]. The issue is worth exploring.

In *Annakumant Pillai v. Muthupayal,*[74] the issue was whether the Rajah of Ramnath by continuous and effective occupation from time immemorial had acquired title to the species of sedentary fishery, the chanks, on the scabed of Palk's Bay and Gulf of Mannar which exist beyond three nautical miles from baseline. The court held that Rajah acquired historic title (customary right) over sedentary fishery on the basis of prescription and acquiescence. The court, thus, applied international custom (customary norms concerning prescriptive title). By recognizing the existence of historic title on the basis of prescription and acquiescence, the court enforced international customary norm concerning the existence of historic title by virtue of prescription and acquiescence of the other States.

In *A.M.S.S.V.M. & Co. v. The State of Madras*[75] the issue was whether the State of Madras was entitled to abolish private rights on the exploration of chank fish in Palk's Bay. According to Madras High Court, chank fish cannot be treated as similar to fisheries proper for the purposes of exploitation in as much as unlike fish, chank fish are animals settled upon the bed of sea from which they are practically unable to move away. Chank fish are practically immobile and can only crawl in constant physical contact with the seabed. The court observed that rulers of the States adjacent to the sea had acquired an immemorial right to exploitation of chank fish in the bay. The court held that the particular part of the bed of the sea. though outside the three mile limit, vested in the Crown and that, according to common law principles, the government was entitled to abolish private rights on the exploitation of chank fish in Palk's Bay. The High Court made it clear that it relied on Principle of English common law as well as on corresponding rules of the law of nations relating to the maritime belt, harbours and estuaries. The importance of this case lies in the fact that like earlier case. the High Court enforced international customary law, i.e. maritime law principles (historic title based on prescription and acquiescence of the other States).

In the above-mentioned cases, Indian courts followed common law doctrine and enforced international customary norms. However, the judgement in *A.D.M. Jabalpur v. Shivkant Shukla*[76] came as a shock for international lawyers. While rejecting the argument that Universal Declaration of Human Rights was a part of the Indian municipal law, Justice Beg observed:

> .....these submissions appear to me to amount to nothing more than appeals to weave certain ethical rules into the fabric of our constitution which is the paramount law of this country and provides the final test of validity and enforceability of rules and rights through courts. To advance such arguments is to forget that our constitution itself embodies these rules and rights. It also governs the conditions of their suspension. Nothing which conflicts with the provisions of our constitution could be enforced here under any disguise.[77]

The thrust of Justice Beg's observation is that the Universal Declaration of Human Rights contains mere ethical rules. This seems to be fallacious in so far as Article 51 of the constitution which is directive principle of State policy and requires the States to foster respect for international law.[78] It is significant to bear in mind that broad spectrum of conceptualization of human rights contained in the Universal Declaration of Human Rights has become international custom with the passage of time. In principle, all States feel themselves bound to protect and promote human rights mentioned in the Universal Declaration of Human Rights, International Covenant on Economic, Social and Cultural Rights, International Covenant on Civil and Political Rights and its Optional Protocol give expression to the undertaking of the States to protect and promote human rights. No state has ever stated that it would not be bound by the international obligation of protection and promotion of human rights. This takes us to the point that according to common law doctrine, municipal courts will enforce Universal Declaration ot Human Riphts in so far as it is not inconsistent with municipal statutes. The common law doctrine requires the municipal courts to harmoniously construe the ambiguous provisions of the municipal statutes so as to avoid conflict between Universal Declaration of Human Rights and municipal law. It is only in case of direct conflict between Universal Declaration of Human Rights and unambiguous statute law that common law doctrine requires the courts to apply statute law and not the Declaration. On the issue of applicability of the common law doctrine in India, Article 372 of the Constitution of India acts as a guiding stone. Article 372 of the constitution of India provides as follows:

> Notwithstanding the repeal by the this constitution of the enactments referred to in Article 395 but subject to the other provisions of this constitution, all the laws in force in the territory of India immediately before the commencement of this constitution shall continue in force there in until altered or repealed or amended by a competent legislature or other competent authority.

Article 372, clause 1 of the Constitution of India enacts that all laws in force in the territory of India immediately before the commencement of the constiuition shall continue to be in force until altered, repealed, or amended by a competent legislature. But this shall be subject to the other provisions of the constitution, which means that if an existing law is repugnant to any provision of the constitution, notwithstanding the present article, that law shall not be saved.[79] It is pertinent to note that the expression law in force' in Article 372 includes not only enactments of the Indian legislature but also common law of the land which was being administered by the courts in India.[80] This leads to the conclusion that common law doctrine is applicable in India. Therefore, international law is enforceable by Indian courts insofar as it is not in consistent with clear and unequivocal Indian statutory law. Thus, rules of international law are not mere ethical rules. These need to be respected and applied by the Indian courts as far as possible.

Interntationat Treaties: There is no provision in the Indian Constitution similar to that in the United States Constitution proclaiming treaties as the supreme law of the land. Under Article 73 of the Constitution of India, the Executive power of Union shall extend to the matters in respect of which Parliament has power to make law. Article 53 provides that the executive power of the Union is vested in the President and shall be exercised by him either directly or through officers subordinate to him in accordance with this constitution. According to Article 246, paragraph I, Parliament has exclusive power to make laws with respect to any of the matters enumerated in List I in the Seventh Schedule (referred to as 'Union List'). Entry 14, List I (Union List) deals with entering into treaties and agreements with foreign countries and implementation of treaties, agreements and conventions with foreign countries. Parliament has not made any laws so far on the subject, and, until it does so, the President's power to enter into treaties (which is after all an executive act) remains unfettered by any internal constitutional restrictions.[81] The Executive Power of the Union being co-extensive with the legislative powers of the Parliament, the treaty-making function is exercised and regulated by the Executive in the absence of legislation on the subject. In practice, the President does not negotiate and conclude a treaty or agreement himself.

Plenipotentiaries are appointed for this purpose, and they act under full power issued by the President. It is, however, the President who ratifies a treaty. By virtue of Article 253 of the Constitution, Parliament has exclusive power to make any law for the whole or any part of the territory of India with a view to implementing treaties and international agreements, notwithstanding the fact that they refer to subjects which under the Constitution are assigned to constituent units for legislative purposes. Article 253 does not give a clear direction as to whether enactment by Parliament is required for implementation of all treaties and agreements. The question whether a particular treaty or agreement calls for an implementing legislation would depend very much upon its subject matter.

In *Union of India v. Manmulla Jain,*[82] the question was whether the Union Executive can exercise its treaty-making power without an authorizing legislation of Parliament. In this case, the court was concerned with the validity of the treaty by which the former possession of Chandernagore was transferred by France to India and the argument was that without Parliamentary legislation the treaty was not valid. The court held:

> Making a treaty is an executive act and not a legislative act. Legislation may be and is often required to give effect to the terms of a treaty. Thus, if a treaty, say, provides for payment of a foreign power, legislation may be necessary before the money can be spent, but the treaty is complete without the legislation.[83]

Referring to Entry 14 of the Union List, the Court said:

> Undoubtedly, this provides for all legislation in connection with entering into treaties. This cannot, however, justify the conclusion that the makers of the constitution intended that no treaty should be entered into unless the Parliament has legislated on the matter. ....The President makes a treaty in exercise of his executive power and no court of law in India can question its validity.[84]

In *Nirmal Base v. Union of India*[85] the court took the position that in view of Entry 14, List I read with Article 73, there can be no doubt that the Union Govemment has the rights by executive action to enter into treaties and agreements with foreign countries. In *Ramjawaya Kapur v. State of Punjab*[86] and *Jayantilal v. Rana*,[87] the Supreme Court held that while under Entry 14 of List I, treaty making is an item of Union Legislation, nevertheless Union Government can enter into treaties with foreign power although no legislation has been passed in pursuance of Entry 14, List 1.

Implementation of Treaties

Treaties Involving Cession of National Territory: There are two cases decided by the Supreme Court relating to the transfer of Berubari Union. The first case is an advisory opinion which involves reference by the President of India under Article 143(1) of the Constitution of India on the implementation of the Indo-Pakistan Agreement relating to Berubari Union and Exchange of Enclaves.[88] The IndoPakistan Agreement was entered into on 10 November 1958 between Prime Minister of India and Pakistan with a view to resolve the border area disputes and problems. One of the items of the agreement related to the division of Berubari Union No. 12 and another to the exchange of old Cooch-Bihar Enclaves. A doubt arose on the question as to whether implementation of the agreement required any legislative action. The Supreme Court came to the conclusion that the agreement amounted to cession or alienation of a part of the Indian territory in favour of Pakistan and was not a mere ascertainment or determination of the boundary. The agreement had the juridical effect of ceding a part of Indian territory to Pakistan. The territory in question had remained in possession of India and had always been treated as part of West Bengal and in view of the court this circumstance lent considerable support to the conclusion that the transaction involved cession of Indian territory. The Supreme Court next considered the legal steps required under domestic law to give effect to the Agreement. The Supreme Court held that the agreement involving cession or alienation of a part of the Indian territory in favour of Pakistan requires legislative act, i.e. incorporation of the agreement in municipal law by the legislature. However, according to Supreme Court, an agreement relating to ascertainment or determination of the boundary does not call for legislative act. Therefore, Supreme Court decided that Agreement in the present case would have to be implemented by Union legislation relatable to Article 368 of the constitution.

Unlike the First Berubari case dealing with transfer of territory which was de facto and dejure Indian territory, the second case, *Ramkishore Sen and others v. Union of India* (popularly known as Berubari Union No. II case)[89] concerned territory which was de facto under the administration of India but dejure that of Pakistan. The Supreme Court pointed out that the territory in question was under the Radcliffc Award, really part of Pakistan though in dividing the territories under the Award the village in question came under West Bengal Administration by a mistake. What the Government of India were now doing was to restore to Pakistan what really belonged to her and as such there was no question of ceding Indian territory. The Supreme Court held that the proposed transfer could take effect by executive action and no legislation was necessary.

In *Maganbhai Ishwarbhai Patel v. Union of India* (Kutch case),[90] the petitioners sought to restrain government of India from ceding without the approval of Parliament areas in Rann of Kutch to Pakistan in accordance with Indo-Pakistan Western Boundary case Tribunal award dated 19 February. 1968. M. Hidayatullah. C.J. in his judgement and Shah, J. in his separate concurring judgement held that the decision to implement the award by exchange of letters treating the award as an operative treaty after the boundary had been marked in this area, was within the constitutional competence of the Union Executive. C.J. Hidayatullah drew the distinction between the two Berubari cases in these words:

> The First Berubari case dealt with transfer of territory which was de facto and de jure Indian territory and therefore as the extent of Indian territories as defined

> in Article I read with the Ist Schedule was reduced, a constitutional amendment was held necessary. The second case concerned territory which was de facto under the administration by India but being de jure that of Pakistan, transfer of that territory was held not to require a constitutional amendment.

Shah J. observed:

> By Article 73, subject to the provisions of the constitution, the executive power of the Union extends to the matters with respect to which the Parliament has power to make laws. Our Constitution makes no provision making legislation a condition of the entry into an international treaty in times either of war or peace. The executive power of the Union is vested in the President and is exercisable in accordance with the constitution. The executive is qua the State competent to represent the State in all matters and may by agreement, convention or treaties incur obligations which in international law are binding upon the State. But the obligations arising under the agreement or treaties are not by their own force binding upon Indian nationals. The power to legislate in respect of treaties lies with the Parliament under Entries 10 and 14 of List I of Seventh Schedule. But making of law under that authority is necessary when the treaty or agreement operates to restrict the rights of citizens or others or modifies the laws of the State. If the rights of the citizens or others which are justiciable and not affected, no legislative measure is needed to give effect to the agreement or treaty.

The effect of Article 253 is that if a treaty, agreement or convention with a foreign State deals with a subject within the competence of the State Legislature, the Parliament alone has, notwithstanding Article 246(3), the power to make laws to implement the treaty, agreement or convention or any decision made at any international conference, association or other body. In terms, the Article deals with legislative power, thereby power is conferred upon the Parliament which it may otherwise possess. But it does not seek to circumscribe the extent of the power conferred by Article 73. If in consequence of the exercise of executive power, rights of the citizens or others are restricted or infringed, or laws are modified, the exercise of power must be supported by legislation: where there is no such restriction, infringement of right or modification of the laws, the executive is competent to exercise the power.[91]

The treaties of cession of territory result in the loss of private property which individuals have in ceded territory and therefore judicial requirement of legislative action for their implementation is based on sound logical considerations.

Extradition Treaties: In Birma v. The State[92] the Rajasthan High Court held that the treaty of extradition in question (not implemented by legislative act) did not have the effect of law within the meaning of Article 21 of the Constitution of India and hence the mode of deprivation of personal liberty followed in that case was not competent under that Article. In the course of its judgement, the High Court made a general statement to the effect that 'treaties which are part of international law do not form part of the law of the land unless expressly made so by legislative authority.' This statement while contextually correct so far as the facts of that case are concerned is, however, misleading.[93]

In *Nanka v. Government of Rajasthan,*[94] the court held:

> Entering into an extradition treaty with British India by Maharaja of Indian State is an executive act and treaty to have a binding effect upon a subject of Maharaja has to be incorporated into municipal law of a State. The mere fact that Maharaja who has executed it was also the legislative authority will not make it binding on the subject.

The above-mentioned cases make it clear that a treaty of extradition by itself cannot legitmate an executive order of arrest and detention of a fugitive in view of the mandatory requirements of Article 21 of the Constitution of India.[95]

On Implementation of treaties, Indian practice appears to be similar to English practice in as much as in India, international treaty calls for legislative action if it affects the application of the existing laws. imposes financial obligations, or otherwise requires specific legislative authority for execution.[96] Legislative action is required in India even in case of treaties affecting private rights, e.g. treaties involving cession of national territory, extradition treaties, etc. The concept of self executing and non self-executing treaties is also recognized by the Supreme Court of India in *Maganbhai Ishwarbhai Patel v. Union of India* in the following words:

> A treaty really concerns the political rather than judicial wines of the State. Where a treaty or award after arbitration comes into existence it has to be implemented and this can only be done after all the three branches of the government, the legislature. the executive and the judiciary, or any one of them possesses the power to implement it. If there is any deficiency in the constitutional system it has to he removed and the State must equip itself with the necessary power. In some jurisdictions the treaty or the compromise read with the award acquires full legal effect automatically in the municipal law notwithstanding. Such treaties or awards are self-executing. Legislation may nevertheless be passed in aid of implementation but is usually not ncccssary.[97]

It is, therefore, beyond doubts that on the issue of implementation of international treaties, Indian practice is similar to English and American practice irrespective of the fact that unlike the Constitution of United States, the Constitution of India does not explicitly provide that international treaties are part of the law of the land in India. The United Nations (Privileges and Immunities) Act. 1947 was enacted to give effect to the Convention on the Privileges and Immunities of the United Nations. 1946. The Geneva Convention Act. 1960 was intended to give effect to the four Geneva Conventions of 12 August 1949 for the Protection of War Victims. The Diplomatic Relations (Vienna Convention) Act, 1972 was enacted to give effect to the Vienna Convention on Diplomatic Relations. 1961. The Tokyo Convention Act, 1975 was enacted to give effect to the Tokyo Convention on Offences and Certain other Acts Committed on Board Aircraft, 1963 and so on.

Implementation of International Human Rights in Domestic Law

The Directive Principles of State Policy under Indian Constitution, like a lodestar gleams in the maze of our constitutional fiats and its myriad mandates, guiding the country fundamentally in its governmance by ordaining the state to apply these principles in making laws. There is an express mandate under Article 51(c) of Indian Constitution that the state shall foster respect for international law treaty obligations. Article 253 has clothed the Parliament with the overiding power to weave any legal attire, the criss-crossing the centre and state lists notwithstanding, for the purposes of implementing any treaty agreement or convention or any decision made at international conferences, association or other body. Entry 14 to list I of the Schedule VII to the Constitution preserves the parliamentary prerogative to enter into treaties and agreements with foreign countries and the implementation therof.[98]

An examination of under mentioned judicial promouncements reflects the role played by the Indian Judiciary in implementing International human rights in domestic jurisprudence.

Arrest and Detention of Judgement Debtor Violates Article 11 of International Covenant on Civil and Political Rights

In *Jolly George Varghese and another v. The Bank of Cochin*[99], the question posed was whether it was right to enforce a contractual liability by imprisoning a debtor in the teeth of Article 11 of the International Covenant on Civil and Political Rights.[100]

V.R. Krishna Iyer J., Pointed out "Right at the beginning, we may take up the bearing of Art. 11 on the law that is to be applied by an Indian Court when there is a specific provision in the Civil Procedure Code, authorising detention for non-payment of a decree debt. The Covenant bans imprisonment merely for not discharging a decree debt. Unless there be some other vice or means rea apart from failure to foot the decree, international law frowns on holding the debtor's person in civil prison, as hostage by the court. India is now a signatory to this Covenant and Art. 51(c) of the Constitution obligates the State to "foster respect for international law and treaty obligations in the dealings of organised peoples with one another". Even so, until the municipal law is changed to accommodate the Covenant what binds the court is the former, not the latter A. H. Robertson. in "Human Rights—in National and International Law" rightly points out that international conventional law must go through the process of trasnformation into the municipal law before the international treaty can become an internal law. From the national point of view the national rules alone count............ with resard to interpretation, however, it is a principle generally recognised in national legal systems that in the event of doubt, the national rule is to be interpreted in accordance with the State's international obligations.

The position has been spelt out correctly in a Kerala ruling (Xavier v. Canara Bank Ltd., 1969 Ker LT 927 at pp. 931, 933) on the same point. In that case, a judgment-debtor was sought to be detained under Order 21, Rules 37, Civil P.C. although he was severty and had spent away on his illness the means he once had to pay off the decree. The observations there made are apposite and may bear experption. The last argument which consumed most of the time of the long arguments of learned counsel for the appellant is that the International Convenants on Civil and Political Rights are part of the law of the land and have to be repsected by the Municipal Courts. Article 11, which I have extracted earlier, grants immunity from imprisonment ot indigent but honest judgement debtors.

The march of civilization has been a story of progressive subordination of property rights to personal freedom; and a by-product of this subordination finds noble expression in the declaration that "No one shall be imprisoned merely on the ground of inability to fulfil a contractual obligation". This revolutionary change in the regard for the human person is spanned by the possible shock that a resuscitated Shylock would suffer if a modern Daniel were to come to judgment when the former asks the pound of flesh from Antonio's bosom according to the tenor of the bond, by fiatly refusing the mayhem on the debtor, because the inability of an impecunious obligee shall not imperil his liberty or person under the new dispensation proclaimed by the Universal Declaration of Human Rights. Viewed in this progressive perspective we may examine whether there is any conflict between S. 51, C. P. C. and Article 11 of the International Covenants quoted above. As already indicated by me, this latter provision only interdicts imprisonment if that is sought solely on the ground of inability to fulfil the obligation. Section 51 also declares that if the debtor has no means to pay he cannot be arrested and detained. If he has and still refuses or neglects to honour his obligation or if he commits acts of bad faith, he incurs the liability to imprisonment under Section 51 of the Code, but this does not violate the mandate of Article 11. However, if he once had the means but now has not or if he has money now on which there are other pressing claims, it is violative of the spirit of Article 11 to arrest and confine him in jail so as to coerce him into payment......."

The judgement dealt with the effect of internaitonal law and the enforceability of such law at the instance of individuals within the State, and observed:

"The remedy for breaches of International Law in general is not to be found in the law courts of the State because International Law per se or proprio vigore has not the force or authority of civil law, till under its inspirational impact actual legislation is undertaken. I agree that the Declaration of Human Rights merely sets a common standard of achievement for all peoples and all nations but cannot create a binding set of rules. Members States may seek, through appropriate agencies, to initiate action when these basic rights are violated, but individual citizens cannot complain about their breach in the municipal courts even if the country concerned has adopted the covenants and ratified the operational protocol. The individual cannot come to the Court but may complain to the HumanRights Committee, which in turn, will set in motion other procedures. In short, the basic human rights enshrined in the International Covenants above referred to may at best inform judicial institutions and inspire legislative action within member-States, but apart from such deep reverence, remedial action at the instance of an aggrieved individual is beyond the area of judicial authority."

While considering the impact of international covenants on municipal law, the decision concluded:

"Indeed the construction I have adopted of S.51 S.P.C. has the flavour of Article 11 of the Human Rights Covenants, Counsel for the appellant inisisted that law and justice must be on speaking terms—by justice he meant, in the present case, that a debtor unable to pay must not be detained in civil prison. But my interpretation does put law and justice on speaking terms. Counsel for the repondent did argue that International Law is the vanishing point of jurisprudence is itself vanishing in a world where humanity is moving steadily, though slowly, towards a world order, led by that intensely active, although yet ineffectual body, the United Nations Organisation. Its resolutions and covenants mirror the conscience of mankind and inseminate, within the member States, progressive legislation, but till his last step of actual enactment of law takes place, the citizen in a world of sovereign States, has only inchoate rights in the domestice Courts under these international covenants. While dealing with the impact of the Dicean rule of law on positive law, Hood Phillips wrote—and this is all that the Covenant means now for Indian courts administering municipal law. The positive commitment of the States parties ignites legislative action at home but does not automatically make the covenant an enforceable part of the corpus juris of India."

He further observed that, "Indeed, the Central Law Commission, in the Fifty-Fourth Report, did cognise the covenant, while dealing with S.51 C.P.C.".

The question to be considered is, whether this mode of execution should be retained on the statute book, particularly in view of the provision in the International Covenant on Civil and Politcal Rights prohibiting imprisonment for a mere non-performance of contract.

The Law Commission, in its unanimous report, quoted the key passages from the Kerala ruling referred to above and endorsed its ratio. 'We agree with this view' said the Law Commission and adopting that meaning as the correct one did not recommend further change on this facet of the Section. It is important to notice that, interpretationally speaking, the Law Commission accepted the dynamics of the changed circumstances of the debtor.

However, if he once had the means but now has not, or if he has money now on which there are other pressing claims, it is violative of the spirit of Art. 11 to arrest and confine him in jail so as to coerce him into payment.

Imprisonment is not to be ordered merely because, like Shylock, the creditor says: "I crave the law, they penalty and forfeit of my bond".

The law does recognise the principle that "Mercy is reasonable in the time of afficition, as clouds of rain in the time of drought."

We concur with the Law Commission in its construction of S.51, C.P.C. It follows that quandam affluence and current indigence without intervening dishonesty or bad faith in liquidating his liability can be consistent with Art. 11 of the Covenant, because then no detention is permissible under S. 51 C.P.C.

Thus the arrest and detention of judgement debtor was held to be violative of Article 21 of the Indian Constitution as well as Article 11 of the Covenant.

Relation between International Law and Municipal Law—Transformation and Incorporation Theories

In *Gramophone Co. of India Ltd. v. Birendra Bahadur Pandey,*[101] the main questions arose before the apex court were (i) whether International law is, of its own force, drawn into the law of the land without the aid of a municipal statute. second, whether, so drawn, it overrides municipal law in case of conflict.

The apex court before deciding the above questions discussed two schools of thoughts prevalent in England. According to one, rules of international law are incorporated into the law of the land automatically and considered to be part of the law of land unless in conflict with an Act of Parliament. This is known as the doctrine of incorporation. According to the other thought, rules of international law are not part of the law of the land, unless adopted so by an Act of Parliament, judicial decision or long established custom. This is called as transformation theory. Lord Denning who had once accepted the transformation doctrine without question, later preferred the doctrine of incorporation and explained how courts were justified in applying modern rules of international law when old rules of international law changed. In fact, the doctrine of incorporation, it appears, was accepted in England long before Lord Denning did so. Lord Denning himself referred to some old cases.[102] The Supreme Court referred the following observations of *West Rand Central Gold Mining Company v. The King.*[103]

"It is quite true that whatever has received the common consent of civilized nations must have received the assent of our country, and that to which we have assented along with other nations in general may properly be called international law, and as such will be acknowledged and applied by our municipal tribunals when legitimate occassion arises for those tribunals to decide questions to which doctrine of international law may be relevant."

Regarding the relation between International law and municipal law, it was held, "There can be no question that nations must march with the international community and the municipal law must respect rules of international law even as nations respect international opinion. The comity of Nations requires that rules of International law may be accommodated in the municipal law even without express legislative sanction provided they do not run into conflict with Acts of parliament. But when do run into such conflict, the sovereignty and the integrity of the Republic and the supremacy of the constituted legislatures in making the laws may not be subjected to external rules except to the extent legitimately accepted by the constituted legislatures themselves. The doctrine of incorporation also recognises the position that the rules of international law are incorporated into national law and considered to be part of the national law, unless they are in conflict with an Act of Parliament, comity of nations or no. Municipal law must prevail in case of conflict. National Courts cannot say yes if Parliament has said no to a principle of international law. National Courts will endorse international law but not if it conflicts with national law. National courts being organs of the national state and not organs of international law must perforce apply national law if international law conflicts with it. But the courts are under an obligation within legitimate limits, to so interpret the municipal statute as to avoid confrontation with the comity of Nations or the well established principles of International law. But if conflict is inevitable, the latter must yield."[104] The proposition has been well stated by Lathama CJ in *Politics v. The Commonwealth*, 70 Commonwealth LR 60: "Every statute is to be interpreted and applied, as for as its language admits, as not to be inconsistent with the comity of nations with the established rules of international law............. It must be held that legislation otherwise within the power of the Commonwealth Parliament does not become invalid because it conflicts with a rule of international law, though every effort should be made to construe commonwealth statutes so as to avoid breaches of international law and of international comity. The question, therefore, is not a question of the power of the commonwealth Parliament to legislate in breach of international law, but is a question whether in fact it has done so.[105] The Supreme Court of India has said practically the same thing in *Tracto Roexport, Moscow v. Tarapore & Company*, (1970) 3 SCR 53, (AIR 1971 SC 1 at p. 8): Now as stated in Halsbury's Laws of England, vol. 36, page 414, there is a presumption that Parliament does not assert or assume jurisdiction which goes beyond the limits established by the common Consent of nations and statutes are to be interpreted provided that their language permits, so as not to be inconsistent with the comity of nations or with the established principles of international law. But this principle applies only where there is an ambiguity and must give way before a clearly expressed intention. If statutory enactments are clear in meaning, they must be construed according to their meaning even though they are contrary to the comity of nations or international Law."

The observations show that the court was only concerned with a principle of interpretation, but, by implication, it may be possible to say that the court preferred the doctrine of incorporation....."

Low Wages to Casual Labourers Violates ICESCR

In *Daily Rated casual Labour employed under P & T Department through Bhartiya Dak Tar Mazdoor Manch v. Union of India and others*[106]; the petitioner's main contention was, first, that the wages paid to casual labourers were very low and far less than the salary and allowances paid to the regular employees of the Posts and Telegraph Department. Secondly, that Union of India had not laid down any plan to regularize their services. as a result they have been denied the benefits of increments, leave facility and pension etc.

On the other hand respondents contended that since the petitioners belong to the category of casual labour and are not being regularly employed, they are not entitled to the same rights or privileges which the regular employees are enjoying.

The apex court observed, "It may be true that the petitioners have not been regularly recruited. But many of them have been working continuously for more than a year in the department and some of them have been engaged as casual labourers for nearly ten years. They are rendering the same kind of service which is being rendered by the regular employees doing the same type of work, clause (2) of Article 38 of the Constitution of India which contains one of the Directive Principles of state policy provides that, "the state shall in particular, strive to minimise the inequalities in income and endeavour to eliminate inequalities in status, facilities and opportunities not only amongst individuals but also amongst groups of people residing in different areas or engaged indifferent vocations." Even though the above Directive Principles may not be enforceable as such by virtue of Article 37 of the constitution of India, it may be relied upon by the petitioners to show that in the instant case they have been subjected to hostile discrimination. It is urged that the state cannot deny at least the minimum pay in the pay scales of regularly employed workman even though the Government may not be compelled to extend all the benefits enjoyed by regularly recruited employees. We are of the view that such denial amounts to exploitation of labour. The government cannot take advantage of its dominant position and compel any worker to work even as a casual labourer on starving wages. It may be that the casual labourer has agreed to work on such low wages. That he has done because he has no other choice. It is poverty that has driven him to that state. The Government should be a model employer. We are of the view that on the facts and in the circumstances of this case the classification of employers into regularly recruited employees and casual employees for the purpose of paying less than the minimum pay payable to employees in the corresponding regular cadres particularly in the lowest rungs of the department where the payscales are the lowest is not tanable. The further classification of casual labourers into three categories namely (i) those who have not completed 720 days of service; (ii) those who have completed 720 days of service and not completed 1200 days of service; (iii) those who have completed more tham 1200 days of service for purpose of payment of different rates of wages is equally untenable. There is clearly no justification for doing so. Such a classification is violative of Articles 14 and 16 of the constitution. It is also opposed to the spirit of Article 7 of the International covenant on Economic, social and cultural Rights, 1966 which exhorts all states parties to ensure fair wages and equal wages for equal work. We feel that there is substance in contention of the petitioners.[107]

Thus it is clear from the above judgement that disparity in pay and allowances of two categories of labourers were held to be violative of Equality clause on the basis of International covenant on Economic social and cultural Rights, 1966.

Preventive Detention of a Foreign National

In *Kubic Dariusz v. Union of India,* AIR 1990 SC 605 the petitioner was a polish national when he arrived in calcutta by air from

Singapore via Bangkok was arrested under section 104 of the customs Act, by the officers of the custom department attached to calcutta Airport on the ground that he was carrying in his possession foreign gold weighing about 70 tolas. During the jail custody, he was served with a detention order passed under section 3(1) of the conservation of Foreign Exchange and Prevention of Smuggling Activities Act (COFEPOSA Act). He challenged his detention order on two grounds, first, that the grounds of detention were communicated to him in a language which he did not know. Secondly, the representation submitted by him was not considered, therefore the detention order was liable to be quashed as violative of Article 22(5) of the Constitution of India.

K.N. Saikia J. said, "Preventive detention of a foreign national who is not resident of the country involves an element of international law and human rights and the appropriate authorities ought not to be seen to have been oblivious of its international obligations in this regard. The Universal Declaration of human rights include the right to life, liberty and security of person, freedom from arbitrary arrest and detention, the right to fair trial by an independent and impartial tribunal, and the right to presume to be an innocent man until proved guilty. When an act of preventive detention involves of foreign national though from the national point of view the municipal law alone count in its application and interpretation, it is generally a recognised principle in national legal system that in the event of doubt the national rule is to be interpreted in accordance with the state's international obligations as was pointed out by Krishna Iyer J. in *Jolly George Verghese v. The Bank of Cochin,* AIR 1980 SC 470. There is need for harmonisation when ever possible bearing in mind the spirit of the covenants. In this context it may not be out of place to bear in mind that the fundamental rights guaranteed under our constitution are in conforming line with those in the declaration and the covenant on civil and Political rights and the covenant on Economic, social and cultural rights to which India has become a party by ratifying them. Crimes trahit personam. The crime carries the person. The commission of a crime gives the court of the place where it is committed jurisdiction over the person of the offender. Legal relations associated with the effecting of legal aid on criminal matters is governed in the international field either by the norms of multilateral international conventions relating to control of crime of an international character or by special treaties concerning legal cooperation. Sumggling may not be regarded as such a crime. The system of extradition of criminals represents an act of legal assistance by one state (the requestee) to another state (requestor) with the aim of carrying out a criminal prosecution finding and arresting a suspected in order to bring him to court or for executing the sentence. In concluding such conventions the states base themselves on principles of humanitarianism in their efforts to contribute to the more effective achievement of the objective of the correction and re-education of violaters of the law."[108]

UDHR and Health of Workers

Regarding the health of the workers employed in asbestos industries the apex court in *Consumer Education & Research Centre v. Union of India,*[109] through K. Ramaswamy J. (on belhalf of himself and A.H. Ahmadi, C.J. & M.M. Punchhi J.) said that Article 1 of the Universal Declaration of Human Rights asserts human sensitivity and moral responsibility of every state that, "all human beings are born free and equal in dignity and rights. They are endowed with reason and conscience and should act towards one another in a spirit of brotherhood. The charter of the United nations thus reinforces the faith in fundamental human rights and in the dignity and worth of the human person envisaged in the directive principles of state policy as part of the constitution. Article 25(2) of the Universal declaration of human rights ensures right to standard of adequate living for health and well being of the individual including medical care, sickness and disability, Art. 2(b) of the International covenant on Political, Social and cultural Rights protects the right of worker to enjoy just and favourable conditions of work ensuring safe and healthy working conditions.... the right to human dignity, development of personality social protection, right to rest and leisure are fundamental human rights to a workman assured by the charter of Human Rights, in the Preamble and Articles 38 and 39 of the constitution..... Health of the worker enables him to enjoy the fruit of his labour, keeping him physically fit and mentally alert for leading a successful life, economically, socially and culturally. Medical facilities to protect the health of the workers are, therefore, the fundamental and human rights to the workman.[110]

Stockholm Declaration: Environmental Principles and Right to Life and Liberty

In *Vellore Citizens Welfare Forum v. Union of India*[111] the petitioner filed a writ petition under Article 32 of the constitution, complaining that the tanneries are discharging untreated effluent in the Palar river which has resulted in scarcity of potable water to the residents of the area.

In the facts and circumstances of the case, Kuldip Singh J.[112], observed, "The traditional concept that development and ecology are opposed to each other, is no longer acceptable. 'Sustainable development' is the answer. In the international sphere 'Sustainable development' as a concept came to be known for the first time in the stockholm Declaration of 1972. Thereafter, in 1987 the concept was given a definite shape by the world commission on environment and development in its report called 'our Common future'. The commission was chaired by the then Prime Minister of Norway, G.H. Brundtland and as such the report is popularly known as 'Brundtland Report'. In 1991 the world conservation union, United Nations Environment Programme and world wide fund for nature, jointly came out with a document called 'caring for the earth' which is a strategy for sustainable living. Finally came the Earth Summit held in June, 1992 at Rio which saw the largest gathering of world leaders ever in the history-deliberating and chalking out a blue print for the survival of the planet. Among the tangible achievements of the Rio conference was signing of two conventions, one on biological diversity and another on climate change. These conventions were signed by 153 nations. The delegates also approved by consensus three non-binding documents namely, a statement on Forestry Principles, a declaration of principles on environmental policy and development initiatives and Agenda 21, a programme of action into the next century in areas like poverty, population and pollution. During the two decades from stockholm to Rio 'Sustainable Development' has come to be accepted as a viable concept to eradicate poverty and improve the quality of human life while living within the carrying capacity of the supporting eco-systems. 'Sustainable Development' as defined by the Brundtland Report means 'Development that meets the needs of the present without compromising the ability of the future generations to meet their own needs.' We have no hesitation in holding that 'Sustainable Development' as a balancing concept between ecology and development has been accepted as a part of the customany International law though its salient features have yet to be finalised by the International law Jurists. Some of the salient principles of 'Sustainable development' as culled out from Brundtland Report and other international documents, are Inter-Generational equity, use and conservation of Natural resources, Environmental protection, the precautionary principle, Polluter pays principle, obligation to assist and co-operate, eradication of poverty and financial assistance to the developing countries.... The Precautionary principle and 'The polluter pays principle are essential features of 'Sustainable development'. The 'Precautionary principle' in the context of the municipal law means:

(i) Environmental measures by the state Government and the statutory authorities must anticipate, prevent and attack the causes of environmental degradation.

(ii) Where there are threats of serious and irrversible damage, lack of scientific certainty should not be used as a reason for postponing measures to prevent environmental degradation.

(iii) The 'onus of proof' is on the actor or the developer industralist to show that this action is enviornamentally benign. "The Polluter pays" principle has been held

> to be a sound principle by this Court in *Indian Council for Enviro Legal Action v. Union of India.*[113] The court observed, "we are of the opinion that any principle evolved in this behalf should be simple, practical and suited to the conditions obtaining in this county. The court ruled that once the activity Carried on is hazardous or inherently dangerous, the person carrying on such activity is liable to make good the loss Caused to any other person by his activity irrespective of the fact whether he took reasonable care while carrying on his activity. The rule is premised upon the very nature of the activity carried on. Consequently the polluting industries are absoulutely liable to compensate for the harm caused by them to villagers in the affected area, to the soil and to the underground water and hence, they are bound to take all necessary measures to remove sludege and other pollutants lying in the affected areas. The 'Polluter pays' principle as interpreted by this court means that the absolute liability for harm to the environment extends not only to compensate the victims of pollution but also the cost of restoring the environmental degradation. Remediation of the damaged environment is part of the process of 'sustainable development' and as such polluter is liable to pay the cost to the individual sufferers as well as the cost of reversing the damaged ecology.

The precautionary principle and the polluter pays principle have been accepted as part of the law of the land. Article 21 of the constitution of India guarantees protection of life and personal liberty.[114]

Convention on the Elimination of all forms of Discriminiation against Women (CEDAW) and Female's Right to Inheritance

In *Madhu Kishwar and Others v. State of Bihar*[115], the customary law applied in the state of Bihar and other parts of the country which excluded tribal women from inheritance of property belonging to the parents of husband, was challenged on the ground that it was discriminatory. A three Judges bench[116] examined the qustion whether female tribal is entitled to parity with male tribal in intestate succession?

K. Ramaswamy J. observed

The General Assembly of the United Nations adopted a Declaration on December 4, 1986 on "The Right to Development" to which India played a crusading role for its adoption and ratified the same. Its preamble recognises that all human rights and fundamental freedoms are indivisible and interdependent. All Nation States are concerned at the existence of serious obstacles to development and complete fulfilment of human beings, denial of civil, political, economic, social and cultural rights. In order to promote development, equal attention should be given to the implementation, promotion and protection of civil, political, economic social and political rights.

Article 1(1) assures right to development, an inalienable human right, by virtue of which every person and all people are entitled to participate in, contribute to, and enjoy economic, social, cultural and political development in which all human rights and fundamental freedoms can be fully realised. Article 6(1) obligated the State to observe all human rights and fundamental freedoms for all without any discrimination as to race, sex, language or religion. Sub-article (2) enjoins that............. equal attention and urgent consideration should be given to the implementation, promotion and protection of civil political, economic, social and political rights. Sub-article (3) thereof enjoins that "State should take steps to eliminate obstacle to development resulting from failure to observe civil and political rights as well as economic, social and cultural rights. Article 8 castes duty on the State to undertake, ...all necessary measures for the realisation of right to development and ensure, inter alia, equality of opportunity for all in their access to basic resources............ and fair distribution of income. Effective measures should be undertaken to ensure that women have an active role in the development process. Appropriate economic and social reforms should be carried out with a view to eradicate all social injustice.

Human Rights are derived from the dignity and worth inherent in the human person. Human Rights and fundamental freedom have been reiterated by the Universal Declaration of Human Rights. Democracy, development and respect for human rights and fundamental freedoms are inter-dependent and have mutual reinforcement. The human rights for woman, including girl child are, therefore, inalienable, integral and indivisible part of universal human rights. The full development of personality and fundamental freedoms and equal participation by women in political, social, economic and cultural life are concomitants for national development, social and family stability and growth, culturally, socially and economically. All forms of discrimination on grounds of gender is violative of fundamental freedoms and human rights. Vienna Convention on the Elimination of all forms of Discrimination Against Women (for short "CEDAW") was ratified by the U.N.O. on December 18, 1979. The Government of India who was an active participant to CEDAW ratified it on June 19, 1993 and acceded to CEDAW on August 8, 1993 with reservation of Articles 5(e), 16(1), 16(2) and 29 thereof. The Preamble of CEDAW reiterates that discrimination against women, violates the principles of equality of rights and respect for human dignity; is an obstacle to the participation on equal terms with men in the political, social, ecomonic and cultural life of their country; hampers the growth of the personality from society and family and makes it more difficult for the full development of potentialities of women in the service of their countries and of humanity. Poverty of women is a handicap. Establishment of new international economic order based on equality and justice will countribute significantly towards the promotion of equality between men and women etc. Article 1 defines discrimination against women to men "any distinction, exclusion or restriction made on the basis of sex which has the effect or purpose on impairing or nullifying the recognized enjoyment or exercise by women, irrespective of their marital status, on a basis of equality of men and women, all human rights and fundamental freedoms in the political, economic, social, cultural, civil or any other field." Article 2(b) enjoins the State parties while condemning discrimination against women in all its forms, to pursue, by appropriate means, without delay, elimination of discrimination against women by adopting "appropriate legislative and other measures including sanctions where appropriate, prohibiting all discriminations against women" to take all appropriate measures including legislation, to modify or abolish existing laws, regulations, customs and practices which constitute discrimination against women. clause (C) enjoins to ensure legal protection of the rights of women on equal basis with men through constituted national tribunals and other public institutions against any act of discrimination to provide effective protection to women. Article 3 enjoins State parties that it shall take, in all fields, in particular in the political social, economic and cultural fields, all appropriate measures including legislation to ensure full development and advancement of women for the purpose of guaranteeing them the exercise and enjoyment of human rights and fundamental freedoms on the basis of equality with men. Article 13 states that "the State parties shall take all appropriate measures to eliminate discrimination against women in other areas of economic and social life in order to ensure on a basis of equality of men and women". Article 14 lays emphasis to eliminate discrimination on the problems faced by rural women so as to enable them to play "in the economic survival of their families including their work in the non-monetized sectors of the economy and shall take... all appropriate measures...." Participation in and benefit from rural development in particular, shall ensure to such women the right to participate in the development programme to organize self groups and co-operatives to obtain equal access to economic opportunities through employment or self-employment etc. Article 15(2) enjoins to accord to women equality with men before the law, in particular, to administer property....."

The Parliament has enacted the Protection of Human Rights Act, 1993. Section 2(b) defines human rights to mean "the rights relating to life, liberty, equality and dignity of the individual guranteed by the Constitution, embodied in the international Conventions and enforceable by courts in India." Thereby the principles embodied in CEDAW and the concomitant Right to Development became integral parts of the Indian Constitution and the Human Rights Act and became enforceable. Section 12 of Protection of Human Rights Act charges the Commission with duty for proper implementation as well as prevention of violation of the human rights and fundamental freedoms.

Article 5(a) of CEDAW to which the Government of India expressed reservation does not stand in its way and in fact Article 2(f) denudes its effect and enjoins to implement Article 2(f) read with its obligation undertaken under Articles 3, 14 and 15 of the Convention *vis-a-vis* Articles 1, 3, 6 and 8 of the Declaration of Right to Development. Though the directive principles and fundamental rights provide the matrix for development of human personality and elimination of discrimination, these conventions add urgency and teeth for immediate implementation. It is, therefore, imperative for the State to eliminate obstacles, prohibit all gender based discriminations as mandated by Articles 14 and 15 of the Constitution of India. By operation of Article 2(f) and other related articles of CEDAW, the State should by appropriate measures including legislation, modify law and abolish gender based discrimination in the existing laws, regulations, customs and practices which constiute discrimination against women.[117]

It was concluded that Covenants of the United nation add impetus and urgency to eliminate gender based obstacles and discrimination. Legislative action should be devised suitably to constitute economic empowerment of women into socio-economic restructure for establishing egalitarian social order. Law is an instrument of social change as well as the defender for social change. Article 2(e) of CEDAW enjoins this court to breath life into dry bones of the constitution, international conventions and the protection of the Human Rights Act, to prevent gender based discrimination and to effectuate right to life including empowerement of economic, social and cultural rights.

International Conventions and Protection of Working Women from Sexual Harassment

In *Vishaka v. State of Rajasthan*[118] certain social activists and NGOs filed a petition for the enforcement of the fundamental rights of working women under Articles 14, 19 and 21 of the constitution. The petitioners draw the attention of the apex court to the increasing incidents of sexual harassment of working women at the working places.

J.S. Verma, C.J.I.[119], Pointed out that:

(1) In the absence of domestic law occupying the field, to formulate effective measures to check the evil of sexual harassment of working women at all work places, the contents of International Conventions and norms are significant for the purpose of interpretation of the guarantee of gender equality, right to work with human dignity in Articles 14, 15, 19(1)(g) and 21 of the constitution and the safeguards against sexual harassment implicit therein Any International Convention not inconsistent with the fundamental rights and in harmony with its spirit must be read into these provisions to enlarge the meaning and content thereof, to promote the object of the constitutional guarantee. This is implicit from Article 51(c) and the enabling power of Parliament to enact laws for implementing the International Conventions and norms by virtue of Article 253 read with entry 14 of the Union list in Seventh Schedule of the Constitution.[120]

(2) The obligation of this court under Article 32 of the constitution for the enforcement of these fundamental rights in the absence of legislation must be viewed along with the role of judiciary envisaged in the Beijing statement of Principles of the independence of the judiciary in the LAWASIA region. These Principles were accepted by the Chief Justices of the Asia and the Pacific at Beijing in 1995 as those representing the minimum standards necessary to be observed in order

to maintain the independence and effective functioning of the judiciary. The objectives of the judiciary mentioned in the Beijing statements are:

"Objectives of the Judiciary:

The objectives and functions of the judiciary include the following:

(a) to ensure that all persons are able to live securely under the rule of law;

(b) to promote, within the proper limits of the judicial function, the observance and the attainment of human rights; and

(c) to administer the law impartially among persons and the state."[121]

(3) Gender equality includes protection from sexual harassment and right to work with dignity, which is a universally recognised basic human right. The common minimum requirement of this right has received global acceptance. The international conventions and norms are, therefore, of great significance in the formulation of the guidelines to achieve this purpose.[122]

(4) Some provisions in the convention on the Elimination of All Forms of Discrimination against women, of significance in the present context are:

Article 11

(1) States parties shall take all appropriate measures to eliminate discrimination against women in the field of employment in order to ensure, on a basis of equality of men and women, the same rights, in particular;

(a) The right to work as an inalienable right of all human beings;

(f) The right to protection of health and to safety in working conditions, including the safeguarding of the function of reproduction.

Article 24

States Parties undertake to adopt all necessary measures at the national level aimed at achieving the full realization of the rights recognised in the present convention.

The general recommendations of CEDAW in this context in respect of Article are:

"Violence and equality in employment:

(i) Equality in employment can be seriously impaired when women are subjected to gender specific violence, such as sexual harassment in the work place.

(ii) Sexual harassment includes such as unwelcome sexually determined behaviour as physical contacts and advances sexually coloured remarks, showing pornography and sexual demands, whether by words or actions. Such conduct can be humiliating and may constitute a health and safety problem; it is discriminatory when the women has reasonable grounds to believe that her objection would disadvantage her in Connection with her employment, including recruiting or promotion, or when it creates a hostile working environment. Effective complaints procedures and remedies, including compensation, should be provided.

States should include in their reports information about sexual harassment, and on measures to protect women from sexual harassment and other forms of violence of coercion in the work place."

The Government of India has ratified the above resolution on June 25, 1993 with some reservations.... At the Fourth World Conference On Women in Beijing, the Government of India has also made an official commitment, inter alia, to formulate and operationalize a national policy on women which will continuously guide and inform action at every level and in every sector; to set up a commission for women's to act as a public defender of women's human rights; to institutionalise a national level mechanism to monitor the implementation of the platform for action.[123]

(5) The meaning and content of the fundamental rights guaranteed in the Constitution of India are of sufficient amplitude to encompass all the facets of gender equality including prevention of sexual harassment Or abuse..... The international Coventions and norms are to be read into them in the absence of enacted domestic law occupying the field when there is no inconsistency between them. It is now accepted rule of judicial construction that regard must be had to international conventions and norms for construing domestic law when there is no inconsistency between them and there is a void in the domestic law.[124]

In *Nilbati Behera v. State of Orissa,*[125] a provisions in the ICC PR was referred to support the view taken that 'an enforceable right to compensation is not alien to the concept of enforcement of a guaranteed right as a public law remedy under Article 32, distinct from the private law remedy in torts. There is no reason why these international conventions and norms cannot therefore, be used for construing the fundamental rights expressly guaranteed in the Constitution of India which embody the basic concept of gender equality in all spheres of human activity.[126]

Keeping in view the definition of Human right,[127] the above mentioned International Conventions and norms for construing municipal law, the Supreme Court laid down the guidlines to be observed by employers of working place to prevent sexual harassment of women.

This important case shows a productive inter-action between international treaties and domestic courts, which has also been seen in other countries, gives domestic activists a blueprint for change that they can take to their own courts, in this case achieving the incorporation of CEDAW standards in to domestic law. The role for NGOs in the solution was especially creative. Legislation binding on non-governmental actors has not yet been passed, and the current polittical climate does not appear favourable to it. Nonetheless, Vishaka sets out firmly on a path that can be followed in other areas in the future, a path that productively combines internal democratic legitimacy with the external suasion supplied by an international treaty.[128]

Compensation to Rape Victim by Applying UDHR and Two Important Conventions

In *Chairman, Rly. Board and others v. Chandrimadas*[129] Mrs.Chandrimadas a practising advocate of the Calcutta High Court, filed a petition under Article 226 of the Constitution against Railway Board and others, claiming compensation for the victim, Smt. Hanuffa Khatoon, a Bangaladeshi national who was gang raped by many including employees of the Railways in room at Yatri Niwas at Howrah Station. The Calcutta High Court awarded a sum of Rupees ten lakhs as compensation to the victim.

As a result an appeal was filed in the Supreme Court contending that the Railway would not be liable to pay compensation to Smt. Khatoon because she was a foreigner and not an Indian national. It was also contended that since it was the individual act of the persons committing the offence, they alone would be punished and may also be liable to pay fine or compensation, the Union of India would not be even vicariously liable.

Considering the first contention that the fundamental right in part III of the Constitution are available only to citizens of this country, it was observed, "This argument must also fail for two reasons : first, on the ground of domestic jurisprudence based on constitutional provisions and secondly, on the ground of human rights jurisprudence based on the Universal Declaration of Human Rights, 1948, which has the international recognition as the "Moral Code of Conduct" having been adopted by the General Assembly of the United Nations. First consider the principles and objects behind the Universal Declaration of Human Rights, 1948, as adopted and proclaimed by the United Nations General Assembly Resoltuion of 10-12-1948. The Preamble, inter alia, sets out as under:

"WHEREAS recognition of the INHERENT DIGNITY and of the equal and inalienable rights of all members of the human family is the foundation of freedom, justice and peace in the world.

"WHEREAS disregard and contempt for human rights have resulted in barbarous acts which have outraged the conscience of mankind, and the advent of a world in which human beings shall enjoy freedom of speech and belief and freedom from fear and want has been proclaimed as the highest aspiration of the common people.

WHEREAS it is essential to promote the development of firendly relation between nation.

WHEREAS the people of the United Nations have in the Charter affirmed their faith in fundamental human rights, IN THE DIGNITY AND WORTH OF THE HUMAN PERSON AND IN THE EQUAL RIGHTS OF MEN AND WOMEN and have determined to promote social progress and better standards of life in large freedom.

WHEREAS member States have pledged themselves to achieve, in cooperation with the United Nations, the promotion of universal respect for an observance of human rights and fundamental freedoms.

WHEREAS a common understanding of these rights and freedoms is of the greatest importance for the full realisation of this plege."

Thereafer, the Declaration sets out, inter alia, in various articles, the following:

1. All human beings are born free and equal in dignity and rights. They are endowed with reason and conscience and should act towards one another in a spirit of brotherhood.
2. Everyone is entitled to all the rights and freedom set forth in this Delcaration, without distinction of any kind, such as race, colour, sex, language, religion, political or other opinion, NATIONAL OR SOCIAL ORIGIN PROPERTY, BIRTH OR OTHER STATUS.

   Furthermore, NO DISTINCTION SHALL BE MADE ON THE BASIS OF THE POLITICAL, JURIDICTIONAL OR INTERNATIONAL STATUS OF THE COUNTRY OR TERRITORY to which a person belongs, whether it be independence, trust, non-self-governing or under any other limitation of sovereignty.

3. Everyone has the right to life, liberty and security of person.
4. No one shall be subjected to torture or to cruel, inhuman or degarding treatment or punishment.
5. All are equal before the law and are entitled wihout any discrimination to equal protection of the law. All are entitled to equal prtoection against any discrimination in violation of this Declaration and against any incitement to such discrimination.
6. No one shall be subject to arbitrary arrest, detention or exile."

Apart from the above, the General Assembly also while adopting the Declaration on the Elimination of Violence against Women, by its resolution dated 20.12.1993, observed in Article 1 that:

> "'violence against women' means any act of gender-based violence that result in, or is likely to result in, physcial, sexual or psychological harm or suffering to women, including threats of such acts, coercion or arbitrary deprivation of liberty, whether occuring in public or in private life".

In Article 2, it was specified that:

> "......violence against women shall be understood to encompass, but not be limited to:

(a) physical, sexual and psychological violence occuring in the family including battering, sexual abuse of female children in the household, dowry-related violence, marital rape, female genital mutilation and other traditional practices harmful to women, non-spousal violence and violence related to exploitation.

(b) physical, sexual and psychological violence occuring within the general community, including rape, sexual abuse, sexual harassment and intimidation at work in educational institutions and elesewhere, trafficking in women and forced positions;

(c) Physical, sexual and psychological violence perpetrated or condoned by the State, wherever it occurs".

In Article 3, it was specified that:

".........women are entitled to the equal enjoyment and protection of all human rights, which would include, inter alia:

(a) the right to life,

(b) the right to equality, and

(c) the right to liberty and secuirty of person."

The International Convenants and Declarations as adopted by the United Nations have to be respected by all signatory States and the meaning given to the above words in those Declarations and Covenants have to be such as would help in effective implementation of those rights. The applicability of the Universal Declaration of Human Rights and the principles thereof may have to be read, if need be, into the domestic jurisprudence.

Lord Diplock in *Salomon v. Commr. of Customs and Excise*[130] said that there is a prima facie presumption that Parliament does not intend to act in breach of international law, including specific treaty obligations. So also Lord Bridge in *Brind v. Secy. of State for the Home Deptt.*[131] observed that it was well settled that, in construing any provision in domestic legislation which was ambiguous in the sense that it was capable of a meaning which either conforms to or conflicts with the Internaional Convention, the courts would presume that Parliament intended to legislate in conformity with the Convention and not in conflict with it.

The domestic application of international human rights and norms was considered by the Judicial Colloquia (Judges and Lawyers) at Bangalore in 1988. It was later affirmed by the Colloquia that it was the vital duty of an independent judiciary to interpret and apply national Constitutions in the light of those principles. Further Colloquia were convened in 1994 at Zimbabwe, in 1996 at Hong Kong and in 1997 at Guyana and in all those Colloquia, the question of domestic application of international and regional human rights specially in relation to women, was considered. The Zimbabwe Declaration 1994, inter alia, stated:

> "Judge and lawyers have duty to familiarise themselves with the growing international jurisprudence of human rights and particularly with the expanding material on the protection and promotion of the human rights of women".

But this situation may not really arise in our country.

Our Constitution guarantees all the basic and fundamental human rights set out in the Universal Declaration of Human Rights, 1948, to its citizens and other persons. The chapter dealing with the fundamental rights is contained in Part III of the Constitution. The purpose of this Part is to safeguard the basic human rights from the vicissitudes of political controversy and to place them beyond the reach of the political parties who, by virtue of their majority, may come to form the Government at the Centre or in the State.

The word "LIFE" has also been used prominently in the Universal Declaration of Human Rights, 1948. (See Article 3 quoted above). The fundamental rights under the Constitution are almost in consonance with the rights contained in the Universal Declaration of Human Rights as also the Declaration and the Covenant of Civil and Political Rights and the Covenants of Economic, Social and Cultural Rights, to which India is party having ratified them, as set out by this Court in *Kubic Darusz v. Union of India*[132]. That being so, since "LIFE" is also recognised as a basic human right in the Universal Declaration of Human Right, 1948 it has to have the same meaning and interpretation as has been palced on that word by this Court in its various decisions relating to Article 21 of the Constitution. The meaning of the word 'life' cannot be narrowed down. According to the tenor of the language used in Article 21, it will be available not only to every citizen of this country, but also to a 'person' who may not be a citizen of the country.[133]

Accordingly, it was held that Smt. Khatoon, who was a foreign national, could not be subjected to a treatment which was below dignity nor could she be subjected to physical violence at the hands of government employees who outraged her modesty. Her right under Article 21 of the Indian Constitution was violated consequently, the state was under a constitutional liability to pay compensation to her.

Custodial Violence-Right to Compensation under International Convention

D. K. Basu v. State of W.B.,[134]

The Facts of the case discloses that the executive Chairman Legal Aid Services, West Bengal, a non-political Organisation addressed a letter to the Chief Justice of India drawing his attention to certain news items published in the Telegraph dated 20th July to 22nd July 1986 and in other leading news papers regarding death in Police lock-ups and custody. The executive Chairman submitted that it was imperative to examine the issue in depth and to develop "Custody jurisprudence" and formulate modalities for awarding compensation to the victim and/or family members of the victim for atrocities and death caused in police custody. The letter was treated as a writ petition.

Emphasising the need for developing the law on compensation to victim, it was observed by Dr. A.S. Anand, J., "Article 9(5) of the International Covenant On Civil and Political Rights, 1966 (ICCPR) provides that any one who has been the victim of unlawful arrest or detention shall have enforceable right to compensation" of course, the Government of India at the time of ratification (of ICCPR) in 1979 had made a specific reservation to the effect that the Indian legal system does not recognise a right to compensation for victims of unlawful arrest or detention and thus did not become a party to the covenant. That reservation, however, has now lost its relevance in view of the law laid down by this court in a number of cases awarding compensation for the infringement of the fundamental right to life of a citizen.[135] There is indeed no express provision in the Constitution of India for grant of compensation for violation of a fundamental right to life, nonetheless, this court has judicially evolved a right to compensation in cases of established unconstitutional deprivation of personal liberty or life.[136]

Reading of International Conventions into Domestic Law

In *People's Union for Civil Liberties v. Union of India*[137] a significant question arose, as to what extent can the provisions of an international covenants/conventions be read into national laws. B.P. Jeevan Reddy J. discussed an Austrialian judgement,[138] the factual position was that the United Nations Convention on the rights of the child was ratified by the commonwealth executive in December, 1990 and had force in Australia from January 17, 1991 pursuant to a declaration made, on December 22, 1992, by the Attorney General pursuant to Section 47(1) of the Human Rights and Equal opportunity Commission Act, 1986 to the effect that the said convention is an international instrument relating to human rights. Respondent Teoh, a Nalaysian Citizen was found to have imported and be in possession of heroin, for which he was convicted. A deportation order was passed on that basis. The Immigration Review Panel opined that deportation of Teoh would deprive his young children (who were Australian Citizens) of their only financial support, landing them in bleak misery. Article 3 of the aforesaid convention provides that, "In all actions concerning children, whether undertaken by public or private social welfare institutions, courts of law, administrative authorities or legislative bodies, the best interests of the child shall be a primary consideration." Teoh invoked this article to ward off his deportation. The matter was carried to High Court where the question of enforceability of the convention by the national courts was thoroughly debated. Mason C. J., speaking for himself and Dean J., stated the position in the following words:

"It is well established that the provisions of any international treaty to which Australia is a party do not form part of Australian law unless these provisions have been validly incorporated into our municipal law by statute.[139] This principle has its foundation in the proposition that in our constitutional system the making and ratification of treaties fall within the province of the executive in the exercise of its prerogative power whereas the making and alteration of the law fall within the province of Parliament, not the executive.[140] So a treaty which has not been incorporated into our municipal law cannot operate as a direct source of individual rights and obligations under that law. In this case, it is common ground that the provisions of the conventions have not been incorporated in this way. It is not suggested that the delcaration made pursuant to Section 47(1) of the Human Rights and Equal opportunity Commission Act has this effect.

But the fact that the convention has not been incorporated into Australian law does not mean that its ratification hold no significance for Australian law. Where a statute or subordinate legislation is ambiguous, the courts should favour that construction which accords with Australia's obligations under a treaty or international convention to which Australia is a party,[141] at least in those cases in which the legislation is enacted after, or, in contemplation of, entry into, or ratification of, the relevant international instrument. That is because Parliament, prima facie, intends to give effect to Australia's obligations under international law.

It is accepted that a statute is to be interpreted and applied, as far as its language permits, so that it is in conformity and not in conflict with the established rules of international law.[142]

Apart from influencing the construction of a statute or subordinate legislation, an international convention may play a part in the development by the courts of the common law. The provisions of International convention to which Australia is a party, especially one which declare universal fundamental rights, may be used by the courts as a legitimate guide in developing the common law.[143] But the courts should act in this fashion with due circumspection when the parliament itself has not seen fit to incorporate the provisions of a convention into our domestic law. Judicial development of the common law by reference to must not be seen as a backdoor means of importing an unincorporated convention into Australian law. A cautious approach to the development of the common law by reference to international conventions would be consistent with the approach which the courts have hitherto adopted to the development of the common law by reference to statutory policy and statutory materials.[144] Much will depend upon the nature of relevant provision, the extent to which it has been accepted by the international community, the purpose which it is intended to serve and its relationship to the existing principle of our domestic law.

Toohey J. and Gaurdon, J. broadly concurred with the above opinion. Toohey J. spoke of such conventions giving rise to legitimate expectation among the people that the executive will honour the commitment while taking any action concerning children while Gaudron, J. relegated the Convention to a subsidiary position vis-a-vis Austrlian Statute law. (Mc Hugh dissented altogether).

The main Criticism against reading such conventions and covenants into national laws is one pointed by Mason, CJ himself, viz. the ratification of these conventions and covenants is done, in most of the countries by the executive acting alone and that the prerogative of making the law is that of the parliament alone; unless the Parliament legislates, no law can come into existence. It is not clear whether our Parliament has approved the action of the Government of India ratifying the said 1966 covenant. Assuming that it has, the question may yet arise whether such approval can be equated to legislation and invests the covenant with the sanctity of a law made by Parliament. As pointed out by this Court in *S.R. Bommai v. Union of India*[145], every action of Parliament cannot be equated to legislation. Legislation is no doubt the main function of the Parliament but it also performs many other functions all of which do not amount to legislation. In our opinion, this aspect requires deeper scrutiny than has been possible in this case. For the present, it would suffice to state that the provisions of the covenant, which elucidate and go to effectuate the fundamental rights guaranteed by our constitution, can certainly be relied upon by courts as facets of those fundamental rights and hence, enforceable as such. So far as multi-lateral treaties are concerned, the law is, of course, different and definite.[146]

Application of International Conventions to Protect the Human Rights of Children

(1) In *Bandhua Mukti Morcha v. Union of India and others,*[147] a writ petition under Article 32 of the constitution was filed by way of Public Interest litigation to issue a writ of mandamus directing the Government to take steps to stop employment of children in carpet industry in the state of U.P. The Supreme court followed the relevant international conventions and pointed out, "....Article 26(1) of the Universal Declaration of Human Rights assures that every one has the right to education which shall be free, at least at the elementary and fundamental stages. Elementary education shall be compulsory. Technical and professional education shall be made available and higher education shall equally be accessible to all on the basis of merit. Education enable development of human personality and strengthens the respect for human rights and fundamental freedoms. It promotes understanding, tolerance and friendship among people. It is, therefore, the duty of the state to provide facilities and opporunities to the children driven to child labour to develop their personality as responsible citizens.

Due to poverty, children and youth are subjected to many visible and invisible sufferings and disabilities, in particular, health, intellectual and social degradation and deprivation. The Convention on the rights of the child which was ratified by the Government of India on November 20, 1989 recognises the rights of the child for full and harmonious development of his or her personality. Child should grow up in a family environment, in an atmosphere of happiness, love and understanding. The Child should be fully prepared to live an individual life in society. Article 3 provides that in all actions concerning children, whether undertaken by public or private social welfare institutions, courts of law, administrative authorities or legislative bodies, the best interests of the child shall be the primary consideration. Article 27(1) provides that the state parties recognise the right of every child to a standard of living adequate for the child's physical, mental, spiritual, moral and social development. Article 28 provides thus:

I. State parties recognises the right of the child to education and with a view to education, and with a view to achieving this right progressively and on the basis of equal opportunity, they shall in particular:

   (a) Make primary education compulsory and available free to all;

   (b) Encourage the development of different forms of secondary education, including general and vocational education, make them available and accessible to every child, and take appropriate measures such as the introduction of free education and offering financial assistance in case of need;

   (c) Making higher education accessible to all on the basis of capacity by every appropriate means;

   (d) Make educational and vocational information and guidance available and accessible to all children.

   (e) Take measures to encourage regular attendance at schools and the reduction of drop-out rates.

II. State Parties shall take all appropriate measures to ensure that school discipline is administered in a manner consistent with the child's human dignity and in conformity with the present convention.

III. States Parties shall promote and encourage international co-operation in matters relating to education, in particular with a view to contributing to the elimination of ignorance and illiteracy throughout the world and facilitating access to scientific and technical knowledge and modern teaching methods in this regard. Particular account shall be taken of the needs of developing countries.

Article 31(1) recognises the right of the child to rest and leisure, to engage in play and recreational activities appropriate to the age of the child and to participate freely in cultural life and the arts. Article 32(1) which is material for the purpose of this case reads as under:

(1) States Parties recognize the right of the child to be protected from economic exploitation and from performing any work that is likely to be hazardous or to interfere with the child's education, or to be harmful to the child's health or physical, mental, spiritual, moral or social development.

(2) States Parties shall take legislative, administrative, social and educational measures to ensure the implementation of the present Article. To this end, and having regard to the relevant provisions of other international instruments. States parties shall in particular:

(a) Provide for a minimum age or minimum ages for admission to employment;

(b) Provide for appropriate regulation of the hours and conditions of employment;

(c) Provide for appropriate penalities or other sanctions to ensure the effective enforcement of the present article. Article 36 states that state parties shall protect the child against all other forms of exploiation prejudicial to any aspects of the child's welfare. No doubt, the Government, while ratifying the convention with a reservation of progressive implementation of the governance, reminded itself of the obligations undertaken there under, but they do not absolve the state in its fundamental governance of the imperatives of Directive Principle of the Constitution particularly, Articles 45, 39(e) and (f), 46 read with the Preamble, Articles 21, 23 and 24 of the constitution rendering socio-economic justice to the child and their empowerement, full growth of their personality-socially, educationally and culturally-with a right to leisure and opportunity for development of the spirit of reform, inquiry humanism and scientific temper to improve excellence-individually and collectively.[148]

(2) In *M.C. Mehta v. State of T.N.*,[149] the public spirited lawyer Sh. M.C. Mehta requested the Supreme Court to invoke its jurisdiction under Article 32 to protect the human rights of children[150] guaranteed by Article 24 of the Constitution in the form of basic inalienable rights. The apex court, highlighted the magnitude of the problem, examined the constitutional, statutory provisions and quoting India's Committment pointed out, "It would be apposite to apprise ourselves also about our commitment to world community. For the case at hand it would be enough to note that India has accepted the convention on the rights of the child, which was concluded by the UN General Assembly on 20th November, 1989. This convention affirms that children's right require special protection and it aims, not only to provide such protection, but also to ensure the continous improvement in the situation of children all over the world, as well as their development and education in conditions of peace and security. Thus the convention not only protectes the child's civil and political right, but also extends protection to child's economic, social, cultural and humanitarian rights. The Government of India deposited its instrument of accession to the above convention on December 11, 1992, with the United Nation's Secretary General. That instrument contains the following declaration: 'while fully subscribing to the objectives and purposes of the convention, realising that certain of the rights of the child, namely those pertaining to the economic, social and cultural rights can only be progressively implemented in the developing countries, subject to the extent of available resources and within the frame work of international co-operation; recognising that the child has to be protected from exploitation of all forms including economic exploitation; noting that for several reasons

children of different ages do work in India; having prescribed minimum ages for employment in hazardous occupations and in certain other areas; having made regulatory provisions regarding hours and conditions of employment, and being aware that it is not practical immediately to prescribe minimum ages for admission to each and every area of employment in India, the Government of India undertakes to take measures to progressively implement the provisions of Article 32,[151] particularly paragraph 2(a), in accordance with its national legislation and relevant international instruments to which it is a state party."[152]

(3) In *Parents Forum for meaningful Education and another v. Union of India,*[153] the petitioners challenged the provision of corporal punishment, which could be imposed on a student, embodied in Rule 37[154] of the Delhi school Education Rules, 1973.

The petitioners contended that infliction of corporal punishment upon children is inhuman. The Rules 37(1)(a) and 37(4) are illegal, arbitrary and violative of Articles 14, 19, 21 and 39(e) and (f) of the Constitution of India. A Division bench[155] examined the above rules and contentions of the parties in the light of provisions of the convention on the rights of the child adopted by the General Assembly of the United nations on November 20, 1989, Articles 14, 21 and 39(f) and (g) of the Constitution and National Policy of Education.

It was pointed out that, "The Preamble to the Convention on the Rights of the Child reflects that the State parties there to, recognising the importance of the child considered the necessity of bringing up the child in the spirit of the ideals proclaimed in the Charter of the United Nations, particularly in the spirit of peace, dignity, tolerance, freedom, equality and solidarity. The Preamble recalls that in the Universal Declaration of Human Rights, the United Nations has proclaimed that childhood is entilted to special care and assistance. From the Preamble to the Convention it appears that the General Assembly while adopting the same kept in view the Geneva Declaration, of the Rights of the Child of 1924, and the Declaration of the Rights of the Child adopted by the General Assembly on November 20, 1950, and recognised in theUniversal Declaration of Human Rights, in the International Covenant on Civil and Political Rights (in particular in articles 23 and 24), in the International Covenant on Economic, Social and Cultural Rights (in particulars in Article (10) and in the statutes and relevant Instruments of specialised agencies and international organisations concerned with the welfare of the Child.

Article 19 of the Convention mandates the States Parties to take appropriate legislative, administrative, social and educational measures to protect the child from all forms of physical or mental violence, injury or absue, neglect, or negligent treatment, maltreatment or exploitation. Article 29 inter alia records the agreement of the States Parties for administering a system of education which developes the child's personality, talents and mental and physical abilities to the fullest potential and the preparation of the child for responsible life in the free society in the system of peace, understanding and friendship among all people. The Convention under Article 37(a) declares that no child be subjected to torture or other cruel, inhuman or degrading treatment or punishment. Articles 39 and 40 recognise the right of the child to be protected from any form of neglect, exploitation, or abuse, or any other form of cruel, inhuman or degrading treatment or punishment and to be treated in a manner consistent with his sense of dignity. At this stage it will be convenient to set out Articles 19, 29, 37, 39 and 40 of the Convention.

"Article 19

1. State Parties shall take all appropriate legislative, administrative, social and educational measures to protect the child from all forms of physical or mental violence. Injury or abuse, neglect or negligent treatment, maltreatment or exploitation including sexual abuse, while in the care of parent(s), legal guardian(s) or any other person who has the care of the child.

2. Such protective measures should, as appropriate, include effective procedures for the establishment of social programmes to provide necessary support for the child and for those who have the care of the child, as well as for other forms of prevention and for indentification, reporting, referral, Investigation, treatment, and follow-up of instances of child maltreatment described heretofore, and, as appropriate, for judicial involvement."

"Article 29

1. States Parties agree that the education of the child shall be directed to:

   (a) The development of the child's personality, talents and mental and physical abilities to their fullest potential:

   (b) The development of respect for human rights and fundamental freedoms, and for the principles enshrined in the Charter of the United Nations;

   (c) The development of respect for the child's parents, his or her own cultural indentity, language and values, for the national values of the country in which the child is living, the country from which he or she may originate, and for civiliations different from his or her own;

   (d) The preparation of the child for responsible life in a free society in the spirit of understanding, peace, tolerance, equality of sexes and friendship among all peoples, ethnic, national and religious groups and persons of indigenous origin:

   (e) The development of respect for the natural environment.

2. No part of the present article or Article 28 shall be construed so as to interfere with the liberty of individuals and bodies to establish and direct educational institutions, subject always to the observance of the principles set forth in paragraph 1 of the present article and to the requirements that the education given in such institutions shall conform

to such minimum standards as may be laid down by the State."

"Article 37

States Parties shall ensure that:

(a) No child shall be subjected to torture or other cruel, inhuman or degrading treatment or punishment. Neither capital punishmeat nor life imprisonment without possibility of release shall be imposed for offences committed by persons below 18 years of age:

(b) No child shall be deprived of his or her liberty unlawfully or arbitrarily. The arrest, detention or imprisonment of a child shall be in conformity with the law and shall be used only as a measure of last resort and for the shortest appropriate period of time.

(c) Every child deprived of liberty shall be treated with humanity" and respect for the inherent dignity of the human person, and in a manner which takes into account the needs of persons of his her age, in particular, every child deprived of liberty shall be separated from adults unless it is considered in the child's best interest not to do so and shall have the right to maintain contact with his or her family through correspondence and visites, save in exceptional circumstances.

(d) Every child deprived of his or her liberty shall have the right to prompt acces to legal and other appropriate assistance, as well as the right to challenge the legality of the deprivation of his or her liberty before a Court or other competent, independent and Impartial authority, and to a prompt decision on any such action."

"Article 39

States Parties shall take all appropriate measures to promote physical and psychological recovery and social reintegration of a child victim of any form of neglect, exploitation, or abuse;

torture or any other form of cruel, inhuman or degrading treatment or punishment; or armed conflicts. Such recovery and re-integration shall take place in an environment which fosters the health, self-respect and dignity of the child.

Artlcle 40

1. States Parties recognise the right of every child alleged as, accused of, or recognised as having infringed the penal law to be treated in a manner consistent with the promotion of the child's sense of dignity and worth, which reinforces the child's respect for the human rights and fundamental freedoms of others and which takes into account the child's age and desirability of promoting the child's re-integration and the child's assuming a constructive role in society.
2. To this end, and having regard to the relevant provisions of international instruments States Parties shall, particular ensure that:
   - (a) No child shall be alleged as, be accused of, or recongised as having infringed the penal law by reason of acts or omissions that were not prohibited by national or international law at the time they were committed:
   - (b) Every child alleged as or accused of having infringed the penal law has at least the following guarantees:
     - (i) To be presumed innocent until proven guilty according to law;
     - (ii) To be informed promptly and directly of the charges against him or her, and if appropriate through his or her parents or legal guardian, and to have legal or other appropriate assistance in the preparation and presentation of his or her defence;
     - (iii) To have the matter determined without delay by a competent, independent and impartial authority or judicial body in a fair hearing according to law, in the presence of legal or other appropriate assistance and, unless it is considered not to be in

the best interest of the child, in particular, taking into account his or her age or situation, his or her parents or legal guardians;

(iv) Not to be compelled to give testimony or to confess guilt; to examine or have examined adverse witnesses and to obtain the participation and examination of witnesses on his or her behalf under conditions of equality;

(v) If cosidered to have infringed the penal law, to have this decision and by measures imposed in consequence thereof reviewed by a higher competent, independent and impartial authority or judicial body according to law;

(vi) To have the free assistance of an interpreter if the child cannot understand or speak the language used;

(vii) To have his or her privacy fully respected at all stages of the proceedings.

3. States Parties shall seek to promote the establishment of laws, procedures, authorities and institutions specifically applicable to children alleged as, accused of or recognised as having infringed the penal law, and in particular :

(a) The establishment of a minimum age below which children shall be presumed not have the capacity to infringe the penal law;

(b) Whenever appropriate and desirable, measures for dealing with such children without resorting to judicial proceedings, providing that human rights and legal safeguards are fully respected.

4. A variety of dispositions, such as care, guidance, and supervision orders; counselling; probation; foster care; education and vocational training programmes and other alternatives to institutional care shall be available to ensure that children are dealt with in a manner appropriate to their wellbeing and proportionate both to their circumstances and the offence."

Thus, in a nut shell the thoughts which pervade the various Articles of the convention are basically protection of the child from all forms of physical or mental violence, injury, neglect, exploitation, abuse, torture or any other form of cruel, inhuman or degrading treatment or punishment and adoption of means for the welfare of the child in every conceivable way and preservation of the dignity of the child.

The Government of India acceded to the Convention on December 11, 1992. National Policy on Education was modified in 1992 before acceding to it. It is significant to note that the National Policy is in tune with the Convention inasmuch as it is against imposition of corporal punishment.

(4) *R.D. Upadhayay v. State of A.P. & Others,*[156] The main issue involved in the case was relating to the direction to be issued in matter of children who were in jail with their mothers, who were in jail either as under trial prisoner or convicts. It was pointed out, "This court has, in several cases, accepted International coventions as enforceable when these conventions elucidate and effectuate the fundamental rights under the constitution. They have also been read as part of domestic law, as long as there is no inconsistency between the convention and domestic law. (see *Vishaka v. State of Raj.* (1997) 6 SCC 241). In *Sheela Barse v. Secretary, Children's Aid Society* [(1987) 3 SCC 50] which dealt with the working of an observation Home that was maintained and managed by the Children's Aid Society, Bombay, it was said:

Children are the citizens of the future era. on the proper bringing up of Children and giving them the proper training to turn out to be good citizens depends the future of the country. In recent years, this position has been well realised. In 1959, the Declaration of all the rights of the child was adopted by the General Assembly of the United Nations and in Article 24 of the International covenant on civil and Political Rights, 1966. The importance of the Child has been appropriately recognised. India as a party to these International charters having ratified the declaration, it is an obligation of the Government of India as also the state machinery to implement the same in the proper way. The Children's Act, 1948 has made elaborate provisions to cover this and if these provisions are properly translated into action and the authorities created under the Act become cognizant of their role, duties and obligation in the performance of the statutory mechanism created under the Act and they are properly motivated to meet the situations that arise in handling the problems, the situation would certainly be very much eased."

UDHR, ICCPR AND RIGHT TO PRIVACY

In *People's Union for Civil Liberties (PUCL) v. Union of India and another*[157] PUCL a voluntary orgainsation, filed a public interest petition under Article 32 of the constitution, highlighting the incidents of telephone tapping, challenged the constitutional validity of section 5(2) of the Indian Telegraph. Act, 1885, in the alternative it was argued that the said provisions be suitably read-down to inclub procedural safeguards to rule out arbitrariness and to prevent the indiscriminate telephone tapping.

Kuldip Singh J. (on behalf of himself and S. Saghir Ahmad J.) observed, "India is a signatory to the International covenant on civil and political Rights, 1966. Article 17 of the said covenart speaks as under:

(1) No one shall be subject to arbitratry or unlawful interference with his privacy, family, human or correspondence, nor to lawful attacks on his honour and reputation.

(2) Every one has the right to the protection of the law against such interference or attacks.

Article 12 of the Universal Declaration of Human Rights, 1948 is almost in similar terms.

International law today is not confinced to regulating the relations between the states. Scope continues to extend. Today matters of social concerns, such as health, education and economics apart from human rights fall within the ambit of International regulations. International law is more than ever aimed at individuals. It is almost accepted proposition of law that the rules of customary internationl law which are not contrary to the municipal law shall be deemed to be incorparated in the domestic law.

Article 51 of the constitution directs that the state shall endeavour to inter alia, foster respect for international law and treaty obligations in the dealings of organised peoples with one another. Relying upon the said Article Sikri, C.J. in *Kesvanand Bharati v. State of Kerala*[158], observed "it seems to me that in view of Article 51 of the directive principles, this court must interpret language of the constitution, if not intractable, which is after all a municipal law, in the light of the United Nations charter and the solemn declaration subscribed to by India." *In A.D.M. Jabalpur v. Shivkant Shukla*[159], Khanna J.[160] Said, "Equally well established is therule of construction that if there be a conflict between the municipal law on one side and the international law or the provisions of any treaty obligations on the other, the courts would give effect to municipal law. If, however, two constructions of the municipal law are possible. the courts should lean in favour of adopting such construction as would make the provisions of the municipal law to be in harmony with the international law on treaty obligations. Every statute, according to this rule is interpreted, so far as its language permits, so as not to be inconsistent with the comity of nations on the established rules of international law and the court will avoid a construction which would give rise to such inconsistency unless compelled to adopt it by plain and unambiguous language. Similary section 51 of the code of civil procedure was interpreted consistently with Article 11 of the International covenant.[161]

Article 17 of the International covenant (quoted above) does not go contrary to any part of our municipal law. Article 21 of the Constitution has, therefore, been interpreted in conformity with the international law.[162]

Right to Development

N.D. Jayal v. Union of India,[163] S. Rajendra Babu J. (on behalf of himself and D.M. Dharmadhikari and G.P. Mathur JJ.) pointed out that the right to development cannot be treated as a mere right to economic betterment cannot be limited to a misnomer to simple construction activities. The right to development encompasses much more than economic well being and includes within its definition the guarantee of fundamental human rights. The development is not related only to the growth of GNP. In the classical work—'Development as Freedom' the nobel prize winner Amartya Sen pointed out that 'the issue of development cannot be separated from the conceptual framework of human right'. This idea is also part of the UN Declaration on the Right to Development. The right to development includes the whole specturum of civil, cultural, economic, political and social process, for the improvement of peoples' well being and realization of their full potential. It is an integral part of human right. (Para 22).

The examination of this case shows that following UN Declaration on the right to development, the Supreme Court of India accepted the right to development as an integral part of human right.

In *Karantaka Industrial Areas Development Board v. Kenchappa and others,*[164] the respondents agriculturists, who were affected by the acquisition of lands of different village filed writ petition under Article 226 of the Constitution with a prayer that the appellant be directed to refrain from converting the lands of the respondents for any industrial or other purposes and to retain the lands for use by the respondents for grazing their cattle. It was contended by the respondents that deprivation of thier land is violative of their fundamental rights guaranteed under Articles 14 and 21 of the Constitution. It was held that, "The right to sustainable development has been declared by the UN General Assembly to be inalienable human right (Declaration on the Right to Development, 1986). Similarly, in 1992 Rio Conference it was declared that human beings are at the centre of concerns for sustainable development. Human beings are entitled to a healthy and productive life in harmony with nature. In order to achieve sustainable development, environmental protection shall constitute an integral part of development process and the same cannot be considered in isolation of it. The same principle was articulated in the '1997

Earth Summit'... In the Rio Conference of 1992 great concern had been shown about sustainable development. 'Sustainable development' means a development which can be sustained by nature with or without mitigation. In otherwords, it is to maintain delicate balance between industrialisation and ecology. While development of industry is essential for the growth of economy, at the same time, the environment and the ecosystem are required to be protected. The pollution created as a consequence of development must not exceed the carrying capacity of the ecosystem. The courts in various judgements have developed the basic and essential features of sustainable development. In order to protect sustainable development, it is necessary to implement and enfore some of its main components and ingredients such as precautionary principle, polluter pays and public trust doctrine. The Supreme Court gave direction to the effect that in future, before acquisition of lands for development, the consequence and adverse impact of development on environment must be properly comprehended and the lands be acquired for development that they do not gravely impair the ecology and environment.[165]

International Conventions and Right to Choose Representative

In *Kuldip Nayar v. Union of India,*[166] the petitioner, by a writ under Article 32 of the Constitution of India, challenged the amendments made in the Representation of the People Act, 1951, through Representation of the People (Amendment) Act 2003. By this amendment, the pre-condition of 'domicile' in the state concerned for getting elected to the 'Rajaya Sabha' was deleted and open ballot system was introduced.

The petitioner contends that the amendment violates the 'federalism' and 'Secrecy' principle which are basic features of the Constitution.

On behalf of the petitioners it was stated that international instruments put emphasis on 'secret ballot' since it lays the foundation for ensuring free and fair election which in turn ensures a democratic Government showing the true will of the people. The significance of this emphasis lies in the recognition that it is a democratic Government that is ultimately responsible for protecting the human rights of the people viz. civil, political, social and economic rights.

In the above context, reference was made to the Universal Declaration of Human Rights and the International convention of civil and political Rights (ICCPR).

Universal Declaration of Human Rights through Article 21 provides as under:

(1) Every one has the right to take part in the Government of his country, directly or through freely chosen representatives.

(2) Every one has the right of equal access to public service in his country.

(3) The will of the people shall be the basis of the authority of Government; this will shall be expressed in periodic and genuine elections which shall be by universal and equal suffrage and shall be held by secret vote or by equivalent free voting procedures."

The International convention on civil and political rights (ICCPR) in its Article 25 provides as under : Every citizen shall have the right and the opportunity, without any of the distinctions mentioned in Article 2 and without unreasonable restrictions:

(a) to take part in the conduct of public affairs, directly or through freely chosen representatives;

(b) to vote and to be elected at genuine periodic elections which shall be by universal and equal suffrage and shall be held by secret ballot guaranteeing the free expression of the will of the electors;

(c) to have access, on general terms of equality to public service in his country."

Both the documents, thus, provide for formation of a Government through secret ballot. Prime importance is given in these two human rights instruments on 'will of the electors' giving basis to the authority of the Government. It may, however, be noticed that in Article 21 of the Universal

Declaration of Human Rights the requirement is satisfied not necessarily by secret ballot but even "by equivalent free voting procedures." The learned counsel would also rely upon the instrument called Inter-American convention, in which the principles of the secret ballot system, as free expression of the will of voter have been accepted. The counsel pointed out that the above mentioned expressions were added in Article 25(b) of ICCPR in the wake of one view of participatory countries in the Third committee, 16th session (1961) to the effect: "......Others held that 'genuine periodic elections' universal and equal sufferage and 'secret ballot' were the elements of genuine elections, which in turn guaranteed the free expression of the will of the electors. These elements should therefore remain grouped together."

The another argument adduced was that the International instructions can be used for interpreting the municipal laws and in support of this certain cases were referred.[167] The emphasis in the above mentioned judgments is that the evolving jurisprudence of human rights is required to be used in interpreting the statutes. This argument is in addition to the general argument that in the absence of any law, this court may lay down guidelines in consonance with the principles laid down in the international instruments so as to effectuate the fundamental rights guaranteed under the constitution. There can be no quarrel with the proposition that the International covenants and Declarations as adopted by the United Nations have to be respected by all signatory states and the meaning given to them has to be such as would help in effective implementation of the rights declared there in. The applicability of the Universal Declaration of Human Rights and the principles thereof may have to be read, if need be, into the domestic jurisprudence.[168]

It was said as early as in *Kesvanand Bharati v. State of Kerala*[169] that, "(I)n view of Article 51 of the directive principles, this court must interpret language of the constitution, if not intractable, which is after all a municipal law, in the light of the United Nations Charter and solemn declaration subscribed to by India."

M. Nagraj v. Union of India,[170] it was observed that 'it is a fallacy to regard fundamental rights as a gift from the state to its citizens. Individuals possess basic human rights independently of any constitution by reason of the basic fact that they are members of the human race. These fundamental rights are important as they possess intrinsic value. Part III of the constitution does not confer fundamental rights. It confirms their existence and gives them protection. Its purpose is to withdraw certain subjects from the area of political controversy to place them beyond the reach of majorities and officials and to establish them as legal principles to be applied by the courts. Every right has a content. Every foundational value is put in Part III as a fundamental rights as it has intrinsic value. The converse does not apply. A right becomes a fundamental right because it has foundational value. Apart from the principles, one has also to see the structure of the article in which the fundamental value is incorporated. A fundamental right is a limitation on the power of the state."[171]

It is submitted that although the process of harmonizing municipal law with internatinal law is a legilsative task and the Parliament by exercising this power has enacted several Acts like, 'The Extradition Act, 1962, the Arbitration and Conclication Act, 1996, The Chemical weapons Convention Act, 2000 and the Information Technology Act, 2000 etc. on the lines of International Conventions and instruments. But a detailed examination of above judical decisions shows that the Indian Judicary has applied the various principles contained in Universal Delcaration of Human Rights, International Covenant on Political and Civil Rights, International Covenant on Economic and Cultural rights and other International instruments in devleoping the law relating to children, women, workers, compensation cases of custodial violence and environmental jurisprudence. The analysis of discussed case law also, reflects the judicial yeomen service towards harmonising municipal law with International law.

NOTES

1. Article 14 says, 'The State shall not deny to any person equality before the law or the equal protection of laws within the territory of India.
2. See Article 15(3), 15(4) and 15(5) of the Constitution of India.
3. See Clause (1) and (2) of Article 16 of the Constitution.
4. Article 16(4) of the Indian Cosntitution.
5. Article 17 lays down, 'Untouchability' is a bolished and its practice in any form is forbiddeen. The enforcement of any disability arising out of 'untouchability' shall be an offence punishable in accordance with law.
6. Article 19(1)(a) to (g) of the Cosntitution of India.
7. Article 19(1)(f) and Article 31 were omitted by the Constitution (Forty-fourth Amendment) Act, 1978. The same amendment inserted Article 300A in the Constitution which lays down, "No person shall be deprived of his property save by authority of law".
8. Granville Austin, The Indian Constitution: Corner Stone of a Nation, (1966) p. 86.
9. Article 28 of the Indian Constitution.
10. Vijayshri Sripat, 'Towards fifty years of Constitutionalism and Fundamental Rights in India: Looking back to see ahead'. 14 Am. U. Int'l L. Rev. 413 at 415.
11. Article 30(2) of the Constitution of India.
12. Granville Austin, The Indian Constitutio: Corner Stone of a Nation, (1966) p. 108
13. Vijayshri Sripat, 'Human Rights in India—Fifty years after Independence' (1997) 26 Denv. J. Int'l Law Policy 93.
14. ICCPR Article 14(3)(c).
15. ICCPR Article 14(3)(d).
16. Article 11 of the Covenant.
17. Article 12 of the Covenant.
18. Article 7 of the Covenant.
19. Article 17 of the Covenant.
20. Article 9(5) of the Covenant.
21. 26 Den. J. Int. law & Policy 93, at 96.

22. A.I.R. 1980 SC 470 at 473-74.
23. Patanjali Sastri J. In *Romesh Thapper v. State of Madras,* AIR 1950 SC 124 at p. 126.
24. *State of Madras v. V.G. Row,* AIR 1952 SC 196, at p. 199
25. *Daryao v. State of U.P.,* AIR 1961 SC 1457.
26. Indu Sing and Ajay Saxena, "Human Rights in India and Pakistan", Ist ed. (2004) at p. 42.
27. *Kumari Shrilekha Vidyarthi v. State of U.P.,* AIR 1991 SC 537.
28. *Food Corporation of India v. Kamdhenu Cattle Breed Industries,* (1993) 1 SCC 71.
29. *SCAOR v. Union of India,* AIR 1994 SC 268.
30. *Lily Thomas v. President of Inida,* AIR 1982 SC 149.
31. *Express Newspaper (P) Ltd. v. Union of India,* AIR 1958 SC 578; *Indian Express Newspapers Pvt. Ltd. v. Union of India,* AIR 1986 SC 515.
32. *A.K. Gopalan v. State of Madras,* AIR 1950 SC 27.
33. AIR 1978 SWC 597.
34. AIR 1974 SC 555.
35. AIR 1952 SC 75.
36. 14 Am. U. Int.'l L. Rev. 413 (1998) at p. 417.
37. AIR 1976 SC 1836.
38. AIR 1978 SC 1675.
39. AIR 1963 SC 1295.
40. AIR 1963 SC 1295, at p. 1306.
41. AIR 1975 SC 1378.
42. (1991) 1 SCC 57.
43. (1994) 6 SCC 632.
44. *P.U.C.L. v. Union of India,* AIR 1997 SC 568.
45. AIR 1983 SC 1473.
46. AIR 1986 SC 180.
47. *H.M. Hoskot v. State of Maharastra,* (1978) 3 SCC 544, *Hussainaira Khatoon v. State of Bihar,* (1980 1 SCC 98.
48. *Khatri v. State of Bihar,* AIR 1981 SC 928.

49. *Suk Das v. Union Territory of Arunachal Pradesh,* AIR 1986 SC 991.
50. AIR 1979 SC 1360.
51. *Kadara Pahadiya v. State of Bihar,* AIR 1982 SC 1167, *Mohd. Salim Khan v. State of U.P.,* AIR 1982 SC 1096; *Mathew v. State of Bihar,* (1985) 2 SCC 102.
52. 1985, Crl.J. (Pat) 584.
53. (1994) 3 SCC 569.
54. AIR 1981 SC 753.
55. (1973) 1 SCC 20.
56. *Bachan Singh v. State of Punjab,* AIR 1980 SC 898.
57. Article 8(3)(a) of the Covenant.
58. AIR 1981 SC 802.
59. *R.P. Ltd., v. Proprietors, Idian Express News Papers, Bombay (P) Ltd.,* AIR 1989 SC 190.
60. *Rudal Shah v. State of Bihar,* (1983) 1 SCC 141; *Bhim Singh v. State of J&K,* (1985) 4 SCC 677; *M.C. Mehta v. Union of India* (1987) 1 SCC 395; *Chairman Rly. Board v. Chandrima Das (MRS.) and others,* (2000) 2 SCC 465.
61. Principle I of the Stockholm declaration, 1972.
62. Article 51(a)(g) of the Constitution of India.
63. AIR 1985 SC 652.
64. *Indian Council for Enviro-legal action v. Union of India,* (1996) 5 SCC 281, at para 31.
65. (2000) 2 SCC 599, at p. 605.
66. (2004) 2 SCC 392, para 27.
67. *Intellectual Forum Tirupathi v. State of A.P.,* AIR 2006 SC 1350.
68. AIR 2006 SC 1350, at p. 1363.
69. *Subhash Kumar v. State of Bihar,* AIR 1991 SC 420; *Virendra Gaur v. State of Haryana,* (1995) 2 SCC 574; *Vellore Citizsens Welfare Forum v. Union of India,* (1996) 5 SCC 647; *S. Jagannath v. Union of India,* AIR 1997 SC 811; *Naramada Bachao Andolan v. Union of India,* (2000) 10 SCC 664.
70. Kelsen, 'The Principles of International Law', 1952, pp. 446-47.
71. Triepel, Volkerrecht Und Landerecht, 1899.

72. Anzilotti, Corso di Diritto Internazionale, 1928, Vol. 1.
73. Gurdip Singh, "International Law", Ist Ed. 2003 at p. 55.
74. *Annakumaru Pillai v. Muthupayal and Others,* 12 L.R., 1907, Madras, p. 551.
75. MLJ, 1953(2), p. 587.
76. AIR 1976 SC 1207.
77. *A.D.M. Jabalpur v. S.K.Shukla,* AIR 1976 SC 1207 at p. 1291.
78. Gurdip Singh, 'International and National Measures of Implementation of Human Right', Indian Journal of International Law, 18, 1978, p. 187.
79. *Sunil Kumar Bose v. Chief Secretary,* AIR 1950 Calcutta, 274, *Brahmeshwar Prasad v. State of Bihar,* AIR 1950 Patna, 25
80. V.N. Shukla, The Constitution of India, p. 610
81. Statement of the Government of India on national laws and practices in the matter of the conclusion of treaties made in response to a circular letter and by the Secretary General of the United Nations to Government in January 1951, UN Doc. ST/LEG/SER. B/3 December 1952, pp. 63-64.
82. *Union of India v. Manmulla Jain,* A.I.R. 1954 Calcutta 615.
83. AIR 1954 Cal. 615 at p. 616
84. AIR 1954 Cal 615, at p. 616-617
85. *Nirmal Bose v. Union of India,* AIR 1959Calcutta, 506.
86. *Ramjawaya Kapur v. State of Punjab,* AIR 1955 SC 549.
87. *Jayantilal v. Rana,* AIR 1964 SC 648.
88. AIR 1960 SC 845.
89. AIR 1966 SC 644
90. *Maganbhai Ishwarbhai Patel v. Union of India,* AIR 1969 SC 783.
91. AIR 1969 SC 783, at p. 784.
92. *Birma v. The State,* AIR 1951 Rajasthan 127.
93. C.G. Raghavan, 'Treaty Making Power under the Constitution of India', in S.K. Agrawala, Essays on the Law of Treaties, p. 217 at p. 232.
94. *Nanka v. Govt. of Rajasthan,* AIR 1951 Rajasthan 153.
95. Gurdip Singh, "International Law", Ist ed. p. 62

96. Dr (Mrs) K. Thakore, a paper presented at the Conference on National Treaty Law and Procedure, Bellagio, 6-10 August 1977.
97. See G.V.G. Krishnamurty, Functioning of International Law and Internal Law of States (Postures. Practices and Perspectives). AIR 1985 p. 17 at p. 23(1985).
98. Role of Indian Judiciary in harmonising Municipal law with International Law, AIR 2003 J.S. 211.
99. AIR 1980 SC 470.
100. Article 11 of the Covenant says, "No one shall be imprisoned merely on the ground of inability to fulfil a contractual obligation."
101. AIR 1984 SC 667, The judgement was delivered by O. Chinnappa Readdy J. on behalf of himself and E.S. Venkataramiah and R.B. Mishra JJ.
102. *Ibid*, p. 670.
103. (1905) 2 KB 391
104. AIR 1984 SC 667, at p. 671 (Para 5).
105. *Ibid* para 6.
106. AIR 1987 SC 2342.
107. F. N. 6 at page 2346.
108. AIR 1990 SC 605 at pp. 614, 615.
109. AIR 1995 SC 922.
110. *Ibid.* at paras 22, 23, 26.
111. AIR 1996 SC 2715
112. On behalf of three Judges bench Comprising Kuldip Singh, Faizanuddin and K. Venkataswami JJ.
113. (1996) 2 JT (SC) 196.
114. AIR 1996 SC 2715, para 10-12
115. AIR 1996 SC 1864.
116. Bench consisted of Kuldip Singh, M.M. Punchhi and K. Ramaswamy. The majority view wastaken by Kuldip Singh and M.M. Punchhi JJ, and the minority view by K. Ramaswamy J.
117. AIR 1996 SC 1864 at pp. 1869-1870.
118. AIR 1997 SC 3011.

119. On behalt of himself and on behalf of Mrs. Sujata v. Manohar and B.N. Kirpal J.

120. AIR 1997 SC 3011 at para 7.

121. AIR 1997 SC 3011, at para 11.

122. AIR 1997 SC 3011, at para 3014

123. at pp. 3014-15 Paras 12, 13.

124. Para 14

125. (1993) 2 SCC 746

126. AIR 1997 SC 3001, at p. 3015 (Para 15).

127. Sec. 2(d), Protection of Human Rights Act, 1993.

128. Martha C. Nussbaum, "International Human Rights Law in Practice : India Implementing Sex Equality through Law" (2001) 2 Chi. J. Int'l L. 35.

129. (2000) 2 SCC 465.

130. (1996) 3 All. E. R. 871.

131. (1991) 1 All. E.R. 720 (HL).

132. (1990) 1 SCC 568 : 1990 SCC (Cri) 227: AIR 1990 SC 605.

133. (2000) 2 SCC 465, at pp. 479-483.

134. AIR 1997 SC 610.

135. Followed *Rudal Shah v. State of Bihar* (1983) 4 SCC 141 (AIR 1983 SC 1086), *S.M. Hongrey v. Union of India, Rajendra Singh v. Usha Rani,* AIR 1984 SC 956; *Bhim Singh v. State of J&K,* 1984 (Supp) SCC 504, *Saheli v. Commission of Police, Delhi,* AIR 1990 SC 513.

136. AIR 1997 SC 610 at page 624-625 (Para 42A).

137. AIR 1997 SC 1203.

138. Minister for Immigration and Ethnic affairs V. Teoh (1995) 69 Australian Law Journal 423.

139. *Chow Hung Ching v. The King,* (1948) 77 CLR 449 at 478; *Brodley v. The Commonwealth,* (1973) 128 CLR 557 at 582; *Simsek v. Macphee,* (1982) 148 CLR 636 at 641-42; *Koowarta v. Bjelke-Peterson* (1982) 153 CLR 168 at 211-212, 224-225; *Kioa v. West* (1985) 159 CLR 550 at 570; *Dietrich v. The Queen* (1992) 177 CLR 292 at 305; *J.H. Rayner Ltd. v. Dept. of Trade* (1990) 2 AC 418 at 500.

140. *Simesk v. Macphee* (1982) 148 CLR at 641-642.

141. *Chukheng Lim v. Minister for Immigration* (1992) 176 CLR 1 at 381.

142. *Polites v. The Commonwealth* (1945) 70 CLR 60 at 68-69, 77, 80-81.

143. *Mabo v. Queensland (No.2),* (1991) 175 CLR 1 at 42, per Brennan J. (with whom Mason CJ and Mc Hugh J., agreed); *Dietricho v. The Queen* (1992) 177 CLR at 321, per Brennan J. at 360, per Toohey J. *Jago v. District Court of New South Wales* (1988) 12 NSW&R 558 at 569, per kirby p., *Derbyshire County Council v. Times Newspapers Ltd.* (1992) QB 770.

144. *Lamb v. Cotogno* (1987) 164 CLRI at 11-12.

145. (1994) 3 SCC 1.

146. AIR 1997 SC 1203 at 1206-1208. See *Elisa Chan v. Korean Airlines Limited* (1989) 104 LED 2 d 113 and *Eastern Air Lines v. Floyd* 113 LE 2d 569 (US Supreme Court decisions); R.V. Secretary of state for employment, Ex-Parte equal opportunities commission, 1994 ICR 317 : 1994 All ER 910 (Decisions of House of Lords).

147. AIR 1997 SC 2218 (Bench coprised of K. Ramaswamy and S. Saghir Ahmad JJ.)

148. AIR 1997 SC 2218, at paras 5-7 (at pp. 2221-2222).

149. AIR 1997 SC 699

150. In Cracker Factories of Sivakasi, 2941 Children were employed as on 31.13.1985.

151. Article 32 of instrument of accession is as under :

(1) State parties recognise the right of the child to be protected from economic exploitation and from performing any work that is likely to be hazardous or to interfere with the child's education, or to be harmful to the child's health or physical, mental, spiritual, moral or social development.

(2) State parties shall take legislative, administrative, social and educational measures to ensure the implementation of the present article. To this end and having regard to the relevant provisions of other international instruments. State parties shall in particular: (a) provide for a minimum age or minimum ages for admission to employment; (b) provide for appropriate regulation of the hours and conditions of employment; (c) provide for appropriate penalties or other sanctions to ensure the effective enforcement of the present article.

152. AIR 1997 SC 699 (paras 15-17 as per Hansaria J.)

153. AIR 2001, Delhi, 212.

154. "Rule 37. Forms of disciplinary measures—

(1) The following shall be the disciplinary measures which may be adopted by a school in dealing with

(a) all students-

(i) detention during the break, for neglect of class work, but no detention shall be made after the school hours.

(ii) corporal puishment.

(b) students who have attained the age of fourteen years—

(i) fine,

(ii) expulsion,

(iii) rustication;

(2) For the avoidance of doubts, it is hereby declared that the disciplinary measures specified in Clause (b) of sub-rule (1) shall not be imposed on any student who has not attained the age of fourteen years.

(3) Fine may be imposed on a student who has attained the age of fourteen years in the following cases, namely:

(i) late attendance;

(ii) absence from class without proper application from the parent or guardian;

(iii) truancy;

(iv) wilful damage to school property;

(v) delay in payment of school fees and dues:

(4) (a) Corporal punishment may be given by the head of the school in cases of persisting impertinence or rude behaviour towards the teachers, physical violence, intemperance and serious form of misbehaviour with other students.

(b) Corporal punishment shall not be inflicted on the students who are in ill health.

(c) Where corporal punishment is imposed, it shall not be severe or excessive and shall be so administered as not to cause bodily injury.

(d) Where cane is used for inflicting any corporal punishment, such punishment shall take the form of storkes not exceeding ten on the plam of the hand.

(e) Every punishment inflicted on a student shall, be recorded in the Conduct Register of such student.

(5) Explusion shall debar a student from being re-admitted to the school from where he is expelled but shall not preclude his admission with the previous sanction of the Director to any other school.

(6) Where a student is rusticated, he shall not be admitted to any school till the expiry of the period of rustication.

(7) No student shall be expelled or rusticated from a school except after giving the parent or guardian of the students a reasonable opportunity of showing cause against the proposed action.

Notes:

(i) Explusion or rustication shall be resorted to only in cases of grave offences where the retention of the student in the school is likely to endanger its moral tone of discipline.

(ii) Except in the case of any explusion or rustication from an unaided minority school, the punishment of explusion and rustication shall not be imposed without the prior approval of the Director.

It also provides that corporal punishment to a student may be adminstered by the Head of School in the event of continous impertinence or rude behaviour by the student towards the teachers and in case he indulges in physical violence, intemperance and serious form of misbehaviour with other students. Where cane is used for inflicting corporal punishment, it imposes a limit of ten strokes on the hand of the student.

155. Bench Comprised of ANIL Dev Singh & Dr. Mukundakam Sharma, JJ.

156. AIR 2006 SC 1946

157. AIR 1997 SC 568.

158. 1973 Supp SCR 1.

159. AIR 1976 SC 1207.

160. Minority opinion, at para 169.

161. AIR 1980 SC 470.

162. AIR 1977 SC 568, at p. 575.

163. AIR 2004 SC 867.

164. f.n. 1, paras 7 to 11.

165. (2006) 6 SCC 371.

166. Supre note , Paras 90, 91, 92 and 99.

167. (2006) 7 SCC 1

168. (2006) 7 SCC 1, at pp. 130-131 (observation made by Y.K. Sabharwal C.J.)

169. *Kesvanand Bharati v. State of Kerala,* AIR 1973 S.C. 1461, *Jolly George Varghese v. Bank of Cochin* (1980) 2 SCC 360, *PUCL v. Union of India* (1997) 1 SCC 301, *Nilabati Behera v. State of Orissa* (1993) 2 SCC 746; *Kapila Hingorani v. State of Bihar* (2003) 6 SCC 1 and *State of W.B. v. Kesoram Industries Ltd.* AIR 2005 SC 1646.

170. (2006) 8 SCC 212.

171. (1973) 4 SCC 225 at p. 333.

7

CONCLUSION AND SUGGESTIONS

The Preamble to the charter of the United Nations in 1945 reaffirmed the faith in the fundamental rights. Article 1 of the charter listed among the purposes of the United Nations, promoting and encouraging respect for human rights and fundamental freedoms. The Universal declaration of Human Rights (UDHR) was well in consonance with the purposes contained in the charter. The preamble to Universal Declaration of Human Rights proclaims the UDHR as a common standard of achievement for all people and all nations, to the end that every individual and every organ of society, keeping this declaration constantly in mind shall strive by teaching and educating to promote respect for these rights and freedoms and by progressive measures, national and international, to secure their universal and effective recognition and observance, both among the people of member states themselves and among the people of territories under their jurisdiction.

The study in preceding chapters presents a clear picture relating to provisions contained in various International Covenants, International instruments, Constitution of India and Domestic law for the protection and implementation of International Human Rights. The following are the main conclusions of this study:

(1) That though the concept of human rights is as old as political philosophy and jurisprudence, the term human rights had its origin in international law, apperatin to the development of the status and diginity of an individual in international legal regime. Thus the concept of human rights has two aspects-national or domestic and international. The domestic aspect of human rights consists protection of certain constitutionally recognized basic and fundamental rights from arbitrainess and tyranny of executive as well as legislative actions. This is known as negative conception of human rights. In a democratic state, it is not enough that the human rights are protected and safeguarded against the violation or encorachment by the state. But a postive obligation is imposed upon the state to take affirmative action to improve the quality of human life in all its dimensions to the level of excellence, not to the privileged few but to all sections of the society. The International aspect of human rights consists largely of identifying certain human rights as a minimum international standard and securing for them widest recognition and protection by largest number of countries of the world and evolving of viable enforcement mechanism at international level. J.G. Starke, an international law jurist, is of the view that international law ensures protection of human rights at three levels : first, a declaration definining the various human rights which ought to be respected; Second, a series of binding covenants on the part of States to respect such rights, and third, measures and machinery for implementation of such rights. The UN charter lay down principles for the protection of human rights. One of the basic purposes as stated in Article 1(3), is promoting and encouraging respect for 'human rights'. Similarly, by Article 55, the members of the UN reaffirm the commitment for promoting universal respect for and observance of human and fundamental

freedoms for all. Under Article 56 : all members of the UN pledge themselves to take joint and separate action in co-operation with the organization for the achievement of the aims set out in Article 55.[1]

(2) That the human rights becomes operative with the birth of a human being so they are also known as birth rights, inherent in all the individuals irrespective of the considerations like, caste, creed, religion, sex, nationality and the place of birth.

The Human rights are not the gift or bounty of any political sovereign through legislation or any edict, but are right inherent in human existance. The purpose of any law dealing with these rights is merely to recognise them, to regulate their exercise and to provide for their enforcement and the anciliary matters.[2]

The expession 'human rights' covers every aspect of human dignity. To achieve this end the definition contained in domestic legislation should be consistent with the international covenants. In India, the Protection of Human Rights Act, 1993 (POHA) defines 'human rights' as rights relating to life, liberty, equality and dignity of the individual guaranteed by the Constitution or embodied in the International covenants and enforceable by Court of India. International Covenants here means the International Covenant on Civil and Political Rights and the International Covenant on Economic, Social and Cultural Rights adopted by the General assembly of the United Nations. Thus it is very clear that the statutory definition of human rights is wide enough to cover the fundamental rights enshrined in the Indian Constitution as well as civil, political, economic, social and cultural rights in the two covenants.

(3) The 'Human Rights' in practice has been redefined to cover every aspect of dignified human existence which makes every human being an equal member of the human family. Human dignity is the quintessence of

human rights. It is wide comprehension of the expression and appreciation of the amplitude of dignity of the individual which must define the true scope of human rights. The modern concepts are "All human rights for all and the 'world is one family', this concept is founded on the expanded meaning of human rights assuring full human dignity to every member of the human race in the global village. Globalization of human rights by making it universally accepted, eradicating the global inequities is the clarion call of human rights movement. It cannot be doubted that any humiliation of a human being is an affront to his human dignity, and, thus, a violation of human rights.

In this regard Mahatama Gandhi said, "It has always been a mystery to me how men can feel themsleves honoured by the humiliation of their fellow beings". Emphasis on the human dignity is laid not only in the charter of United Nations, the Universal Declaration of Human Rights[3] and several other international covenants[4] but also in the Constitution of India which mentions 'dignity of the individual' as a core value in its preamble. Empowerement of the people through human development is the aim of human rights. The Human Development Index is the new measure of development and it is said, "A nation's ability to convert knowledge into wealth and social good through the process of innovation is going to determine its future." The Human Developments reports in the last decade have analyzed and focused on the new vistas of human rights while integrating human rights with human development as the true measure of progress. The four essentials of human development paradigm are : Productivity-economic growth with people's participation in income generation; Equity-people's access to equal opportunities; sustainability-access to opportunities must be not only for present generations but also for future generations to all forms of capital i.e. physical, human, environmental; and Empowerment-opportunity with developed capabilities as all people to participate in policy and decision making processes that shape and affect their lives.[5]

(4) As far as globalization and its effect on human rights is concerned it has not only affected the nature and contents of human rights but also the safeguards and the implementation mechanism laid down in the international law and the municipal law. The copenhagen Declaration states, "Globalisation, which is a consequence of increased human mobility ehanced communciations, greatly increased trade and capital flows and technological developments, open new opportunities for sustained economic growth and development of the world economy, particularly in developing countries..... At the same time, the rapid processes of change and adjustment have been accompanied by intensified poverty, unemployment and social disintegration. Threats to human well - being, such as environmental risks, have also been globalised. Furthermore, the global transformations of the world economy are profoundly changing the parameters of social development in all countries. The challenge is how to manage these processes and threats so as to enhance their benefits and mitigate their negative effects upon people."[6] To achieve the goal of social development, the programme of Action lays down that it is essential to take measures to ensure that every human being and people are entitled to participate, contribute to and to enjoy economic, social, cultural and political development; encouraging all human persons to take responsibility for development, individually and collectively; and recognizing that state have the primary responsibility for the cretation of national and international conditions favourable for the realization of the rights to development......"[7]

In the opinion of Prof. S.K. Verma, the states are under a duty to meet the basic needs for their surging population by creating favourable conditions which will be an uphill task in the market-economy under globalisation and it lays down the agenda for recasting and re-interpreting various constitutioal and statutory provisions, which should aim at overcoming the ill effects of globalisation and enhancing and reaping its benefits. Prof. Verma further says that the main element of the role making of the state in the market economy model is the constitutional regulation of the economy, the problem area of economic constitutionality and its attended consequences on the human resource development by ensuring the realization of human rights. A very significant component of economic constitutionality is the constitutional protection of the basic economic and social rights of citizens.[8]

The basic rights like the right to work, the right of free choice of profession, the right to social security, the right to strike and leisure should be founded on the goals of social justice. In India the Government has launched an employment guarantee scheme to provide employment minimum for hundred days in a year, and social security scheme for the organized as well as unorganized sector. Now the state is obliged to provide free and compulsory education to all children of the age of six to fourteen years.[9] This provision has been inserted in part III of the Constitution which guarantees the protection of basic human rights. The Government has released a charter on corporate responsibility for environmental protection and it has made environmental clearance mandatory for new big urban projects so as to meet out the ill effects of globalization.

(5) That the charter of United Nations clearly recognizes that the maintenance of 'international peace and security' and the protection of human rights are dependent on each other, and declares the promotion

of human rights as one of the Chief object of the United Nations. It casts upon both the memebr states and the organization a legal duty to promote and protect human rights. This is reflected in various provisions of the charter. In the preamble, the people of the United Nations express determination to raffirm faith in fundamental human rights, in the equal rights of men and women and of nations large and small. The expression 'promoting and encouraging respect for human rights' and 'assisting in the realization of human rights and fundamental freedoms' appear with certain variations in Article 1, on the purposes and principles of the United Nations, Article 13, on the General Assembly; Article 62, on the Economic and Social Council, and Article 76 on the International Trusteeship System. Article 55 and 56 read together say, "All members pledge themselves to take joint and separate action in cooperation with the organization for the achievement', of a number of purposes which the United Nations shall promote, among them 'universal respect for, and observance of human rights and fundamental freedoms for all without distinction as to race, sex, language or religion.

Thus the provisions of the United Nations Charter concerning human rights provide a foundation for and an impetus to further improvement in the protection of human rights.[10] They indicate the wide possibilities of the international recognition of human rights.[11] Article 55 and 56 bind member states to observe and respect human rights. This view is supported by the interpretation given to these provisions by the International Court of Justice.[12] The court gave its opinion in the context of the observation of human rights in a territory having an international status but as observed by Egon Schwelb, the pledge contained in Article 55 and 56 is of wider significance and is not confined to the observance of human rights in a territory having international importance.[13]

There is a difference of opinion as to whether the provisions of the UN Charter relating to human rights create duty on the members. The one view is that the clauses of the charter only contain a pious injunction to co-operate and do not impose any duty or obligation.[14] The others contend that the charter 'imposes upon the members of moral and, however imperfect, probably a legal duty'.[15] The latter view seems to be appropriate and justified beacuse of 'members' pledge to take joint and separate action in co-operation.

(6) That the Universal declaration of human rights is the first major elucidation of the provisions contained in the UN charter relating to human rights, it was drafted after two years of study of the Commission on Human Rights which was established under Article 68 of the charter by the Economic and Social council, and approved by the General Assembly on December 10, 1948. The rights stipulated in it are most comprehensive. This declaration was not designed or proposed as an enforceable treaty obligation but rather as a broad classification and recommendation of policy. The rights proclaimed in the Universal Declaration of Human Rights are divided into Civil and Political rights and economic, social and cultural rights.

The Declaration has been hailed 'as a historic event of the profound significance and as one of the greatest achievements of the United Nations'.[16] The declaration is the mine from which other conventions as well as national Constitutions protecting these rights have been and are being quarried.[17] Theprovisions of the declaration has influenced various national Constitutions enacted after the adoption of the declaration. For example, the Constitution of Algeria, Burundi, Cameroon, Chad, Democratic Republic of Congo, Dhaomey, Guniea, Gabon, Mali, Niger, Togo and upper volta, the people of these Countries solemnly affirmed their devotion to the principles and ideals of the Universal Declaration.[18] The Indian Constitution also bears the impact of the UDHR which is reflected by the observations made by Sikri, C.J., "I am unable to hold that these provisions show that some rights are not natural or inalienable rights. As a matter of fact, India was a party to the Universal Declaration of Human Rights.... and the declaration describes some fundamental rights as inalienable.[19]

There is no unanimity regarding the legal importance of the declaration. Some jurists are of the view that the declaration is not a legally binding instrument. On contrary, the other jurists have taken the view that the declaration might not have been binding effect when it was adopted in the year 1948 but in due course of time it has assumed legal significance containing elements of legal binding. According to starke the declaration could not and did not purport to be more than manifesto, a statement of ideals, a path finding instrument, yet it has had a remarkable influence on further developments, at both the international and domestic levels, as is reflected in the number of instances of conventions and other instruments referring to, or invoking, its provisions.[20] In the view of oppenheim, 'in the years since its adoption, the widespread acceptance of the authority of declaration has led some to the opinion that while the declaration as an instrument is not a treaty, its provisions may have come to the embodiment of new rules of customary law in the matter.[21] Palmer and Perkins subscribe to the view that the declaration is merely a statement of principles, not a legally binding instrument; but it has become one of the best known international documents and its has often been referred to in resolutions of the UN, the specialized agencies, regional arrangements, other international organizations, in national Constitutions, legislation and the decisions of the Courts. It is a becaon light for all mankind even though it has been honoured more often in the breach than in the observance.[22] In the opinion of J.L. Brierly the declaration is not a legally binding instrument, however it has gained considerable authority as a general guide to the content of fundamental rights and freedoms as understood by members of the United Nations and it is important as providing a connecting link between different concepts of human rights in different parts of the world. Ian Brownline points out that declaration is not a legally binding instrument as such and some of its provisions depart from existing and generally accepted rules. Nevertheless some of its provisions either constitute general principles of law or represent elementary considerations of humanity. More important is the status as an authoritative guide produced by the General Assembly to the interpretation of the charter. In this capacity, the declaration has considerably indirect legal effect and is regarded by the Assembly and by some jurists as a part of the law of the United Nations.[23]

(7) That the idea of international implementation of human rights does not violate Article 2, paragraph 7 of the United Nations Charter.[24] This conclusion is supported by the view taken by Lauterpacht, Jessup, Myres McDougal, Quincy Wright and Paul Guggenheim. In this regard Richard B. Bilder pointed out, "Now it is universally agreed that human rights are proper subjects of international concern. It has been affirmantively assumed by the United Nations Charter, international conventions, declarations and more than three decades of international practice.[25]

The International Covenant on Civil and Political Rights establishes, the Human Rights Committee as a principal international organ of implementation. The committee consists of eighteen persons of high moral character and professional competency in the field of human rights. According to the Draft of the

Commission on Human Rights, the members of the Committee should be elected by the International court of Justice but the Covenant lays down that members of the committee shall be elected by state parties. The role of the committee has been discussed in detail in Chapter Second of the research work. Regarding the finding of the committee John P. Hamphrey rightly observed, "Legally, the views formulated by the Human Rights Committee are not binding on the State party concerned which remains free to criticize them. Nonetheless any state party will find it hard to reject such findings in so for as they are based on orderly proceedings during which the defendant party had ample opportunity to present its submissions. The views of the Human Rights Committee gain their authority from their inner qualities of impartiality, objectiveness and soberness. If such requirements are met, the views of the Human Rights Committee can have a far reaching impact, at least vis-a-vis such governments which have not outrightly broken with the international community and ceased to care any more for concern expressed by international bodies. If such a situation arose, however, even a legally binding decision would not be likely to be respected.[26]

As discussed in Chatper II the Human Rights Committee implement the human rights embodied in the civil covenant by reporting system, inter-state communication system and conciliation procedure. It is submitted that although under the civil covenant there is an obligation on the state parties to submit reports but there is no express obligation to comply with the reports and comments of the committee. Similarly the Inter-communication system has some defects. First, the function of the committee is limited to making available to state parties concerned its good offices. It is not empowered to pass any comment on the communication relating to the non-compliance of the rights stated in the covenant. Secondly, a state party is free to withdraw its declaration by notification, weakens the system. In the conciliation mechanism solution of the matter referred to the commission dependes upon the consent of the parties. The another defect of the mechanism is that without resort to inter-state communication procedure the conciliation mechanism cannot be used.

One more method of implementation of human rights recognised under the optional protocol to the International Covenant on Civil and Political Rights is the method of 'Individual's communication system'. With regard to this procedure Egon Schwelb rightly remarked, "From the point of view of principle the entry into force of the option protocol on the right of individual petition is probably the most revolutionary of the series of events.... In the course of the many years during which the United Nations dealt with the International Bill of Rights, there had until 1966, never been a majority for making the right of individual petition a part of it. Proposals to recognise the right to petition an international authority were made on several occassions, but none was accepted.[27]

(8) That the European Convention on Human Rights, 1950 may be considered as first significant regional convention on human rights which gives protection to civil and political rights embodied therein by a positive commitment. The convention accurately defines civil and political rights and specifies the contents of the rights by incorporating exceptions, limitations or restrictions to which such rights are subject to. It also provides machinery for the implementation of rights in the form of commission, Court and the Committee of ministers.

A detailed analysis of the working of the commission shows that it has proved, itself to be more effective body in compare to 'Human Rights Committee' established under International Covenant on Civil and Political Rights because the commission made attempt to resolve friendly. If it was not resolved in this manner, it transmitted its report to the Committee of ministers. This committee is a political as well as known as executive wing of the council of Europe and such an effective body which could decide whether there had been a violation of the convention, if decided so, it prescribes a time limit within which the state party concerned must take measures required by the committee of ministers. It is to be noted here that the decision of the committee of ministers has a binding effect on the state parties.

As far as European court of Human Rights (ECHR) is concerned it has very wide jurisdiction, contentious as well as advisory jurisdiction. With the enlargement of the powers of the court by protocols and abolition of the commission on 31st October, 1998, the court has become the only body who can enforce the rights stated in the European convention. If a national of contracting party is a victim of a violation of a human right than he may file a case in the court and the parties are bound by the decision of the court because under the convention the state parties have undertaken to bound by the final verdict of the court. The final verdict is transmitted to the committee of ministers which shall supervise its execution.

Like the European convention, the American convention on Human Rights, 1969 also contains the provisions for implementation of Human rights through an Inter-American Commission of Human Rights and Inter-American Court of Human Rights. The study in Chatper III reveals that the Inter-American Commission has effectively performed its functions, first, to develop an awareness of human rights among the people of America and, second, to make recommendations to the Governments of member states, to prepare, report, requesting Government to furnish information, rendering advisory services, considering and deciding individual petitions and to submit annual reports to the GeneralAssembly. Inter-American Commission and state parties who have expressly recognised its jurisdiction can approach the Inter-American court of Human Rights. The Court in its advisory opinion on effect of reservation on entry into force of the American convention very aptly observed, "That the object and purpose of American Covention is the protection of the basic rights of individual human beings, irrespective of their nationality, both against the state of their nationality and all other contracting states under Human Rights treaties, the states can be deemed to submit themselves to a legal order which they, for the common good assume various obligations not in relation to other states but towards all individuals within their jurisdiction..... the convention must be seen for what in reality it is a mulitilateral legal instrument of framework enabling state to make binding unilateral commitments not to violate the human rights of individual within their jurisdiction."[28] The African charter also provides three procedures of implementation, namely, reporting, inter-state communications and communication other than those of state parties including individuals. A close scrutiny of the charter reflects that this charter differs to other regional charter because of the inclusion of collective or people's rights, such as the rights to peace and development, and the particuarly prominent place the charter gives to individual duties.

(9) That the United Commission on Human rights[29] established by the Economic and Social Council may be said to be "the nearest approach to permanent machinery for the supervision of the issues relating to protection of human rights."[30] The commission can be expressed as 'universal' because the nature and the

scope of the remedy available under it is wider than that available under the optional protocol to International Covenant on Civil and Political Rights. The commission can exercise its jurisdiction in case of any individual belonging to member state of United Nations while under option protocol the jurisdiction can be exercised in case of an individual belonging to state parties of the civil covenant which are parties to optional protocol.

As examined under the Third Chapter, initially the mandate of the UN commission on human rights was limited to promotional role of norm creation rather than an open-ended protection role. Even its norm creating function was full of hardship because of the political and economic ambition of influential countries. The UN Commission was criticized for its failure to create sense of priorities in terms of standard setting, complete neglect of organs other than itself, for lack of procedure during the drafting process and for lack of any substantive role. Regarding the role of dealing with specific human right violations, the UN commission stated assumption of responsibility of dealing with specific violation after 1960's. It is after the adoption of two procedures, i.e. procedure 1235 which established the principle that violations could be examined and responded to and provided the necessary authorization for the commission to engage in public debate on the issue each year, and procedure 1503 which provided the individuals to submit their petition as to the violation of human rights by states, that the UN Commission started to deal with specific human right violations. It is possible to say that it is after 1966 that the UN commission became legally competent to deal with all violations.[30a] The UN commission's thematic procedures were effective as compared to the 1503 and 1235 procedure, but the procedures have been criticized since they ignored many other important issues to be dealt. Therefore,

United Nations must examine this procedure again and must take appropriate measures which can eliminate the said criticisms. Despite the above criticism it is submitted that the commission has played an important role by preparing the texts of the Universal Declaration of Human Rights, the Convention on the Political rights of women, drafted covenants on human rights supplementing the Universal Declaration. The year book on Human rights is regularly published by the commission.

(10) That in order to implement the 'Paris Principles of 1991', (endorsed by United Nations Commission on Human Rights, United Nations General Assembly and the Vienna Conference) in India the Protection of Human Rights Act, 1993 was enacted and the National Human Rights commission was established for better protection of human rights. The commission has been entrusted with an all-India role and responsibility of protecting and promoting human rights of the citizens. According to Vijayshri Sripati, "The NHRC is, in essence, a purely recommendatory body that has in its arsenal only the powers to recommend and to initiate litigation. It does not have the power to make determination and enforceable order. In cases where its inquiry discloses the violation of human rights or negligence in the prevention of its violation by a public servant, it can neither initiate proceedings for prosecution against delinquent official nor can it award appropriate compensation to the victim or his family members. All that it can do is to recommend to the appropriate authorities : (a) to prosecute the errant public servants; (b) to take any other action with a view towards remedying or preventing a fundamental right violation and (c) to grant interim relief to the victim or the members of the family. In addition, the Human Rights Act does not specifically make the recommendations of the commission bindining on the concerned Government or the authority. But it lays

down a time frame (one month) within which the government or authority must respond to the commission about the action it has taken on the commission's recommendations..... It was adverse international opinion against the armed forces' brutal atrocities that led to the establishment of NHRC. The armed forces have sweeping powers when they are called to quell internal distrubance giving them ample scope to commit human rights absuses. Despite these factors, the POHRA precludes the NHRC from investigating violations committed by the armed forces. When the commission receives a complaint of human rights violations by the armed forces, the only weapon in its meager arsenal it to call for a report from the government. The commission may make recommendations, on the basis of the report. Indeed, this restrictive procedure that it lays down for the commission's investigation into violations by the armed forces has "driven a huge hole in the jurisdiction of the Commission. The Human Rights Act unarguably renders the commission a deeply ineffectual institution for checking human rights violations by both public servants and the armed forces."[31] Thus Sripat has pointed out normative and structural weaknesses of the Commission, particularly relating to enforcement and implementation.

Regarding the functions and powers of the National Human Rights Commission, P. Venkatarama Reddi J., Observed, "The commission which is a unique expert body, is no doubt entrusted with a very important function of protecting the human rights, but it is needless to point out that the commission has no unlimited jurisdiction nor does it exercise plenary powers in derogation of the statutory limitations. The commission which is the creature of statute is bound by its provisions. Its duties and functions are defined and circumscribed by the Act. Of course, as any other statutory functionary it undoubtedly has incidental or ancillary powers to effectively exercise its jurisdiction in respect of powers confided to it but the commission should necessarily act within the parameters prescribed by the Act creating it and the confines of jurisdiction vested in by the Act. The commission is one of the fora which can redress the grievances arising out of the violation of Human Rights. If it is not in a position to take up the enquiry and to afford redressal on account of certain statutory fetters or handicaps the aggrieved persons are not without other remedies.[32]

Despite the above weaknesses, the efforts made by the commission had concrete results. First, The Chairman of the commission publicly voiced against the decision of the Supreme Court upholding TADA's validity. In a letter addressed to all members of Parliament including the Prime Minister, the Chairman of the commission, strongly recommended the removal of TADA from the statue book. What really maked the commission's recommendations was the categorical impact of its conclusions. Thus the commssion was decisive force for the demise of TADA and was perhaps its earliest and most tangible achievement. Secondly, The commission repeatedly drew the then govt.'s attention to the rampant use of torture in detention centers that contributed to the phenomenal rise in incidents of custodial deaths. Advising the Govt. of the desirability of and its obligations to adhere to, international standards in the treatment of detainees, the commission boldly urged the then Prime Minister, Mr. P.V. Narsimharao to accede to the United Nations Convention on torture. Ultimately the United front Govt. signed the UN convention on torture on 14th Oct., 1997.[33] Thirdly, The Preventive of Child Marraige Bill, 2004 introduced in the Rajaya Sabha on 20.12.04 and amendments suggested in the draft Bill are the result of continous positive efforts made by the commission: Fourthly, the commission had recommended that the Government of India should become a party to optional Protocols 1 and 2 to the convention on the Rights of the child, dealing with the involvement of children in armed conflict, sale of children, child prostituion and child pornography. Ultimately the Govt. of India signed the above two optional protocols on November 15, 04. Fifthly, the Commission carefully examined the Protection from domestic violence Bill, 2002 along with the report of standing committee of Parliament and made comments and recommendations. Now the bill has taken the form of an Act.

From the above discussion it can be concluded that the Commission has certainly attempted to develop a human rights culture in India. In addition, there have been serious attempts to create accountability mechanisms for human rights violations at different levels of the Indian Government to ensure that human rights remain the central focus of India political and governemnt discourse. The commission remains a forum in which people can seek justice for human rights violations.[34]

J.S. Verma, J. subscribes to the view that a significant trend is the development of complimentarity between the Supreme Court and the National Human Rights Commission of India in enforcement of human rights. The better capacity of the NHRC to directly monitor performance of institution in certain situations, has been utilized by the Supreme Court to aid its functions of issuing directions in appropriate cases. Such instances are of monitoring the mental homes, protective homes, child labour, bonded labour etc. The Complimentarity make the mechanism more effective in the enforcement of human rights.[35]

It is submitted that in order to dispose complaints expeditiously and also deal and deliberate upon other related issues, the commission in its meeting held on

21st Nov., 2006 decided to hold its meeting in the State Capitals. It was felt that such a meetings would help to get information about the status of complaints to the parties, help to receive fresh complaints and sensitize the state functionaries on the issues concerning human rights. It will also help to review the progress made by each state on the recommendations of the commission, particularly those related to Economic, Social and cultural rights. Pursuant to this decision, the commission held its first sitting outside Delhi in Lucknow from 18th to 20th January, 2007. During its three days sitting, the commission drew the attention of the UP authorities to a number of issues including failure to file FIRs, delay in compliance with its recommendations and delay in sending requisite details of reports on custodial deaths.[36]

Dr. Shiv Raj Patil, acting Chairperson of NHRC, recently said, "that the provisions of Juvenile Justice Act, 2000 along with its amendments in 2006 have to be looked into and forcefully enforced to get the maximum result. He said there has to be a development–oriented culture for the rights of Children."[37]

This shows the commitment of the commission towards the cause of human rights relating to children and efforts to develop a human rights culture in every walks of life.

(11) With the globalization of human rights, it has become important for the judicial systems around the world, to examine the posssibility of and the need for application in their domestic jurisdiction, of human rights law.[38] The relevant principles, in this regard are 'Bangalore principles', which were summarized by the convenor of the 'Judicial Colliquim', were as under:

(a) Fundamental human rights and freedoms are inherent in all human kind and find expression in Constitution and legal systems throughout the world and in the international human rights instruments.

(b) These international human rights instruments provide important guidance in cases concerning fundamental human rights and freedoms.

(c) There is an impressive body of jurisdprudence, both international and national, concerning the interpretation of particular human rights and freedoms and their application. This body of jurisdprudence is of practical relevance and value to judges and lawyers generally.

(d) In most countries whose legal systems are based upon comon law, International conventions are not directly enforceable in national courts unless their provisions have been incorporated by legislation into domestic law. However, there is a growing tendency for national courts to have regard to these international norms for the purpose of deciding cases where the domestic law—Whether constitutional, statute or common law is uncertain or incomplete.

(e) This tendency is entirely welcomed because it respects the universality of fundamental human rights and freedoms and the vital role of an independent judiciary in reconciling the competing claims of individuals and groups of persons with the general interests of the community.

(f) While it is desirable for the norms contained in the international human rights instruments to be still more widely recognised and applied by national courts, this process must take fully into account local laws, traditions, circumstances and needs.

(g) It is within the proper nature of the judicial process and well established judicial functions for national courts to have regard to international obligations which a country undertakes. Whether or not they have been incorporated into domestic law for the purpose of removing ambiguity or uncertainty from national Constitutions, legislation or common law.

(h) However, where national law is clear and inconsistent with the international obligations of the state concerned in common law countries the national court is obliged to give effect to national law. In such cases the court should draw such inconsistency to the attention of the appropriate authorities since the supremacy of national law in no way mitigates a breach of an international legal obligation, which is undertaken by a country.[39]

It is submitted that the Bangalore principles do not undermine the sovereignty of national laws making institutions. They acknowledge that if those institutions have made a rule which is unambiguous and binding no international human rights principle can undermine or overrule the applicable domestic law. To introduce such a principle requires the opportunity of a gap in the common law or of an ambiguity of a local statute. Far from being a negation of sovereignity, this is an application of it.[39a]

(12) That regarding the international custom India has not followed the Blackstonian doctrine stating that the law of nations is part of the law of the land. This conclusion is based upon Article 51(c) of the Indian Constitution. The Article states that the state shall endeavour to 'foster respect for international law and treaty obligations. It is submitted that the difference in Article 51(c) between international law and treaty obligation is that the expression 'international law' refers to international customary law. The aceptance of such an approach would mean that customary International

Law is not incorporated into Indian domestic law ipso facto.

The Constitution of United States of America explicitly declares 'treaties as supreme law of the land'. But the Indian Constitution does not specifically states so. The Indian Parliament, under Article 246(1), has exclusive power to make laws with respect to any of the matters enumerated in List I in the 7th Schedule. Entry 14, List I (Union list) deals with entering into treaties and agreements with foreign countries under Article 253 the Parliament is empowered to make any law for the whole or any part of the Territory of India to implement treaties and international agreements, notwithstanding the fact that they refer to subjects which falls in List II (State List) of the 7th Schedule. On implementation of treaties, Indian practice resembles English practise, if a treaty affects the application of existing laws, imposes financial obligations or otherwise requires specific legislative authority for execution than its needs a legislative action.[40]

(13) The Judicial March from Kesvanand Bharati,[41] A.D.M. Jabalpur (Minority view),[42] Jolly George Verghese,[43] Gramophone Co.'s Case[44] to R.D. Upadhayay[45] passing through D.K. Basu,[46] Vishakha[47] and Chandrimadas[48] reflects the principles applied by the courts in harmonising municipal law with International law, the principles may be summarized as under:

(a) International law today is not limited to regulating, the relations between the state. Today matters of social concerns such as health, education, economics and environment falls within the area of international regulations. The undisputed proposition of law in this regard is that the rules of customary international law which are not contrary to the municipal law shall be deemed to be incorporated in the domestic law.[49]

(b) The United Nations charter, Universal Declaration of Human rights, the two International Covenants – ICCPR and ICESR, various international instruments, international treaties and declaration have been utlized by the apex court to promote the cause of casual labourers,[50] to protect the health of workers,[51] to grant females the right to inheritance,[52] to protect working women from sexual harassment,[53] to grant compensation to rape victim,[54] to compensate for custodial violence,[55] to protect the Human rights of children,[56] declaring the right to development as an integral part of human right[57] and enriching the environmental law to protect the environment from pollution.[58]

(c) The International human rights norms have been used for expanding the connotation of fundamental rights and for covering areas not covered by existing domestic legislation provided this does not conflict with any existing domestic legislation. This has enabled the Supreme Court of India to lay down guidelines for prevention of sexual harassment of women at the work place, this being treated as denial of the right of equality and discrimination at the Workplace.[59]

(d) The comity of nations requires that rules of International law may be accomodated in the municipal law even without express legislative sanction provided they do not run into conflict with Parliamentary legislation. The doctrine of incorporation also recognises the position that the rules of International law are incorporated into national law and considered to be part of the national law unless they are contrary to an Act of Parliament. Certainly the national Courts will endorse the International law but not if it conflicts with the national law. National Courts being organs of the national state and not organs of international law must perforce apply national law if international law conflicts with it. But the courts are under an obligation within legitimate limits to so interpret the domestic statute as to avoid the confrontation with the comity of nations or the well established principles of Interntional Law.[60]

(e) That Article 1 of the Universal Declaration of Human Rights asserts human sensitivity and obligation on every state that, "all human beings are born free and equal in dignity and rights. They are endowed with reason and conscience and should act towards one another in a spirit of brotherhood. The Charter of the United nations thus reinforces the faith in fundamental human rights and in the dignity and worth of the human person envisaged in the Directive Principles of state policy as a part of the Constitution.[61] Preventive detention of a foreign national who is a foreign national involves the application of the principles of International human rights law. The UDHR include the right to life, liberty and security of person, freedom from arbitrary arrest and dentention, the right to fair trial by an independent and impartial tribunal, and the right to presume to be an innocent man until proved guilty.[62]

(f) It is generally a recognised principle in national legal system that in the event of doubt the domestic rule is to be interpreted in accordance with the State's international obligations. In fact there is need for harmonisation whenever possible bearing in mind the spirit of the Covenants. In this context it should be kept in mind that the fundamental rights guaranteed by Part III of the Indian Constitution are in conforming line with

> those in the UDHR and the Covenant on Civil and Political Rights and the Covenant on Economic, Social and cultural rights to which India has become a party by ratifying them.[63]

The following suggestions of far reaching consequences are made on the basis of study in the foregoing chatpers:

(1) The state party to the covenant on civil and Political Rights, 1966 undertook to respect and to ensure to all individuals within its territory.... the rights recognised in the covenant without distinction of any kind and to take the necessary steps, in accordance with its constitutional process and with the provisions on the covenant to adopt such legislative and other measures as may be necessary to give effect to the rights recognized in the covenant. The reporting procedure is the primary method of implementation provided under the civil covenant. But there is unwillingness on the part of member states to submit genuine reports. Thus there is a need to persuade the states to adopt and follow the procedure properly.

(2) The most important instrumetns on human rights, are the Covenant on Civil and Political Rights, 1966 containing the civil and political rights, and Covenant On Economic, Social and Cultural Rights, 1966 recognising economic, social and cultrual rights essential for human being for maintaining the human dignity. It is very unfortunate that these covenants have yet not been ratified by many countries. It is suggested that a special convention should be called by the United Nations for Convincing the states to ratify these international instruments.

(3) The 'Human Rights Committee', is a principal body to implement the International Human Rights, established under International Covenant on Civil and Political Rights. The structure and anatomy of the commission reveals that it consists of eighteen members having expertise in the field of Human

Rights and they are elected by the state parties. It is suggested that for ensuring impartiality and independence the members of the committee should be elected by the World Court, i.e. International Court of Justice.

The Human Rights Committee implement the human rights contained in the Civil and Political Covenant by adopting the reporting, inter-state Communication and Conciliation procedures. It is pointed out here that under the covenant the state parties are obliged to submit the reports but there is no explicit obligation to comply the reports, comments and suggestions made by the committee. This provision weakens the reporting procedure. Similarly, the Inter-State communication procedure also suffers from some defects. First, the Function of the committee is limited to making available to state parties concerned its good offices. The committee cannot pass any comment on the communciation relating to non-observance of rights enshrined in the covenant. Secondly, the inter-communication procedure is applicable only if a state party declares that it recognises the competence of the HumanRights Committee to receive and consider communications. Thirdly, the exhaustion of domestic remedies is another obstacle affecting the proper enforcement of the procedure. Fourthly, in conciliation mechanism solution on the matter referred to the commission depends upon the consent of the parties and this mechanism can be adopted only after using the Inter-state communication procedure.

To strengthen the above procedures or mechanism, following suggstions are made by the researcher : First, an express provision should be inserted in the civil covenant making it obligatory, on the state parties, to comply with the reports, comments and suggestions made by the Human Rights Committee. Secondly, a provision should be made that one can resort to conciliation mechanism at first instance, even without resort to Inter-state communication mechanism. Thirdly, the fetter relating to exhaustion of domestic remedies should be removed to impart justice in a real sense. Fourthly, the decisions of Human rights committee under individual complaints procedure should be treated as formally binding under the law of the Nations in the same way as a judgement of the European Court of Human rights or Inter-American Court of Human Rights. The suggestion is supported by the finding in *Ameeruddy-Ziffra v. Mauritius*[64] in which it was held that the general comments and the view of the Human Rights Committee is a main source of interpretation of the International Covenant on Civil and Political Rights. A similar view was taken by the High Court of Australia, the Court pointed out that, "the opening up of international remedies to individuals brings to bear on the common law the powerful influence of the ICCPR and the international standards it imposes."[65]

(4) The regional systems i.e. the European convention on Human rights, the American convention on Human Rights and the African charter on Human and People's rights have their own implementation mechanisms, however the efficiency of one is different from the other due to various factors. It is suggested that the more mechanism has to be employed by the organization of American states and the organization of African unity in order to make their regional convention more competent as comparable to the European counter part.

(5) The National Human Rights Commission lacks power to prosecute the delinquent public servants, to award compensation to the Victims and to make recommendations, the commission as it stands today, remains a shackled institution. In actual practise, it is an ineffective and woefully feeble protector of human rights.[66]

It is suggested that the commission should be empowered to procsecute delinquent public servants when a prima facie case is made out of human rights violation. Although under Section 18 of Protection of Human Rights Act, 1993, the commission on an inquiry where it discloses the commission of violation of human rights or negligence in the prevention of violation of human rights or abetment thereof by a public servant, it may recommend to the concerned Government or authority to initiate proceedings for prosecution or such other suitable action as the commission may deem fit against the concerned person or persons. It is submitted that this provision is not sufficient for an erring public servant. Secondly, the commission's recommendations to the concerned Government must have a binding effect. For this purpose the present provision[67] is not enough, a provision should be made in the Protection of Human Rights Act, 1993 to the effect that the recommendations of the commission shall be considered 'fully and faithfully' by the Government. Besides it there is a need to fix a time limit to consider and implement to recommenda-tions of the commission. Thirdly, Sec. 11 lays down that the Central Government shall make available to the commission such police and investigative staff under an officer not below the rank of a Director General of Police and according to Section 14 of the POHRA, 1993, the commission may, for the puprose of conducting any investigation pertaining to the inquiry utilise the services of any officer or investigating agency of the Central Government or any state Government with the concurrence of the Central Government or the State Government as the case may be.

These provisions show that the commission has no independent investigation team of its own. It is suggested that to conduct an effective investigation, the commission must have it own independent investigation agency manned by trained officials. The officials to such agency should be appointed by the Central Government with the consultation of the Chairman of the commission. If such an agency or team is provided to the Commission, it will certainly contribute immensely to make it a real and powerful guarantor of human rights.

Fourthly, the Human Rights Committee while assessing the India's report on implementation of International Covenant on Civil and Political rights, pointed out, "The committee regrets that the National Human Rights Commission is prevented by section 19 of the Human Rights Act from investigating directly complaints of human rights violations against the armed forces, but must request a report from the central Government..."

In the light of the above observation of the committee an amendment in Section 19 is suggested that the commission should be empowered to inquire into the complaints of violations of Human Rights by the armed forces in areas where they have been deployed by the Central government and on the completion of such enquiry to send a copy of inquiry report together with its recomendations to the Central Government on concerned authority to take appropriate action.

(6) The apex court held in N.C. Dhoundial Case that National Human Rights Commission in India is a unique expert body, it is no doubt entrusted with a very important function of protecting the human rights, but it is pointed out that it has no unlimited jurisdiction nor does it exercise plenary powers in derogation of the statutory limitations. The commission which is the creature of state is bound by its provisions. Its duties and functions are defined and circumscribed by the Act.

It is suggested that it would have been better if the Supereme Court, looking to the objects of Protection of Human Rights Act and Universal Declaration of Human Rights, had interpreted the powers of the Commission widely. It is also suggested that the restriction imposed by caluse (2) of Section 36 of the Act.[68] Which prevent the commission from inquiring complaints filed one year after the alleged violation of human rights, should be removed as in many cases it may cause hardship or injustice to a victim. Although this limitation does not apply in a matter referred to the commission by the apex court.

(7) The Human Rights courts as proposed by Section 30 of the Protection of Human Rights Act, should be set up at district level to try the offences arising out of violation of Human rights. These courts should be presided by an officer not below the rank of Sessions Judge and should be conferred exclusive jurisdiction in the matters of violation of human rights so that these cases may be decided speedily.

(8) As far as harmonisation of municipal law with International Law is concerned it is suggested that whenever there is a doubt about a domestic rule it should be interpreted in the light of International obligations of the state concenred. This suggestion is founded on the observations of Krishna Iyer, J., he pointed out, "There is need for harmonisation whenever possible bearing in mind the spirit of the convenants.[69] Secondly, the fundamental rights guaranteed by the Indian Constitution should be read and interpreted in the light of the Universal Declaration of Human Rights, covenant on civil and political rights and the covenant on Economic, Social and Cultural Rights to which India has become a party by ratifying them. Thirdly, any international covenant not inconsistent with the fundamental rights and in harmony with its spirit should be read into these provisions so as to enlarge the meaning, nature and contents of these fundamental human rights. It will

promote the aims and objects of the constitutional guarantee. This is implicit from Article 51(c) of the Constitution and the power of Parliament to make laws for implementing the International Conventions by virtue of Article 253 read together with entry 14 of the first list (Union List) of the Seventh Schedule of the Constitution. In this regard in *Visakha v. State of Rajasthan,*[70] it was observed, "...... it is now accepted rule of judicial construction that regard must be had to international conventions and norms for consturing domestic law when there is no inconsistency between them and there is a void in the domestic law. Fourthly, it is suggested that the nations much march with the international community and the domestic law must respect rules of international law even as nations respect international opinion. The comity of nations requires that rules of International Law may be adopted in the domestic law even without express legislative enactment. Fifthly, even though the doctrine of incorporation recognises the position that the rules of international law are incorporated into national law and considered to be part of the national law, unless they are in conflict with an Act of Parliament. In other words Municipal law must prevail in case of conflict. But the reasearcher is of the view if the violation of human rights is involved then the domestic law, even if in confilict with the UDHR, two important covenants or other international documents securing human rights, should be amended and the judiciary should lean towards an interpretation which promotoes the human rights. It will enrich our domestic jurisprudence. In this regard Michal Kirby J., subscribes to the view that the process which Bangalore Principles endorse is an inevitable one. As countries submit themselves to the external scrutiny and criticism of their laws by the UN Human Rights committee, the results must be addressed. If a domestic law is measured and found wanting, a country must bring its law into conformity or be revealed as engaged in nothing but window dressing.[71]

(9) It is suggested that if a state is found negligent in preventing violations of human rights of its citizens or non-citizens should be held internationally accountable and responsible. From it follows that the state must train its police, investigation agency, its judiciary and medical experts in matters relating to violation of human rights. The state must set up a machinery to provide legal and other kind of assistance and services to the victims. It must also appoint officers or should engage NGOs in data collecting and conducting research on the problem of violence, educational programmes to raise awareness and prevent harmful practices.

Similar view was taken at Judicial Colloquium in Bangalore[72] stating. "It is essential to redress a situation where, by reason of traditional legal training, which has tended to ignore the international dimensions, Judges and practising lawyers are often unaware of the remarkable and comprehensive developments of statements of international human rights norms. For the practical implementation of these views it is desirable to make provision for appropriate courses in universities and colleges, and for lawyers and law enforcement officials; provision in libararies of relevant materials; promotion of expert advisory bodies knowledgeable about developments in this field; better dissemination of information to judges, lawyers and law enforcement officials; and meetings for exchange of relevant information and experience.

In this context it is submitted that the Human Rights movement in the present scenario requires to focuss on and be pro-active rather than reactive in evolving a new 'Human Rights Culture'. There is a need to impose restrictions or fetters on the processes which violates or disrespect the human rights. For developing such a culture our emphasis must be on spreading awareness amongst weaker sections, downtroddens and vulnerable groups, about their human rights.

NOTES

1. Dr. B. Hydervali (2003), "The Jurisprudence of Human Rights", *Indian Bar Review*, Volume XXX (4).
2. J.S. Verma J. (2004), "The New Universe of Human Rights", Ist ed. (p. 42).
3. Art. 1 of the Universal Declaration of Human Rights says "All Human beings are born free and equal in dignity and rights......".
4. For example, Article 10(1) of ICCPR, 1966 read as under, "All persons deprived of their liberty shall be treated with humanity and with respect for the inherent dignity of the human persons".
5. J.S. Verma J. (2004), "The New Universe of Human Rights", Ist ed. at pp. 43, 48.
6. United Nations (1995), "The Copenhagen Declaration Adopted at the World Summit for Social Development, 6th to 12th March.
7. The Copenhagen Declaration and Programme of Actions 5 (1995), para 14(c).
8. Prof. S.K. Verma (2000), 'Globalisation, Marketisation and Constitutional Mandate', 42 JILI, p. 398.
9. Article 21A Inserted by Constitution (86th Amendment) Act, 2002.
10. Jan Brownlie (1973), "Principles of Public International Law, (2nd ed. p. 552.
11. Oppenheim, "International Law", (ed. 1992) p. 988.
12. Legal Consequences of the continued presence of South Africa in Nambia (I.C.J.R. 1971, p.16)
13. The International Court of Justice and the Human Right clauses of the Charter, *A.J.I.L.* Vol. 62 (1972) p. 346.
14. Mike M.K.Yin (1972), "Charter provisions Concerning Human Rights", *India* Quarterly, Vol. 28.
15. Oppeheim, "*International Law*" Eighth edition, Vol. 1, p. 740.
16. Lauterpacht, "*International Law and Human Rights*", p. 394.
17. J.E.S. Facett (1968), "The Law of Nations", p. 158.

18. S.K. Kapoor, *"International Law and Human Rights"*, 14th ed., p. 777.
19. *Kesvanand Bharrati v. State of Kerala,* AIR 1973 SC 1461 at p. 1536.
20. *"International Law"*, 11th edition, ed. by I.A. Shearer, at p. 330.
21. *"International Law"*, 9th edition (1992) p. 1003.
22. International Relations, 3rd ed. (1970) p. 370.
23. Ian Brownili (1973), *"Principles of Public International Law"*, p. 554.
24. Article 2, para 7 speaks as under: Nothing contained in the present charter shall authorize the United Nations to intervene in matters which are essentially within the domestic jurisdiction of any state or shall require the members to submit such matters to the settlement under the present charter; but this principle shall not prejudice the application of enforcement measures under Chatper VII".
25. Richard B. Bilder (1969), "Rethinking International Human Rights", *Human Right Journal,* 2, p. 567.
26. John P. Humphery, "The International Law of Human Rights in the Middle Twentieth Century", *The Present State of International Law and other Essays,* p. 255.
27. 'Entry into force of the International Covenant on Human Rights and the Optional Protocol to the ICCPR,' *A.J.I.L.* Vol. 70 (1976) pp. 514-515.
28. (1982) 67 ILR 559.
29. See for details Chapter III of the Research work.
30. Jan Brownlie (1973), Principles of Public International Law, p. 554.

30a. Philip Alston (ed.) (1995), The UN and Human Rights: A Critical Appraisal p. 180-181.

31. Vijayshri Sripat, "India's National Human Rights Commission: A Schackled Commission?" 18 *B.U. Int. Law J.* 1 (2000).
32. *N.C. Dhoundial v. Union of India and other,* 2004(1) UJ 746 (SC) at p. 752.
33. 18 B.U. Int'L.J. 1 (Spring 2000).
34. C. Raj Kumar (2005), "Human Rights Implications of National Security Laws in India: Combating Terrorism while preserving Civil Liberties, 33 Den.J. Int'L & Policy, 195.

35. J. S. Verma (1st ed.) , (2004), "The New Universe of Human Rights", p. 36.
36. Human Rights News Letter, Vol. 14 No. 2, Feb., 2007.
37. Speech of Dr. Justice Shiv Raj Patil at two day national Conference on "Juvenile Justice System in India" Organized by NHRC on Feb. 3 & 4, 2007.
38. Sujata Manohar J. (2003), "International Human Rights Law in Domestic Courts: Violence against Women and Administration of Justice", *Journal of the NHRC,* Vol. 2, at p. 11.
39. From 24th to 26th Feb., 1988, there was convened in Bangalore, a high level judicialcolliquim on the domestic application of International Human Rights norms. The participants were: P.N. Bhagwati (former C.J.I.) Convenor; M.P. Chandra Kanatraj Urs. J. (from India); Michael D Kirby J. (Australia); Tun Mohmd. Salleh Bin Bas J. (Malaysia); Rajsoomer Lallah, J. (Mauritius); Muhammad Haleen, C.J., (Pakistan); Sir Mari Kapi, Dy C.J. (Papua New Guinea); P. Ramanathan J., (Sri Lanka); Recorder Anthony Lester, QC (U.K.); Ruth Badar Ginsburg (U.S.A.) and E. Dumbutshena, C.J. (Zimbabwe).

39a. Speech delivered by Michael Kirby J. at a conference on "Implementing International Human Rights: Domestic implementation of International Human Rights norms", 6th Dec., 1997.

40. See fordetails Chapter VI, Point 3B—Indian Practise Regarding the Relationship between International Law amd Municipal Law.
41. AIR 1973 SC 1461.
42. AIR 1976 SC 1207.
43. AIR 1980 SC 470.
44. AIR 1984 SC 667.
45. AIR 2006 SC 1946.
46. AIR 1998 SC 610.
47 AIR 1998 SC 3011.
48. (2000) 2 SCC 465.
49. See *Kuldeep Singh J. in PUCL v. Union of India,* AIR 1991 SC 568.
50. AIR 1987 SC 2342.
51. *Consumer Education & Research Centre v. Union of India,* AIR 1995 SC 922.

52. *Madhu Kishwar v. State of Bihar,* AIR 1996 SC 1864.
53. *Vishaka v. State of Rajasthan,* AIR 1997 SC 3011
54. *Chairman Rly. Board V. Chandrimadas,* (2000) 2 SCC 465.
55. AIR 1997 SC 610
56. *Bandhua Mukti Morcha v. U.I.,* AIR 1997 SC 2218; *M.C. Mehta v. State of T.N.,* AIR 1997 SC 699; *Parents Forum for Meaningful Education v. U.I.,* AIR 2001 Delhi 212.
57. *N.D. Jayal v. Union of India,* AIR 2004 SC 867.
58 *Vellore Citizens Welfare Forum v. Union of India,* AIR 1996 SC 2715; *Karnataka Industrial Area Development Board v. Kenchappa,* (2006) 6 SCC 371.
59. f.n. 53.
60. *Gramophone Co. of India Ltd. v. Birendra Bahadur Pandey,* AIR
61. See for details *Consumer Education & Research Centre v. Union of India,* AIR 1995 SC 922 (Chapter VI of the research work)
62. *Kubic Dariusz v. Union of India,* AIR 1990 SC 605.
63. See for details Chatper VI of this work : Observation made by Krishna Iyer J. in *Jolly George Verghese v. The Bank of Cochin,* AIR 1980 SC 470 and K.N. Saikia J. in *Kubic Darisuz v. Union of India,* AIR 1990 SC 605.1984 SC 677, at p. 641.
64. Extracts stated in 1995, 38 Japanese Manual of International Law, 118 at 129-131, Quoted by Sujata Manohar J. in article 'International Human Rights Law in domestic Courts', *Journal of the NHRC,* Vol. 2, 2003, p. 23.
65. *Mabo v. Queensland* (1992) 175 CLR 1 at 42.
66. Vijayshri Sripati, "India's NHRC: A Shackled Commission? 18 B.U. Int.'L J.1, p. 44-45.
67. Sec. 18(a)(e) speaks, "The Commission shall send a copy of its inquiry report together with its recommendations to the concerned Government or authority and the concerned. Government or authority shall, within a period of one month or such further time as the commission may allow, forward its comments on the report, including the action taken or proposed to be taken thereon, to the commission. Sub-clause (f) says, "the commission shall publish its inquiry report together with the comments of the concerned Government or authority, if any, and the action taken or proposed to be taken by the concerned

Government or authority on the recommendation of the commission.

67a. 2004 (1) UJ 746 (SC) at p. 752.

68. Sec. 36(2) of the POHA reads as under, "The commission or the State Commission shall not inquire into any matter after the expiry of one year from the date on which the act constituting violation of human rights is alleged to have been committed."

69. *Jolly George Verghese v. The Bank of Cochin,* AIR 1980 SC 470

70. AIR 1997 SC 3011, at para 24.

71. Speeche delivered at the confrenece on "Implementating International Human Rights: Domestic implementation of international human rights norms", 6th Dec. 1997, Faculty of Law, Australian National University.

72. Conclusions of Judicial Colloquia, on domestic application of International Human Rights norms, held in Bangalore from 24th to 26th Feb., 1988.

APPENDIX

LAW RELATING TO PROTECTION OF HUMAN RIGHTS

UNIVERSAL DECLARATION, OF HUMAN RIGHTS, 1948

This Universal Declaration of Human Rights as a common standard of achievement for all peoples and all nations, to the end that every individual and every organ of society, keeping this declaration constantly in mind, shall strive by teaching and educating to promote respect for these rights and freedoms and by progressive measures, national and international, to secure their universal and effective recognition and observance, both among the peoples of Member States themselves and among the peoples of territories under their jurisdiction:

Article 1 – All human beings are born free and equal in dignity and rights. They are endowed with reason and conscience and should act towards one another in a spirit of brotherhood.

Article 2 – Everyone is entitled to all the rights and freedoms set forth in this declaration, without distinction of any kind, such as race, colour, sex, language, religion, political or other opinion, national or social origin, property, birth or other status.

Furthermore, no distinction shall be made on the basis of the political, jurisdictional or international status of the country or territory to which a person belongs, whether it be independent, trust, non-self-governing or under any other limitation of sovereignty.

Article 3 – Everyone has the right of life, liberty and security of person.

Article 4 – No one shall be held in slavery or servitude; slavery and the slave trade shall be prohibited in all their forms.

Article 5 – No one shall be subjected to torture or to cruel, inhuman or degrading treatment or punishment.

Article 6 – Everyone has the right to recognition everywhere as a person before the law.

Article 7 – All are equal before the law and are entitled without any discrimination to equal protection of the law. All are entitled to equal protection against any discrimination in violation of this declaration and against any incitement to such discrimination.

Article 8 – Everyone has the right to an effective remedy by the competent national tribunals for act violating the funda-mental rights granted to him by the Constitution or by law.

Article 9 – No one shall be subjected to arbitrary arrest, detention or exile.

Article 10 – Everyone is entitled in full equality to a fair and public hearing by an independent and impartial tribunal, in the determination of his rights, and obligations and of any criminal charge against him.

Article 11 – Everyone charged with a penal offence has the right to be presumed innocent until proved guilty according to law in a public trial at which he has had all the guarantees necessary for his defence.

No one shall be held guilty of any penal offence on account of any act or omission which did not constitute a penal offence, under national or international law, at the time when it was committed. Nor shall a heavier penalty be imposed than the one that was applicable at the time the penal offence was committed.

Article 12 – *No* one shall be subjected to arbitrary interference with his privacy family home or correspondence,, nor to attacks upon his honour and reputation. Everyone has the right to the protection of the law against such interference or attacks.

Article 13 – 1. Everyone has the right to freedom of movement and residence within the borders of each State.

Everyone has the right to leave any country, including his own, and to return to his country.

Article 14 – Everyone has the right to seek and to enjoy in other countries asylum from prosecution.

This right may not be invoked in the case of prosecutions genuinely arising from non-political crimes or from acts contrary to the purposes and principles of the United Nations.

Article 15 – Everyone has the right to a nationality.

No one shall be arbitrarily deprived of his nationality nor denied the right to change his nationality.

Article 16 – Men and women of full age, without limitation due to race, nationality or religion, have the right to marry and to found a ramiljL. They are entitled to equal rights as to marriage, during marriage and4fits dissolution.

Marriage shall be entered into only with the free and full consent of the intending spouses.

The family is the natural and fundamental group unit of society and is entitled to protection by society and the State.

Article 17 – Everyone has the right to own property alone as well as in association with others.

No one shall be arbitrarily deprived of his property.

Article 18 – Everyone has the right to freedom of thought, conscience and religion; this right includes freedom to change his religion or belief, and freedom, either alone or in community with others and in public or private to manifest his religion or belief in teaching, practice, worship and observance.

Article 19 – Everyone has the right to freedom of opinion and expression; this right includes freedom to hold opinions without interference and to seek, receive and impart information and ideas through any media and regardless of frontiers.

Article 20 – Everyone has the right to freedom of peaceful assembly and association.

No one may be compelled to belong to an association.

Article 22 – Everyone has the right to take part in the Government of his country, directly or through freely chosen representatives.

Everyone has the right of equal access to public service/s in his country.

The will of the people shall be the basis of the authority of Government; this will shall be expressed in periodic and genuine elections which shall be by universal and equal suffrage and shall be held by secret vote or by equivalent free voting procedures.

Article 22 – Everyone,- as a member of society, has the right to social security and is entitled to realisation through national effort and international co-operation and in accordance with the organisation and resources of each State, of the economic, social and cultural rights indispensable for his dignity and the free development of his personality.

Article 23 – Everyone has the right to work, to free choice of employment, to just and favourable conditions of work to protection against unemployment.

Everyone, without any discrimination, has the right to equal pay for equal work.

Everyone who works has the right to just and favourable remuneration ensuring for himself and his family an existence worthy of human dignity, and supplemented, if necessary, by other means of social protection.

Everyone has the right to form and to join trade unions for the protection of his interests.

Article 24 – Everyone has the right to rest and leisure including reasonable limitation of working hours and periodic holidays with pay.

Article 25 – Everyone has the right to a standard of living adequate for the health and well-being" of himself and of his family, including food, clothing, nousing and medical care and necessary social services, and the right to security in the event of unemployment, sickness, disability, widowhood, old age or other lack of livelihood in circumstances beyond his control.

Motherhood and childhood are entitled to special care and assistance. All children, whether born in or out of wedlock, shall enjoy the same social protection.

Article 26 – Everyone has the right to education, education shall be free, at least in the elementary and fundamental stages. Elementary education shall be compulsory, technical and professional education shall be made generally available and higher education shall be equally accessible to all on the basis of merit.

Education shall be directed to the full development of the human personality and to the strengthening of respect for human rights and fundamental freedoms. It shall promote understanding, tolerance and friendship among all nations, racial or religious groups, and shall further the activities of the United Nations for the maintenance of peace.

Parents have a prior right to choose the kind of education that shall be given to their children.

Article 27 – Everyone has the right freely to participate in the cultural life'of the community, to enjoy the arts and to share in scientific advancement and its benefits.

Everyone has the right to protection of the moral arid material interests resulting from any scientific, literary or artistic production of which, he is the author.

Article 28 – Everyone is entitled to a social and international order in which the rights and freedoms set forth in the declaration can be fully realised.

Article 29 – Everyone has duties to the community in which alone the free and full development of his personality is possible.

In the exercise of his rights and freedoms, everyone shall be subject only to such limitations as are determined by law solely for the purpose of security due recognition and respect for the rights and freedoms of others and of meeting the just requirements of morality, public order and the general welfare in a democratic society.

These rights and freedoms may in no case be exercised contrary to the purposes and principles of the United Nations.

Nothing in this Declaration may be interpreted as implying for any State, group or person any right to engage in any activity or to perform any act aimed at the destruction of any of the rights and freedoms set forth herein.

INTERNATIONAL COVENANT ON CIVIL AND POLITICAL RIGHTS, 1966

Article 1 – All people have the right of self-determination by virtue of that right they freely determine their political status and freely pursue their economic, social and cultural development.

All peoples may, for their own ends, freely dispose of their natural wealth and resources without prejudice to any obligations arising out of International Economic Co-operation, based upon the principle of mutual benefit and international law. In no case may a people be deprived of its own means of subsistence.

The States Parties to the present Covenant, including those having responsibility for the administration of Non-Self-Governing and Trust Territories, shall promote the realisation of the right of self-determination, and shall respect that right, in conformity with the provisions of the Charter of the United Nations.

Article 2 – Each State Party to the present Covenant undertakes to respect and to ensure to all individuals within its territory and subject to its jurisdiction the rights recognised in the present Covenant, political or other opinion, national or social origin, property, birth or other status.

Where not already provided for by existing legislative or other measures, each State Party to the present Covenant undertakes to take the necessary steps, in accordance with its constitutional processes and with the provisions of the present Covenant, to adopt such legislative or other measures as may be necessary to give effect to the rights recognised in the present Covenant.

Each State Party to the present Covenant undertakes–

(a) To ensure that any person whose rights or freedoms as herein recognised are violated shall have an effective remedy, notwithstanding that the violation has been committed by persons acting in an official capacity;

(b) To ensure that any person claiming such a remedy shall have his right thereto determined by competent judicial, administrative or legislative authorities, or by any other competent authority provided for by the legal system of the State, and to develop the possibilities of judicial remedy;

(c) To ensure that the competent authorities shall enforce such remedies when granted.

Article 3 – The States Parties to the present Covenant undertake to ensure the equal right of men and women to the enjoyment of all civil and political rights set forth in the present Covenant.

Article 4 – In time of public emergency which threatens the life of the nation and the existence of which is officially proclaimed, the State Parties to the present Covenant may take measures derogating from their obligations under the present Covenant to the existent strictly required by the exigencies of the situation, provided that such measures are not inconsistent with their other obligations under international law and -do not involve discrimination solely on the ground of race, colour, sex, language, religion or social origin.

No derogation from Articles 6, 7, 8 (paragraphs 1 and 2), 11,15,16 and 18, may be made under this provision.

Any State Party to the present Covenant availing itself of the right of derogation shall immediately inform the other States Parties to the present Covenant, through the intermediary of the Secretary-General of the United Nations, of the provisions from which it has derogated and of the United Nations of the provisions from which it has derogated and of the reasons by which it was actuated. A further communication shall be made, through the same intermediary, on the date on which it terminates such derogation.

Article 5 – Nothing in the present Covenant may be interpreted as implying for any State, group or person any right to engage in any activity or perform any act aimed at the destruction of any of the rights and freedoms recognised herein or at their limitation to a greater extent than is provided for in the present Covenant.

There shall be no restriction upon or derogation from any of the fundamental human rights recognised or existing in any State Party to the present Covenant pursuant to law, conventions, regulations or custom on the pretext that the present Covenant does not recognise such rights or that it recognises them to a lesser extent.

Article 6 – Every human being has the inherent right to life. This right shall be protected by law. No one shall be arbitrarily deprived of his life.

In countries which have not abolished the death penalty, sentence of death may be imposed only for the most serious crimes in accordance with the law in force at the time of the commission of the crime and not contrary to the provisions of the present Covenant and to the Convention on the Prevention and Punishment of the Crime of Genocide. This penalty can only be carried out pursuant to a final judgment rendered by a competent Court.

When deprivation of life constitutes the Crime of Genocide, it is understood that nothing in this Article, shall authorise any State Party to the present Covenant to derogation in any way from any obligation assumed under the provisions of the Convention on the Prevention and Punishment of the Crime of Genocide.

Anyone sentenced to death shall have the right to seek pardon or commutation of the sentence. Amnesty, pardon or commutation of the sentence of death may be granted in all cases.

Sentence of death shall not be imposed for crimes committed by persons below 18 years of age and shall not be carried out on pregnant women.

Nothing in this Article, shall be invoked to delay or to prevent the abolition of capital punishment by any State Party to the present Covenant.

Article 7—No one shall be subjected to torture or to cruel, inhuman or degrad | ngjreatment or punishment. In particular, no one shall be subjected without his free consent to medical or scientific experimentation.

Article 8 —No one shall be held in slavery, and the slave-trade in all their forms shall be prohibited.

No one shall be held in servitude.

(a) No one shall be required to perform forced or compulsory labour;

(b) paragraph 3(a), shall not be held to preclude, in countries where imprisonment with hard labour may be imposed as a punishment for a crime, the performance of hard labour in pursuance of a sentence to such punishment by a competent Court;

(c) For the purpose of this paragraph the term "forced" or "compulsory labour" shall not include;

(i) Any work or service, not referred to in sub-paragraph *(b),* normally required of a person who is under detention in consequence of a lawful order of a Court, or of a person during conditional release from such detention;

(ii) Any service of a military character and, in countries where conscientious objection is recognised, any national service required by law of conscientious objectors;

(iii) Any service exacted in cases of emergency or calamity-threatening the life or well-being of the community;

(iv) Any work or service which forms part of normal civil obligations.

Article 9— Everyone has the right to liberty and security of person.

No one shall be subjected to arbitrary arrest or detention. No one shall be deprived of his liberty except on such grounds and m accordance with such procedure as are established by law.

Anyone who is arrested shall be informed, at the time of arrest, of the reasons for his arrest and shall be promptly informed of any charges against him.

Anyone arrested or detained on a criminal charge shall be brought promptly before a Judge or other officer authorised by law to exercise judicial power and shall be entitled to trial within a reasonable time or to release. It shall not be the general rule that persons awaiting trial shall be detained in custody but release may be subject to guarantees to appear for trial, at any other stage or but release may be subject to guarantees or appear for trial, at any other stage or the judicial proceedings, and should occasion arise, for execution of the judgment.

Anyone who is deprived of his liberty by arrest or detention shall be entitled to take proceedings before a Court, in order that Court may decide without delay on the lawfulness of his detention and order his release if the detention is not lawful.

Anyone who has been the victim of unlawful arrest or detention shall have an enforceable right to compensation.

Article 10 – All persons deprived of their liberty shall be treated with humanity and with respect for the inherent dignity of the human persons.

(a) Accused persons shall, save in exceptional circumstances, be segregated from convicted persons and shall be subject to separate treatment appropriate to their status as unconvicted persons;

(b) Accused juvenile persons shall be separated from adults and brought as speedily as possible from adjudication.

The penitentiary system shall comprise treatment of prisoners the essential aim of which shall be their reformation and social rehabilitation. Juvenile offenders shall be segregated from adults and be accorded treatment appropriate to their age and legal status.

Article 11 – No one shall be imposed merely on the ground of inability to fulfil a contractual obligation.

Article 12 – Everyone lawfully within the territory of a State shall, within that territory, have the right to liberty of movement and freedom to choose his residence.

Everyone shall be free to leave any country, including his own.

The above-mentioned rights shall not be subject to any restrictions except those which are provided by law, are necessary to protect national security, public order (order public), public health or morals or the rights and freedoms of others, and are consistent with the other rights recognised in the present Covenant.

No one shall be arbitrarily deprived of the right to enter his own country.

Article 13 – An alien lawfully in the territory of a State Party to the present Covenant may be expelled therefrom only in pursuance of a decision reached in accordance with law and shall, except where compelling reasons of national security otherwise require, be allowed to submit the reasons against his expulsion and to have his case reviewed by, and be represented for the purpose before the competent authority or a person or persons especially designated by the competent authority.

Article 14 – All persons shall be equal before the Courts and tribunals. In the determination of any criminal charge against him, or of his rights and obligations in a suit of law, everyone shall be entitled to a fair and public hearing of a competent, independent and impartial tribunal established by law. The press and the public may be excluded from all or part of a trial for reasons of morals, public order (ordre public) or national security in a democratic society, or where the interest of the private lives of the parties so requires, or the extent strictly necessary in the opinion of the Court in special circumstances where publicity would prejudice the interests of justice, but any judgment rendered in a criminal case or in a suit at law shall be made public except where the interest of juvenile persons otherwise requires or the proceedings concern matrimonial disputes or the guardianship of children.

Everyone charged with a criminal offence shall have the right to be presumed innocent until proved guilty, according to law.

In the determination of any criminal charge against him, everyone shall be entitled to the following minimum guarantees, in full equality:

(a) To be informed promptly and in detail in a language which he understands of the nature and cause of the charge against him;

(b) To have adequate time and facilities for the preparation of his defence and to communicate with counsel of his own choosing;

(c) To be tried without undue delay;

(d) To be tried in his presence, and to defend himself in person or through legal assistance of his own choosing; to be informed, if he does not have legal assistance of this right; and to have legal assistance assigned to him, in any case where the interests of justice so require; and without payment by him in any such case if he does not have sufficient means to pay for it;

(e) To examine, or have examined, the witnesses against him and to obtain the attendance and examination of witnesses on his behalf under the same conditions as witnesses against him;

(f) To have have the free assistance of an interpreter if he cannot understand or speak the language used in Court;

(g) Not to be compelled to testify against himself or to confess guilt.

In the case of juvenile persons, the procedure shall be such as will take account of their age and the desirability of promoting their rehabilitation.

Everyone convicted of a crime shall have the right to his conviction and sentence being reviewed by a higher tribunal according to law.

When a person has by a final decision been convicted of a criminal offence and when subsequently his conviction has been reversed or he has been pardoned on the ground that a new or newly discovered fact shows conclusively that there has been a miscarriage of justice, the person who has suffered punishment as a result of such conviction shall be compensated according to law, unless it is proved that the non-disclosure of the unknown fact in time is wholly or partly attributable to him.

No one shall be liable to be tried or punished again for an offence for which he has already been finally convicted or acquitted in accordance with each country.

Article 15 – No one shall be held guilty of any criminal offence on account of any act or omission which did not constitute a criminal offence, under national or international law, at the time when it was committed. Nor shall a heavier penalty be imposed than the one that was applicable at the time when the criminal offence was committed. If, subsequent to the commission of the offence, provision is made by law for imposition of a lighter penalty, the offender shall benefit thereby.

Nothing in this Article, shall prejudice the trial and punishment of any person for any act or omission which, at the time when it was committed, was criminal according to the general principles of law recognised by the community of nations.

Article 16 – Everyone shall have the right to recognition everywhere as a person before the law.

Article 17 – No one shall be subjected to arbitrary or unlawful interference with his privacy, family, home or correspondence, nor to unlawful attacks on his honour and reputation.

Everyone has the right to the protection of the law against such interference or attacks.

Article 18 – Everyone shall have the right to freedom of thought, conscience and religion. This right shall include freedom to have or adopt a religion or belief of his choice and freedom, either individually or in community with others and in public or private, to manifest his religion or belief in worship, observance, practice and teaching.

No one shall be subject to coercion which would impair his freedom to have or to adopt a religion or belief of his choice.

Freedom to manifest one's religion or beliefs may be subject only to such limitations as are prescribed by law and are necessary to protect public safety, order, health or morals or the fundamental rights and freedoms of others.

The States Parties to the present Covenant undertake to have respect for the liberty of parents and, when applicable, legal guardians to ensure the religious and moral education of their children in conformity with their own convictions.

Article 19 – Everyone shall have the right to hold opinions without interference.

Everyone shall have the right to freedom of expression; this right shall include' freedom to seek, receive and impart information and ideas of all kinds, regardless of frontiers, either orally, in writing or in print, in the form of art, or through any other media of his choice.

The exercise of the rights provided for in paragraph 2 of this Article carries with it special duties and responsibilities. It may, therefore, be subject to certain restrictions, but these shall only be such as are provided by law and are necessary:

(a) for respect of the rights or reputations of others;

(b) for the protection of national security or of public order (ordre public) or of public health or morals.

Article 20 – Any propaganda for war shall be prohibited by law.

Any advocacy of national, racial or religious hatred that constitutes incitement to discrimination, hostility or violence shall be prohibited by law.

Article 21 – The right of peaceful assembly shall be recognised. No restrictions may be placed on the exercise of this right other than those imposed in conformity with the law and which are necessary in a democratic society in the interests of national security or public safety, public order (order public), the protection of public health or morals-or the protection of the rights and freedoms of others.

Article 22 – Everyone shall have the right to freedom of association with others, including the right to form and join trade unions for the protection of his interests.

No restrictions may be placed on the exercise of this right other than those which are prescribed by law and which are necessary in a democratic society in the interests of national security or public safety, public order (ordre public) the protection of public health or morals or the protection of the rights and freedoms of others. This Article shall not prevent the imposition of lawful restrictions on members of the armed forces and of the police in their exercise of this right.

No tiling in this Article, shall authorise States Parties to the International Labour Organisation Convention of 1948, concerning Freedom of Association and Protection of the Right to organise to take legislative measures which would prejudice, or to apply the law in such a manner as to prejudice, the guarantees provided for in that convention.

Article 23 – The family is the natural and fundamental group unit of society and is entitled to protection by society and the State.

The right of men and women of marriageable age to marry and to found a family shall be recognised.

No marriage shall be entered into without the free and full consent of the intending spouses.

State Parties to the present Covenant shall take appropriate steps to ensure equality of rights and responsibilities of spouses as to marriage, during marriage and at its dissolution. In the case of dissolution, provision shall be made for the necessary protection of any children.

Article 24 – Every child shall have, without any discrimination as to race, colour, sex, language, religion, national or social origin, property or birth, the right to such measures of protection as are required by his status as a minor, on the part of his family, society and the State.

Every child shall be registered immediately after birth and shall have a name.

Every child has the right to acquire a nationality.

Article 25 – Every citizen shall have the right and the opportunity, without any of the distinctions mentioned in Article 2, and without unreasonable restrictions :

(a) to take part in the conduct of public affairs, directly or through freely chosen representatives;

(b) to vote and to be elected at genuine periodic elections which shall be by universal and equal suffrage and shall be held by secret ballot, guaranteeing the free expression of the will of the electors;

(c) to have access, on general terms of equality, to public service in his country.

Article 26 – All persons are equal before the law and are entitled without any discrimination to the equal protection of the law. In this respect, the law shall prohibit any discrimination and guarantee to all persons equal and effective protection against discrimination on any ground such as race, colour, sex, language, political or other opinion, national or social origin, property, birth or other status.

Article 27—In those States in which ethnic, religious or linguistic minorities exists, persons belonging to such minorities shall not be denied the right, in community with the other members of their group, to enjoy their own culture, to profess and practice their own religion, or to use their own language.

Article 47 – Nothing in the present Covenant shall be interpreted as impairing the inherent right of all peoples to enjoy and utilise fully and freely their natural wealth and resources.

Article 50—The provisions of the present Covenant shall extend to all parts of federal States without any limitations or exceptions.

INTERNATIONAL COVENANT ON ECONOMIC SOCIAL AND CULTURAL RIGHTS, 1966

Article 1 – All people have the right of self-determination. By virtue of that right they freely determine their political status and freely pursue their economic, social and cultural development.

All peoples may, for their own ends, freely dispose of their natural wealth and resources without prejudice to any obligations arising out of International economic co-operation, based upon the principle of mutual benefit and International Law. In no case, may a people be deprived of its own means of subsistence.

The States Parties to the present Covenant, including those having responsibility for the administration of Non-Self-Governing and trust territories, shall promote the realisation of the right of self-determination, and shall respect that right, in conformity with the provisions of the Charter of the United Nations.

Article 2 – Each State Party to the present Covenant undertakes to take steps, individually and through International assistance and co-operation, especially economic and technical, to the maximum of its available resources, with a view to acliieving progressively the full realisation of the rights recognised in the present Covenant by all appropriate means, including particularly the adoption of legislative measures.

The States Parties to the present Covenant undertake to guarantee that the rights enunciated in the present Covenant will be exercised without discrimination of any kind"as to race, colour, sex, language, religion, political or other opinion, national or social origin, property, birth or other status.

Developing countries, with due regard to human rights and their National Economy, may determine to what extent they would guarantee the economic right recognised in the present Covenant to non-nationals.

Article 3 —The States Parties to the present Covenant undertake to ensure the equal right *of* men and women to the enjoyment of all economic, social and cultural rights set forth in the present Covenant.

Article 4 – The States Parties to the present Covenant recognise that, in the enjoyment of those rights provided by the State in conformity with the present Covenant, the State may subject such rights only to such limitations as are determined by law only in so far as this may be compatible with the nature of these rights and solely for the purpose of promoting the general welfare in a democratic society.

Article 5 – Nothing in the present Covenant may be interpreted as implying for any State, group or person any right to engage in any activity or to perform any act aimed at the destruction of any of the rights or freedoms recognised herein, or at their limitation to a greater extent than is provided for in the present Covenant.

No restriction upon or derogation from any of the fundamental human rights recognised or existing in any country in virtue of law, conventions, regulations or custom shall be admitted on the pretext that the present Covenant does not recognise such rights or that it recognises them to a lesser extent.

Article 6 – The States Parties to the present Covenant recognise the right to work, which includes the right of everyone to the opportunity to gain his living by work which he freely chooses or accepts, and will take appropriate steps to safeguard this right.

The steps to be taken by a State Party to the present Covenant to achieve the full realisation of this right shall include technical and vocational guidance and training programmes, policies and techniques to achieve steady economic, social and cultural development and full and productive employment under conditions safeguarding fundamental, political and economic freedoms to the individual.

Article 7 – The States Parties to the present Covenant recognise the right of everyone to the enjoyment of just and favourable conditions of work, which ensure, in particular –

(a) Remuneration which provides all workers, as a minimum, with;

  (i) fair wages and equal remuneration for work of equal value without distinction of any kind, in particular women being guaranteed conditions of work not inferior to those enjoyed by men, with equal pay for equal work;

  (ii) a decent living for themselves and their families in accordance with the provisions of the present Covenant;

(b) Safe and healthy working conditions;

(c) Equal opportunity for everyone to be promoted in his employment to an appropriate higher level, subject to no considerations other than those of seniority and competence;

(d) Rest, leisure and reasonable limitation of working hours and periodic holidays with pay, as well as remuneration for public holidays.

Article 8 – The States Parties to the present Covenant undertake to ensure –

(a) The right of everyone to form trade unions and join the trade union of his choice, subject only to the rules of the organisation concerned, for the promotion and protection of his economic and social interest. No restrictions may be placed on the exercise of this right other than those prescribed by law and which are necessary in a democratic society in the interests of national security or public order or for the protection of the rights and freedoms of others;

(b) The right of trade unions to establish national federations or confederations and the right of the latter to form or join international trade union organisations;

(c) The right of trade unions to function freely subject to no limitations other than those prescribed by law and which are necessary in a democratic society in the interests of national security or public order or for the protection of the rights and freedoms of others;

(d) The right to strike, provided that it is exercised in conformity with the laws of the particular country.

This Article shall not prevent the imposition of lawful restrictions on the exercise of these rights by members of the armed forces or other police or of the administration of the State.

Nothing in this Article shall authorise States Parties to the International Labour Organization Convention of 1948, concerning Freedom of Association and Protection of the Right to organise to take legislative measures which would prejudice or apply the law in such a manner as would prejudice, the guarantees provided for in that convention.

Article 9 – The States Parties to the present Covenant recognise the right of everyone to social security, including social insurance.

Article 10 – The States Parties to the present Covenant recognise that:

1. The widest possible protection and assistance should be accorded to the family, which is the natural and fundamental group unit of society, particularly, for its establishment and while it is responsible for the care and education of dependent children. Marriage must be

entered into with the free consent of the intending spouses.

2. Special protection should be accorded to mothers during a reasonable period before and after child birth. During such period working mothers should be accorded paid leave or leave with adequate social security benefits.
3. Special measures of protection and assistance should be taken on behalf of all children and young persons without any discrimination for reasons of parentage or other conditions. Children and young persons should be protected from economic and social exploitation. Their employment in work harmful to their morals or health or dangerous to like or likely to hamper their normal development should be punishable by law. States should also set age limits below which the paid employment of child labour should be prohibited and punishable by law.

Article 11 – The States Parties to the present Covenant recognise the right of everyone to an adequate standard of living for himself and his family including adequate food, clothing and house, and to the continuous improvement of living conditions. The States Parties will take appropriate steps to ensure the realisation of this right, recognising to this effect the essential importance of international co-operation based on free consent.

The States Parties to the present Covenant, recognising the fundamental right of everyone to be free from hunger, shall take, individually and through international co-operation, the measures, including specific programmes, which are needed –

(a) to improve methods of production, conservation and distribution of food by making full use of technical and scientific knowledge by disseminating knowledge of the principles of nutrition and by developing or reforming agrarian systems in such a way as to achieve the most efficient development and utilisation of natural resources;

(b) taking into account the problems of both food-importing and food-exporting countries, to ensure an equitable distribution of world food supplies in relation to need.

Article 12 – The States Parties to the present Covenant recognise the right of everyone to the enjoyment of the highest attainable standard of physical and mental health.

The steps to be taken by the States Parties to the present Covenant to achieve the full realisation of this right shall include those necessary for –

(a) the provision for the reduction of the still birth rate and of infant mortality and for the healthy development of the child;

(b) the improvement of all aspects of environmental and industrial hygiene;

(c) the prevention, treatment and control of epidemic, endemic, occupational and other diseases;

(d) the creation of conditions which would assure to all medical service and medical attention in the event of sickness.

Article 13 – The States Parties to the present Covenant recognise the right of everyone to education. They agree that education shall be directed to the full development of the Human personality and the sense of its dignity, and shall strengthen the respect for human rights and fundamental freedoms. They further agree that education shall enable all persons to participate effectively in a free society, promote understanding, tolerance and friendship among all nations and all racial, ethnic or religious groups, and further the activities of the United Nations for the maintenance of peace.

The States Parties to the present Covenant recognise that, with a view to achieving the full realisation of this right –

(a) Primary education shall be compulsory and available free to all;

(b) Secondary education in its different forms, including technical and vocational secondary education, shall be made generally available and accessible to all by every appropriate means, and in particular by the progressive introduction of free education;

(c) Higher education shall be made equally accessible to all, on the basis of capacity, by every appropriate means, and in particular by the progressive introduction of free education;

(d) Fundamental education shall be encouraged or intensified as far as possible for those persons who have not received or completed the whole period of their primary education;
(e) The development of a system of schools at all levels shall be actively pursued, an adequate fellowship system shall be established, and the material conditions of teaching staff shall be continuously improved.

The States Parties to the present Covenant undertake to have respect for the liberty of parents and when applicable, legal guardians, to choose for their children schools, other than those established by the public authorities, which conform to such minimum educational standards as may be laid down or approved by the State and to ensure the religious and moral education of their children in conformity with their own convictions.

No part of this Article shall be construed so as to interfere with the liberty of individuals and bodies to establish and direct educational institutions, subject always to the observance of the principles set forth in paragraph 1 of this Article and to the requirement that the education given in such institutions shall conform to such minimum standards as may be laid down by the State.

Article 24 – Each State Party to the present Covenant which, at the time of becoming a Party, has not been able to secure in its metropolitan territory or other territories under its jurisdiction compulsory primary education, free of charge, undertakes, within two years, to work out and adopt a detailed plan of action for the progressive implementation, within a reasonable number of years, to be fixed in the plan, of the principle of compulsory education free of charge for all.

Article 15 – The States Parties to the present Covenant recognise the right of everyone:

(a) To take part in cultural life;
(b) To enjoy the benefits of scientific progress and its applications;
(c) To benefit from the protection of the moral and material interests resulting from any scientific, literary or artistic production of which he is the author.

The steps to be taken by the States Parties to the present Covenant to achieve the full realisation of this right shall include those necessary for the conservation, the development and the diffusion of science and culture.

The States Parties to the present Covenant undertake to respect the freedom indispensable for scientific research and creative activity.

The States Parties to the present Covenant recognise the benefits to be derived from the encouragement and development of international contacts and co-operation in the scientific and cultural fields.

Article 23 – The States Parties to the present Covenant agree that international action for the achievement of the rights recognised in the present Covenant includes such methods as the conclusion of conventions, the adoption of recommendations, the furnishing of technical assistance and the holding of regional meetings and technical meetings for the purpose of consultation and study organised in conjunction with the Governments concerned.

Article 25 – Every citizen shall have the right and the opportunity, without any of the distinctions mentioned in Article 2 and without unreasonable restrictions –

(a) To take part in the conduct of public affairs, directly or through freely chosen representatives;

(b) To vote and to be elected at genuine periodic elections which shall be by Universal and equal suffrage and shall be held by secret ballot, guaranteeing the free expression of the will of the electors;

(c) To have access, on general terms of equality, to public service in his country.

Article 28 – To provisions of the present Covenant shall extend *to* all *parts of* federal States without any limitations or exceptions.

AMERICAN CONVENTION ON HUMAN RIGHTS, 1969

Article 1 – The States Parties to the Convention undertake to respect the rights and freedoms recognised herein and to ensure to all persons subject to their jurisdiction the freed and full exercise of those rights and freedoms, without any discrimination for reasons of race, colour, sex, language, religion, political or other opinion, national or social origin, economic status, birth, or any other social condition.

For the purposes of this convention, "person" means every human being.

Article 2 – Where the exercise of any of the rights or freedoms referred to in Article I is not already ensured by legislative or other provisions, the States Parties undertake to adopt, in accordance with their constitutional processes and the provisions of this Convention, such legislative or other measures as may be necessary to give effect to those rights or freedoms.

Article 3 – Every person has the right to recognition as a person before the law.

Article 4 – Every person has the right to have his life respected. This right shall be protected by law, and, in general, from the moment of conception. No one shall be arbitrarily deprived of his life.

In countries that have not abolished the death penalty, it may be imposed only for the most serious crimes and pursuant to final a judgment rendered by a competent Court and in accordance with a law establishing such punishment enacted prior to the commission of the crime. The application of such punishment shall not be extended to crimes to which it does not presently apply.

The death penalty shall not be re-established in States that have abolished it.

In no case shall capital punishment be inflicted for political offences or related common crimes.

Capital punishment shall not be imposed upon persons who, at the time the crime was committed, were under 18 years of age or over 70 years of age; nor shall it be applied to pregnant women.

Every person condemned to death shall have the right to apply for amnesty, pardon, or commutation of sentence, which may be granted in all cases. Capital punishment shall not be imposed while such a petition is pending decision by the competent authority.

Article 5 – Every person has the right to have his physical, mental, and moral integrity respected.

No one shall be subjected to torture or to cruel, inhuman, or degrading punishment or treatment. All persons deprived of their liberty shall be treated with respect for the inherent dignity of the human person.

Punishment shall not be extended to any person other than the criminal.

Accused persons shall, save in exceptional circumstances, be segregated from convicted persons, and shall be subject to separate treatment appropriate to their status as unconvicted persons.

Minors while subject to criminal proceedings shall be separated from adults and brought before specialised tribunals, as speedily as possible, so that they may be treated in accordance with their status as minors.

Punishments consisting of deprivation of liberty shall have as an essential aim the reform and social readaptation of the prisoners.

Article 6 – No one shall be subject to slavery or to involuntary servitude, which are prohibited in all their forms, as are the slave trade and traffic in women.

No one shall be required to perform forced or compulsory labour. This provision shall not be interpreted to mean that in those countries in which the penalty established for certain crimes in deprivation of liberty at forced labour, the carrying out of such a sentence imposed by a competent Court is prohibited. Forced labour shall not adversely affect the dignity or the physical or intellectual capacity of the prisoners.

For the purposes of this Article the following do not constitute forced or compulsory labour, –

(a) work or service normally required of a person imprisoned in execution of a sentence or formal decision passed by the competent judicial authority. Such work or service shall be carried out under the supervision and control of public authorities, and any persons performing such work or service shall not be placed at the disposal of any private party, company, or judicial person;

(b) military service and, in countries in which conscientious objectors are recognised, national service that the law may provide for in lieu of military service;

(c) service exacted in time of danger or calamity that threatens the existence or the well-being of the community; or

(d) work of service that forms part of normal civic obligations.

Article 7 – Every person has the right to personal liberty and security.

No one shall be deprived of his physical liberty except for the reasons and under the conditions established before hand by the constitution of the State Party concerned or by a law established pursuant thereto.

No one shall be subject to arbitrary arrest or imprisonment.

Anyone who is detained shall be informed of the reasons for his detention and shall be promptly notified of the charge or charge against him.

Any person detained shall be brought promptly before a Judge or other officer authorised by law to exercise judicial power and shall be entitled to trial within a reasonable time or to be released without prejudice to the continuation of the proceedings. His release may be subject to guarantees to assure his appearance for trial.

Anyone who is deprived of his liberty shall be entitled to recourse to a competent Court, in order that the Court may decide without delay on the lawfulness of his arrest or detention and order his release if the arrest or detention is unlawful. In States Parties whose laws provide that anyone who believes himself to be threatened with deprivation of his liberty is entitled to recourse to a competent Court in order that it may decide on the lawfulness of such threat, this remedy may not be restricted or abolished. The interested party or another person in his behalf is entitled to seek these remedies.

No one shall be detained for debt. This principle shall not limit the orders of a competent judicial authority issued for non-fulfilment of duties of support.

Article 8 – Every person has the right to a hearing, with the due guarantees and within a reasonable time, by a competent independent, and impartial tribunal, previously established by law, in the substantiation of any accusation of a criminal nature made against him or for the determination of his rights and obligations of a civil, labour, fiscal, or any other nature.

Every person accused of a criminal offence has the right to be sumed innocent so long as his guilt has not been proven according to law. During the proceedings, every person is entitled, with full equality, to the following minimum guarantees,–

(a) the right of the accused to be assisted without charge by a translator or interpreter, if he does not understand or does not speak the language of the tribunal or Court;

(b) prior notification in detail to the accused of the charges against him;

(c) adequate time and means for the preparation of his defence;

(d) the right of the accused to defend himself personally or to be assisted by legal counsel of his own choosing, and to communicate freely and privately with his counsel;

(e) the inalienable right to be assisted by counsel provided by the State, paid or not as the domestic law provides, if the accused does not defend himself personally or engage his own counsel within the time period established by law;

(f) the right of the defence to examine witnesses present in the Court and to obtain the appearance as witness, of experts or other persons who may throw light on the facts;

(g) the right not to be compelled to be a witness against himself or to plead guilty; and

(h) the right to appeal the judgment to a higher Court.

A confession of guilt by the accused shall be valid only if it is made without coercion of any kind.

An accused person acquitted by a non-appealable judgment shall not be subjected to a new trial for the same cause.

Criminal proceedings shall be public, except in so far as may be necessary to protect the, interests of justice.

Article 9 – No one shall be convicted of any act or omission that did not constitute a criminal offence, under the applicable law, at the time it was committed. A the heavier penalty shall not be imposed than the one that was applicable at the time the criminal offence was committed. If subsequent to the commission of the offence the law provides for the imposition of a lighter punishment, the guilty person shall benefit therefrom.

Article 10 – Every person has the right to be compensated in accordance with the law in the event he has been sentenced by a final judgment through a miscarriage of justice.

Article 11 – Everyone has the right to have his honour respected and his dignity recognised.

No one may be the object of arbitrary or abusive interference with his private life, his family, his home.

Everyone has the right to the protection of the law against such interference or attacks.

Article 12 – Everyone has the right to freedom of conscience and of religion. This includes freedom to maintain or to change one's religion or beliefs, and freedom to profess or disseminate one's religion or beliefs either individually or together with others, in public or in private.

No one shall be subject to restrictions that might impair his freedom to maintain or to change his religion or beliefs.

Freedom to manifest one's religion and beliefs may be subject only to the limitations prescribed by law that are necessary to protect public safety, order, health or morals, or the rights or freedoms of others.

Parents or guardians, as the case may be, have the right to provide for the religious and moral education of their children or wards that is in accord with their own convictions.

Article 13 – Everyone shall have the right to freedom of thought and expressions. This right shall include freedom to seek, receive, and impart information and ideas of all kinds, regardless of frontiers, either orally, in writing, in print, in the form of art, or through any other medium of one's choice.

The exercise of the right provided for in the foregoing paragraph shall not be subject to prior censorship but shall be subject to subsequent imposition of liability, which shall be expressly established by law to the extent necessary in order to ensure,–

(a) respect for the rights or reputations of others; or

(b) the protection of national security, public order, or public health or morals.

The right of expression may not be restricted by indirect methods or means, such as the abuse of Government or private controls over newsprint, radio broadcasting frequencies, or equipment used in the dissemination of information, or by any other means tending to impede the communication and circulation of ideas and opinions.

Notwithstanding the provisions of paragraph 2 above, public entertainments may be subject by law to prior censorship for the sole purpose of regulating access to them for the moral protection of childhood and adolescence.

Any propaganda for war and any advocacy of national, racial, or religious hatred that constitute incitements to lawless violence or to any other similar illegal action against any person or group of persons on any grounds including those of race, colour, religion, language, or national origin shall be considered as offences punishable by law.

Article 14 – Anyone injured by inaccurate or offensive statements of ideas disseminated to the public in general by a legally regulated medium of communication has the right to reply or make a correction using the same communications outlet, under such conditions as the law may establish.

The correction or reply shall not in any case remit other legal liabilities that may have been incurred.

For the effective protection of honour and reputation, every publisher, and every newspaper, motion picture, radio and television company shall have a person responsible, who is not protected by immunities or special privileges.

Article 15 – The right of peaceful assembly, without arms, is recognised. No restrictions may be placed on the exercise of this right other than those imposed in conformity with the law and necessary in a democratic society in the'interest of national security, public safety or public order, or to protect public health or morals or the rights or freedoms of others.

Article 16 – Everyone has the right to associate freely for ideological, religious, political, economic, labour, social, cultural sports, or other purposes.

The exercise of'this right shall be subject only to such restrictions established by law as may be necessary in a democratic society, in the interest of national security, public safety or public order, or to protect public health or morals or the rights and freedoms of others.

The provisions of this Article do not bar the imposition of legal restrictions, including even deprivation of the exercise of the right of association, on members of the armed forces, ana the police.

Article 17 – The family is the natural and fundamental group unit of society and is entitled to protection by society and the State.

The right of men and women of marriageable age to marry and to raise a family shall be recognised, if they meet the conditions required by domestic laws, in so far as such conditions do not affect the principle of non-discrimination established in this Convention.

No marriage shall be entered into without the free and full consent of the intending spouses.

The States Parties shall take appropriate steps to ensure the equality of rights and the adequate balancing of responsibilities of the spouses as to marriage, and in the event of its dissolution. In case of dissolution, provision shall be made for the necessary protection of any children solely on the basis of their own best interests.

The law shall recognise equal rights for children born out of wedlock and those born in wedlock.

Article 18 – Every person has the right to a given name and to the surnames of his parents or that of one of them. The law shall regulate the manner in which this right shall be ensured for all, by the use of assumed names if necessary.

Article 19 – Every minor child has the right to the measures of protection required by his condition as a minor on the part of his family, society, and the State.

Article 20 – Every person has the right to a nationality.

Every person has the right to the nationality of the State in whose territory he was born if he does not have the right to any other nationality.

No one shall be arbitrarily deprived of his nationality or of the right to change it.

Article 21 – Everyone has the right to the use and enjoyment of his property. The law may subordinate such use and enjoyment to the interest of society.

No one shall be deprived of his property except upon payment of just compensation, for reasons of public utility or social interest, and in the cases and according to the forms established by law.

Usury and any other form of exploitation of man shall be prohibited by law.

Article 22 – Every person lawfully in the territory of a State Party has the right to move about it and to reside in it subject to the provisions of the law.

Every person has the right to leave any country freely, including his own.

The exercise of the foregoing rights may be restricted only pursuant to a law to extent necessary in a democratic society to prevent crime or to protect national security public safety, public order, public morals, public health or the rights or freedoms of others.

The exercise of the rights recognised in paragraph 1 may also be restricted by law in designated zones for reasons of public interest.

No one can be expelled from the territory of a State of which he is a national or be deprived of the right to enter it.

An alien lawfully in the territory of a State Party to this Convention may be expelled from it only pursuant to a decision reached in accordance with law.

Every person has the right to seek and be granted asylum in a foreign territory, in accordance with the legislation of the State and international conventions, in the event he is being pursued for political offences or related common crimes.

In no case may an alien be deported or returned to a country regardless of whether or not it is his country of origin, if in that country his right to life or personal freedom is in danger of being violated because of his race, nationality, religion, social status, or political opinions.

The collective expulsion of aliens is prohibited.

Article 23 – Every citizen shall enjoy the following rights and opportunities, –

(a) to take part in the conduct of public affairs, directly or through freely chosen representatives;

(b) to vote and to be elected in genuine periodic elections, which shall be by universal and equal suffrage and by secret ballot that guarantees the free expression of the will of the voters; and

(c) to have access, under general conditions of equality, to the public service of his country.

The law may regulate the exercise of the rights and opportunities referred to in the preceding paragraph only on the basis of age, nationality, residence, language, education, civil and mental capacity, *or* sentencing by a competent Court in criminal proceedings.

Article 24 – All persons are equal before the law. Consequently, they are entitled without discrimination, to equal protection of the law.

Article 25 – Everyone has the right to simple and prompt recourse, or any other effective recourse, to a competent Court or tribunal for protection against acts that violate his fundamental rights recognised by the Constitution or laws of the State concerned or by this Convention, even though such violation may have been committed by persons acting in the course of their official duties.

The States Parties undertake,–

(a) to ensure that any person claiming such remedy shall have his rights determined by the competent authority provided for by the legal system of the State;

(b) to develop the possibilities of judicial remedy; and

(c) to ensure that the competent authorities shall enforce such remedies when granted.

Article 26 – The States Parties undertake to adopt measures, both internally and through international co-operation, especially those of an economic and technical nature, with a view to achieving progressively, by legislation or other appropriate means, the full realisation of the rights implicit in the economic, social, educational, scientific, and cultural standards set forth in the Charter of the Organisation of American States as amended by the Protocol of Buenos Aires.

Article 27 – In time of war, public danger, or other emergency that threatens the independence or security of a State Party, it may take measures, derogating from its obligations under the present Convention to the extent and for the period of time strictly required by the exigencies of the situation, provided that such measures are not inconsistent with its other obligations under international law and do not involve discrimination on the ground of race, colour, sex, language, religion or social origin.

The foregoing provision does not authorise any suspension of the following Articles: Article 3 (Right to Judicial Personality), Article 4 (Right to Life), Article 5 (Right to Human Treatment), Article 6 (Freedom from Slavery), Article 9 (Freedom from *Ex Post Facto* Laws), Article 12 (Freedom of Conscience and Religion), Article 17 (Rights *of* the Family), Article 18 (Right to a Name), Article 19 (Rights of the Child), Article 20 (Right to Nationality), and Article 23 (Right to Participate in Government), or of the judicial guarantees essential for the protection of such rights.

Any State Party availing itself of the right of suspension shall immediately inform the other States Parties, through the Secretary General of the Organization of American States, of the provisions the application of which it has suspended, the reasons that gave rise to the suspension, and the date set for the termination of such suspension.

Article 28 – Where a State Party is constituted as a federal State, the national Government of such State Party shall implement all the provisions of the Convention over whose subject-matter it exercises legislative and judicial jurisdiction.

With respect to the provisions over whose subject-matter the constituent units of the federal State have jurisdiction, the national Government shall immediately take suitable measures/in *accordance* with its Constitution and its laws, to the end that the competent authorities of the constituent units may adopt appropriate provisions for the fulfillment of this Convention.

Whenever two or more States Parties agree to form a federation or other type of association they shall take care that the resulting federal or other compact contains the provisions necessary for continuing and rendering effective the standards of this Convention in the new State that is organised.

Article 29 – No provision of this Convention shall be interpreted as, –

(a) permitting any State Party, group, or persons to suppress the enjoyment or exercise of right and freedoms recognised in this Convention or restrict them to a greater extent than is provided for herein;

(b) restricting the enjoyment or exercise of any right or freedom recognised by virtue of the laws of any State Party or by virtue of another Convention to which one of the said States is a party;

(c) precluding other rights or guarantees that are inherent in the human personality or derived from representative democracy as a form of Government; or

(d) excluding or limiting the effect that the American Declaration of the Rights and Duties of Man and other international acts of the same nature may have.

Article 30 – The restrictions that, pursuant to this Convention, may be placed on the enjoyment or exercise of the rights or freedoms recognised herein may not be applied except in accordance with the laws enacted for reasons of general interest and in accordance with the purpose for which such restrictions have been established.

Article 31 – Other rights and freedoms recognised in accordance with the procedures established in Articles *76* and *77* may be included in the system of protection of this Convention.

Article 32 – Every person has responsibilities to his family, his community and mankind.

The rights of each person are limited by the rights of others,.by the security of all, and by the just demands of the general welfare, in a democratic society.

AFRICAN CHARTER OF HUMAN RIGHTS ANA PEOPLES RIGNTS 1981

Article 1 – The Member States of the Organization of African Unity parties to the present Charter shall recognise the right, duties and freedoms enshrined in this Charier and shall undertake to adopt legislative or other measures to give effect to them.

Article 2 – Every individual shall be entitled to the enjoyment of the rights and freedoms recognised and guaranteed in the present Charter without distinction of any kind such as race, ethnic group, colour, sex, language, religion, political or any other opinion, national and social origin, fortune, birth or other status.

Article 3 – Every individual shall be equal before the law.

Every individual shall be entitled to equal protection of the law.

Article 4 – Human beings are inviolable. Every human being shall be enfitled-to respect for his life and the integrity of his person. No one may be arbitrarily deprived of this right.

Article 5 – Every individual shall have the right to the respect of the dignity inherent in a human being and to the recognition of his legal status. All forms of exploitation and degradation of man particularly slavery, slave trade, torture, cruel, inhuman or degrading punishment and treatment shall be prohibited.

Article 6 – Every individual shall have the right to liberty and to the security of his person. No one may be deprived of his freedom except for reasons and conditions previously laid down by law. In particular, no one may be arbitrarily arrested or detained.

Article 7 – Every individual shall have the right to have his cause heard. This comprises,–

(a) The right to an appeal to competent national organs against acts violating his fundamental rights as recognised and guaranteed by conventions, laws, regulations and customs in force;

(b) the right to be presumed innocent until proved guilty by a competent Court or tribunal;

(c) the right to defence, including the right to be defended by counsel of his choice;

(d) the right to be tried within a reasonable time by an impartial Court or tribunal.

No one may be condemned for an act or omission which did not constitute a legally punishable offence at the time it was committed. No penalty may be inflicted for an offence for which no provision was made at the time it was committed. Punishment is personal and can be imposed only on the offender.

Article 8 – Freedom of conscience, the profession and free practice of religion shall be guaranteed. No one may, subject to law and order, be submitted to measures restricting the exercise of these freedoms.

Article 9 – Every individual shall have the right to receive information.

Every individual shall have the right to express and disseminate his opinions within the law.

Article 10 – Every individual shall have the right to free association provided that he abides by the law.

Subject to the obligation of solidarity provided for in Article 29 no one may be compelled to join an association.

Article 11 – Every individual shall have the right to assemble freely with others. The exercise of this right shall be subject only to necessary restrictions provided for by law in particular those enacted in the interest of national security, the safety, health, ethics and rights and freedoms of others.

Article 12 – Every individual shall have the right to freedom of movement and residence within the borders of a State provided he abides by the law.

Every individual shall have the right to leave any country including his own, and to return to his country. This right may only be subject to restrictions, provided for by law for the protection of national security, law and order, public health or morality.

Every individual shall have the right, when prosecuted, to seek and obtain asylum in other countries in accordance with the laws of those countries and international conventions.

A non-national legally admitted in a territory of a State Party to the present Charter, may only be expelled from it by virtue of a decision taken in accordance with law.

The mass expulsion of non-nationals shall be prohibited. Mass expulsion shall be that which is aimed at national, racial, ethnic or religious groups.

Article 13 – Every citizen shall have the right to freely participate in the Government of his country, either directly or through freely chosen representatives in accordance with the provisions of the law.

Every citizen shall have the right of equal access to the public service of his country.

Every individual shall have the right of access to public property and services in strict equality of all persons before the law.

Article 14 – The right to property shall be guaranteed. It may only be encroached upon in the interest of public need or in the general interest of the community and in accordance with the provisions of appropriate laws.

Article 15 – Every individual shall have the right to work under equitable and satisfactory conditions and shall receive equal pay for equal work.

Article 16 – Every individual shall have the right to enjoy the best attainable state of physical and mental health.

State Parties to the present Charter shall take the necessary measures to protect the health of their people and to ensure that they receive medical attention when they are sick.

Article 17 – 1. Every individual shall have the right to education.

Every individual may freely, take part in the cultural life of his community.

The promotion and protection of morals and traditional values recognised by the community shall be the duty of the State.

Article 28 – The family shall be the natural unit and basis of society. It shall be protected by the State.

The State shall have the duty to assist the family which is the custodian of morals and traditional values recognised by the community.

The State shall ensure the elimination of every discrimination against women and also ensure the protection of the rights of the woman and the child as stipulated in international declarations and conventions.

The aged and the disabled shall also have the right to special measures of protection in keeping with their physical or moral needs.

Article 19 – All peoples shall be equal; they shall enjoy the same respect and shall have the same rights. Nothing shall justify the domination of a people by another.

Article 20 – All people shall have the right to existence. They shall have the unquestionable and inalienable right to self-determination. They shall freely determine their political status and shall pursue their economic and social development according to the policy they have freely chosen.

Colonised or oppressed peoples shall have the right to free themselves from the bonds of domination by resorting to any means recognised by the international community.

All peoples shall have the right to the assistance of the States Parties to the present Charter in their liberation struggle against foreign domination, be it political, economic or cultural.

Article 22 – All peoples shall freely dispose of their wealth and natural resources. This right shall be exercised in the exclusive interest of the people. In no case shall a pe6ple be deprived of it.

In the case of spoliation the dispossessed people shall have the right to the lawful recovery of its property as well as an adequate compensation.

The free disposal of wealth and natural resources shall be exercised without prejudice to the obligation of promoting international economic co-operation based on mutual respect, equitable exchange and the principles of international law.

States Parties to the present Charter shall individually and collectively exercise the right to free disposal of their wealth and natural resources with a view to strengthening African unity and solidarity.

States Parties to the present Charter shall undertake to eliminate all forms of foreign economic exploitation particularly that practised by international monopolies so as to enable their peoples to fully benefit from the advantages derived from their natural resources.

Article 22 – All peoples shall have the right to their economic, social and cultural development with due regard to their freedom and identity and in the equal enjoyment of the common heritage of mankind.

States shall have the duty, individually or collectively, to erisure the exercise of the right to development.

Article 23 – All peoples shall have the right to national and international peace and security. The principles of solidarity and friendly relations implicitly affirmed by the Charter of the United Nations and reaffirmed by that of the Organization of African Unity shall govern relations between States.

For the purpose of strengthening peace, solidarity and friendly relations, States Parties to the present Charter shall ensure that, –

(a) any individual enjoying the right of asylum under Article 12 of the present Charter shall not engage in subversive activities against his country of origin or any other State Party to the present Charter;

(b) their territories shall not be used as bases for subversive or terrorist activities against the people of any other State Party to the present Charter.

Article 24 – All peoples have the right to a general satisfactory environment favourable to their development.

Article 25 – States Parties to the present Charter shall have the duty to promote and ensure through teaching, education and publication, the respect of the rights and freedoms contained in the present Charter and to see to it that these freedoms and rights as well as corresponding obligations and duties are understood.

Article 26 – States Parties to the present Charter shall have the duty to guarantee the independence of the Courts and shall allow the establishment and improvement of appropriate national institutions entrusted with the promotion and protection of the right and freedoms guaranteed by the present Charter.

CHAPTER II

DUTIES

Article 27 – Every individual shall have duties towards his family and society, the State and other legally recognised communities and the international community.

The rights and freedoms of each individual shall be exercised with due regard to the rights of others, collective security, morality and common interest.

Article 28 – Every individual shall have the duty to respect and consider liis fellow beings without discrimination, and to maintain relations aimed-at promoting, safeguarding and reinforcing mutual respect and tolerance.

Article 29 – The individual shall also have the duty, –

1. To preserve the harmonious development of the family and to work of the cohesion and respect of the family, to respect his parents at all times, to maintain them in case of need;
2. To serve his national community by placing his physical and intellectual abilities at its service;
3. Not to compromise the security of the State whose national or resident he is;
4. To preserve and strengthen social and national solidarity, particularly when the later is threatened;
5. To preserve and strengthen the national independence and the territorial integrity of his country and to contribute to its defence in accordance with the law;
6. To work to the best of his abilities and competence, and to pay taxes imposed by law in the interest of the society;
7. To preserve and strengthen positive African cultural values in his relations with other members of the society, in the spirit of tolerance, dialogue and consultation and, in general, to contribute to the promotion of the moral well being of society;
8. To contribute to the best of his abilities, at all levels, to the promotion and achievement of African unity.

Article 30 – An African Commission on Human and Peoples' Rights, hereinafter called "the Commission", shall be established within the Organisation of African Unity to promote human and peoples' rights and ensure their protection in Africa.

*** *** *** *** ***

Article 56 – Communication relating to human and peoples' rights referred to in Article 55 received by the Commission, shall be considered if they, –

1. indicate their authors even if the latter request anonymity,
2. are compatible with the Charter of the Organisation of African Unity or with the present Charter,
3. are not written in disparaging or insulting language directed against the State concerned and its institutions or to the Organisation of African Unity,
4. are not based exclusively on news disseminated through the mass media,
5. are sent after exhausting local remedies, if any, unless it is obvious that this procedure is unduly prolonged,
6. are submitted within a reasonable period from the time local remedies are exhausted or from the date the Commission is seized with the matter, and
7. do not deal with cases which have been settled by the State involved in accordance with the principles of the Charter of the United Nations or the Charter of the Organisation of African Unity or the provisions of the present Charter.

Article 60 – The commission shall draw inspiration from international law on human and peoples' rights, particularly from the provisions of various African Instruments on human and peoples rights, the Charter of the United Nations, the Charter of the Organisations of African Unity, the Universal Declaration of Human Rights, other instruments adopted by the United Nations and by African countries in the field of human and peoples' rights as well as from the provisions of various instruments adopted within the Specialised Agencies of the United Nations of which the parties to the present Charter are members.

Article 61 – The Commission shall also take into consideration, as subsidiary measures to determine the principles of law, other general or special international conventions, laying down rules expressly recognised by member States of the Organisation of African Unity, African practices consistent with international norms on human and peoples' rights, customs generally accepted as law, general principles of law recognised by African States as well as legal precedents and doctrine.

THE PROTECTION OF HUMAN RIGHTS ACT, 1993

[As amended by the Protection of Human Rights (Amaendment) Act, 2005 – No. 43 of 2006]

THE PROTECTION OF HUMAN RIGHTS ACT, 1993*

No. 10 of 1994

(8th January, 1994)

An Act to provide for the constitution of a National Human Rights Commission, State Human Rights Commission in States and Human Rights Courts for better protection of human rights and for matters connected therewith or incidental thereto.

Be it enacted by Parliament in the forty-fourth year of the Republic of India as follows:

* *As amended by the Protection of Human Rights (Amendment) Act, 2006-No. 43 of 2006.*

CONTENTS

CHAPTER VIII

MISCELLANEOUS

36. Matters not subject to jurisdiction of the Commission

37. Constitution of special investigation teams

38. Protection of action taken in good faith

39. Members and officers to be public servants

40. Power of Central Government to make rules

40(a). Power to make rules retrospectively 40(B). Power of Commission to make Regulations

41. Power of State Government to make rules

42. Power to remove difficulties

43. Repeal and Savings

CHAPTER I

PRELIMINARY

1. *Short title, extent and commencement*

(1) This Act may be called the Protection of Human Rights Act, 1993.*

(2) It extends to the whole of India.

Provided that it shall apply to the State of Jammu and Kashmir only in so far as it pertains to the matters relatable to any of the entries enumerated in List I or List HI in the Seventh Schedule to the Constitution as applicable to that State.

(3) It shall be deemed to have come into force on the 28th day of September, 1993.

2. *Definitions*

(1) In this Act, unless the context otherwise requires-

(a) "armed forces" means the naval, military and air forces and includes any other armed forces of the Union;

(b) "Chairperson" means the Chairperson of the Commission or of the State Commission, as the case may be;

(c) "Commission" means the National Human Rights Commission under section 3;

(d) "human rights" means the rights relating to life, liberty, equality and dignity of the individual guaranteed by the Constitution or embodied in the International Covenants and enforceable by courts in India.

(e) "Human Rights Court" means the Human Rights Court specified under section 30;

(f) "International Covenants" means the International Covenant on Civil and Political Rights and the International Covenant on Economic, Social and Cultural rights adopted by the General Assembly of the United Nations on the 16th December, 1966 [and such other Covenant or Convention adopted by the General

Assembly of the United Nations as the Central Government may, by notification, specify"][1];

(g) "Member" means a Member of the Commission or of the State Commission, as the case may be[2];

(h) "National Commission for Minorities" means the National Commission for Minorities constituted under section 3 of the National Commission for Minorities Act, 1992;

(i) "National Commission for the Scheduled Castes" means the National Commission for the Scheduled Castes referred to in Article 338 of the Constitution1; 43 of 2006

(ia) "National Commission for the Scheduled Tribes" means the National Commission for the Scheduled Tribes referred to in Article 338A of the Constitution; 43 of 2006

(j) "National Commission for Women" means the National Commission for Women constituted under section 3 of the National Commission for Women Act, 1990; 20 of 1990

(k) "Notification" means a notification published in the official Gazette;

(l) "Prescribed" means prescribed by rules made under this Act;

(m) "Public servant" shall have the meaning assigned to it in section 21 of the Indian Penal Code; 45 of 1860;

(n) "State Commission" means a State Human Rights Commission constituted under section 21.

(2) Any reference in this Act to a law, which is not in force in the State of Jammu and Kashmir, shall, in relation to that State, be construed as a reference to a corresponding law, if any, in force in that State.

Chapter II

THE NATIONAL HUMAN RIGHTS COMMISSION

3. *Constitution of a National Human Rights Commission*

(1) The Central Government shall constitute a body to be known as the National Human Rights Commission to exercise the powers conferred upon, and to perform the functions assigned to it, under this Act.

(2) The Commission shall consist of:

(a) a Chairperson who has been a Chief Justice of the Supreme Court;

(b) one Member who is or has been, a Judge of the Supreme Court;

(c) one Member who is, or has been, the Chief Justice of a High Court;

(d) two Members to be appointed from amongst persons having knowledge of, or practical experience in, matters relating to human rights.

(3) The Chairperson of the National Commission for Minorities, [3][the National Commission for the Scheduled Castes, the National Commission for the Scheduled Tribes] and the National Commission for Women shall be deemed to be Members of the Commission for the discharge of functions specified in clauses (b) to (j) of section 12.

(4) There shall be a Secretary-General who shall be the Chief Executive Officer of the Commission and shall exercise such powers and discharge such functions of the Commission[4] [except judicial functions and the power to make regulations under section 40 B], as may be delegated to him by the Commission or the Chairperson as the case may be.

(5) The headquarters of the Commission shall be at Delhi and the Commission may, with the previous approval of the Central Government, establish offices at other places in India.

4. *Appointment of Chairperson and other Members*

(1) The Chairperson and [the Members][5] shall be appointed by the President by warrant under his hand and seal;

Provided that every appointment under this sub-section shall be made after obtaining the recommendations of a Committee consisting of-

(a) The Prime Minister – Chairperson

(b) Speaker of the House of the People – Member

(c) Minister in-charge of the Ministry of Home Affairs in the Government of India – Member

(d) Leader of the Opposition in the House of the People – Member

(e) Leader of the Opposition in the Council of States – Member

(f) Deputy Chairman of the Council of States – Member

Provided further that no sitting Judge of the Supreme Court or sitting Chief Justice of a High Court shall be appointed except after consultation with the Chief Justice of India.

(2) No appointment of a Chairperson or a Member shall be invalid merely by reason of any [vacancy of any member in the Committee referred to in the first proviso to sub-section (1)][6].

5. *Resignation and removal of Chairperson and Members*[7]

(1) The Chairperson or any Member may, by notice in writing under his hand addressed to the President of India, resign his office.

(2) Subject to the provisions of sub-section (3), the Chairperson or any Member shall only be removed from his office by order of the President of India on the ground of proved misbehaviour or incapacity after the Supreme Court, on reference being made to it by the President, has, on inquiry held in accordance with the procedure prescribed in that behalf by the Supreme Court, reported that the Chairperson or the Member, as the case may be, ought on any such ground to be removed.

(3) Notwithstanding anything in sub-section (2), the President may, by order, remove from office the Chairperson or any

Member if the Chairperson or such Member, as the case may be-

(a) is adjudged an insolvent; or

(b) engages during his term of office in any paid employment outside the duties of his office; or

(c) is unfit to continue in office by reason of infirmity of mind or body; or

(d) is of unsound mind and stands so declared by a competent court; or

(e) is convicted and sentenced to imprisonment for an offence which in the opinion of the President involves moral turpitude.

6. Term of office of Chairperson and Members[8]

(1) A person appointed as Chairperson shall hold office for a term of five years from the date on which he enters upon his office or until he attains the age of seventy years, whichever is earlier.

(2) A person appointed as a Member shall hold office for a term of five years from the date on which he enters upon his office and shall be eligible for re-appointment for another term of five years.

Provided that no Member shall hold office after he has attained the age of seventy years.

(3) On ceasing to hold office, a Chairperson or a Member shall be ineligible for further employment under the Government of India or under the Government of any State.

7. Member to act as Chairperson or to discharge his functions in certain circumstances

(1) In the event of the occurrence of any vacancy in the office of the Chairperson by reason of his death, resignation or otherwise, the

President may, by notification, authorise one of the Members to act as the Chairperson until the appointment of a new Chairperson to fill such vacancy.

(2) When the Chairperson is unable to discharge his functions owing to absence on leave or otherwise, such one of the

Members as the President may, by notification, authorise in this behalf, shall discharge the functions of the Chairperson until the date on which the Chairperson resumes his duties.

8. Terms and conditions of service of Chairperson and Members

The salaries and allowances payable to, and other terms and conditions of service of, the[9] [Chairperson and] Members shall be such as may be prescribed.

Provided that neither the salary and allowances nor the other terms and conditions of service of[10] [the Chairperson or] a Member shall be varied to his disadvantage after his appointment.]

9. Vacancies, etc., not to invalidate the proceedings of the Commission

No act or proceedings of the Commission shall be questioned or shall be invalidated merely on the ground of existence of any vacancy or defect in the constitution of the Commission.

20. Procedure to be regulated by the Commission

(1) The Commission shall meet at such time and place as the Chairperson may think fit.

(2) Subject to the provisions of this Act and the rules made thereunder, the Commission shall have the power to lay down by regulations its own procedure[11].

(3) All orders and decisions of the Commission shall be authenticated by the Secretary-General or any other officer of the Commission duly authorised by the Chairperson in this behalf.

11. Officers and other staff of the Commission

(1) The Central Government shall make available to the Commission:

  (a) an officer of the rank of the Secretary to the Government of India who shall be the Secretary-General of the Commission; and

  (b) such police and investigative staff under an officer not below the rank of a Director General of Police and such other officers and staff as may be necessary for the efficient performance of the functions of the Commission.

(2) Subject to such rules as may be made by the Central Government in this behalf, the Commission may appoint such other administrative, technical and scientific staff as it may consider necessary.

(3) The salaries, allowances and conditions of service of the officers and other staff appointed under sub-section (2) shall be such as may be prescribed.

Chapter III

FUNCTIONS AND POWERS OF THE COMMISSION

12. *Functions of the Commission*

The Commission shall perform all or any of the following functions, namely:

(a) inquire, suo motu or on a petition presented to it by a victim or any person on his behalf [or on a direction or order of any court][12], into complaint of

 (i) violation of human rights or abetment thereof; or

 (ii) negligence in the prevention of such violation, by a public servant;

(b) intervene in any proceeding involving any allegation of violation of human rights pending before a court with the approval of such court;

(c) [13]visit, notwithstanding anything contained in any other law for the time being in force, any jail or other institution under the control of the State Government, where persons are detained or lodged for purposes of treatment, reformation or protection, for the study of the living conditions of the inmates thereof and make recommendations thereon to the Government;

(d) review the safeguards provided by or under the Constitution or any law for the time being in force for the protection of human rights and recommend measures for their effective implementation;

(e) review the factors, including acts of terrorism that inhibit the enjoyment of human rights and recommend appropriate remedial measures;

(f) study treaties and other international instruments on human rights and make recommendations for their effective implementation;

(g) undertake and promote research in the field of human rights;

(h) spread human rights literacy among various sections of society and promote awareness of the safeguards available for the protection of these rights through publications, the media, seminars and other available means;

(i) encourage the efforts of non-governmental organisations and institutions working in the field of human rights;

(j) such other functions as it may consider necessary for the protection of human rights.

13. Powers relating to inquiries

(1) The Commission shall, while inquiring into complaints under this Act, have all the powers of a civil court trying a suit under the Code of Civil Procedure, 1908, and in particular in respect of the following matters, namely:

(a) summoning and enforcing the attendance of witnesses and examining them on oath;

(b) discovery and production of any document;

(c) receiving evidence on affidavits;

(d) requisitioning any public record or copy thereof from any court or office;

(e) issuing commissions for the examination of witnesses or documents;

(f) any other matter which may be prescribed.

(2) The Commission shall have power to require any person, subject to any privilege which may be claimed by that person under any law for the time being in force, to furnish information on such points or matters as, in the opinion of the Commission, may be useful for, or relevant to, the subject matter of the inquiry and any person so required shall be deemed to be legally bound to furnish such information within the meaning of section 176 and section 177 of the Indian Penal Code.

(3) The Commission or any other officer, not below the rank of a Gazetted Officer, specially authorised in this behalf by the Commission may enter any building or place where the Commission has reason to believe that any document relating

to the subject matter of the inquiry may be found, and may seize any such document or take extracts or copies therefrom subject to the provisions of section 100 of the Code of Criminal Procedure, 1973, in so far as it may be applicable.

(4) The Commission shall be deemed to be a civil court and when any offence as is described in section 175, section 178, section 179, section 180 or section 228 of the Indian Penal Code is committed in the view or presence of the Commission, the Commission may, after recording the facts constituting the offence and the statement of the accused as provided for in the Code of Criminal Procedure, 1973, forward the case to a Magistrate having jurisdiction to try the same and the Magistrate to whom any such case is forwarded shall proceed to hear the complaint against the accused as if the case has been forwarded to him under section 346 of the Code of Criminal Procedure, 1973.

(5) Every proceeding before the Commission shall be deemed to be a judicial proceeding within the meaning of sections 193 and 228, and for the purposes of section 196, of the Indian Penal Code, and the Commission shall be deemed to be a civil court for all the purposes of section 195 and Chapter XXVI of the Code of Criminal Procedure, 1973.

(6) [14] Where the Commission considers it necessary or expedient so to do, it may, by order, transfer any complaint filed or pending before it to the State Commission of the State from which the complaint arises, for disposal in accordance with the provisions of this Act;

Provided that no such complaint shall be transferred unless the same is one respecting which the State Commission has jurisdiction to entertain the same.

(7) [14] Every complaint transferred under sub-section{6) shall be dealt with and disposed of by the State Commission as if it were a complaint initially filed before it.

14. Investigation

(1) The Commission may, for the purpose of conducting any investigation pertaining to the inquiry, utilise the services of any officer or investigation agency of the Central Government

or any State Government with the concurrence of the Central Government or the State Government, as the case may be.

(2) For the purpose of investigating into any matter pertaining to the inquiry, any officer or agency whose services are utilised under subsection (1) may, subject to the direction and control of the Commission:

(a) summon and enforce the attendance of any person and examine him;

(b) require the discovery and production of any document; and

(c) requisition any public record or copy thereof from any office.

(3) The provisions of section 15 shall apply in relation to any statement made by a person before any officer or agency whose services are utilised under sub-section (1) as they apply in relation to any statement made by a person in the course of giving evidence before the Commission.

(4) The officer or agency whose services are utilised under subsection (1) shall investigate into any matter pertaining to the inquiry and submit a report thereon to the Commission within such period as may be specified by the Commission in this behalf.

(5) The Commission shall satisfy itself about the correctness of the facts stated and the conclusion, if any, arrived at in the report submitted to it under sub-section (4) and for this purpose the Commission may make such inquiry (including the examination of the person or persons who conducted or assisted in the investigation) as it thinks fit.

15. Statement made by persons to the Commission

No statement made by a person in the course of giving evidence before the Commission shall subject him to, or be used against him in, any civil or criminal proceeding except a prosecution for giving false evidence by such statement:

Provided that the statement:

(a) is made in reply to the question which he is required by the Commission to answer; or

(b) is relevant to the subject matter of the inquiry.

16. Persons likely to be prejudicially affected to be heard

If, at any stage of the inquiry, the Commission:-

(a) considers it necessary to inquire into the conduct of any person; or

(b) is of the opinion that the reputation of any person is likely to be prejudicially affected by the inquiry;

it shall give to that person a reasonable opportunity of being heard in the inquiry and to produce evidence in his defence:

Provided that nothing in this section shall apply where the credit of a witness is being impeached.

CHAPTER IV

PROCEDURE

17. Inquiry into complaints

The Commission while inquiring into the complaints of violations of human rights may:

(i) call for information or report from the Central Government or any State Government or any other authority or organisation subordinate thereto within such time as may be specified by it-

Provided that-

(a) if the information or report is not received within the time stipulated by the Commission, it may proceed to inquire into the complaint on its own;

(b) if on receipt of information or report, the Commission is satisfied either that no further inquiry is required or that the required action has been initiated or taken by the concerned Government or authority, it may not proceed with the complaint and inform the complainant accordingly;

(ii) without prejudice to anything contained in clause (i), if it considers necessary, having regard to the nature of the complaint, initiate an inquiry.

18. Steps during and after inquiry[16]

[The Commission may take any of the following steps during or upon the completion of an inquiry held under this Act, namely:-

(a) where the inquiry discloses the commission of violation of human rights or negligence in the prevention of violation of human rights or abetment thereof by a public servant, it may recommend to the concerned Government or authority-

(i) to make payment of compensation or damages to the complainant or to the victim or the members of his family as the Commission may consider necessary;

(ii) to initiate proceedings for prosecution or such other suitable action as the Commission may deem fit against the concerned person or persons;

(iii) to take such further action as it may think fit;

(b) approach the Supreme Court or the High Court concerned for such directions, orders or writs as that Court may deem necessary;

(c) recommend to the concerned Government or authority at any stage of the inquiry for the grant of such immediate interim relief to the victim or the members of his family as the Commission may consider necessary;

(d) subject to the provisions of clause (e), provide a copy of the inquiry report to the petitioner or his representative;

(e) the Commission shall send a copy of its inquiry report together with its recommendations to the concerned Government or authority and the concerned Government or authority shall, within a period of one month, or such further time as the Commission may allow, forward its comments on the report, including the action taken or proposed to be taken thereon, to the Commission;

(f) the Commission shall publish its inquiry report together with the comments of the concerned Government or authority, if any, and the action taken or proposed to be taken by the concerned Government or authority on the recommendations of the Commission.][17]

19. Procedure with respect to armed forces

(1) Notwithstanding anything contained in this Act, while dealing with complaints of violation of human rights by members of the armed forces, the Commission shall adopt the following procedure, namely:

(a) it may, either on its own motion or on receipt of a petition, seek a report from the Central Government;

(b) after the receipt of the report, it may, either not proceed with the complaint or, as the case may be, make its recommendations to that Government.

(2) The Central Government shall inform the Commission of the action taken on the recommendations within three months or such further time as the Commission may allow.

(3) The Commission shall publish its report together with its recommendations made to the Central Government and the action taken by that Government on such recommendations.

(4) The Commission shall provide a copy of the report published under sub-section (3) to the petitioner or his representative.

20. Annual and special reports of the Commission

(1) The Commission shall submit an annual report to the Central Government and to the State Government concerned and may at any time submit special reports on any matter which, in its opinion, is of such urgency or importance that it should not be deferred till submission of the annual report.

(2) The Central Government and the State Government, as the case may be, shall cause the annual and special reports of the Commission to be laid before each House of Parliament or the State Legislature respectively, as the case may be, along with a memorandum of action taken or proposed to be taken on the recommendations of the Commission and the reasons for non-acceptance of the recommendations, if any.

CHAPTER V

STATE HUMAN RIGHTS COMMISSIONS

21. Constitution of State Human Rights Commissions

(1) A State Government may constitute a body to be known as the ....(name of the State) Human Rights Commission to exercise the powers conferred upon, and to perform the functions assigned to, a State Commission under this chapter.

(2) [18][The State Commission shall, with effect from such date as the State Government may by notification specify, consist of—

- (a) a Chairperson who has been a Chief Justice of a High Court;
- (b) one Member who is, or has been, a Judge of a High Court or District Judge in the State with a minimum of seven years experience as District Judge;
- (c) one Member to be appointed from amongst persons having knowledge of, or practical experience in, matters relating to human rights.]

(3) There shall be a Secretary who shall be the Chief Executive Officer of the State Commission and shall exercise such powers and discharge such functions of the State Commission as it may delegate to him.

(4) The headquarters of the State Commission shall be at such place as the State Government may, by notification, specify.

(5) A State Commission may inquire into violation of human rights only in respect of matters relatable to any of the entries enumerated in List II and List III in the Seventh Schedule to the Constitution:

Provided that if any such matter is already being inquired into by the Commission or any other Commission duly constituted under any law for the time being in force, the State Commission shall not inquire into the said matter:

Provided further that in relation to the Jammu and Kashmir Human Rights Commission, this sub-section shall have effect as if for the words and figures "List II and List III in the Seventh Schedule to the Constitution", the words and figures "List III in the Seventh Schedule to the Constitution as applicable to the State of Jammu and Kashmir and in respect of matters in relation to which the Legislature of that State has power to make laws" had been substituted.

(6) [Two or more State Governments may, with the consent of a Chairperson or Member of a State Commission, appoint such Chairperson or, as the case may be, such Member of another State Commission simultaneously if such Chairperson or Member consents to such appointment:

Provided that every appointment made under this sub-section shall be made after obtaining the recommendations of the Committee referred to in sub-section(l) of section 22 in respect of the State for which a common Chairperson or Member, or both, as the case may be, is to be appointed.][19]

22. *Appointment of Chairperson and [Membersf of State Commission*

(1) The Chairperson and [Members][20] shall be appointed by the Governor by warrant under his hand and seal:

Provided that every appointment under this sub-section shall be made after obtaining the recommendation of a Committee consisting of

(a) the Chief Minister – Chairperson

(b) Speaker of the Legislative Assembly – Member

(c) Minister in-charge of the Department of Home, in that State – Member

(d) Leader of the Opposition in the Legislative Assembly – Member

Provided further that where there is a Legislative Council in a State, the Chairman of that Council and the Leader of the Opposition in that Council shall also be members of the Committee.

Provided also that no sitting Judge of a High Court or a sitting District Judge shall be appointed except after consultation with the Chief Justice of the High Court of the concerned State.

(2) No appointment of a Chairperson or a Member of the State Commission shall be invalid merely by reason of [any vacancy of any Member in the Committee referred to in sub-section(l)].[21]

23. *[Resignation and Removal of Chairperson or a Member of the State Commission]*[22]

[23][(1) The Chairperson or a Member of a State Commission may, by notice in writing under his hand addressed to the Governor, resign his office

(1A) Subject to the provisions of sub-section (2), the Chairperson or any Member of the State Commission shall only be removed from his office by order of the President on the ground of proved misbehaviour or incapacity after the Supreme Court, on a reference being made to it by the President, has, on inquiry held in accordance with the procedure prescribed in that behalf by the Supreme Court, reported that the Chairperson or such Member, as the case may be, ought on any such ground to be removed.]

(2) Notwithstanding anything in sub-section (1A), the President may by order remove from office the Chairperson or any [Member][24] if the Chairperson or such [Member][25], as the case may be-

- (a) is adjudged an insolvent; or
- (b) engages during his term of office in any paid employment outside the duties of his office; or
- (c) is unfit to continue in office by reason of infirmity of mind or body; or
- (d) is of unsound mind and stands so declared by a competent court; or
- (e) is convicted and sentenced to imprisonment for an offence which in the opinion of the President involves moral turpitude.

24. *Term of office of [Chairperson and]*[26] *Members of the State Commission*

(1) A person appointed as Chairperson shall hold office for a term of five years from the date on which he enters upon his office or until he attains the age of seventy years, whichever is earlier;

(2) A person appointed as a Member shall hold office for a term of five years from the date on which he enters upon his office and shall be eligible for re-appointment for another term of five years;

Provided that no Member shall hold office after he has attained the age of seventy years.

(3) On ceasing to hold office, a Chairperson or a Member shall be ineligible for further employment under the Government of a State or under the Government of India.

25. Member to act as Chairperson or to discharge his functions in certain circumstances

(1) In the event of the occurrence of any vacancy in the office of the Chairperson by reason of his death, resignation or otherwise, the Governor may, by notification, authorise one of the Members to act as the Chairperson until the appointment of a new Chairperson to fill such vacancy.

(2) When the Chairperson is unable to discharge his functions owing to absence on leave or otherwise, such one of the Members as the Governor may, by notification, authorise in this behalf, shall discharge the functions of the Chairperson until the date on which the Chairperson resumes his duties.

26. [Terms and conditions of service of Chairperson and Members of the State Commissions

The salaries and allowances payable to, and other terms and conditions of service of, the Chairperson and Members shall be such as may be prescribed by the State Government;

Provided that neither the salary and allowances nor the other terms and conditions of service of the Chairperson or a Member shall be varied to his disadvantage after his appointment.][27]

27. Officers and other staff of the State Commission

(1) The State Government shall make available to the Commission

- (a) an officer not below the rank of a Secretary to the State Government who shall be the Secretary of the State Commission; and
- (b) such police and investigative staff under an officer not below the rank of an Inspector General of Police and such

other officers and staff as may be necessary for the efficient performance of the functions of the State Commission.

(2) Subject to such rules as may be made by the State Government in this behalf, the State Commission may appoint such other addministrative, technical and scientific staff as it may consider necessary.

(3) The salaries, allowances and conditions of service of the officers and other staff appointed under sub-section (2) shall be such as may be prescribed by the State Government.

28. Annual and special reports of State Commission

(1) The State Commission shall submit an annual report to the State Government and may at any time submit special reports on any matter which, in its opinion, is of such urgency or importance that it should not be deferred till submission of the annual report.

(2) The State Government shall cause the annual and special reports of the State Commission to be laid before each House of State Legislature where it consists of two Houses, or where such Legislature consists of one House, before that House along with a memorandum of action taken or proposed to be taken on the recommendations of the State Commission and the reasons for non-acceptance of the recommendations, if any.

29. Application of certain provisions relating to National Human Rights Commission to State Commissions

The provisions of sections 9, 10, 12, 13, 14, 15, 16, 17 and 18 shall apply to a State Commission and shall have effect, subject to the following modifications, namely:

(a) references to "Commission" shall be construed as references to "State Commission";

(b) in section 10, in sub-section (3), for the word "Secretary General", the word "Secretary" shall be substituted;

(c) in section 12, clause (f) shall be omitted;

(d) in section 17, in clause (i), the words "Central Government or any" shall be omitted;

CHAPTER VI

HUMAN RIGHTS COURTS

30. For the purpose of providing speedy trial of offences arising out of violation of human rights, the State Government may, with the concurrence of the Chief Justice of the High Court, by notification, specify for each district a Court of Session to be a Human Rights Court to try the said offences.

Provided that nothing in this section shall apply if

(a) a Court of Session is already specified as a special court; or

(b) a special court is already constituted, for such offences under any other law for the time being in force.

31. Special Public Prosecutor

For every Human Rights Court, the State Government shall, by notification, specify a Public Prosecutor or appoint an advocate who has been in practice as an advocate for not less than seven years, as a Special Public Prosecutor for the purpose of conducting cases in that Court.

CHAPTER VII

FINANCE, ACCOUNTS AND AUDIT

32. *Grants by the Central Government*

(1) The Central Government shall after due appropriation made by Parliament by law in this behalf, pay to the Commission by way of grants such sums of money as the Central Government may think fit for being utilised for the purposes of this Act.

(2) The Commission may spend such sums as it thinks fit for performing the functions under this Act, and such sums shall be treated as expenditure payable out of the grants referred to in sub-section (1).

33. *Grants by the State Government*

(1) The State Government shall, after due appropriation made by Legislature by law in this behalf, pay to the State Commission by way of grants such sums of money as the State Government may think fit for being utilised for the purposes of this Act.

(2) The State Commission may spend such sums as it thinks fit for performing the functions under Chapter V, and such sums shall be treated as expenditure payable out of the grants referred to in sub-section (1).

34. *Accounts and Audit*

(1) The Commission shall maintain proper accounts and other relevant records and prepare an annual statement of accounts in such form as may be prescribed by the Central Government in consultation with the Comptroller and Auditor-General of India.

(2) The Accounts of the Commission shall be audited by the Comptroller and Auditor-General at such intervals as may be specified by him and any expenditure incurred in connection with such audit shall be payable by the Commission to the Comptroller and Auditor-General.

(3) The Comptroller and Auditor-General or any person appointed by him in connection with the audit of the accounts of the Commision under this Act shall have the same rights and privileges and the authority in connection with such audit as the Comptroller and Auditor-General generally has in connection with the audit of Government accounts and, in particular, shall have the right to demand the production of books, accounts, connected vouchers and other documents and papers and to inspect any of the offices of the Commission.

(4) The accounts of the Commission as certified by the Comptroller and Auditor-General or any other person appointed by him in this behalf, together with the audit report thereon shall be forwarded annually to the Central Government by the Commission and the Central Government shall cause the audit report to be laid as soon as may be after it is received before each House of Parliament.

35. ***Accounts and Audit of State Commission***

(1) The State Commission shall maintain proper accounts and other relevant records and prepare an annual statement of accounts in such form as may be prescribed by the State Government in consultation with the Comptroller and Auditor-General of India.

(2) The accounts of the State Commission shall be audited by the Comptroller and Auditor-General at such intervals as may be specified by him and any expenditure incurred in connection with such audit shall be payable by the State Commission to the Comptroller and Auditor-General.

(3) The Comptroller and Auditor-General or any person appointed by him in connection with the audit of the accounts of the State Commission under this Act shall have the same rights and privileges and the authority in connection with such audit as the Comptroller and Auditor-General generally has in connection with the audit of Government accounts and, in particular, shall have the right to demand the production of books, accounts, connected vouchers and other documents and papers and to inspect any of the offices of the State Commission.

(4) The accounts of the State Commission, as certified by the Comptroller and Auditor-General or any other person appointed by him in this behalf, together with the audit report thereon, shall be forwarded annually to the State Government by the State Commission and the State Government shall cause the audit report to be laid, as soon as may be after it is received, before the State Legislature.

CHAPTER VIII
MISCELLANEOUS

36. Matters not subject to jurisdiction of the Commission

(1) The Commission shall not inquire into any matter which is pending before a State Commission or any other Commission duly constituted under any law for the time being in force.

(2) The Commission or the State Commission shall not inquire into any matter after the expiry of one year from the date on which the act constituting violation of human rights is alleged to have been commited.

37. Constitution of special investigation teams

Notwithstanding anything contained in any other law for the time being in force, where the Government considers it necessary so to do, it may constitute one or more special investigation teams, consisting of such police officers as it thinks necessary for purposes of investigation and prosecution of offences arising out of violations of human rights.

38. Protection of action taken in good faith

No suit or other legal proceeding shall lie against the Central Government, State Government, Commission, the State Commission or any Member thereof or any person acting under the direction either of the Central Government, State Government, Commission or the State Commission in respect of anything which is in good faith done or intended to be done in pursuance of this Act or of any rules or any order made thereunder or in respect of the publication by or under the authority of the Central Government, State Government, Commission or the State Commission of any report paper or proceedings.

39. Members and officers to be public servants

Every Member of the Commission, State Commission and every officer appointed or authorised by the Commission or the State Commission to exercise functions under this Act shall be deemed to be a public servant within the meaning of section 21 of the Indian Penal Code.

40. Power of Central Government to make rules

(1) The Central Government may, by notification, make rules to carry out the provisions of this Act.

(2) In particular and without prejudice to the generality of the foregoing power, such rules may provide for all or any of the following matters namely:

(a) the salaries and allowances and other terms and conditions of service of the [Chairperson and Members][28] under section 8;

(b) the conditions subject to which other administrative, technical and scientific staff may be appointed by the Commission and the salaries and allowances of officers and other staff under subsection (3) of section 11;

(c) any other power of a civil court required to be prescribed under clause (f) of sub-section (1) of section 13;

(d) the form in which the annual statement of accounts is to be prepared by the Commission under sub-section (1) of section 34; and

(e) any other matter which has to be, or may be, prescribed.

(3) Every rule made under this Act shall be laid, as soon as may be after it is made, before each House of Parliament, while it is in session, for a total period of thirty days which may be comprised in one session or in two or more successive sessions, and if, before the expiry of the session immediately following the session or the successive sessions aforesaid, both Houses agree in making any modification in the rule or both Houses agree that the rule should not be made, the rule shall thereafter have effect only in such modified form or be of no effect, as the case may be; so however, that any such modification or annulment shall be without prejudice to the validity of anything previously done under that rule.

40 A. Power to make rules retrospectively—The power to make rules under clause (b) of sub-section (2) of section 40 shall include the power to make such rules or any of them retrospectively from a date not earlier than the date on which this Act received the assent of the President, but no such retrospective effect shall be given to any such rule so as to prejudicially affect the interests of any person to whom such rule may be applicable.

POWER OF COMMISSION TO MAKE REGULATIONS[29]

[30]*[40(B)]*

(1) Subject to the provisions of this Act and the rules made thereunder, the Commission may, with the previous approval of the Central Government, by notification, make regulations to carry out the provisions of this Act.

(2) In particular and without prejudice to the generality of the foregoing power, such regulations may provide for all or any of the following matters, namely:-

(a) the procedure to be followed by the Commission under subsection^) of Section 10;

(b) the returns and statistics to be furnished by the State Commission;

(c) any other matter which has to be, or may be, specified by regulations.

(3) Every regulation made by the Commission under this Act shall be laid, as soon as may be after it is made, before each House of Parliament, while it is in session, for a total period of thirty days which may be comprised in one session or in two or more successive sessions, and if, before the expiry of the session or the successive sessions aforesaid, both Houses agree in making any modification in the regulations or both Houses agree that the regulation should not be made, the regulation shall thereafter have effect only in such modified form or be of no effect, as the case may be; so however, that any such modification or annulment shall be without prejudice to the validity of anything previously done under that regulation.]

41. Power of State Government to make rules

(1) The State Government may, by notification, make rules to carry out the provisions of this Act.

(2) In particular and without prejudice to the generality of the foregoing power, such rules may provide for all or any of the following matters, namely:

(a) the salaries and allowances and other terms and conditions of service of the Chairperson and Members under section 26;

(b) the conditions subject to which other administrative, technical and scientific staff may be appointed by the State Commission and the salaries and allowances of officers and other staff under sub-section (3) of section 27;

(c) the form in which the annual statement of accounts is to be prepared under sub-section (1) of section 35.

(3) Every rule made by the State Government under this section shall be laid, as soon as may be after it is made, before each House of the State Legislature where it consists of two Houses, or where such Legislature consists of one House, before that House.

42. *Power to remove difficulties*

(1) If any difficulty arises in giving effect to the provisions of this Act, the Central Government, may by order published in the Official Gazette, make such provisions, not inconsistent with the provisions of this Act as appear to it to be necessary or expedient for removing the difficulty.

Provided that no such order shall be made after the expiry of the period of two years from the date of commencement of this Act.

(2) Every order made under this section shall, as soon as may be after it is made, be laid before each house of Parliament.

43. *Repeal and Savings*

(1) The Protection of Human Rights Ordinance, 1993 is hereby repealed.

(2) Notwithstanding such repeal, anything done or any action taken uiader the said Ordinance, shall be deemed to hcive been done or taken under the corresponding provisions of this Act.

* Amended vide Protection of Human Rights (Amendment) Act, 2006 (No. 43 of 2006).

1. Added by Act 43 of 2006
2. Subs, by Act 43 of 2006
3. Subs, by Act 43 of 2006 for "The National Commission for the Scheduled Castes and Scheduled Tribes."
4. Subs, by Act 43 of 2006 for "as it may delegate to him."
5. Subs, by Act 43 of 2006 for "other members"
6. Subs, by Act 43 of 2006 for "vacancy in the Committee"
7. Subs, by Act 43 of 2006
8. Subs, by Act 43 of 2006
9. Inserted by Act 43 of 2006
10. Inserted by Act 43 of 2006
11. Subs, by Act 43 of 2006
12. Inserted by Act 43 of 2006
13. Sub. by Act 43 of 2006
14. Inserted by Act 43 of 2006
15. Inserted by Act 43 of 2006
16. Subs, by Act 43 of 2006
17. Subs, by Act 43 of 2006
18. Subs, by Act 43 of 2006
19. Subs, by Act 43 of 2006
20. Subs, by Act 43 of 2006 for "other Members"
21. Subs, by Act 43 of 2006 for "any vacancy in the Committee"
22. Subs, by Act 43 of 2006 for "Removal of a member of the State Commission
23. Subs, by Act 43 of 2006
24. Subs, by Act 43 of 2006 for "other member"
25. Subs, by Act 43 of 2006 for "other member"
26. Inserted by Act 43 of 2006
27. Subs, by Act 43 of 2006
28. Subs, by Act 43 of 2006 for "members"
29. Inserted by Act 43 of 2006
30. Inserted by Act 43 of 2006

Bibliography

A. C. Kapur (1981), Principles of Political Science. S. Chand & Company Ltd., Ramnagar, New Delhi, 611.

A. H. Robertson (1961), The law of International Institution in Europe.

A. K. Merchant (1998), Atrocious Forms of Human Rights at p. 311.

A. M. Ahmadi (1995), Inagural Speech at a Workshop on "Judicial Process, Social Legitimacy and Institutional Viability", The Institute of Advanced Legal Studies, Pune, December 16.

A. P. Singh (1999) , Human Rights and Protective Discrimination, the Academy Law Review, Vol. XXIII, 209.

A. S. Anand CJI (1999), Address at the 135th Anniversary of the Madras Bar Association, Chennai, April 24, 1999, See The Times of India April 26.

A.V. Raghwan (1997), Association of NGOs with the Human Rights Machinery, at p. 112.

Abdulrahim P. Vijapur (1996), The UN at Fifty : Studies in Human Rights, p. 64.

Alston (1995), 'The U.N. and Human Rights' A Critical Appraisal, p. 128.

Altor Chand (1985), Politics of Human Rights and Civil Liberties-A Global Survey, 45

Anand Mehta (1999) , Right of Life and Personal Liberty, at page 281.

Ansuman Singh (1999), Valedictory Address at the Golden Jubilee Celebrations of the Rajasthan High Court, Jaipur, on September 26, 1999, *The Times of India*, Monday, September 27.

Antony Anghie (2000), "Time present and time past; Globaliazation, International Financial Institutions and the Third World. New York University *Journal of International Law and Policy,* 243.

Anzilotti (1928), Corso di Diritto Internazionale, Vol. 1.

Arun Mahajan (1999), The Role of NGOs in Implementing and Enforcing Human Rights Law, at p. 148.

Arun Ray (2004), 'National Human Rights commission of India'.

Asghar Ali Engineer (1997), "Globalization, Democracy and Threat to Diversity," Mainstre am 10, Nov. 1.

Ashok H. Desai (1997), Law Day Speech, November 26, 1996 in the Supreme Court Premises; 2 SCC (*Journal*) 10.

Attar Chand (1985), Politics of Hainan Rights and Civil Liberties at page 248.

B.G. Ramcharon (1997) , The Principles of Legality in International Human Rights Institutions: Selected Legal Opinions, p. 23-26.

Badri Prasad Jalan (1995), Discrimination Against Women in Specific Areas: Some Momentous Socio-Legal Issues, at page 21.

Bharat H. Desai (1996), Expansion of NGOs Pro-Active Role: Credibility and Acceptance, The Hindustan Times, 18 August.

Blackstone (1982), Personal Liberty and other Human Rights: Community Expectations, at page 36-37

C. Raj Kumar (2005), "Human Rights Implications of National Security Laws in India: Combating Terrorism while preserving Civil Liberties", 33 *Denv. J. Int'l. L. & Pol'y* 195.

C. G. Raghavan, 'Treaty Making Power under the Constitution of India', in S.K. Agrawala, Essays on the Law of Treaties, p. 217 at p. 232.

C. M. Lodha (1983), Judiciary-Fumes Flames and Fire. Unique Traders. Jaipur, p. vii

C. R. Parthsarthi (1999), Civil Liberties and Human Rights: A Challenging Issues, at page 144.

C. Raj Kumar (2005), "Human Rights Implications of National Security Laws in India: Combating Terrorism while Preserving Civil Liberties," 33 *Den.J. Int'L & Policy,* 195.

C.V.N. Sastri J. (1999), Role of the Bench and the Bar in the Administration of Justice, A.I.R., *Journal* 155.

Chakradhar Jha (1993), Judicial Review of Legislative Acts, at page 422.

Charlotle Bunch (1997), NGOs: Cultural and Ideological Perspectives, Human Rights Quarterly, Volume IX, at p. 468.

Claire Archbold (2004), "Incorporation of Rights in Domestic Law" in Globalization of Human Rights", edited by Jean Marc, Coiacud, Michal W. Doyee Annie Mari Gardner, at pp. 58-65.

Claire Archbold (2004), "The Incorporation of Civic and Social Rights in Domestic Law", in Globalization of Human Rights ed. by Jean Marc, colcared, Michael W. Doyee and Anne Mari Gardner, pp. 56-58.

D. D. Basu (2003), "Human Rights in Constitutional Law', 2nd ed., at pp. 16-17.

David P. Forsythe, "The Internationalisation of Human Rights"

Dr (Mrs.) K. Thakore (1977), A Paper Presented at the Conference on National Treaty Law and Procedure, Bellagio, 6-10 August.

Dr. B. Hydervali (2003), "The Jurisprudence of Human Rights", *Indian Bar Review*, Volume XXX (4).

Dr. H.O. Aggrawal (2005), 'International Law and Human Rights'.

Dr. S. K. Kapoor, International Law and Human Rights, 14th ed. p. 765.

Edward Lawson (ed) (1969) , Encyclopedia of Human Rights (2nd ed), p. 1484.

Frank E. Holman (1948), An International Bill of Rights; Proposals have Dangerous Implications for USA, ABAJ, pp. 984-86 and pp. 107-81.

G. H. Gutjals (1986), "Human Rights the Indian Law", 26.1 and 2 *Indian Journal of International Law*, 55, Jan.-June.

G.V.G. Krishnamurty (1985), Functioning of International Law and Internal Law of States (Postures. Practices and Perspectives). AIR 1985 p. 17 at p. 23.

Gavison (2004), 'Relation between Rights' in Globalization of Human Rights (ed.) by Marc, Gardner at p. 26-27.

Gidden (1990), "The Consequences of Modernity, Polity Canabridge, 64.

Granville Austin (1966) , "The Indian Constitution: Cornerstone of a Nation", pp. 59-60.

Gurdip Singh (2003), "International Law", pp. 534-540.

H.O. Aggrawal (2005), "International Law & Human Rights; 12th ed. p. 706-707

Hans Kelsen (1950), The Law of the United Nations, New York, pp. 29 and 179.

Hertz (2001), "The Silent Takeover, Global Capitalism and the Death of Democracy.

Human Rights Manual, Department of Foreign Affairs and Trade (1993).

Humphrey (1967), 'The U.N. Charter and the UN Declaration of Human Rights' in Laurd (ed.) The International Protection of Human Rights.

Imtiaz Ahmed (1998), People's Movement and Role of NGOs: A Critical Overview, at p. 177.

J. L. Brierly (1963), 'The Law of Nations' Sixthed.

J. C. Johari (1996), Human Rights and New World Order: Towards Perfection of the Democracticway of Life.

J. E. S. Fawcett (1968), The Law of Nations.

J. E. S. Facett (1968), "The Law of Nations", p. 158.

J.G. Starke (1989), Introduction to International Law, 10th ed., p. 311.

J.S. Verma J. (2004), "The New Universe of Human Rights, Ist ed., p. 42.

J.S. Verma (1st ed.), (2004), "The New Universe of Human Rights" , p. 36.

Jacobs and White (1996), The European Convention on Human Rights, 2nd ed., p. 2.

Jan Brownlie (2nd ed.), (1973), "Principles of Public International Law, p. 552.

Jan Brownlie (2nd ed.), (1973), "Principles of Public International Law", p. 554.

Jan Brownlie (1973), Principles of Public International Law, p. 554.

Jane A. Peddicord, "The American Convention on Human Rights: Potential Defects and Remedies" *Texas International Law Journal*. Vol. 19, No. 2, p. 141.

Jeremy Waldron (1992), Human Rights and the Search for Community Conciousness, The Oxford Amnesty Lecturers, London.

John Braithwaite and Peter Drahos (2000), "Global Business Regulation", p. 511-12.

John H. Dunning (2003), "Making Globalization Good-The Moral Challenges of Global Capitalism".

John H. Dunning (2003), "The Moral Imperative of Global Capitalism", p. 12.

John K. Ebiasah (1970), "In Africa Black Dictatorships have Demonstrated a Talent for Oppression Equal to that of the White", *American Bar Assoication,* Vol. 8, No. 2, p. 12.

John P. Humphery "The International Law of Human Rights in the Middle Twentieth Century", *The Present State of International Law and other Essays,* p. 255.

John R. Crook "The Fifty-First Session of the UN Commission on Human Rights", *American Journal of International Law,* Vol. 90, No 1, p. 127.

Joseph E. Stiglitz (2002), "Globalization and its Discontents".

K. Chockalingam (2007), Human Rights, Justice and Constitutional Empowerement, p. 245.

K. R. Narayana (1996), "Liberal Values and Human Rights", Mainstream, Vol. XXXIV, No. 21, February 24, p. 7-10.

Kay and Bradley (1995), European Human Rights Law: Text and Materials, p. 30.

Kelsen (1952), 'The Principles of International Law', pp. 446-47.

Kumar Suresh (1999), Dialogue on Ancient Wrongs: NGOs Role at p. 231.

L. Henkin (1979), "The Right of Man Today", p. 18-19.

Lauterpacht, "International Law and Human Rights", p. 394.

LM. Singhvi (1973), Law and Poverty, N.M. Tripathi Pvt Ltd., 287.

Louterpach (1950), International Law and Human Rights, p. 244-51.

Lowson (1969), 'Encylopedia of Human Rights' p. 790-91.

Luke Clements (1994), European Human Rights: Taking a case under the Convention, p. 6-7.

M Shiviah (1995), "Human Rights and the Third World: Towards a Reassessment of Ideological Dynamics", *Economic and Political Weekly,* Nov. 18, p. 2937-46.

M. P. Rana (2002), Human Rights and Societal Changes at p. 122.

M. P. Singh (2007), "Constitualization and Human Rights in India" in Human Rights, Justice and constitutional empowerement (e.d.) by C. Raj Kumar and K. Chockalingam, p. 32.

M.S. Mc Dougal and Bebr (1964), "Human Rights in the United Nations, *A.J.I.L.*, Vol. 56, p. 604.

Madhva Menon (1973), Justice for the Poor: Rationale Retrospect and Prospect, in Law and Poverty edited by L.M. Singhvi, N.M. Tripalhi Pvl, Ltd., 218.

Manual of the Council of Europe, its structure functions and achievements, (London, 1970) Art. 1 (a) (b).

Maurice Cranston, What are Human Rights, p. 36.

Michal Kirby (1999), "Domestic Implementation of International Human Rights Norms", *AJHR*, 27.

Mike M. K. Yin (1972), "Charter Provisions Concerning Human Rights", *India* Quarterly, Vol. 28.

Mohammad A. Ansari (1998) , People's Movements and Protection of Human Rights at p. 41.

Mukundan K. (2002), NGOs and Human Rights Culture, at p. 113.

N. V. Reddy (1995), Human Rights Organisations and Activists, at p. 2.

Noam Chomsky (1999), 'Profit Over People Neoliberalism and Global Order .

Nyaya Deep, Vol. U Oct.-Dec. (1999) page 47

Oiusola Ojo (ed.), (1990), Understanding Human Rights in Africa", Human Rights in Pluralist World : Individuals and Collectivities, Jan. Berting *et al* , p. 116.

Oppeheim, "*International Law*" Eighth edition, Vol. 1, p. 740.

Oppenheim, "*International Law*" (ed. 1992) p. 988.

P. Gopalaswamy (2000), Non-Governmental Organisations : A Challenging Perspective at p. 218.

P.L. Mehta and Neena Verma (1999), Human Rights under the Indian Constitution 4 , Deep & Deep Publication Pvt. Ltd. New Delhi.

P.N. Mishra (1995), Civilized Life and Human Dignity, at page 32.

P. R. Dasgupta (1996), The Significant Role of the NGO's in the Protection of Human Rights: A critical Perspective at p. 224.

P.R. Ghandhi (1987), "The Human Rights Committee and the Right of Individual Communication" The British Year Book of International Law.

Paras Diwan (1998), Human Rights and the Law: Universal and Indian, p. 31.

Peter H. Schuck (1997), Non-Governmental Organisations and Policy Process, Public Administration Review, New York, Vol. XI.

Philip Alston (ed.) (1995) , 'The UN and Human Rights: A Critical Appraisal, p. 180-181.

Philip Alston (ed.), (1995), The UN and Human Rights: A Critical Appraisal, p. 126.

Pollock (1974), The English Legal Aid System, Orient Longman Ltd. N. Delhi.

Prabhakar Sharma (1999), NGOs and Human Rights Activists, at p. 72.

Pratibha Sharma (1999), Social Backwardness and Yeomen Service of NGOs at p. 65.

Priya Prakash (2001), Functional Aspects of Non-Governmental Organisations and Institutions Towards Promotion of Human Rights, *The Times of India* 22, January.

Priya Prakash (2001), NGOs Towards Redressing Societal Wrongs at page 36.

Prof. S. K. Verma (2000), "Globalisation, marketistation and Cosntitutional Mandate', 42, *JILI*, 401-402.

Prof. S. K. Verma (2000), 'Globalisation, Marketisation and constitutional mandate', 42, *JILI*, p. 398.

R. Dhavan, "The Lesser Evil ? Judges and Indian Democracy" (PIL SARC Working Paper no. 152).

R. A. Diwaker (2000), Englightened Social Activists and Human Rights Perspective, at p. 113-114.

R. C. Mishra (2001), NGOs and Human Rights Activism at p. 179.

R. K. Gupta (2001), Implementation of Human Rights: A Realistic Approach Needed to be Adopted at p. 54.

R. M. Pal (1996), Social Welfare Programmes and Role of National Institutions, at p. 27.

Rachel Brett (1995), The Role and Limits of Human Rights NGOs at the United Nations, *Political Studies*, Vol. XIII, at p. 96.

Raj Kumar and K. Chockalingam (2007), "Human Rights, Justice and Constitutional Empowerement, 250-251.

Raj Kumar (2007), "Human Rights, Justice and Constitutional Environment, p. 246.

Rajagopal (2003), 'International Law and Social movements Challenge of Theorising Resistance' *Columbia Journal of Transnational Law*, 41 397.

Rajeev Dhawn (1999), Step by Step: 4th Annual Report of NHRC: 1996-97 41 *J.I. : L.I.*, p. 193-194.

Ravi Nair (1988), Co-operation of Non-Governmental Organisations in Human Rights Perspective at p. 423.

Richard B. Bilder (1969), 'Rethinking International Human Rights: Some Basic Questions', *Human Rights Journal*, 2, p. 567

Richard B. Bilder (1969), "Rethinking International Human Rights" *Human Right Journal*, 2, p. 567.

Richard Peet (2003), "World Bank and WTO, p.1

Robertson (1961), The Law of International Institutions in Europe, p. 73.

S. Bandopadhyay (2000), Role of NGOs : Home and Abroad, at p. 32.

S. Gopalaswamy (1998), Non-Governmental Organisations and Redressing Social Wrongs, at page 372.

S. Lukes (1996), Human Rights NGOs in Third World, at p. 145.

S. K. Kapoor, "International Law and Human Rights", 14th ed., p. 777.

S. L. Bhalla (1991), Human Rights and Institutional Frame Work for Imblementation, p. 10

S.L. Bhalla (1991), Human Rights and Institutional Frame Work for Imblementation, p. 43.

Saskia Sassen (1996), Losing Control? Sovereignity in an age of Globalization.

Schwetb and Alstan (1982), "The Principal Institutions and other Bodies Founded under the Charter, in vasak and Alston (eds), International Dimensions of Human Rights, p. 271-72.

Scott Davidson (2003), Human Rights, Open University Press, Buckingham, Philadelphia.

Stephen S. Goodspeed (2nd ed). (1967) , 'The Nature and Functions of International Organisation.

Steven R. Rother (2001), 'Corporation and Human Rights: A Theory of Legal Responsibility, *Yale Law Journal*, 443.

Stock-Taking on the European Convention on Human Rights. The first Thirty Years (1984) p. 312.

Subhash C. Kashyap (1977), Human Rights and Parliament, 33 (Metropolitan, New Delhi.

Sudarshan Sharma (2000), Socio-Political Genesis of Human Rights Organisations, at p. 112

Sujata Manohar J. (2003), "International Human Rights Law in Domestic Courts: Violence Against Women and Administration of Justice", *Journal of the NHRC*, Vol. 2, at p. 11.

Surendra Pratap Rana (2001), Non-Governmental Bodies and Human Rigths Conspectus, at p. 228.

Surya Deva (2007), "Globalization and its impact on the relization of Human Rights - Indian Perspective on a global Canvas' in Human Rights, Justice and Constitution Empowerment by Raj Kumar, p. 240-241.

Surya Deva (2004), "The Sangam of Foreign investment, Multinational corporations and Human Rights : An Indian perspective for a developing Asia, Singapore Journal of Legal Studies.

Surya Deva (2007), Globalization and its Impact on the Realization of Human Rights' in Human Right, Justice and Constitutional Empowerement, p. 252-253.

Surya Deva (2003), Human Rights Violations by Multinational Corporation and International Law, Jounral of International Law, 19, 1.

T. Howard (1994), Globalisation and Latin America, Cambridge, OUP Vol. III.

Tarun Bose (1997), NGOs as Instruments of Humanitarian Mission, at p.22.

Triepel (1899), Volkerrecht Und Landerecht.

Upendra Baxi (2003), "The Future of Human Rights".

Upendra Baxi (2002) , "The Future of Human Rights".

V.B. Rawat (1999), Societal Aspects of the Protection and Promotion of Human Rights, at p. 242.

V. N. Shukla, The Constitution of India, p. 610

V. R. Dasgupta (2001), NGOs and Human Rights Activism: Continuing the Discussion, at p. 263.

V. S. Mani (1981), "Regional approaches to the implementation of Human Rights, IJIL Vol. 21 No. 1, p. 105.

VE. Moray (2001), Struggle for Human Rights and Community Consciousness at p. 318.

Venkataraman Chandrasekhran (1996), Domestic Violence and Indian Social Structure, at page 221.

Vijay Pal Arora (1996), Right to Life, Freedom and Equality, at page 5.

Vijayashri, Sripat (2000), "India's National Human Rights Commission: A Shackled Commission; 18 B.U. Int'.L. J. 1.

Vijayshri Sripat, 'Towards Fifty years of Constitutionalism and Fundamental Rights in India: Looking back to see ahead'. 14 Am. U. Int'l L. Rev. 413 at 415.

Vijayshri Sripati, "India's NHRC: A Shackled Commission? 18 B.U. Int.'L. J. 1, p. 44-45.

Will Kymlicka (1994), Multicultural Citizenship, Cambridge, OUP, Vol. IX.

INDEX

J

K

P

Q

R